Understanding the Legal Aspects of Design/Build

Timothy R. Twomey, Esq., AIA

R.S. Means Company, Inc.

Understanding the Legal Aspects *of* Design/Build

Timothy R. Twomey, Esq., AIA

R.S. MEANS COMPANY, INC.
CONSTRUCTION CONSULTANTS & PUBLISHERS
100 Construction Plaza
P.O. Box 800
Kingston, Massachusetts 02364-0800
(617) 585-7880

The editors for this book were Jill Farinelli and Dwayne Lehigh. Typesetting was supervised by Helen Marcella. The book and jacket were designed by Norman R. Forgit.

Printed in the United States of America

10 9 8 7 6 5 4 3 2 1

Library of Congress Cataloging in Publication Data

ISBN 0-87629-137-X

To
Nancy

For
Ryan, Colin, and Kevin

In Memory
of
Henry Pierce Sheldon

You were a flash of profound emotions,
A rush to the heart,
A wrench to the soul,
A song to be sung with love and great joy
Again and again and again!

Table of Contents

Foreword

This book is for architects, engineers, designers, builders, contractors, potential developers or property owners, and attorneys who are unfamiliar with the design/build process. This book includes the most comprehensive overview currently available of the opportunities and legal aspects of the design/build process. It also provides detailed discussions of many of the problems and practical concerns commonly encountered by parties involved in this increasingly popular method of project delivery.

There is currently very little information conveniently available on the design/build process. To date, published commentary has been limited to magazine articles and brief discussions of the subject in books devoted to general construction matters, or legal manuals and treatises on construction law. This is surprising in light of the many and often-times heated debates that this subject generated in the late 1970s and '80s. The goal of this book is to explore, in a systematic and organized manner, many of the issues raised by these commentaries, as well as other issues not yet addressed to any significant degree in the published literature to date.

This book is organized into five parts. Part I, "Defining Design/Build," describes, defines, and differentiates design/build and other construction methods. Chapter 1 traces the evolution of the design/build method and compares it to other traditional and nontraditional methods of construction. It is important to understand the context in which the design/build process exists in order to appreciate the opportunities it offers and the legal issues it raises. Chapter 2 contains a detailed discussion of the four principal design/build arrangements, in terms of structure and lines of responsibility in each model.

Part II, "Design/Build—Advantages and Disadvantages," reviews both the positive and negative aspects of design/build from the perspectives of each project participant: the client in Chapter 3, the contractor in Chapter 4, and in Chapter 5, the design professional.

Part III, "Procuring Design/Build Services," discusses the process by which design/build services are contracted. (It should be noted that the word "client" as used throughout this book refers to the owner or developer of the property.) Chapter 6 points out that while the various types of private-sector clients have, over the years, chosen the design/build method for their projects, the public sector in recent times has been expressing increasing interest in this process. Federal, state, and local agencies are beginning to explore the possibilities offered by design/build, and the number of such projects actually constructed using this method is growing. Chapter 7 concludes this section with a discussion of the methods and evaluation criteria that a private- or public-sector client might employ in selecting a design/build firm.

Part IV, "Liability," focuses on the liability and legal issues applicable to the design/build process. Chapter 8 describes the theories of liability that are employed in the construction industry in general, as well as those that apply particularly to design/build projects. This chapter also includes a discussion of traditional legal defenses that may be unavailable to design/build participants.

Other legal issues surrounding the imposition of liability are examined in Chapter 9. These include the time frame in which claims may be filed, the type and amount of damages that may be awarded, the ability to collect all or a portion of the claim from one or more of the parties, and methods of resolving the disputes that inevitably arise on every construction project.

Part V, "Administration," examines the administrative steps necessary to engage in design/build: insurance, bonding, licensing, registration, and contract agreements. Chapter 10 identifies the various types of insurance and bonds that may be required of design/build participants. Included is a discussion of the gaps and exclusions that may exist in a construction professional's coverage when insurance policies designed for traditionally structured projects are applied to design/build projects, and when construction professionals practice outside their traditional disciplines.

Chapter 11 discusses the licensing and registration requirements of design professionals and contractors, and how these requirements may vary depending on the laws of the jurisdiction in which the project is located. This chapter also examines certain ethical constraints that are placed on design professionals who wish to engage in design/build, and the court decisions that have removed some of these obstacles.

Finally, Chapter 12 examines the standard form design/build contract agreements published by the various professional and national associations. The chapter describes the benefits of using these preprinted contracts and recommends specific documents for particular situations. The structure of each form, the relationships they represent, and areas of special concern are identified. The chapter concludes with a brief discussion of the use of nonstandard form agreements.

The book includes five appendices. The first two list the applicable codes of ethics, as established by the American Institute of Architects (AIA) and the National Society of Professional Engineers (NSPE). The last three appendices contain copies of the standard form design/build contract agreements published by the AIA, NSPE, and the Associated General Contractors of America (AGC). A comprehensive glossary of pertinent legal and construction terms follows.

This book should provide those who are contemplating involvement in design/build with an objective view of this evolving construction method. The conscientious reader will use this book as a reference tool, mindful that there is no substitute for appropriate professional legal consultation.

Part One

Defining Design/Build

Design/build is both an old and a new method of project delivery. In order to understand design/build, it is helpful, first, to review the evolution of construction—from antiquity to the 20th century; second, to compare design/build method to other forms of project delivery; and finally, to witness how the flexibility of design/build enables it to adapt to a variety of project requirements and client needs. Chapter 1 begins with a brief overview of the ancient origins of this construction method, and a comparison of design/build to other methods of construction commonly used today.

Chapter One

Comparing Construction Methods

The Design/Build Method

The practice of design/build is rooted in antiquity, when the *master builder* was usually both the designer and the assembler of the projects he envisioned. Manual laborers were used to haul large blocks of stone that skilled craftsmen would later fashion into useful components of a structure. Throughout this process, their efforts were controlled by the individual responsible for the project's design. Often the "plans" were little more than an image in the designer's mind, realized only in the course of the actual construction. It was essential, therefore, that the designer be the builder as well.

Today the term *design/build* refers to a method of project delivery in which a single entity provides to the client all of the services necessary to both design and construct all or a portion of the project. This *single point of responsibility* fundamentally distinguishes design/build from other forms of project delivery (see Figure 1.1).

Figure 1.1

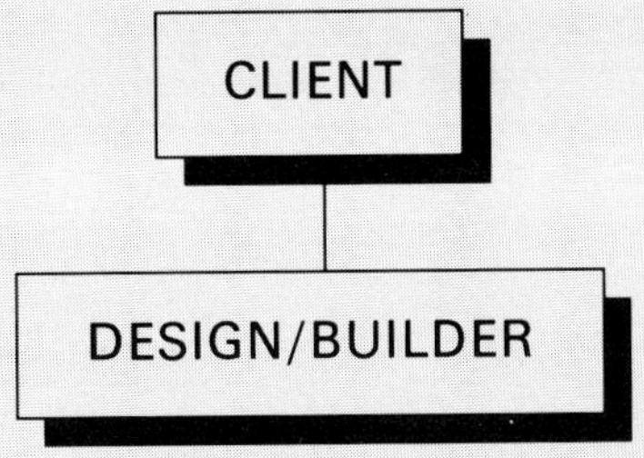

The Design/Build Method of Project Delivery

Client Responsibility

On a design/build project, the client has a number of important responsibilities. These include providing pre-design site data such as site surveys, topographical information, and soil characteristics. Generally, the client is also responsible for procuring regulatory permits, although the design/builder typically assists the client in this regard. The client also provides or works closely with the design/build team to develop a program that identifies the character, size, type, and functional relationships of the various spaces included in the project.

Licensing

A design/build project, like any other construction project, is subject to licensing and regulation by the jurisdiction in which the project is located. In most states, both the design professional and the contractor are required by law to be licensed, regardless of the method of project delivery. In some instances, however, design/build projects may require additional licensing and registration. Chapter 11 explores these requirements in greater detail.

The Traditional Method

During the Renaissance, a divergence occurred between the parties responsible for design, and those responsible for construction. Increasingly complex structures required greater expertise in design, construction analysis, and construction techniques. The term *master builder* was applied less frequently to those who acted as design/builder, and was more often associated solely with the builder. Increasingly, the terms *architect*, and sometimes *engineer*, were used to describe the designer. This separation of roles, now referred to as the *traditional method of project delivery*, was well established by the 19th century and continues today to represent the single most often used method. Figure 1.2 shows the relationships of the three parties in a traditional project.

The Design Professional's Traditional Role

In the traditional method of project delivery, both the design professional and the contractor are retained separately by the client. Each construction professional maintains a separate contract with the client. The design professional's role is to develop a design plan in response to client-defined needs or goals, to weigh the alternative solutions, and to recommend a plan to the client. The design professional then documents

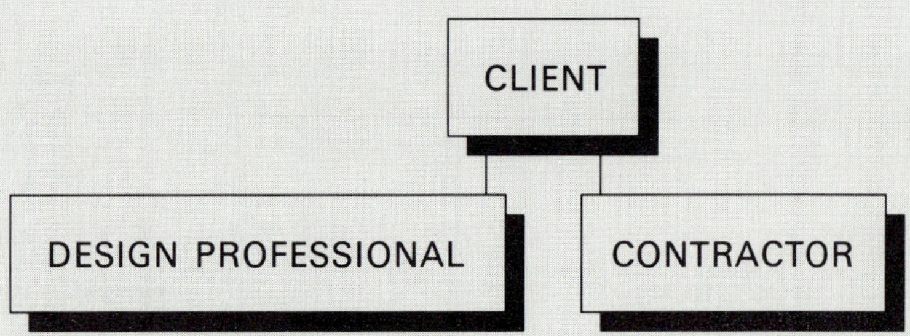

The Traditional Method of Project Delivery

Figure 1.2

the client's choices and presents this information to the contractor(s). During the construction phase, the design professional acts as a *fiduciary*, or representative, of the client, guarding the client against potential defects and deficiencies in the contractor's work. The design professional must exercise good judgment and discretion on behalf of the client.

The Contractor's Traditional Role

The contractor has a different role and relationship with the client. The contractor is not expected to represent the client's wishes but, rather, to determine the most efficient and cost-effective methods by which the design intent (represented by the drawings and specifications prepared by the design professional) can be achieved. The contractor has a contractual obligation to the client to complete the project in accordance with the plans and specifications within the agreed-upon limits of time and cost.

Turnkey Projects

The *turnkey project delivery method*, shown in Figure 1.3, is similar to the design/build project delivery method in that a single source, in this case the turnkey contractor, provides all design and construction services for the project. The significant difference between design/build and turnkey construction is that the turnkey contractor provides a comprehensive set of project-related services beyond design and construction. These services may include (in the order in which they are typically provided):

- Financing the project
- Identifying and procuring the construction site and site data
- Obtaining regulatory permits
- Designing and constructing the project
- Operating and maintaining the facility for a period of time to determine that the various systems are functioning properly

The turnkey contractor then essentially turns over to the client the keys of a fully functioning and operating facility. Specialized industrial design projects and large-scale engineering and construction projects such as sewage treatment plants, public utilities, and process plants are typical examples of turnkey projects.

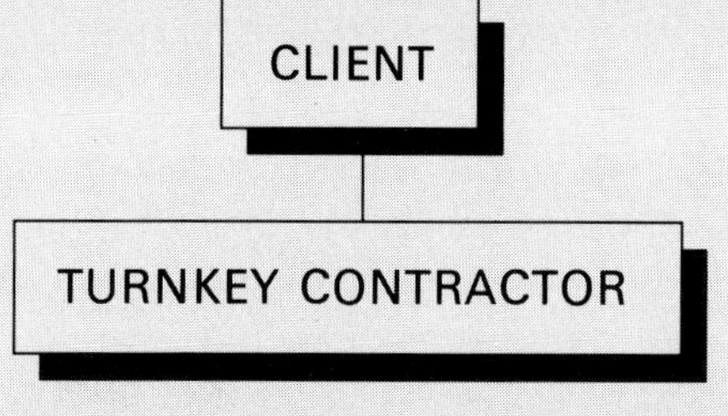

The Turnkey Method of Project Delivery

Figure 1.3

Construction Management

There are a number of other approaches to project delivery in addition to the design/build, traditional, and turnkey methods. Some introduce new parties to the traditional triad of client, design professional, and contractor. Others involve the client in a far more active role.

The *construction management* method of project delivery became popular in the early 1970s, at about the same time that the design/build method gained momentum. Both methods grew out of the client's desire to find more economical methods of project delivery. In construction management, however, the client hires an "outsider," or construction manager, to maintain objective control over the project's schedule and cost.

Currently, there are two principal methods by which construction management services are performed:

- Construction manager as independent professional consultant
- Construction manager as contractor

Both arrangements add a fourth player to the traditional three-party structure, although the relationship between the client and the contractor (and possibly the subcontractors) may vary.

Construction Manager as Independent Professional Consultant

In this approach, the construction manager is retained by the client and has no contractual obligation to either the design professional or the general contractor. The construction manager acts as independent professional advisor to the client, lending expertise in certain pre-construction activities, such as cost estimating, value engineering, and scheduling. Other responsibilities include assisting the client and design professional in achieving the program, design, and budget requirements of the project.

The construction manager is paid a fee by the client for his or her services, but has no financial interest in the project itself. During the construction phase of the project, the construction manager furnishes business administration and management services, and coordinates an overall plan of activities for the general contractor, as indicated by the dotted line in Figure 1.4. The independent construction manager is not, however, responsible for the means and methods of construction, nor does he or she hire subcontractors or trade contractors. The construction manager is not contractually bound to the general contractor. This individual is also not responsible for the general contractor's failure to meet project requirements, or for safety precautions in connection with construction. He or she may, however, recommend a course of action to the client when the requirements of a construction contract are not being met.

Construction Manager as General Contractor

In this approach, the construction manager is retained by the client and assumes the role of general contractor. He or she also provides many services normally performed by an independent professional construction manager, including advising the client and performing scheduling, cost analysis, and value engineering. The construction manager as general contractor also performs services normally carried out by the project's general contractor, including choosing the means and methods of the construction and hiring sub- and trade contractors.

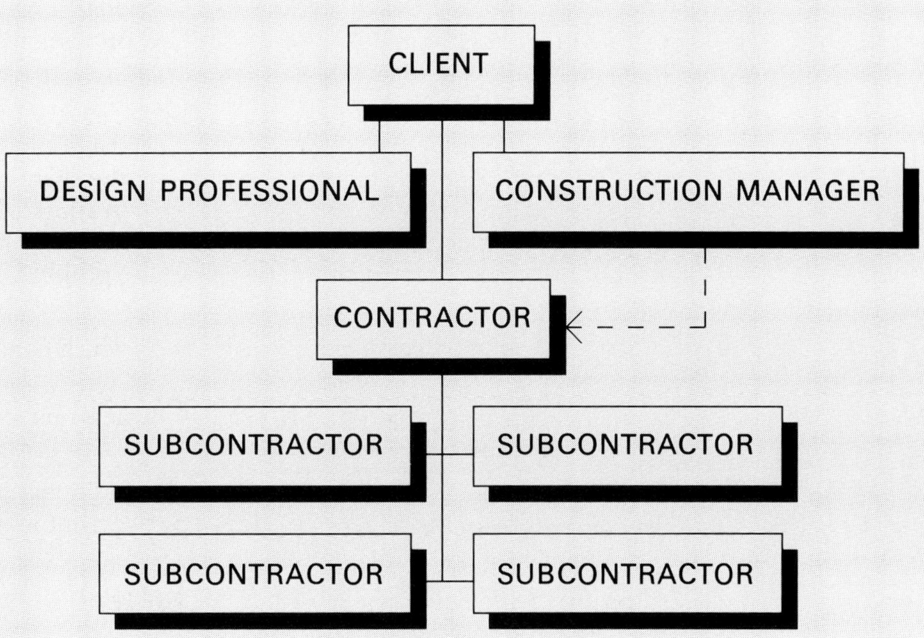

Construction Manager as Independent Professional Consultant

Figure 1.4

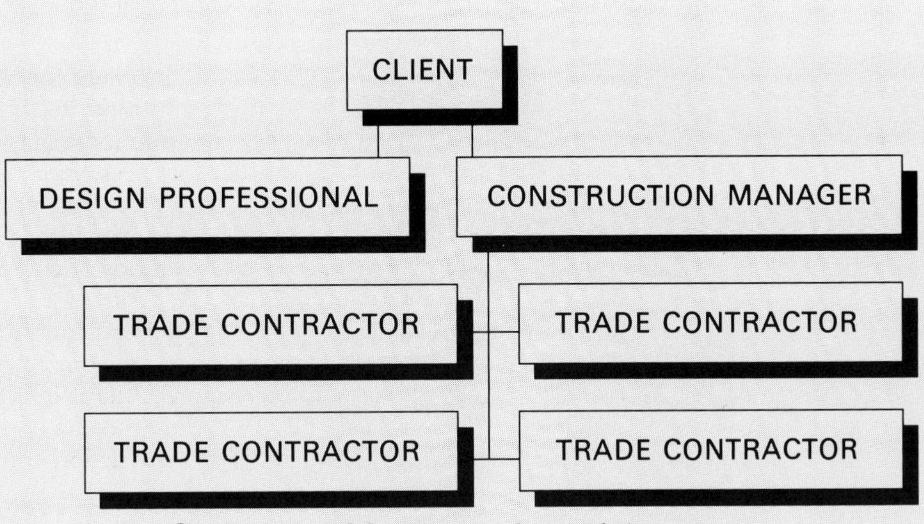

Construction Manager as General Contractor

Figure 1.5

The solid line in Figure 1.5 connecting the construction manager with the trade contractor represents the contractual relationship between these individuals and responsibility for construction activities. Unlike the construction manager as independent professional consultant, the construction manager as general contractor has a financial interest in the project. Here lies a major source of controversy in this common method of construction management.

Defining the Construction Manager's Role

Clients, design professionals, and construction managers each have a different view of the construction manager's role. Should the construction manager be considered the client's independent professional consultant when he or she actually assumes the responsibilities of a contractor on traditionally structured projects? Or should the construction manager be considered a contractor who happens to provide certain pre-construction services not normally provided by contractors on traditional projects? Can the construction manager be properly characterized as an independent professional consultant during the pre-construction period, but as a general contractor during construction? Can a party be truly independent early in the life of a project when that party has a significant interest in the economic outcome of the completed structure? These are important issues to consider when procuring or performing construction management services.

Fast Track Construction

This method of project delivery is less concerned with the *relationships* among the various parties than with the *sequencing* of construction activities. In *fast track construction*, construction activities on some portions of the project may begin before the design is completed on other portions. For example, the contractor may begin early site work and foundation construction before the design professional has completed the construction documents for the remainder of the project. It is possible to fast track portions of a project under virtually any of the forms of project delivery described above.

Like construction management, fast track construction became popular in the late 1960s and early 1970s in response to high interest rates and the need to reduce the overall cost of projects. Clients found ways to complete a project quickly so that their property could begin producing income sooner. They realized that the total design and construction period of the project could be reduced if certain design and construction activities were performed *concurrently* instead of *consecutively*.

Fast track construction presents a greater risk than other project delivery methods. The reason is that design documents are incomplete at the start of construction and the design professional has no opportunity to coordinate the complete package of construction documents prior to their release to the contractor.

Variations of the Design/Build Method

There are variations in the structure of all project delivery methods, including design/build. Several of the more typical variations are discussed below for purposes of comparison.

Design/Build-Construction Management

In jurisdictions where it is not possible, due to state licensing or registration laws, for a firm to provide both design and construction services, a "hybrid" method of design/build may be employed. Figure 1.6 shows the design/build-construction management structure. In this arrangement, a single entity provides to the client all design and construction *management* and *coordination* services. The design/build-construction manager and the contractor are retained separately by the client, and have no contractual obligation to each other. The design/build-construction manager oversees the activities of the contractor and ensures that the project conforms to the design documents and that costs do not exceed the project's budget.

The difference between design/build-construction management and design/build is that the design/build-construction manager coordinates a plan of activities for the contractor, but does not perform the actual construction, nor subcontract to others for construction services. Instead, all construction services are performed by the contractor who is responsible to the client.

This approach could be seen as a combination of design and construction management services except that the design/build-construction manager typically assumes and is responsible for overseeing all of the *construction activities* of the general contractor (or the separate trade contractors) in the same way that the contractor has this responsibility on traditionally structured projects. In addition, the design/build-construction manager is responsible for keeping the construction of the project within the construction budget. The design/build-construction management structure differs from the construction manager/contractor structure in that it is responsible for the *design* of the project as well as its construction.

Design/Build Fast Track Construction

Some argue that the design/build method of project delivery accommodates fast track construction activities more easily than other methods of project delivery. This may be true since the close communication between design professional and contractor that is inherent in the design/build arrangement enables different portions of the

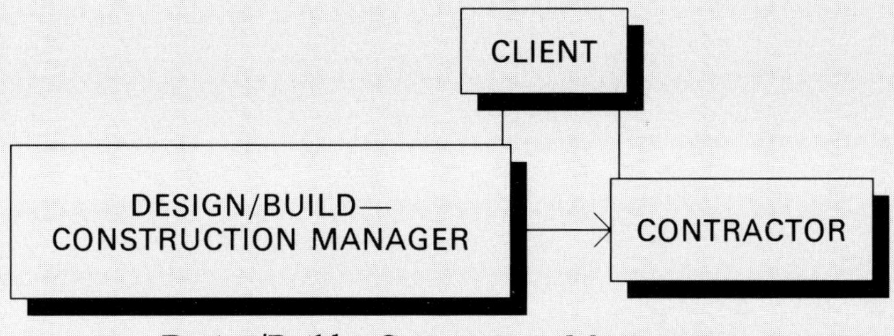

Design/Build—Construction Management

Figure 1.6

project to proceed at different rates with a minimum of confusion and conflict. As a single point of responsibility for all design and construction activities, the participants in design/build must resolve conflicts in-house and keep informed of design developments as they are approved.

Design/Build a Portion of the Project

Increasingly, certain building types are employing design/build services for a portion of the project. For example, speculative office buildings may be designed and constructed using the traditional method, while the mechanical and electrical components are constructed using the design/build method.

In this limited design/build approach (Figure 1.7), the design professional provides mechanical and electrical performance specifications and/or systems descriptions to outline the project's requirements. Using this information, the contractor requests bids from various mechanical/electrical design/build subcontractors to both prepare the plans and construct the mechanical and electrical portions of the project. The independent design professional may be called on to review the various design/build subcontractors' proposals, as well as the chosen design/build subcontractor's construction documents, to assure their general conformance to the original specifications. In some cases there may be no independent design professional involved at all. At any rate, it is the contractor, through the design/build subcontractor, who provides all required design and construction services for the mechanical and electrical portions of the project.

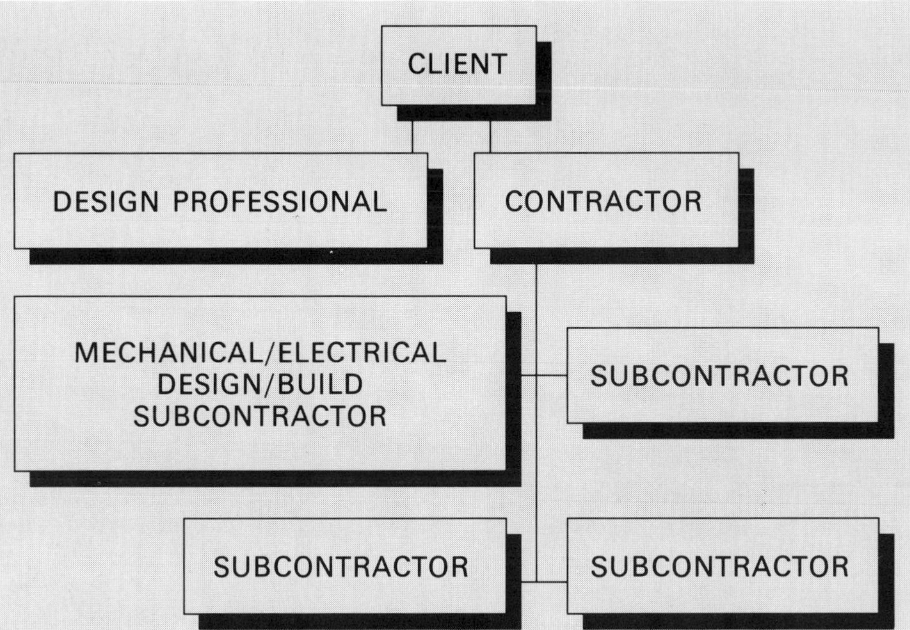

Design/Build a Portion of the Project

Figure 1.7

Finance/Design/Build

Sometimes a design/build firm will procure the project's financing and/or equity investors on behalf of the client. For example, a design/build firm with an established track record for a particular type of building might develop a relationship with one or more parties who are interested in providing financing or investing in such projects. The design/build firm then develops a marketing strategy to identify potential projects and clients who meet the lender/investor's investment criteria.

This arrangement provides the design/build firm with an enormous advantage over its competitors, in that it can offer the client the financial means to realize the project. The lender/investor, in turn, has the opportunity to evaluate the credentials of the design/build team, to analyze the projected quality level of the project and, subsequently, the value and security of its investment. The client benefits because the project's financing is secured by others. If, through no fault of his or her own, the financing falls through or cannot ultimately be secured, the client is free from any financial obligation to the design/build firm for services rendered or expenses incurred.

This arrangement differs from the turnkey method in that the finance/design/build firm does not finance the construction of the project itself. Rather, its obligation is to secure project financing from others for potential clients. The finance/design/build firm never owns or takes title of the project, as the turnkey contractor does prior to turning it over to the client.

In-House Design and Construction (Client/Design/Build)

This is a common form of design/build project delivery. (See Figure 1.8.) Any parent who is coaxed into building a backyard playhouse is participating in client/design/build. Any building owner who designs and implements additions or modifications to its facilities using in-house forces is also utilizing this method of construction.

The distinguishing feature between this approach and standard design/build is that in client/design/build, the *client* provides the design and construction services, not a design/build firm. This is the most cost-effective method of construction, but clients must have the resources to design, schedule, purchase, coordinate, and construct the project to benefit from use of this method. Repetitive or relatively simple construction projects, such as internal repartitioning, are often carried out in this manner.

In-House Design and Construction (Client/Design/Build)

Figure 1.8

The in-house design and construction approach can be somewhat restrictive to a client who desires greater creativity or a wider range of options for a particular project. This is because in-house capabilities tend to be geared toward solving a limited range of design and construction requirements. Shopping for outside services enables the client to tailor the services available from third parties to the needs of the project.

In-House Design Services Only (Client/Design)

The in-house design approach works well where a project is too complex for in-house construction capabilities, but where the design requirements of the project are not so unique (see Figure 1.9). For example, a large medical facility's in-house design and construction staff may be perfectly capable of performing interior renovations or additions to "stick-built" construction, but multi-story additions, or the use of steel or concrete framing, may be beyond this client's in-house construction capabilities. The client, in this case, would contract those services to an independent contractor.

Depending on the particular project, the client/designer may:

- Act as general contractor, assuming responsibility for retaining and coordinating trade subcontractors
- Retain a construction manager to manage and coordinate the contractor
- Retain a construction manager to manage the various trade contractors
- Retain a construction manager who, in turn, retains a contractor

Summary

Design/build refers to a method of project delivery in which a single entity provides the client (owner) with all design and construction services. This method is rooted in antiquity, when the master builder was both designer and builder. During the Renaissance, building design became so complex that the master builder could no longer be responsible for both the design and construction of a project. The traditional method of project delivery grew out of this need for more extensive resources, and is the most widely used method of construction today. The design/build method once practiced by the master builder regained popularity in the 1960s and 1970s when clients sought ways to control project costs and reduce delivery time.

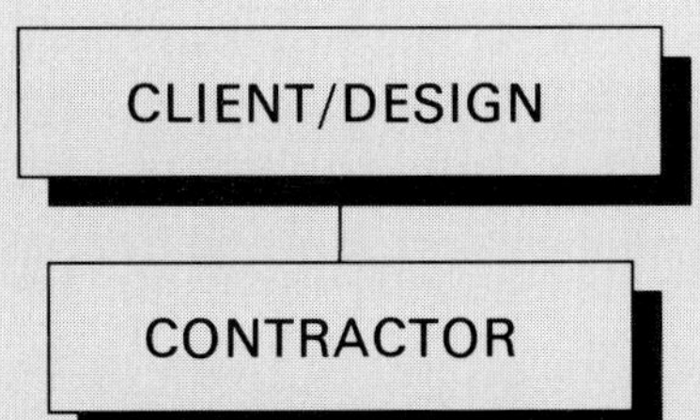

In-House Design Services Only (Client/Design)

Figure 1.9

Other construction methods include turnkey, construction management and fast track project delivery. In turnkey projects, the contractor not only provides all the services necessary to design and build the project, but also operates and maintains the structure for a time before turning the keys of a fully functioning facility over to the client. Construction management is another method of construction in which the client hires an "outside" party to maintain objective control over many aspects of the project including cost, scheduling, and the various construction activities. Construction managers can operate as independent professional consultants or as general contractors. Finally, in fast track construction, some portions of a project are built before others are completely designed.

There are as many variations in the structure and assignment of responsibility in these construction methods as there are individual participants. This is also true for design/build. Some of the variations include projects built using a combination of design/build and traditional methods, design/build-construction management, fast track design/build, finance/design/build, in-house design and construction (client/design/build), and in-house design services only (client/design). These are just a few of the ways in which the design/build method has been adapted to the needs of particular projects. Chapter 2 narrows the focus and explores the four basic ways in which design/build firms are arranged.

Chapter Two

Comparing Design/Build Methods

There are four basic organizational forms through which design/build services are provided to clients. They can be easily distinguished from one another by identifying the *primary contractor*, or the party who contracts directly with the client for the design/build services. While there are many variations in the structure of design/build organizations, the four types listed below represent the basic arrangements used in this type of construction.

- Type A: Design Professional as Primary Contractor
- Type B: Contractor as Primary Contractor
- Type C: Design Professional/Contractor Joint Venture as Primary Contractor
- Type D: Design/Build Organization as Primary Contractor

Type A: The Design Professional as Primary Contractor

Structure

In Type A design/build, the client contracts directly with the design professional for all design and construction services required to complete the project. The design professional performs the necessary design services and contracts directly with the contractor to provide all required construction services (see Figure 2.1). This design/build arrangement is used less frequently than other design/build formats due, in part, to the typically large disparity in size between design and construction firms. A small design firm has fewer resources than a large construction firm and, as a result, may have greater difficulty competing for design/build projects.

The basic relationships illustrated in Figure 2.1 may vary depending on the design professional's strengths and weaknesses, client requirements, and marketing or economic trends. For instance, a design professional who cannot perform all of the design services required for the project has two options: joining forces with one or more design professionals to provide the required design work (see Figure 2.2), or contracting directly with one or more consulting design professionals for design services that the primary design professional cannot perform (see Figure 2.3).

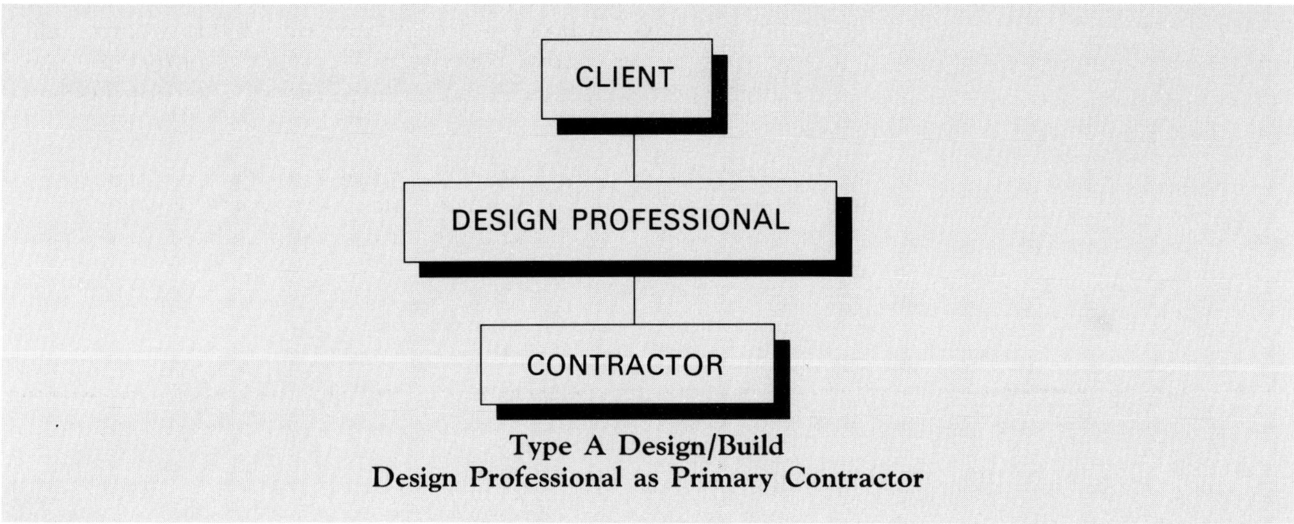

Figure 2.1

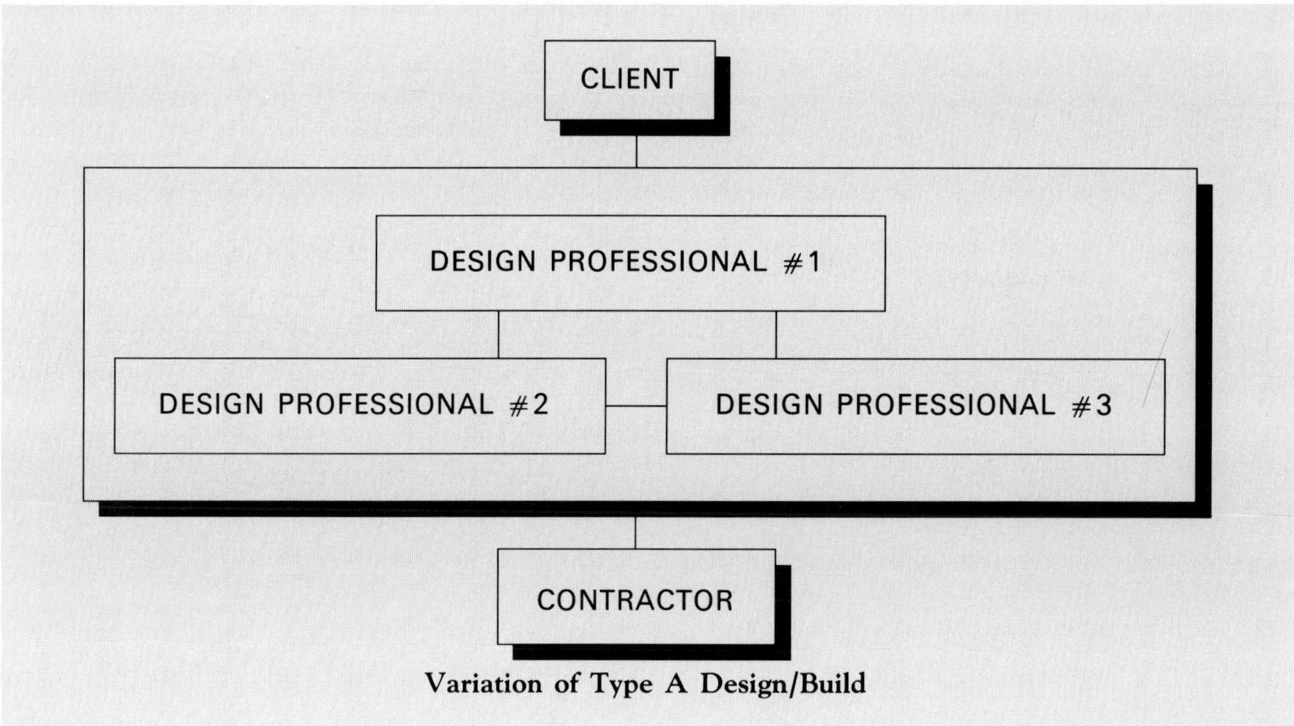

Figure 2.2

Alternatively, a design professional with strong construction management skills may decide to function as a general contractor and subcontract all construction activities to trade contractors. These trade contractors then have a direct contractual relationship with the design professional (see Figure 2.4).

The Design Professional's Responsibilities

In a Type A design/build arrangement, the design professional is contractually responsible to the client for all aspects of both the design

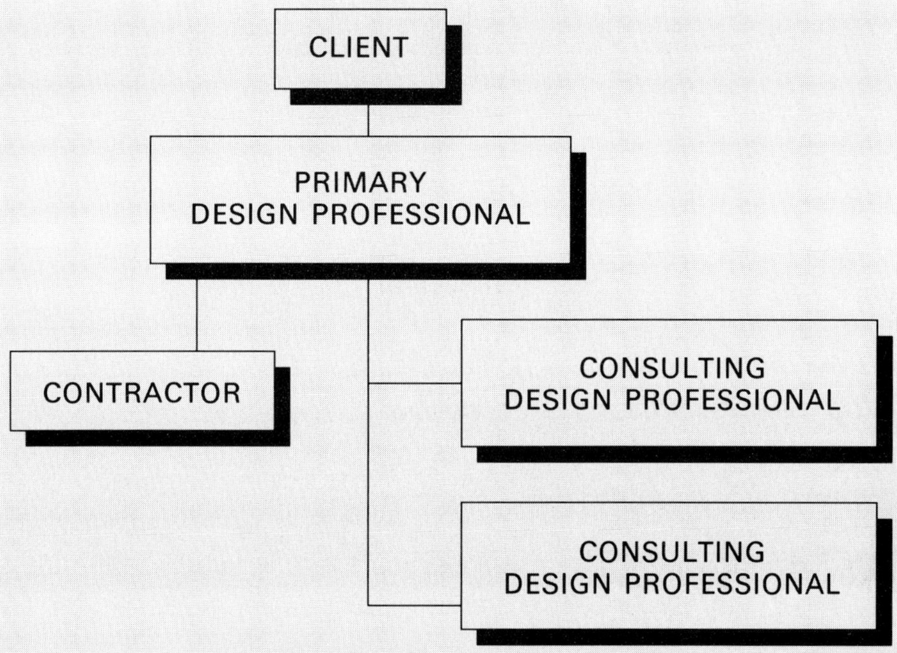

Variation of Type A Design/Build

Figure 2.3

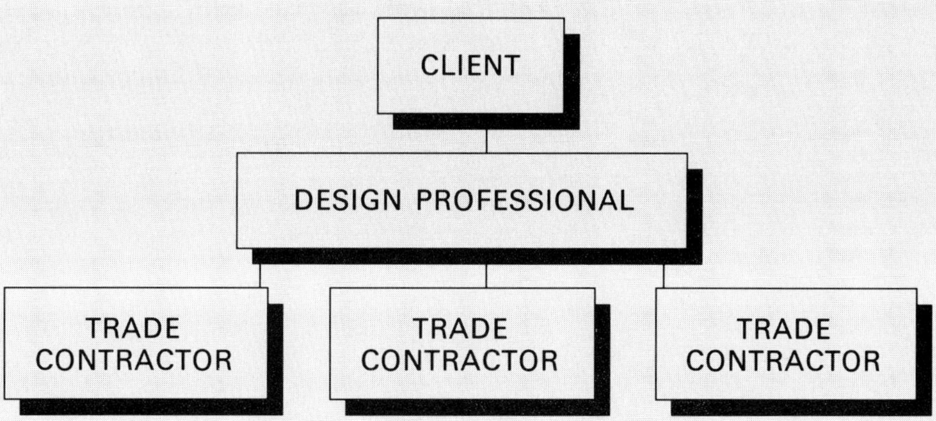

Variation of Type A Design/Build

Figure 2.4

and construction of the project. Like traditional methods of project delivery, the design professional is responsible for any failure of the project's design to conform to applicable codes, standards of professional practice, or other requirements pertaining to professional services stated in the agreement between the client and the design professional. In addition, the design professional is responsible to the client for all construction-related matters, including the failure of a contractor to comply with the construction-related requirements of the contract between the design professional and the client.

Depending on the jurisdiction in which the project is located, and the specific terms of the contractual arrangement between the client and the design professional, the design professional may also be responsible to the general public for construction-related matters. In traditional projects, for instance, a contractor is responsible to the public for site safety measures and compliance with state and federal safety regulations. In Type A design/build, the design professional may also share this responsibility through its contract with the client. Applicable law may also hold the design professional liable for the acts or omissions of those with whom he or she contracts to provide a portion of the services owed to the client.

While the design professional's responsibilities in the traditional method of project delivery are limited to project design and administration of the construction contract, the Type A design/build arrangement holds the design professional responsible if the project fails to conform to the requirements of the construction documents as approved by the client. In addition, the Type A design professional is likely to be responsible for any failure to construct the project in a good and workmanlike manner, and in accordance with applicable industry standards and building codes, and other laws, rules, and regulations.

In traditional forms of project delivery, the design professional's cost obligations are typically limited to redesigning the project to conform to any contractual limit of construction cost. The design professional is not obliged to bear the amount by which actual construction costs exceed the limit established in his or her agreement with the client. In a Type A design/build arrangement, however, the design professional assumes financial responsibility for costs exceeding the contractual limit or guaranteed maximum construction costs.

The Contractor's Responsibilities

In traditional methods of project delivery, the contractor has a direct contractual relationship with the client to provide required construction services. In a Type A design/build arrangement, the client does not contract with the contractor for such services and therefore cannot hold the contractor contractually responsible for compliance with the requirements of the construction documents prepared by the design professional. Neither is the contractor responsible to the client for compliance with applicable codes, rules, laws, or other regulations. Since the design professional contracts with the contractor for required construction services, it is the design professional to whom the contractor is responsible, not the client.

The Type A design/build contractor may be responsible to the general public regardless of the parties involved in the construction contract, although the specific terms of the contract may affect the extent of that responsibility. The contractor's responsibility to the general public under this arrangement is not diminished merely because the contractor is engaged by the design professional rather than by the client.

Type B: The Contractor as Primary Contractor

Structure

The Type B design/build arrangement is one of the most frequently used design/build structures, due largely to the ease with which it can be created. In this arrangement, the client contracts directly with the contractor for all design and construction services required to complete the project. The contractor then contracts directly with the design professional, who supplies the contractor with all required design services. The contractor provides the client with all required construction services based on the design professional's documentation (see Figure 2.5).

There are many variations of the basic Type B design/build arrangement, depending on the contractor's strengths and weaknesses, client requirements, and marketing, economic, or other factors. In some instances, a contractor may prefer to function as a construction manager rather than a traditional contractor, (see Figure 2.6); or a client may prefer to contract with a construction manager rather than a contractor for all required design and construction services (see Figure 2.7). These options are both possible given the flexibility of the design/build method.

If, under the Type B arrangement, the contractor's design professional cannot provide all design services required for the project, the contractor has at least three options. First, the contractor may retain a primary design professional to provide most of the required design services, and stipulate that the remaining design services be provided by design professionals acting as subconsultants to the primary design consultant (see Figure 2.8). This arrangement is similar to many traditionally structured projects, where the primary design professional is the architect who, in turn, separately retains professional consultants to provide expertise in structural engineering, mechanical and electrical engineering, landscaping, site utilities, and civil engineering.

Second, the contractor may contract separately with two or more design professionals to provide all required design services for the project. In this scenario, however, there is no primary design professional. The contractor is required to manage and coordinate the services of each (see Figure 2.9).

The third option is to have two or more design professionals join forces to provide the contractor with all required design services (Figure 2.10).

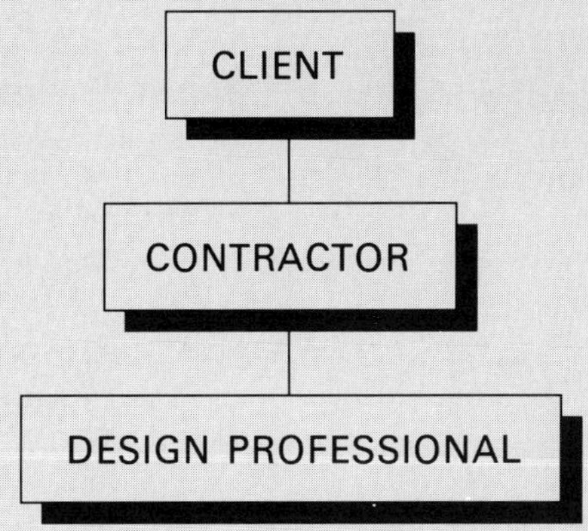

Type B Design/Build
Contractor as Primary Contractor

Figure 2.5

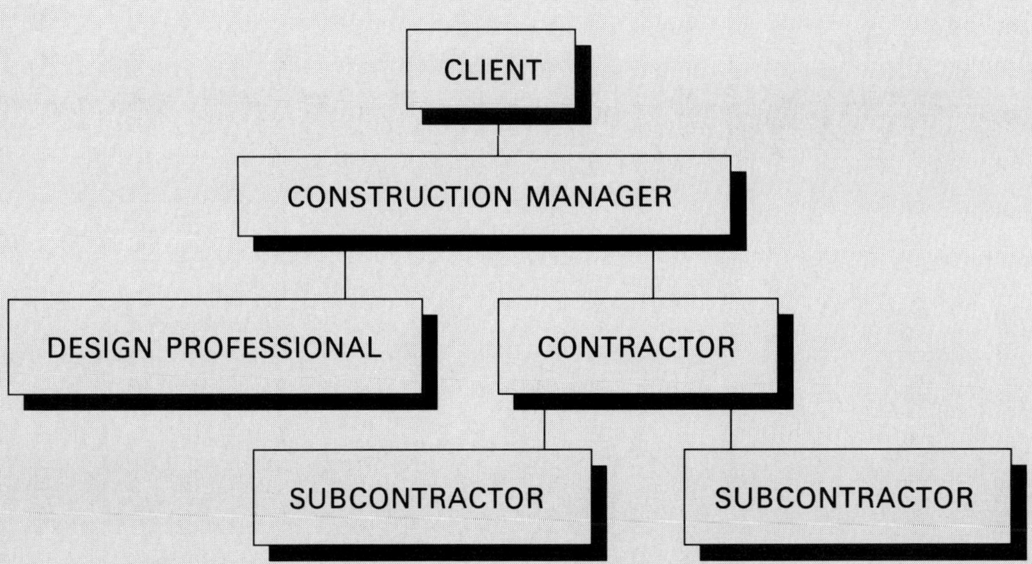

Variation of Type B Design/Build

Figure 2.6

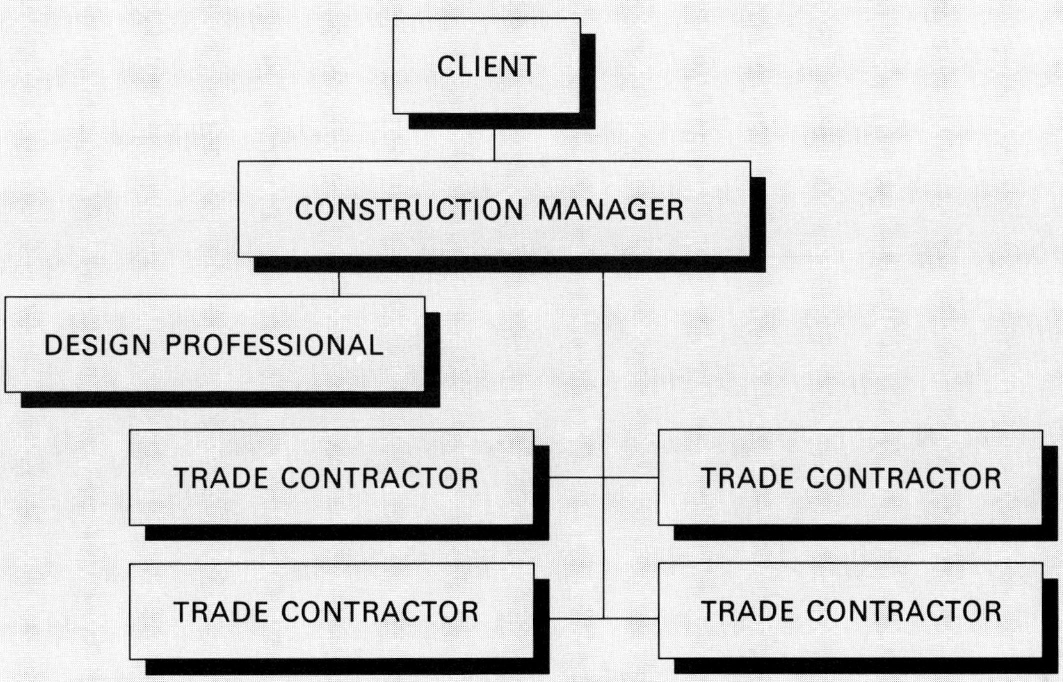

Variation of Type B Design/Build

Figure 2.7

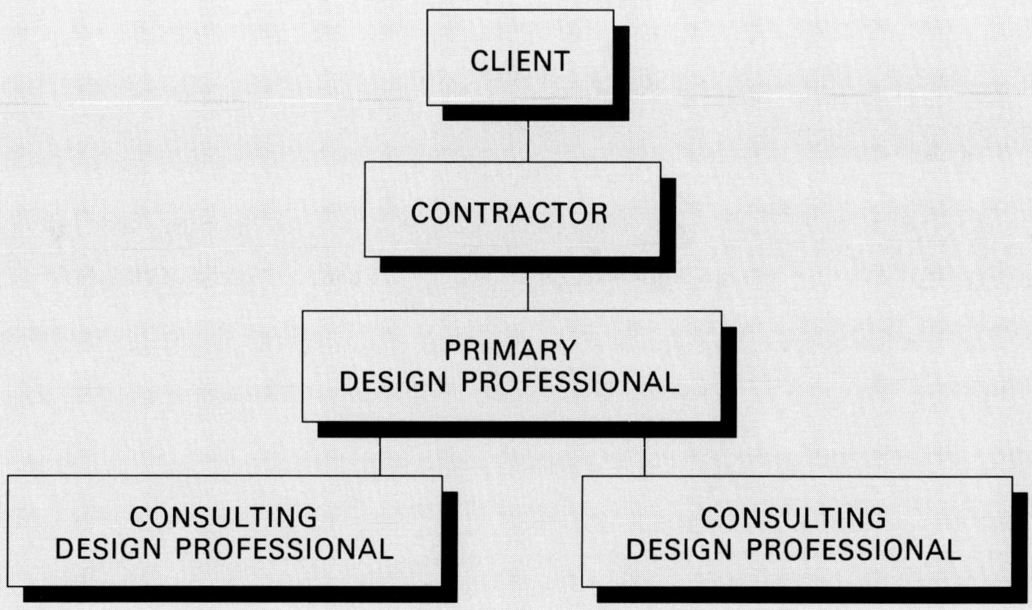

Variation of Type B Design/Build

Figure 2.8

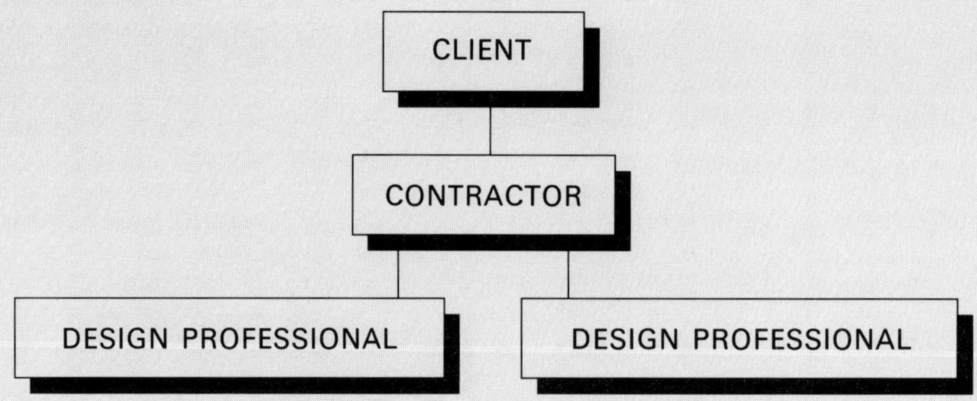

Variation of Type B Design/Build

Figure 2.9

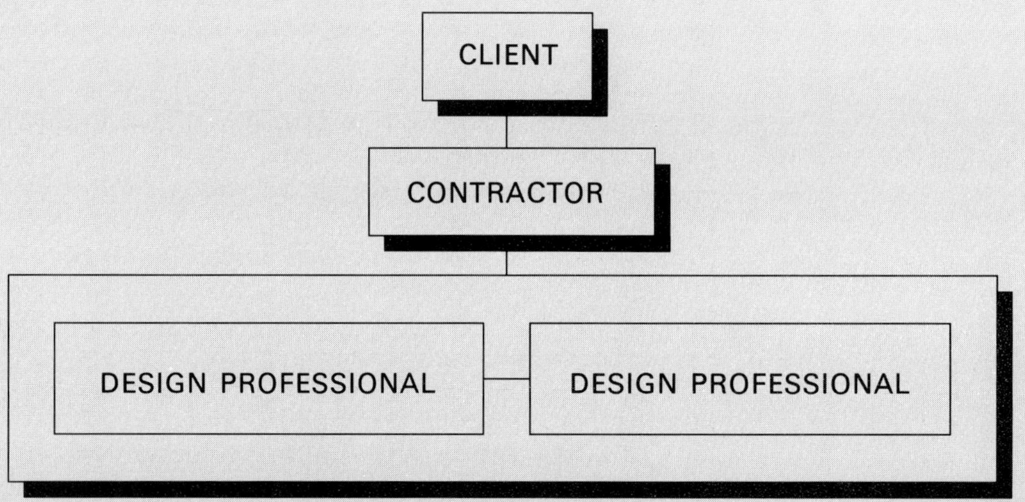

Variation of Type B Design/Build

Figure 2.10

The Design Professional's Responsibilities

In Type B design/build, the design professional is accountable to the contractor for any failure of the project's design to conform to applicable codes, standards of professional practice, or other services stated in the agreement between the contractor and the design professional. The design professional is not contractually responsible to the client, however, for any design-related services, nor for any of the contractor's construction-related activities. The design professional's responsibility to the public under Type B design/build, however, is not diminished merely because the contractor, rather than the client, retained the services of the design professional.

If the project's construction costs exceed its budget, the design professional's responsibilities in the Type B structure are typically limited to redesigning the project at no additional cost to the contractor in order to bring it within the project's budget or any fixed limit of construction cost.

The Contractor's Responsibilities

In Type B design/build, the contractor is responsible to the client for both the design and construction of the project. This includes responsibility for failure of the project's design to conform to applicable codes, standards of professional practice, or other professional services stated in the agreement between the contractor and the client. Furthermore, the contractor is responsible for failure to construct the project in a good and workmanlike manner, in accordance with applicable industry standards, building codes, and other laws, rules, and regulations.

Depending on the language of the contract between the contractor and the client in Type B design/build, the contractor may not be responsible to the client for failure of the project's construction to conform to the construction documents. This is because the construction documents are prepared by the design professional, who is retained by the contractor. Although the client may be entitled to review and approve the design documents and perhaps the outline specification for major building systems, such approval may not extend to the detailed construction documents and specifications. In fact, the client may never see such documents, which are often prepared chiefly for the convenience of the contractor who might use them in soliciting bids from subcontractors or trade contractors.

Type C: The Joint Venture as Primary Contractor

Structure

The Type C design/build arrangement is somewhat more complicated and time consuming to organize and manage than either a Type A or Type B design/build arrangement. Nevertheless, it is an approach employed frequently by design professionals and contractors who wish to engage in design/build. In simple terms, the design professional and contractor enter into a *joint venture agreement* in which they contract with the client to perform all design and construction services required for the project (see Figure 2.11). The joint venture agreement then delegates responsibility for the performance of these services to one or the other of these parties.

Some joint ventures have their own substance, or existence. They may have employees, rent or own space and equipment, and generate profits and losses like any other business organization. Other joint ventures are purely contractual arrangements between two or more parties. Such arrangements may exist only on paper. These joint ventures are referred to as *pass-through joint ventures* because they do not perform services, employ personnel, or rent or own space or equipment, although they could certainly generate profits or losses. Instead, the joint venture subcontracts out to the design professional and the contractor all design and construction services required for the project (see Figure 2.12). All administrative, management, and financial services required by the joint venture, and all professional services required by the project, are provided by one or the other joint venture members according to their respective subcontract arrangements. All profits and losses are passed through the joint venture to its members. No assets are retained at the joint venture level.

Variations of the joint venture relationship may depend on the individual strengths and weaknesses of the design professional and the contractor, on client requirements, or marketing or economic conditions. If the design professional and/or the contractor are not capable of performing all required design and construction services themselves, they each may subcontract to other qualified consulting design professionals and subcontractors portions of the required services (see Figure 2.13). It is important to note that it is the individual joint venture *members*, and not the joint venture shell, who are subcontracting to provide the professional consulting or subcontracting services. On the other hand, the joint venture shell itself might subcontract to one or more consulting design professionals and/or subcontractors for selected portions of the required services (see Figure 2.14).

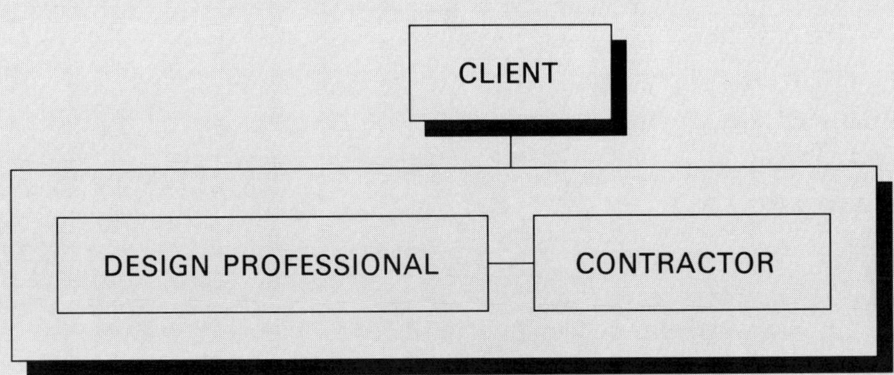

Type C Design/Build
Design Professional/Contractor Joint Venture as Primary Contractor

Figure 2.11

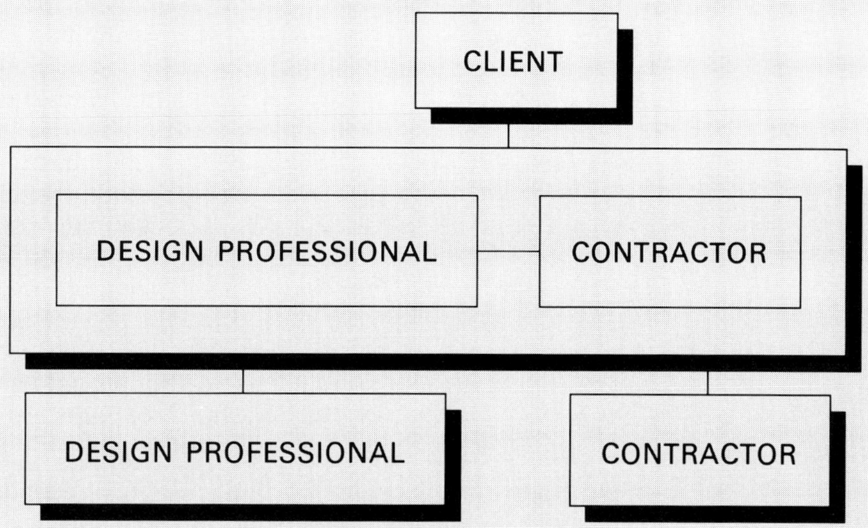

Type C Design/Build
Pass-Through Joint Venture

Figure 2.12

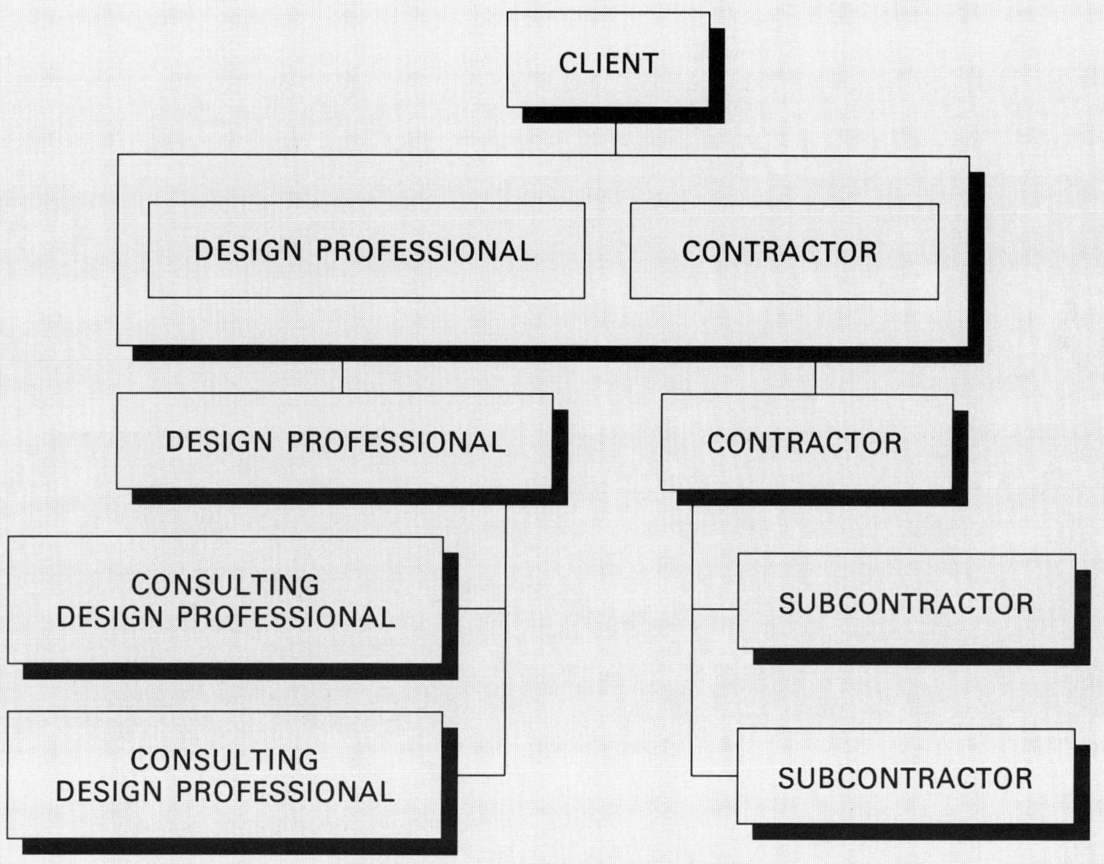

Variation of Type C Design/Build

Figure 2.13

Joint venture design/build organizations structured like Figures 2.11 and 2.14 are typically established in anticipation of a long business relationship, perhaps in connection with a number of projects. The joint venture design/build arrangements described in Figures 2.12 and 2.13, however, are typically established for purposes of a single project. This flexibility is useful for those who do not want to create whole new administrative, management, and financial structures for relationships with other parties when those relationships are likely not to extend beyond a single project.

The Responsibilities of the Design Professional and Contractor

In Type C design/build, both the design professional and the contractor are contractually responsible to the client for the design and construction of the project. Both of these parties are responsible to the client for any failure of the project's design to conform to applicable codes, standards of professional practice, or other professional requirements stated in the agreement between the client and the design professional/contractor joint venture. Both parties are also responsible to the client for all construction-related matters, and for failure of the construction to comply with either accepted construction practices or with the construction-related requirements of the contract between the client and the joint venture.

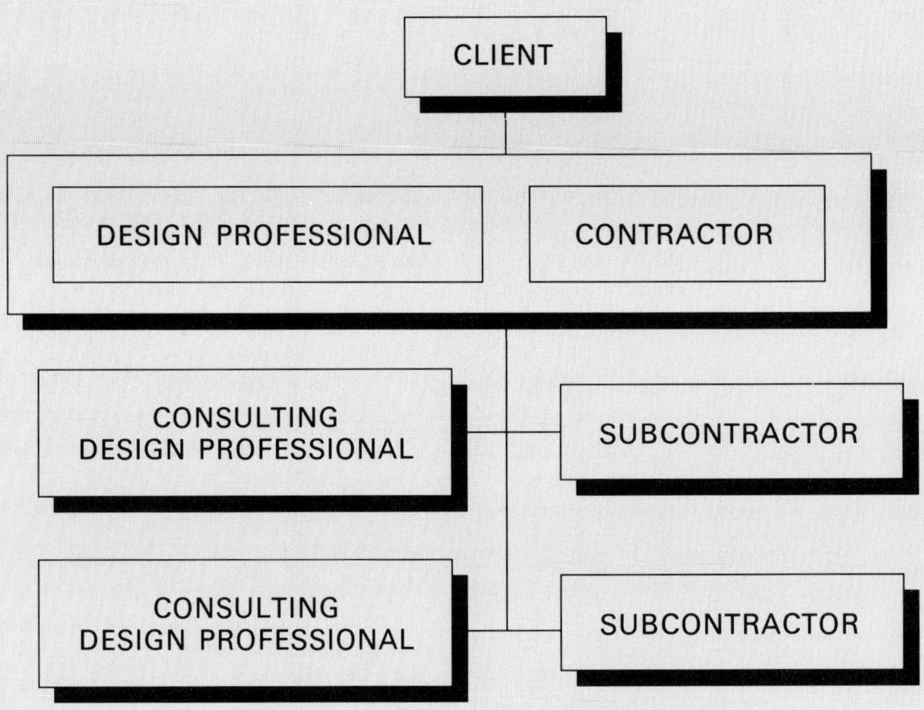

Variation of Type C Design/Build

Figure 2.14

What distinguishes Type C design/build from types A and B is the legal relationship between the design professional and the contractor. A joint venture is considered a form of partnership between two or more parties. As such, joint ventures are governed, to a large extent, by the same laws that govern partnerships. A fundamental tenet of partnership law is that each partner is responsible not only for its own acts and omissions, but also for the acts and omissions of each of its partners. There is no limitation to the extent of one partner's responsibility to third parties for the acts and omissions of the other partners. Each partner is *jointly and severally liable* for the acts and omissions of its partners.

Joint ventures are typically created by agreement between the parties with respect to a specific purpose, such as the design and construction of a single project. When that goal or purpose is realized, the joint venture formally goes out of business or otherwise ceases to exist. Regular partnerships are more often created by parties who have general business or professional objectives in mind and who contemplate a longer term relationship with no predetermined point of termination. A partnership would likely be created by parties whose interests lay in the design and/or construction of many projects, rather than a single project.

Throughout history, individual architects and engineers have joined together in partnership to practice their respective disciplines. There may or may not have been a written partnership agreement between the parties, but the nature of their relationship and how they conducted their business and professional affairs is what characterized their relationship as a partnership.

A joint venture, on the other hand, is often created by a written agreement between the parties. Since it is the parties' intent to limit their relationship to specific projects, and not to have their relationship construed as a general business partnership, a written agreement describing in detail the extent and limitations of that relationship is often used to achieve that purpose. Sometimes the term *contractual joint venture* is used to distinguish the purpose and the nature of the joint venture from other entities, which may be referred to as *partnerships*.

This distinction between a partnership and a contractual joint venture may be significant with respect to the joint venture members' responsibility to the general public. Depending on the laws of the jurisdiction in which the project is located, and the specific terms of the contractual agreements between these parties, the design professional and the contractor may be jointly and severally responsible to the general public for any failure of the project's design to conform to applicable codes or standards of professional practice, or for failure to construct the project in a good and workmanlike manner in accordance with applicable industry standards, building codes, and other laws, rules, and regulations. They may also be jointly responsible for failure to comply with other requirements pertaining to professional services or construction-related matters stated in the agreement between the client and the design professional/contractor joint venture.

While the design professional and the contractor may be jointly and severally liable to the client and the general public for their acts, errors, omissions, or failures to comply with the requirements of their agreement with the client or with the requirements of applicable codes or laws, they may nevertheless each be entitled to *indemnification* by the other to the extent that the act or omission was found to be the other's fault. For example, if a Type C contractor was found liable based on joint and several responsibility for damages incurred by the client as a result of some error on the part of the design professional, the contractor could, either by operation of law or by the terms of the joint venture agreement, be entitled to recover from the design professional all sums which the contractor was required to pay to the client.

Indemnification occurs most often in organizations like that in Figure 2.12, where the joint venture is merely a shell and contracts separately with the design professional and the contractor. (See Chapter 9 for more information on indemnification.)

Type D: The Design/Build Organization as Primary Contractor

Structure

In this arrangement, the design/build organization as a single legal entity, (neither solely a design professional nor a contractor), agrees to provide all design and construction services required for the project. The design/build organization may employ staff made up of sufficiently knowledgeable and capable design professionals, construction managers, and administrators, and a sufficiently skilled construction labor force, to perform all services required for project completion (see Figure 2.15).

Often, however, the design/build organization itself is not capable of performing all required design and construction services. In such cases the design/build organization may subcontract portions of required services to consulting design professionals and/or subcontractors, who would then provide these services to the design/build firm (see Figure 2.16).

Figures 2.15 and 2.16 suggest that the design/build organization has a certain physical existence of its own, with employees, space, and equipment with which to perform at least some of the services required for the project. However, it may be the case that the design/build organization provides no services itself, either because it chooses not to, or because it does not have on staff sufficiently skilled or experienced individuals in the design and construction disciplines, or because the design/build organization is, in fact, nothing more than "paper deep." In this situation, the design/build organization acts like a shell, performing

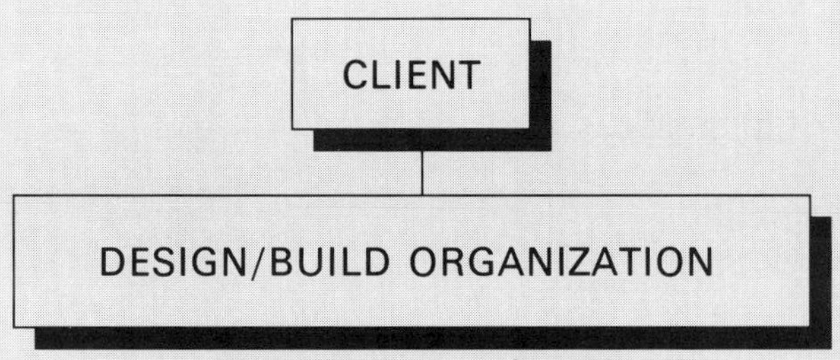

Type D Design/Build
The Design/Build Organization as Primary Contractor

Figure 2.15

none of the services itself and subcontracting all required design and construction services to others (see Figure 2.17). This design/build organization is similar to certain Type C joint venture design/build entities that are purely legal creations with little physical presence other than the legal papers executed by the joint venture members to establish the existence of the organization.

A Type D design/build organization may be owned by a single individual, called a *sole proprietor*, or by a single entity, such as a design or construction firm. Or, it may be owned by a partnership of individuals and/or entities (other than a contractual joint venture). Such partnerships may or may not be owned by design professionals or contractors. A Type D design/build organization may also be a corporation, owned by all of its shareholders just like any other corporation. Regardless of how ownership is established, what is important to note is that it is a legal entity separate and distinct from those who own it. The design/build organization stands on its own, independent of its owners' separate identities.

Unlike the Type C joint venture, where the design professional and contractor, as joint venture members, may choose to subcontract all or portions of required services to themselves, in a Type D design/build organization, such subcontracting activities cannot occur. This is because the design/build organization exists independent of its owners and therefore has no members to whom services may be subcontracted.

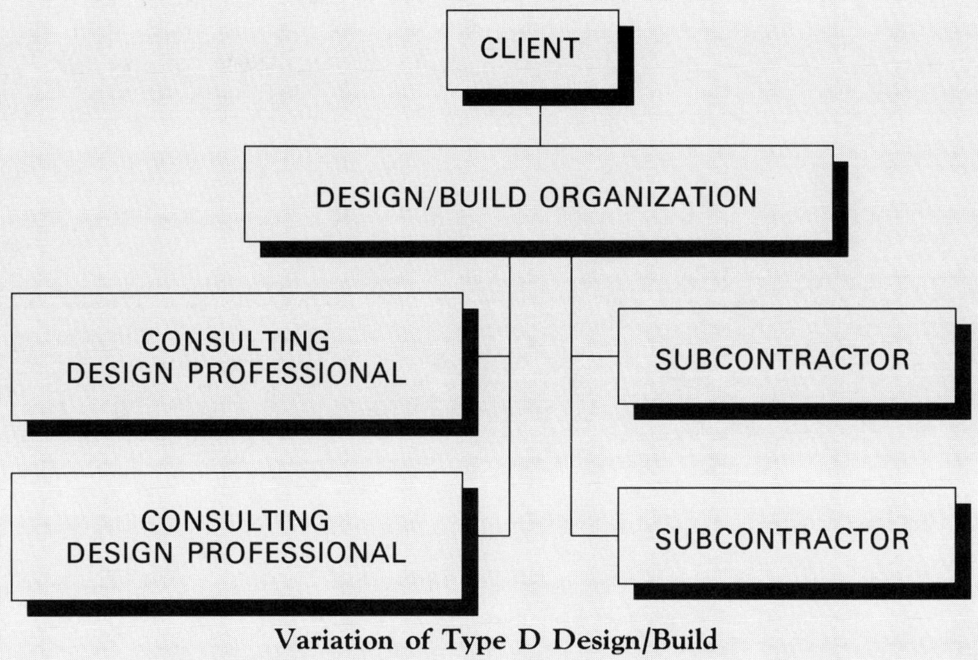

Variation of Type D Design/Build

Figure 2.16

The Design/Build Organization's Responsibilities

A Type D design/build organization is contractually responsible to the client for any failure of the project's design to conform to applicable codes, standards of professional practice, or other requirements pertaining to professional services stated in the agreement between the design/build organization and the client. The design/build organization is also responsible for all construction-related matters and for the failure of the construction to comply with accepted construction practices and the construction requirements of the contract with the client. In turn, all design professionals, contractors, subconsultants, and subcontractors who are retained *by* the design/build organization are responsible *to* the design/build organization for their work. The design/build organization may also be responsible to the general public for any omissions in or failures of its work.

When subconsultants or subcontractors are retained by the design/build organization, as in Figure 2.16, or a separate design professional and contractor are retained, as in Figure 2.17, the responsibility of these parties to the design/build organization and the general public are determined in much the same manner as the contractor's responsibility under a Type A design/build arrangement, or the design professional's responsibility under a Type B design/build arrangement. For instance, in Type D design/build, the design/build organization is responsible to the client for all design and construction-related matters, while the design professional is responsible to the design/build organization for design issues only, and the contractor is responsible to the design/build organization only for construction matters.

Because, theoretically, there are no separate identities in a Type D design/build organization, there can be no legally meaningful or enforceable allocation of design or construction responsibility *within* the organization. Therefore, joint and several responsibility and possible indemnification (which may be applicable between parties comprising a joint venture), is not legally possible in a Type D arrangement.

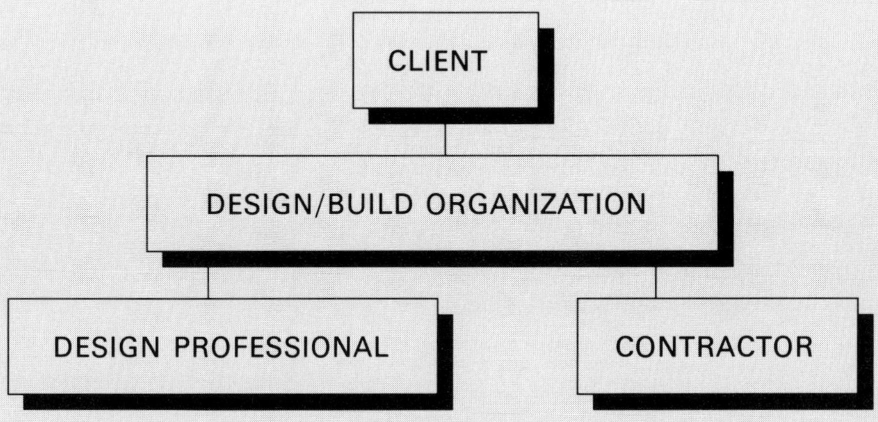

Variation of Type D Design/Build

Figure 2.17

Summary

There are four basic arrangements through which design/build services are provided to clients. They are distinguished from one another by the primary contractor, or party who contracts directly with the client. In the Type A arrangement, the client contracts directly with the design professional for both design and construction services. The designer may then solicit the services of contractors to construct the project. In Type B design/build, the client contracts with the contractor for both design and construction services. The contractor may then contract with one or more design professionals or consultants to provide design services. In Type C, the client contracts with a joint venture that is comprised of one or more design professionals and contractors. The joint venture is a separate legal entity, similar to a partnership, but usually operating on a temporary, project-by-project basis. Finally, in the Type D arrangement, the client contracts with a design/build organization which has, on staff, or solicits the services of, the necessary design professionals and contractors to complete a project. Type D differs from Type C in that it is generally a corporation established on a long-term basis.

As a general rule, the primary contractor, whether the design professional, contractor, joint venture, or design/build organization, is responsible to both the client and the public for the satisfactory completion of a project. Parties who are hired by the primary contractor to provide ancillary design or subcontracting services are usually responsible to the primary contractor, not the client, but may be held accountable on an indemnity basis for conflicts that occur between the client and the primary contractor as a result of deficiencies in their work (see Figure 2.18).

There are variations to these four arrangements, and liability may vary depending on the particular contract or project. Part II explores the advantages and disadvantages to each of the participants of the design/build method of project delivery. Chapter 3 begins with the client.

Allocation of Responsibility in the Four Design/Build Arrangements

	Design Professional	Contractor
Type A Design Professional as Primary Contractor	• Responsible to client for design *and* construction. • Responsible to public for design *and* construction.	• Responsible to design professional for construction. • Responsible to public for construction.
Type B Contractor as Primary Contractor	• Responsible to contractor for design. • Responsible to public for design.	• Responsible to client for design *and* construction. • Responsible to public for design *and* construction.
Type C Design Professional/Contractor Joint Venture as Primary Contractor	• Design professional and contractor are responsible to the client and the public for design and construction of project. Each party to the joint venture is jointly and severally liable for errors and omissions caused by their associates. • According to applicable indemnification laws, either party may hold the other responsible for that party's demonstrated errors and omissions.	
Type D Design/Build Organization as Primary Contractor	• Organization is a single entity; no individual is recognized within the entity. As such, the organization as a whole is responsible to the client and the public for design and construction services. • Because there is no allocation of responsibility in-house, joint and several liability and indemnification do not apply.	

Figure 2.18

Part Two

Design/Build Advantages and Disadvantages

We now know what the design/build process is, how to distinguish it from other methods of project delivery, and the four basic structures of design/build firms. The next question is, what are the advantages and disadvantages of using this method over other methods of project delivery and, more specifically, what benefits and pitfalls are involved in each design/build arrangement? Part II explores these matters from the perspectives of the principal participants: the client, the contractor, and the design professional. Chapter 3 begins with the client.

Chapter Three

The Client

In any given situation, what one party perceives as an advantage or an opportunity may be viewed as a disadvantage by another. This is no less true for the participants in design/build. The internal structure of the design/build firm, each participant's level of expertise, the manner in which the design/build services are procured, and even the political and economic climate at the time of project delivery, may all have a significant impact on the participant's experience. This chapter examines the advantages and disadvantages of design/build from the client's perspective.

Advantages to the Client

What prompts an increasing number of clients to choose design/build over other methods of project delivery? It may vary, depending on the client and the specific circumstances of the project. The following represent some of the more common reasons why clients may favor design/build over traditional construction methods.

Reduction in Total Project Delivery Time

Many clients choose the design/build process in an attempt to reduce total project delivery time—from inception to completion. There are a number of reasons why design/build may complete a project more quickly than other methods. The reason cited most often is that construction documentation need not be as extensive as that normally prepared in traditionally structured projects. Collaborative decision-making by the design professional and the contractor, a reduction in schedule delays, and the elimination of responsibility for preparation of the bid package are other ways in which the design/build method reduces total project delivery time. These time-saving measures are discussed in more detail in the following sections.

Reducing the Extent of Construction Documentation

Many traditionally structured projects use the fast track approach to reduce total project delivery time. In fast track construction the *sequencing* of the design professional's services may determine how quickly the project is realized. Overlapping certain design phases, for instance, enables the contractor to break ground sooner than if the he or she had to wait until all construction documents were completed in the usual sequence by the design professional.

Using the design/build approach, however (and depending on a number of factors including the structure of the design/build firm), it may be possible not only to overlap the sequencing of the design professional's services but to *vary the content or extent* of design services, enabling the construction phase of the project to begin sooner. For instance, if the design/build firm has experience constructing a particular building type, it may be possible to simplify the documentation for early site work and foundations. In this way, the design/build firm's contractor can begin rough site grading and foundation construction earlier.

Collaborative Decision-Making

The design and construction in many design/build projects is based on ongoing, collaborative decision-making by the design professional and the contractor, as opposed to the hierarchical approach that is characteristic of most other project delivery methods. Traditionally structured projects typically require that the design professional first determine his or her approach, and then either require contractors to competitively bid that approach or negotiate with one or more preselected contractors.

In design/build, the contractor has input—from the start—on what might normally be considered basic design decisions. For instance, a design/build firm may determine the structural and foundation systems of the building much earlier than a traditional design professional, since the design/build firm generally focuses more on *how* the project will be built rather than *what* should be built. Since decisions are made more quickly, work can begin sooner, and questions that arise during construction can be resolved more expediently.

There may be certain disadvantages to this collaborative decision-making approach. Clients may feel that they are trading quality for time. For some clients, the circumstances of a particular project may warrant such a compromise, while for others, it may not be the best approach. The fact is that in many instances, the design/build process may simply be a more efficient method of arriving at the same conclusions that would be reached using more traditional methods of project delivery.

Reducing Schedule Delays

In traditionally structured projects, problems concerning the coordination, clarity, completeness, and constructability of the drawings and specifications may create a legally charged atmosphere of allegation and denial concerning the state of the documents. Such disputes can sometimes result in schedule delays. Because responsibility for both design and construction is contained within the design/build firm, these problems are less likely to occur. Matters can be handled less formally, within the design/build firm, in many cases without the client's awareness.

It is also possible to reduce schedule delays in design/build projects by keeping the number of changes during the course of construction to a minimum. When both design and construction responsibility reside within the same design/build entity, it is in the best interests of both disciplines to maintain a cooperative and harmonious relationship. There are likely to be fewer changes in situations where the participants share common goals and are in constant communication with each other.

Changes are inevitable in every project, however. In the traditional method, project changes during construction are typically handled in a sequential manner. The change is first proposed by the proponent of the change, and is then reviewed by the design professional if someone other than the design professional initiated the proposed change. The design professional provides the client with recommendations and prepares the necessary drawings and specifications to document the change. If approved by the client, the design professional issues a *change order*. Only then is the contractor permitted to proceed with the approved change.

The process for effecting change can be simplified, and the time required to implement the change can be reduced when the project is delivered using the design/build approach. The design/build entity may be better able to respond and adapt to changes during construction than parties using traditional methods of project delivery. The link between the discovery of a problem or changed circumstances, and the solution to the problem or change, is much closer in a design/build project, since both design and construction activity takes place under one roof. Finding a solution and then communicating that solution to those responsible for implementing the change may be done less formally and more quickly.

The design professional's involvement in the change process is significantly reduced, or may be eliminated altogether. Usually the client's approval is all that is required to effect the change. Formal documentation may not be necessary, or may be less extensive than on traditional projects. Documentation can often be prepared while the change is being implemented, since its primary purpose is to *record* the change rather than *instruct* the contractor. Depending on the contractual arrangement between the design/build entity and the client, and the extent of client involvement in certain project decisions, client approval may not be necessary at all.

Eliminating Responsibility for Preparation of the Bid Package

The bidding process often used to procure design/build services may be faster and easier for the client than the competitive bidding method used to procure traditional projects. In traditional project delivery, projects are bid based on a very detailed set of drawings and specifications prepared by the client's independently retained design professional. Everything the contractor needs to know to prepare the cost proposal is contained in those plans.

In design/build, the capability to both design and construct a project is inherent in the design/build entity. The design/build team submits both the design concept (which may be less detailed than is necessary on traditional projects) and the cost proposal, or bid, to the client. Procurement for design/build involves fewer individuals, shifts the responsibility for bid package preparation from the client and independent design professional to the design/build team, and simplifies the bid package. As a result, the procurement process is simplified, and the time spent waiting for construction to begin may be reduced by several weeks or even months. (See Chapter 7 for more information on procurement methods.)

Reduction in Total Project Costs

The design/build client can reduce not only total project delivery time, but also costs. This goal can be achieved by reducing project delivery time and design costs.

Reducing Project Delivery Time

In construction, as in other industries, time is money. Most projects are financed in one way or another, with the cost of borrowing money increasing the longer it is borrowed. Naturally, the sooner a project can begin construction and the shorter the duration of the construction process, the less costly the project will be. Reducing project delivery time reduces total project costs.

Reducing Design Costs

Another area of potential savings, although relatively small in terms of total project cost, is the savings realized by reducing design costs. Design costs may be reduced in design/build since the designer in the design/build firm has to spend less time preparing drawings and specifications and administrating the construction of the project. Not all design/build projects can be performed with reduced documentation or less time spent in construction administration. These requirements depend, in large measure, on the resources of the design/build firm, local licensing and practice laws, the type and complexity of the project, and the client's expectations. Nevertheless, in the majority of projects, a savings in design costs is certainly possible.

Single Source of Responsibility

Another advantage to the client of the design/build method is the establishment of a single source of responsibility for virtually all design and construction activity. A single source of responsibility eliminates arguments over responsibility, reduces the client's management and administrative burden, and, in some instances, protects the client from liability. The following section explains these benefits in more detail.

Eliminating Arguments Over Responsibility

Certainly the principal advantage of design/build's single source of responsibility is the elimination of arguments over responsibility for errors or omissions, faulty performance, or coordination problems that inevitably arise during the course of the project. The finger pointing that sometimes occurs between design professionals and contractors on traditionally structured projects is avoided in design/build projects because the primary contractor, regardless of the design/build arrangement, is responsible to the client for errors and omissions in both the design and construction of the project. The client need not be concerned with the source of the problem.

Reducing the Client's Management and Administrative Burden

With the establishment of a single point of responsibility, the client need deal with only one entity with respect to all decision-making activities. In traditionally structured projects, the client's role often becomes that of manager or facilitator of communication between the design professional and the contractor. This task is eliminated using the design/build approach.

The client's administrative responsibilities are also reduced in design/build. A single set of accounts is kept for the design/build project, as opposed to the separate accounts that must be maintained for both the design professional and the contractor in traditionally structured projects.

Protection From Liability

A single source of responsibility may protect a design/build client from liability in certain situations by limiting his or her exposure to claims by the contractor. On a traditional project, clients are considered to have *impliedly warranted* (a legal term referring to the guarantee that is *inferred* based on the client's relationship with the contractor) to the contractor the accuracy, completeness, or sufficiency of the plans and specifications prepared for the project. If there is a serious fault with the documents prepared by the client's independently retained design professional, and the contractor incurs extra expense as a result, the contractor would probably be reimbursed by the client based on the theory that the client owed and failed to give to the contractor a proper set of plans and specification.

Using the design/build approach to construction, however, the client does not impliedly warrant the quality of the design drawings and specifications because the contractor obtains the drawings and specifications from his or her design/build associate (the design professional), not from the client. Any problem that stems from inadequate drawings is the responsibility of the design/build entity, not the client, and must be resolved in-house.

A single source of responsibility may afford the design/build client liability protection based on the legal conclusion that the liability that a *principal* owes to another (on account of the acts of its *agent*) does not occur in design/build. [An agent is a fiduciary, owing to its principal (in this case, the client) loyalty and service untainted by any conflict of interest.] During the construction phase of a traditionally structured project, the design professional acts as the client's agent in various matters involving the contractor. Among the design professional's responsibilities is determining contractor conformance with the requirements of the project.

If the design professional, acting as the client's agent, fails to advise the client of defects in the construction of the project, regardless of the reason for such failure, the client, in certain circumstances, may not be able to hold the design professional or the contractor responsible for the defects. Agency law states that the acts of the agent (in this case the design professional) are treated as the acts of the principal (the client). As such, the client is not permitted to benefit from the mistakes of his or her agent. In the case, the agent is the design professional who failed to notice the defects in construction.

This situation cannot occur in design/build, however, for the following reasons. The courts reason that the design professional cannot act as the client's agent in a design/build project because there is no fiduciary relationship between the two parties. Any loyalty to the client expressed by the design professional would compromise the design professional's primary interest in the design/build firm. Because there is no agency relationship between the client and the design professional (or the client and the contractor for that matter) in a design/build project, the client is free to hold the design professional and/or the contractor, as appropriate, liable for defects in the drawings and specifications, or any other acts and omissions in the design and construction of the project.

Inventive Design Solutions

Many clients believe that the design professional and the contractor may work together more creatively in a design/build setting to solve the various programmatic, design, and construction problems that typically arise on a project. One reason is that the design professional and the contractor on design/build projects are in close communication from the start of the project, long before completion of the design professional's drawings and specifications. Inventive design solutions may also be the product of common goals and increased responsibility assumed by the design professional and/or the contractor, depending on the design/build arrangement. Furthermore, the marriage of design and construction activities within a single organization makes each member of the organization aware of the skills, talents, and constraints of the others.

In short, the coordination and cooperation that design/build requires from its participants may lead to more inventive solutions to design problems than the traditional approach to design and construction. This distinction may be most noticeable on public-sector projects, where the traditional method of project delivery has not proved particularly conducive to inventive problem solving.

Reduction in Project Management Stress

Every project generates a certain amount of stress for the client, regardless of the manner in which it is delivered. The greatest concerns for most clients are whether or not the project will be completed on time and on budget, the extent to which the completed project will meet the client's expectations, and whether market trends will shift during the course of construction, with disastrous effects on the project's financial success. The multitude of individuals and government agencies who must be consulted, the questions that they, in turn, will ask, the decisions that must be made, and milestone events beyond the client's control which must pass before a project is considered complete can be a source of anxiety for even the most sophisticated client.

While no construction method can guarantee the client a trouble-free project, the design/build method may substantially reduce the level of stress, particularly for the relatively inexperienced client. First, as we have already seen, the design/build method reduces total project delivery time and costs—perhaps the two greatest concerns of every client. Project management stress may also be reduced in design/build by reducing the number of principal players with whom the client must interact. Because the design/build entity provides a single point of responsibility for most aspects of the project, the number of meetings with key project personnel and the coordination and scheduling conflicts that come with managing a number of individuals are reduced. Questions concerning the responsibilities of the design professional and contractor, which might involve the client in traditionally structured projects, are also reduced in design/build.

Reducing the Incidence of Claims in Projects Procured Through Negotiation

Many of the problems inherent in traditional bidding procurement practices are imported into the design/build process when the design/build firm is chosen in this manner. However, if the firm is selected after careful negotiation and discussion between the client and the design/build firm, many of the issues likely to give rise to problems on projects that are bid can be resolved during the design/build negotiation stage. As a result, the incidence of claims between clients and construction professionals is likely to be significantly reduced in design/build when the project is secured through negotiation. Negotiations give the parties the opportunity to get to know one other and to understand their mutual concerns and goals, to create and foster good communication channels among the parties, and to become familiar with project requirements, constraints, and probable costs—before any agreements are signed.

Advantages of Each Arrangement

The aforementioned advantages that design/build offers a client may vary somewhat, depending on the specific design/build arrangement chosen to deliver the project. The following discussion examines the advantages of each of the four basic design/build arrangements—types A, B, C, and D—from the client's perspective. (Each of these types is defined in the following sections. For a more detailed discussion of these organizational structures, see Chapter 2.)

Type A: Design Professional as Primary Contractor

In Type A design/build, the client contracts with a design professional who, as *primary contractor*, is responsible for all design and construction services required to complete the project. The client in this arrangement is likely to benefit from a reduction in total project delivery time and total project costs, as well as a single source of project responsibility. There are additional advantages to clients who engage in this design/build arrangement that may not be available under other design/build formats. The principal advantage is that the client is obtaining the design professional as an "independent professional advisor."

"Independent Professional Advisor" to the Client

The most important feature of the Type A design/build arrangement is that it offers the client the best opportunity of the four design/build arrangements to employ a design professional in the traditional role of professional advisor to the client. Of course the Type A design professional is not truly independent, since he or she maintains involvement in construction activities and has a financial interest in the project. However, in this type of arrangement, the project is more likely to be influenced by the design professional than the contractor. A Type A design/build structure is likely to satisfy the client who wants to maintain some semblance of the traditional fiduciary role between the design professional and the client.

Type B: Contractor as Primary Contractor

In Type B design/build, the client contracts directly with the contractor for all design and construction services required for the project. The contractor, in turn, retains the design professional for needed design services. Like Type A design/build, the client employing Type B is likely to benefit from a reduction in total project delivery time and total project costs, a single point of responsibility for all design and construction activities, and the flexibility gained by "marrying" the most qualified independent design professional and independent contractor best suited to the client's unique project requirements. Type B clients may also benefit from an emphasis on construction management, as explained below.

Emphasis on Construction Management

For clients who are more concerned with construction than design issues, Type B design/build places responsibility for these concerns in the hands of the party best able to handle them: the contractor. At the same time, this arrangement enables the client to directly control his or her relationship with the construction manager/contractor. This may be a critical factor on projects that demand a reduction in project delivery time. In the development of suburban low-rise speculative office projects, for example, market analyses may indicate a demand for space, available at a certain point in time. In such cases, the design/build client may be better served by a capable and experienced contractor and/or construction manager in the lead role, rather than a design professional.

In Type B design/build, all critical aspects of the project delivery process are driven by construction-related requirements. For instance, structural and mechanical systems, bay spacing, floor-to-floor heights, and exterior skin treatments can be established quickly by the construction manager/contractor based on experience and familiarity with these project components. Long lead items can be identified and ordered immediately.

Depending on the construction manager/contractor's experience, it may be possible to reduce design services, requiring only that the design professional adapt the construction manager/contractor's requirements to the site and prepare construction documents in just enough detail to bid or negotiate the job with trade contractors or subcontractors. In fact, there may be no need for the design professional to provide construction administration services. The design professional may only be required to interpret the design documents and review shop drawings.

Type C: Design Professional/Contractor Joint Venture as Primary Contractor

Type C design/build offers clients certain advantages that may not be available in other design/build arrangements. The Type C client contracts with the joint venture for all design and construction services required for the project. Like both Type A and Type B design/build arrangements, the client may enjoy a reduction in total project delivery time and total project costs, as well as the benefits of a single point of responsibility. In addition, clients who choose this method of design/build may enjoy direct access to both the design professional and the contractor. The benefits of this access are discussed in the next section.

Direct Access to Both the Design Professional and the Contractor

A client retaining a Type C design/build firm enjoys direct communication with and control over both the design and construction components of the project, a position not unlike that in a traditionally structured construction project, where the design professional and the contractor are retained separately by the client. However, in this form of design/build, as with all design/build arrangements, the client retains a single point of responsibility for all design- and construction-related matters. This may be of great significance to clients who do not wish to relinquish access to or control over one of the parties, as would be required with either a Type A or Type B design/build arrangement.

Type C clients may receive responses more quickly, regardless of the nature of their inquiries. In Type A design/build, clients may feel as though they are too far removed from the contractor, or from the design professional in Type B design/build. These clients may feel that their questions and concerns are not being communicated adequately through the primary contractor to the appropriate party. In Type C design/build, however, the client may obtain direct access to *both* the design professional and the contractor.

Type D: Design/Build Organization as Primary Contractor

Like types A, B, and C design/build, the Type D organization reduces total project delivery time and costs and provides the client with a single source of responsibility. Type D design/build also provides advantages that are unavailable in other design/build arrangements. This is because in Type D design/build, the design professional and the contractor form a separate legal entity (often a corporation or some form of partnership) which has a legal existence all its own. The client contracts with this organization for all design and construction services required for the project. The Type D client is often working with a design/build organization that has an experienced internal management structure, a proven track record on similar projects, and highly efficient in-house communication.

Experienced Internal Management Structure

A Type D design/build organization may afford the client an organization with a more experienced and stable internal management structure than other design/build arrangements and may therefore be better able to entirely focus on project-related issues. Internal management issues that may arise in Type C structures, for example, are likely to have already been resolved in Type D organizations, so that more time and energy can be focused on the project's requirements.

The Type D firm is also likely to have been in existence longer than the other design/build arrangements, since the latter are generally formed on an *ad hoc* basis for specific projects.

Design/Build with a Proven Track Record

A Type D arrangement offers the client an organization with a proven design/build track record. The *ad hoc* relationships of the other three design/build arrangements, while arguably permitting the most suitably qualified design professionals and contractors to work together on a given project, are usually temporary. These design/build entities are not able to develop the same kind of in-house, long-term working relationships that a Type D organization fosters. An established Type D design/build organization should have a record of work on similar projects that the client is able to review.

For example, a design professional may have successfully designed a number of medical facilities, and a given contractor may have participated in the construction of many such structures, but if the two individuals have never worked together before, it is difficult for the client to predict the success of their working relationship. Any strain between these two parties is bound to have a negative impact on the client, regardless of the contract language in the client's agreements with the design professional and the contractor.

Efficient In-House Communication

A Type D design/build organization is composed not of separate legal entities, but possesses all required design and construction services in-house. Communication between the design and construction components of that organization may be more efficient than in any other method of project delivery, including other design/build arrangements.

Disputes between the design and construction elements are less likely to occur in Type D than in types A, B, or C design/build, where not only the channels of communication between various parties have to be established, but the separate professional, business, and management approaches of each of the firms composing types A, B, or C design/build must be reconciled. While effective communication between the design and the construction components of a design/build organization does not in and of itself guarantee a successful project, certainly it is an important factor in the efficient and effective delivery of the project.

Figure 3.1 is a summary of the advantages that the design/build method offers the client, categorized according to the four design/build organizational structures.

Disadvantages to the Client

Prospective clients should be aware of the disadvantages of the design/build method. Naturally the effect of these characteristics varies depending on the circumstances in which the client conducts his or her activities, the client's goals and expectations for the project, and the design/build arrangement through which the project is delivered. The principal disadvantage a client may experience in employing the design/build method over other methods of project delivery is the loss of the design professional as a truly independent professional advisor. The ramifications of this change are explored in the following section.

Loss of Independent Professional Advisor

Perhaps the single greatest disadvantage to the client using the design/build method is the loss of the design professional in the traditional role as independent professional advisor to the client. This is true for all four design/build arrangements, although to a lesser extent in the Type A model. This view is based on the theory that the design

Advantages to the Client of the Design/Build Method

Advantages	Type A	Type B	Type C	Type D
Reduction in Total Project Delivery Time	✓	✓	✓	✓
Reduction in Total Project Costs	✓	✓	✓	✓
Single Source of Responsibility	✓	✓	✓	✓
Inventive Design Solutions	✓	✓	✓	✓
Reduction in Project Management Stress	✓	✓	✓	✓
Reducing the Incidence of Claims Through Negotiation	✓	✓	✓	✓
"Independent Professional Advisor" to the Client	✓			
Emphasis on Construction Management		✓		
Direct Access to Both the Design Professional and Contractor			✓	
Experienced Internal Management Structure				✓
Design/Build with a Proven Track Record				✓
Efficient In-House Communication				✓

Figure 3.1

professional cannot represent the client fairly if he or she has a financial interest in the project. This is a strong and widespread belief among the various design professionals' associations, such as the American Institute of Architects (AIA). Interestingly, the various contractors' associations, such as the Associated General Contractors of America (AGC), do not fully share this view.

Employment of the design professional as independent professional advisor to the client is a concept deeply rooted in the history of this country's professional associations, and supported by legal theories governing the duties of fiduciaries (agents who are contractually obligated to uphold the interests of the client). To support the design professional in a competitive industry, and out of a moral obligation to the client and the public, professional societies (chiefly the AIA) sought to establish ethical guidelines for the relationship between the design professional and the client, and between the design professional and the public at large.

These guidelines are based on the supposition that the design professional has a duty to work solely for the best interests of the client in the design and preparation of the construction documents for the project, consistent with the client's programmatic, budgetary, and other constraints. The design professional was to function much as a trustee acting on behalf of the trust's beneficiaries. The design professional was to represent the client during the construction of the project to ensure that the client did indeed receive the project as described in the contract. The design professional was prohibited from financial participation in the project, other than the professional fee it received from the client. According to these standards, the design professional could not own stock or other interests in any product specified for the project's completion. Any such connection might be seen as a potential conflict of interest, and would need to be disclosed to the client.

Acting on behalf of the client during the construction phase, the design professional could reject a portion of the contractor's work if it did not conform to the construction documents. The design professional was also responsible for approving the contractor's payment application and was to act as the impartial initial arbitrator in disputes between the client and contractor.

Because the design professional was expected to act as the client's representative during construction, and as impartial interpreter of the construction documents, any financial relationship between the design professional and either the contractor or any of the contractor's subcontractors, was strictly forbidden. It was not until the late 1970s, in response to anti-trust actions filed by the United States Department of Justice against several of the professional associations, that it became legally and ethically permissible for design professionals and other members of these professional associations to form contractual working relationships with contractors to share the financial rewards of a completed project. Only after these obstacles were removed could design professionals engage in the design/build method of project delivery.

But how could a design professional fulfill these responsibilities in an objective manner when contractually bound to the contracting arm of the project, and with a financial stake in the outcome of the project? Can the client possibly expect professional guidance and objective advice from a design professional who has a monetary interest in the project? Many argue that this is simply not possible. Clients who feel that they need an independent advisor to assist them in designing and monitoring the construction of the project, and to make decisions on their behalf, are urged to consider methods of project delivery other than design/build.

Many construction professionals feel that the design/build design professional cannot properly act as advisor and protector of the interests of the public either, and that the design professional may not be able to fulfill his or her customary obligations to the public or maintain the high level of public trust and confidence that has been accorded design professionals. The public, the argument goes, has come to rely on design professionals to exercise their professional judgment not only in the client's best interests, but in the greater interests of the community as a whole.

The design professional's decisions must address both public issues, such as conformance to regulations and codes and the quality of the public's built environment, and private concerns, such as compliance with the client's program and budgetary constraints. It is often both a professional and conceptual struggle to balance the client's private wishes with the design professional's perception of the public's needs. But if the design professional is no longer able to represent the interests of the client, how can that design professional protect the public's interests?

A design professional's diminished sense of obligation toward the public is a key issue. While it will always be possible to require by law that design professionals comply with rules and regulations of professional conduct as a precondition to professional licensing, it is still the design professional's sense of obligation and responsibility to the public at large that determines the quality and appropriateness of the built environment.

Disadvantages of Each Arrangement

A client who may be interested in using the design/build method should be aware of the disadvantages inherent in each design/build arrangement. The effect of these disadvantages may vary, depending on the experience of the project participants and the political and economic environment at the time of project delivery. Again, refer to Chapter 2 for a detailed discussion of each design/build arrangement.

Type A: Design Professional as Primary Contractor

The client may enjoy a contractual and close working relationship with the design professional in Type A design/build, but his or her relationship to the party performing the actual construction may be diminished. There is no contractual relationship between the client and the contractor in Type A design/build, and their working relationship may be reduced as well, since it is not entirely in the design professional's best interest to permit the client to communicate directly with the contractor. The client's relationship to the party performing construction management services may also be significantly reduced, as the following discussion illustrates.

Limited Connection with the Party Responsible for Construction Management

It may be necessary for clients employing Type A design/build to rely on the design professional's construction management capabilities to manage and coordinate the construction of the project. If the design professional is inexperienced or lacks the resources necessary to fulfill these responsibilities, the project and the client are both likely to suffer.

Under these circumstances, the design professional and the client may turn to the construction management capabilities of the contractor. This may not necessarily be a bad choice, provided the contractor is properly qualified. From the client's perspective, however, it moves the party responsible for the project's construction one step further from the client's influence. For the client, this may be too tenuous and too problematic a connection with the management of the project's construction.

The design professional could retain a qualified construction manager to act as independent consultant in construction matters. Legally, the client still maintains a single point of responsibility (in the design professional) for all design and construction-related activities on the project. In practice, however, the client may need to consult with the design professional's construction manager on many of the construction management issues arising during the course of the project. Having to obtain information from a party over whom he or she has no direct control may make the Type A design/build arrangement less attractive to the client.

Type B: Contractor as Primary Contractor

In Type B design/build, the design professional has no contractual relationship with the client whatsoever. This arrangement presents two major drawbacks to the client: loss of the design professional as independent professional advisor—more so here than in any other design/build arrangement—and a possible reduction in design quality.

Loss of Independent Professional Advisor

A tremendous conflict of interest exists when a Type B design professional attempts to perform on behalf of the client. The design professional simply cannot represent the interests of the client with the same degree of conviction, certitude, and success when retained by the contractor.

The client need merely ask the question, how can a design professional reject incorrect shop drawings, reject improperly performed construction work, withhold recommendation for payment for the work, or refuse to recommend approval of unnecessary change orders, when the design professional is retained by the contractor? Clearly, it would be extremely difficult for the design professional to do so without straining his or her relationship with the contractor.

Reduction in Design Quality

It is possible that the design quality of a Type B design/build project may be inferior to that of either a Type A design/build project or a traditionally structured project. Of course, this is based on the assumption that contractors do not generally make design decisions as competently as design professionals, and that the design professional's role in a Type B design/build project may be reduced. Unfortunately, clients will have to judge the validity of this theory for themselves.

Type C: Design Professional/Contractor Joint Venture as Primary Contractor

There are certain disadvantages to the client who chooses Type C design/build over other design/build arrangements. One obvious drawback is the loss of the design professional as independent professional advisor to the client. Another disadvantage that clients may overlook is the difficulty in dealing with a potentially fractured management structure. The following discussion explores these issues.

Loss of Independent Professional Advisor

The Type C design/build client does not have the luxury of an independent professional design consultant. The design professional's economic interests in the project and the obligations owed to the contractor as a member of the joint venture make it difficult for the design professional to provide the client with that degree of loyalty characteristic of the traditional client-design professional relationship. Even if the design professional could demonstrate convincingly that he or she had put the client's interests first, such an approach would probably be at the expense of the contractor.

Fractured Management Structure

Design/build clients should understand that a single point of legal responsibility (offered by all forms of design/build) is not the same as a single point of management responsibility. While a single point of legal responsibility exists in a Type C design/build firm, management responsibility must somehow be allocated between the design professional and the contractor as members of that joint venture. Unless the joint venture is structured internally to "speak with one voice" on administrative and management issues, the management structure may appear fractured, and the client may end up interacting with one or the other of the parties, or perhaps with both parties, on various design or construction issues. This puts the design/build client in the very same position as the client in a traditionally structured project, but with one big disadvantage: the client in Type C design/build has no independent professional advisor to serve as his or her representative in construction matters. The client retaining a Type C design/build organization is well advised to examine the internal management and administrative structure of the joint venture to avoid the possibility of bouncing from one joint venture member to the other for information.

Type D: Design/Build Organization as Primary Contractor

Type D design/build, like the other design/build arrangements, presents disadvantages of which potential clients should be aware. Once again, there is no design professional as independent professional advisor to the client. More specific to Type D arrangements is the potential inflexibility of the organization that makes it difficult to adapt to project needs.

Loss of Independent Professional Advisor

It is even more apparent in Type D design/build than in other design/build arrangements that the designer is in no position to act as independent professional advisor to the client during the course of the project. What exacerbates the problem is that the design and construction components of a Type D organization form a single legal identity, each inseparable from the other. In types B and C design/build, where the design professional and the contractor clearly are separate entities drawn together by contract, the design professional may follow his or her traditional instincts and feel obligated to act in the best interests of the client, regardless of any contractual, legal, or ethical restrictions. It is far less likely that the design component of a Type D design/build organization will feel this level of client loyalty. Clients who desire independent advice from design professionals should turn to other methods of project delivery.

Inflexibility

Of the four basic design/build structures, Type D design/build is least able to adapt to the particular needs of a client or project. Each of the other design/build structures, because they are *ad hoc* contractual arrangements formed for a specific project, can set up relationships relatively quickly, with appropriately qualified and experienced design professionals and contractors. When a specific project is completed, the type A, B, or C design/build team dissolves, with each party then free to associate with other parties on other projects.

The organizational and management structure and selection of staff in Type D design/build is geared more toward a long-term or permanent, rather than a temporary or short-term association. Type D design/build firms could associate contractually with other design professionals or contractors to meet the needs of a given project, but are not likely to do so since their business objectives are to develop such capabilities and experience in-house. Therefore, while a Type D design/build organization's strength lies in its tested internal working relationships and experience on certain projects, these qualities can also be limiting in situations where a project's specific requirements do not match the design/build organization's in-house skills or expertise.

Figure 3.2 is a summary of the disadvantages to the client of the design/build method of project delivery.

Disadvantages to the Client of the Design/Build Method

Disadvantages	Type A	Type B	Type C	Type D
Loss of Design Professional as Independent Professional Advisor	✓	✓	✓	✓
Limited Connection with the Party Responsible for Construction Management	✓			
Reduction in Design Quality		✓		
Fractured Management Structure			✓	
Inflexibility to Meet Specific Project's Needs				✓

Figure 3.2

Summary

Design/build offers certain advantages and disadvantages to potential clients. These are determined based on the requirements of the particular project, the experience level of the participants, and the method by which the design/build services are procured. Generally, the client chooses the design/build method of project delivery for the following reasons: reduction in total project delivery time, reduction in total project costs, provision of a single source of responsibility, possibly more inventive design solutions, reduction in management stress, and a reduction in the incidence of claims when design/build services are procured through methods other than traditional competitive bidding.

Each design/build arrangement presents its own advantages. Of the four design/build formats, Type A provides clients with the closest relationship with design professionals. Type B projects are best suited to clients seeking strong construction management services. In Type C design/build, clients have direct access to both the design professional and the contractor, and Type D clients are afforded a design/build firm with an experienced internal management structure, a proven track record, and efficient in-house communication.

The client should be aware of certain disadvantages inherent in the design/build process. Clearly, loss of the design professional as a truly independent professional advisor to the client is a major drawback that occurs in all four of the basic design/build arrangements.

There are also specific disadvantages associated with each design/build arrangement. In Type A, the client's connection with the contractor is limited. Type B clients have the least access to the design professional. In addition, some argue that the design quality is reduced in projects that are structured in this manner. Type C design/build also removes the client from the advice of the design professional. The management structure of the joint venture may be such that the client finds him or herself in direct contact with both the design and construction elements—a position similar to that of a traditional client. Finally, the Type D design/build firm may prove inflexible in some cases, and unable to adapt to the needs of a specific project.

The client should fully understand these factors before entering into any construction contract. Chapter 4 examines the advantages and disadvantages of the design/build method from the contractor's perspective.

Chapter Four

The Contractor

There are advantages and disadvantages of every method of project delivery. Just as the client must weigh the pros and cons of a particular method used to construct his or her project, so too must contractors and design professionals choose the method of project delivery best suited to their needs and skills. Naturally, what one participant perceives to be an advantage may not be an advantage to another at all. There will also be variables that are unique to each project which may determine the suitability and attractiveness of one method over another. This chapter examines the advantages and disadvantages of the design/build method from the contractor's perspective.

Advantages to the Contractor

There are a number of reasons why contractors choose the design/build method over other methods of project delivery. The reasons they give may depend on the types of clients with which each contractor enjoys working, how familiar the contractor is with the particular building type, the size and scale of the project, and to what extent the contractor wants to be involved in the design of the project. The following are reasons cited most often by contractors for entering the design/build market.

Increased Control Over the Project

One of the most important reasons contractors give for engaging in design/build is the increased control they may have over a greater range of project-related activities—the most significant of which is the design process.

Some contractors see a project's construction as the continuation of the art and science of design: the translation of ideas from two to three dimensions (the physical embodiment of social, economic, political, psychological, and philosophical attitudes), and not merely the attachment of seemingly disparate elements. Unfortunately, contemporary American society has stereotyped the design professional as the expert gifted in the art of design, and the contractor as skilled in the craft of construction. We know that it is possible, however, for an individual to excel at more than one activity, and that rigid roles stifle human potential.

Many other countries, notably Japan, recognize the importance of diversity and embrace the concept openly. The percentage of projects in Japan that are built using the design/build method is staggering compared to the United States. In Japan, design/build projects are perhaps even the norm, with most of that country's design professionals practicing their profession within construction companies that offer design services routinely as part of a broad spectrum of project delivery services.

For the contractor who wants to make rather than respond to design decisions, design/build offers an opportunity that is otherwise unavailable in more traditional methods of project delivery.

Greater Job Satisfaction

A contractor may experience greater job satisfaction by participating in a design/build project. This is undoubtedly due to the greater control the contractor assumes over the design and construction of the project. In fact, job satisfaction may be the primary motivation for many contractors involved in design/build.

Minimizing Risk and Project Uncertainty

All construction projects contain a number of unknowns. On a conventionally bid project, for example, the contractor will not have had the opportunity to meet the client or design professional beforehand to discuss their requirements and expectations for the project. The contractor does not participate in the development of the construction documents on which the bids are based. Indeed, it is likely that the contractor will have had little time to review those documents in detail before the bid is submitted. The traditional contractor responds to construction documents that reflect an inestimable number of decisions and assumptions on the part of the design professional, while the design professional may be responding to often vague or imprecise client requirements. A contractor's bid on a traditionally structured project, therefore, must necessarily include a significant "margin of error," or an amount to cover the economic risk of uncertainty.

Design/build projects, however, may be procured through negotiation, design competition, or a form of bidding that requires the design/build team to submit drawings as well as estimates. (See Chapter 7 for more information on procurement methods.) In each procurement method, the client meets with the design/build firm or its representative to discuss the project's requirements. The design/build contractor is in direct communication with the design professional from the start in assessing how the project can best be completed. The design/build firm is chosen not just on price but on its willingness and ability to meet project requirements. This may reduce much of the uncertainty that plagues traditional competitively bid projects. Naturally, when these uncertainties are reduced or eliminated, the cost to protect against them goes down, and any savings can then be shared in varying percentages by the design/build participants.

Improved Communication with the Design Professional

Effective communication is a critical ingredient in the success of any project, particularly communication between the design professional and the contractor. No set of construction documents, regardless of how detailed they are or how competent the design professional may be, is absolutely complete. The contractor will always need additional information. There will always be coordination issues to resolve and a significant interpretive role for someone (usually the design professional) to play during construction of the project. The design professional is often called on to interpret and apply both the design intent as well as the specific requirements of the construction documents to changes that occur during the course of a project.

The more closely linked the design professional and the contractor are, the more effective the communication between them will be. The different emphasis or goals that a design professional and a contractor bring to a traditionally structured project are likely to be synchronized in a design/build project. Certainly economic motivations contribute to improved communication. But unless the design/build firm is the product of a forced marriage of the design and construction components, their relationship is based on shared philosophical, professional, as well as commercial interests. This type of relationship engenders an eagerness to work together to resolve problems when they do arise, and to do so expediently.

Opportunity to Increase Profits

The design/build process may afford the contractor an opportunity to increase profits over those which might normally be earned using traditional methods of project delivery. The contractor may do this not just by participating in whatever design fees might be charged, but by assuming greater control over a wider range of project-related activities, including the selection of construction materials and methods, reducing design services, and responding quickly to unanticipated changes.

Controlling the Selection of Construction Materials and Methods

Design fees may vary tremendously from one design professional to the next, depending on the approach each design professional employs to provide its services. Regardless of the method by which designers arrive at their fees, the fees themselves are usually very small in relation to total project costs. A design/build firm's income on a given project is usually not significantly increased simply by including design services as part of the total package of project-related services. Rather, a design/build firm's profits are increased because the contractor has assumed greater control over the selection of construction materials and methods, and chooses those that are cost-effective and with which the contractor is most familiar.

The contractor on a traditional project is not always able to determine the availability or the price of a specific item at the time the bid is submitted or the contract negotiated with the client, and may feel that an alternate item is sufficient and that any variations between the original item and the proposed substitute are insignificant. But substitutions on traditionally structured projects must first be approved by the design professional. The design professional may not be inclined to accept the contractor's substitution if it varies materially from the item specified in the design documents.

In a design/build project, differences concerning materials are more often resolved in the contractor's favor, permitting the contractor to control costs and, ultimately, increase profits. Depending on the particular structure of the design/build firm, the client might never be aware that a substitution has occurred.

Reducing Design- and Construction-Related Activities

A design/build contractor may increase profits by reducing the extent of design services. The level of documentation required to inform the contractor of the design professional's intentions may be less on a design/build project than on a traditionally structured project, since the contractor in many instances only needs to know certain basic information, such as the general configuration and relationship of project components, with many specific decisions to be determined by the contractor at a later date. If the contractor charges the client what would otherwise be a typical design fee, but pays less in design fees to the design professional, the contractor saves money and increases profits.

There may also be many construction-related activities normally performed by design professionals and contractors alike which can be reduced or eliminated. For instance, the process of preparing and documenting change orders can be streamlined. Construction administration services performed by the design professional on a traditionally structured arrangement, and the time spent by the contractor conforming to the administrative procedures, may be reduced or eliminated on a design/build project.

Responding Quickly to Unanticipated Changes

The design/build contractor may increase profits by responding more quickly to unanticipated or changed circumstances. Unlike the traditional contractor, the design/build contractor need not confer with the design professional and may proceed as soon as the appropriate course of action is determined. The contractor in design/build is able to maintain the construction schedule with as little disruption as possible. Minimizing the negative impact of unanticipated or changed circumstances on scheduled construction activities increases the contractor's ability to maintain contingency funds as profit on the project.

Advantages of Each Arrangement

There are differences among individual design/build arrangements just as there are differences among methods of project delivery in general. The contractor who is contemplating involvement in a design/build project should be aware of the advantages and disadvantages of each of the four methods of design/build. The following is a discussion of the advantages of each design/build arrangement from the perspective of the contractor. For a discussion of the structure of each design/build arrangement, see Chapter 2.

Type A: Design Professional as Primary Contractor

Admittedly, there are few advantages to contractors engaged in Type A design/build, since the contractor has no direct contractual relationship with the client but, rather, is subcontracted by the design professional to provide construction expertise. In fact, the level of control a contractor possesses in Type A design/build may not be significantly different than in traditional methods of project delivery. Particularly in those situations where the contractor and the design professional have not worked together before, the design professional may be cautious and attempt to structure their relationship in a manner similar to the client-contractor relationship on a traditional project. The design professional may not recognize the flexibility that can evolve in a working relationship on design/build projects or that their interests in the project are more closely linked than on traditionally structured projects. Despite the design professional's caution, there may still be advantages to the contractor in this type of design/build arrangement. The most important advantage is an increased level of communication between the contractor and the design professional.

Increased Level of Communication with the Design Professional

In Type A design/build, it is imperative to the design professional's financial as well as professional interest in the project that communication problems with the contractor be reduced to an absolute minimum. Since the design professional in Type A design/build is primarily responsible to the client for all project-related design and construction activities, the design professional is more likely to provide clear and complete written and graphic information to the contractor.

The design professional has a strong financial incentive to provide timely, accurate, and sufficiently detailed information to the contractor so that the contractor can build the project on schedule and with a minimum of time spent by the design professional interpreting construction documents, and with a minimum of changes later on. There is likely to be less competition and combativeness between the design professional and the contractor on a design/build project than on traditionally structured projects. Communication problems reduce the project's efficiency and increase project costs. In short, the contractor's problems become the design professional's problems in Type A design/build. One of the best ways to reduce problems is to increase the level of communication between the participants.

Type B: Contractor as Primary Contractor

There are several advantages to contractors engaged in Type B design/build arrangements. These include the opportunity to assume the greatest degree of control over the project than in any other design/build arrangement and, as corollaries, selection of the most appropriate design professional and a reduction in in-house staff requirements.

Greatest Degree of Project Control

The single most important advantage to the contractor engaged in Type B design/build is the opportunity to assume control over every aspect of the project. In Type B design/build, the contractor may control significant design decisions by determining at the outset major building systems and components. In this way, the Type B contractor can substantially reduce project uncertainties and, subsequently, project delivery time and costs. Additionally, since the Type B contractor controls the project schedule, it is far easier to influence the structure of that schedule, taking into consideration the contractor's labor supply and fabrication requirements, than to arrange the schedule exclusively around the needs of the client or the design professional. The design professional's traditional construction-phase authority is subordinate to the authority of the contractor in Type B design/build. The opportunity for greater control is particularly evident in the construction phase, where field decisions can be made more quickly and as the contractor sees fit.

The contractor in Type B design/build also has greater control over cost-versus-quality issues. For instance, the contractor may recommend that the client use steel construction instead of concrete, basing that decision on cost factors that may have a direct impact on the contractor's profit margin. The contractor may make these decisions free from the potentially conflicting opinions of the design professional.

Selection of the Most Appropriate Design Professional

In Type B design/build, a contractor selects the most qualified design professional to meet the design requirements of the project. The contractor need not have a fixed relationship with any given design professional if that relationship reduces the contractor's ability to seek work from a variety of potential clients. For each project, the Type B design/build contractor assesses the type of design services necessary to successfully compete for the work. The flexibility as well as the temporary nature of the Type B arrangement permits the contractor to work with a number of design professionals on a variety of projects, using that design professional whom the contractor believes is best suited for each project. The Type B design/build contractor who is free to associate with a variety of design professionals expands his or her scope of services, thereby increasing the number and types of projects for which he or she is qualified to compete.

Reducing In-House Staff

Contractors may find the Type B organization attractive because it neither requires them to become subordinate to the design professional, as in Type A design/build, nor to expand the contractor's organization by adding and maintaining design staff. The addition of design staff may be particularly unattractive to contractors who are not capable of, or interested in, providing oversight, control, and coordination of design activities. Furthermore, when design/build activity is slow, there is no need to maintain idle staff. When business improves, the contractor need merely contract for the required services. Keeping overhead low and reducing the size of the staff is one way that Type B contractors can increase their flexibility, reduce expenses, and increase profits.

Type C: Design Professional/Contractor Joint Venture as Primary Contractor

In Type C design/build, the contractor and design professional combine forces to form a joint venture. As joint venture members, they share equal status, since neither is a subconsultant nor subcontracted to the other. Many of the advantages of this arrangement, therefore, are shared by both parties. Some of the advantages to the contractor include a decrease in communication problems with the design professional, since it is usually to both parties' advantage to reduce coordination, scheduling, and other problems that result from poor communication; a decrease in the risk of project uncertainties due, in large part, to better communication and the ability to resolve unknowns within the joint venture; a probable reduction in the number of claims by the joint venture members against one another; and the opportunity for increased profits. There are two additional advantages described below of which a contractor contemplating Type C design/build should be aware: increased marketing strength, and sharing control over the project with the design professional.

Increased Marketing Strength

While the requirements of the project or the needs of the client may significantly determine the success of a particular method of project delivery, a contractor may find that the Type C design/build joint venture is viewed more favorably by clients than either Type A or B design/build formats. This may be because the internal structure of the Type C organization is what the average client expects from the term "design/build," and may be what the client actively searches for in a project delivery system.

A Type C joint venture also allows the contractor and design professional to present themselves more convincingly to prospective clients as a team—established, knowledgeable, and dedicated to pursuing this method of project delivery. Types A and B design/build arrangements, their individual merits notwithstanding, may be viewed by prospective clients as too transitory in nature, formed quickly and perhaps merely for the purpose of increasing its chances of being chosen to deliver the project, or with perhaps too much emphasis placed on one or the other disciplines.

Sharing Control Over the Project

The contractor in Type C design/build may not enjoy the same degree of autonomy as in a Type B arrangement, but instead shares control over aspects of the project for which he or she normally does not have influence. The contractor in a Type C design/build firm is better able to influence design decisions than in traditionally structured projects. In a joint venture, one party will usually rely on the expertise of the other. But each has a voice in the discussion of any given issue. Of course the extent to which each party exercises control over the other party depends on the contractual arrangements between the joint venture parties. It is not unusual for major decisions affecting either the design or the construction of the project to be made by a policy board or management group composed of representatives from each discipline.

Type D: Design/Build Organization as Primary Contractor

Because a Type D design/build organization is composed not of separate design and construction elements, as in types A, B, and C design/build, but is considered a separate legal entity, the advantages to one partner in the organization will undoubtedly apply to the others. Design and construction activities are likely to be integrated, affording the project the greatest opportunity for success. A single management structure governs not only all design and construction activities, but project management and client relations as well. What this means for the Type D design/build contractor is involvement in an organization that fosters team spirit and is capable of managing cost-effective projects through efficient evaluation of budget, schedule, and quality issues.

Fostering Team Spirit

In a Type D design/build organization, the staff on the design and construction components of a project are employees of the same company, subject to a single management structure that sets goals and priorities for both the company and its projects. These goals are established taking into account the attitudes and experiences of the organization's diverse members. This type of design/build arrangement fosters the team spirit among staff that is so critical to the success of any project. Team spirit is more difficult to achieve in other design/build arrangements in which the separate design and construction elements have very different business, professional, or commercial goals. Conflicts that sometimes arise between the design and construction components may be less prevalent in a Type D design/build organization. When conflicts between design and construction professionals do arise, they are likely to be resolved quickly and fairly.

Evaluating Cost, Schedule, and Quality Issues

The Type D contractor is part of a tightly knit organization that is better able than the other three design/build arrangements to evaluate the cost and schedule implications of not only his or her own work but of requested changes by the client as well. This is because, first, individuals involved in an evaluation are likely to be working in the same building, rather than scattered among several separate consulting or subcontracting organizations. This alone facilitates frequent discussion about project issues.

Second, and more importantly, a Type D design/build organization has established a set of design, construction, and quality standards based on years of in-house experience. The separate design and construction elements in types A, B, or C design/build firms may not have that same degree of familiarity or experience, since they generally have not had the opportunity to establish standards of practice. For participants of these design/build arrangements, this translates into time spent developing methods through trial and error.

Third, when conflicts over cost, schedule, and quality issues do arise, they are likely to be resolved more quickly since the same management structure and philosophy which guides individual design and construction decisions also governs in conflict situations. Contrast this with other design/build organizational structures in which either a separate management structure resolves conflicts, as in Type C joint ventures, or in types A and B design/build, where the management structure of either the design or construction discipline resolves the conflict.

The advantages to the contractor of the design/build method are summarized in Figure 4.1.

Advantages to the Contractor of the Design/Build Method

Advantages	Type A	Type B	Type C	Type D
Increased Control Over the Project		✓	✓	✓
Greater Job Satisfaction		✓	✓	✓
Minimizing Risk and Project Uncertainty	✓	✓	✓	✓
Improved Communication with the Design Professional	✓	✓	✓	✓
Opportunity to Increase Profits	✓	✓	✓	✓
Selection of Most Appropriate Design Professional		✓		
Reducing In-House Staff		✓		
Increased Marketing Strength			✓	✓
Fostering Team Spirit				✓
Evaluating Cost, Schedule, and Quality Issues				✓

Figure 4.1

Disadvantages to the Contractor

There are disadvantages of the design/build method of which every contractor should be aware. Naturally these depend to some extent on the particular design/build arrangement, the needs of the client, and project requirements. The greatest concerns for the contractor contemplating involvement in design/build are the increased risk of liability and gaps in or difficulty obtaining liability insurance. The following discussion explains these concerns in more detail.

Responsibility for the Acts and Omissions of the Design Professional

Contractors and design professionals have separate legal concerns over the risk of liability associated with their respective practices. When the two parties form a design/build firm of any kind, the nature of the legal relationships between client, contractor, and design professional may change, exposing one or more of the parties to additional risks of liability, or denying them use of certain liability defenses. (Liability issues are discussed in more detail in Chapter 8. Refer to Chapter 2 for an explanation of the responsibilities of the parties in each design/build arrangement.)

In traditionally structured projects, contractors are generally liable only for their failure to perform their work in compliance with good building practices and according to the information contained in the design professional's drawings and specifications, and the requirements of the other contract documents. Contractors are not normally responsible for the design professional's errors or omissions. In some design/build arrangements, however, the contractor may be liable to the client and to the public not only for his or her own errors, but for the errors and omissions of the design professional as well.

Gaps in Insurance Coverage

Even though it is usually possible to structure the relationships between the contractor and design professional in such a way that each will bear the risk of liability associated with its own activities, there is always the danger that in a lawsuit, the loss may exceed the ability of the negligent party to pay, with the balance then falling on the negligent party's business associate. For example, if the design professional either does not have adequate professional liability insurance coverage, has insufficient assets to cover the cost of his or her errors, or is otherwise "judgment proof," the contractor may be responsible for compensating the client or third parties for damages incurred as a result of that design professional's errors and omissions.

Contractors should also be aware of the scope of their own insurance coverage, because while insurance protects against some risks of liability, gaps may exist, particularly when construction professionals assume responsibility beyond their traditional roles. Construction surety companies do not consider design activities or the services typically performed by design professionals to be the type of activities performed by contractors in general, and may refuse coverage for contractors who provide design services or who are responsible for the design of a project. (See Chapter 10 for more information on insurance and bonding.)

Both contractors and design professionals contemplating design/build should consult with a qualified professional advisor concerning the risks and liabilities associated with the various design/build arrangements. It is essential that each party not only understand how and to what extent liability laws applicable to design/build projects differ from those of traditionally structured projects, but also to be able to choose the design/build arrangement that minimizes the risk.

Disadvantages of Each Arrangement

Any contractor who is contemplating participation in a design/build project should be aware of the disadvantages of each of the four design/build arrangements in order to choose the method best suited to his or her needs. The following section examines these drawbacks. See Chapter 2 for an in-depth discussion of the four design/build arrangements.

Type A: Design Professional as Primary Contractor

There are two major drawbacks for the contractor engaged in Type A design/build: an increased risk of nonpayment from the design professional for construction services, and a decrease in the contractor's authority and credibility with the client.

Increased Risk of Nonpayment

In Type A design/build, the contractor has no contractual relationship with the client. The contractor's legal agreement is with the design professional, and it is the design professional to whom the contractor must look for payment. The contractor has no legal grounds for action against the client if the design professional cannot or will not pay for the services performed by the contractor. The contractor may, in some states and under limited conditions, be entitled to claim a right to payment directly by the client as a third party beneficiary of the contract between the design professional and the client. However, this usually depends on the specific language of the contract between the client and the design professional, the negotiations of which the contractor seldom participates.

The contractor's attempt to collect payment from the design professional, either through the dispute resolution clause in its contract with the design professional or though litigation, may prove fruitless if the design professional simply does not have the money. Design professionals are very often only marginally capitalized. That is, they usually have few assets—liquid or otherwise—since most of their income goes to salaries and overhead expenses. Design professionals are therefore not in a position to pay the contractor for construction services until the design professional is first paid by the client. Any dispute between the design professional and the client that results in delays in compensation to the design professional, whether or not the dispute involves the contractor, may result in a default in payment to the contractor by the design professional. As a practical matter, the contractor may need to invoke its lien rights under applicable state laws. (See Chapter 9 for more information on lien laws.) This can be problematic if the contractor is not persistent in or knowledgeable about the enforcement of his or her lien rights. Furthermore, the enforcement of lien rights requires the contractor to go to court which, in itself, is expensive and time-consuming.

Decreased Authority and Credibility with the Client

Perhaps the single greatest disadvantage to the contractor who engages in Type A design/build is being relegated to a position beneath that which the contractor traditionally enjoys. The contractor in Type A design/build is insulated from direct contact with the client; all communication between the contractor and client takes place through the design professional. The design professional may wield considerable control over the flow of information. As a result, solutions to problems in the normal course of project delivery may appear to be more the result of the design professional's initiative and expertise than the contractor's participation. Furthermore, the only immediate forum in which to air grievances, short of arbitration or litigation, is through the design professional.

Type B: Contractor as Primary Contractor

While there are a number of potential economic advantages to this design/build arrangement, there are also several disadvantages that could have a significant legal impact on the contractor. These include liability for the acts and omissions of the design professional, and loss of certain legal defenses.

Liability for the Acts and Omissions of the Design Professional

One of the most significant disadvantages in Type B design/build is the direct exposure to liability for the acts and omissions of the design professional—a result of the contractor's direct contractual relationship with the client and the assumption of responsibility for all design and construction activities.

Design professionals are not infallible. There will always be changes to the construction drawings and specifications that they prepare. Fortunately, most of those changes are usually minor, or are made by the design professional in the normal course of the project. However, the later in the life of the project that the changes are made, the more expensive these changes are likely to be. In Type B design/build, the contractor may bear the economic consequences of design changes, at least initially.

The design/build contractor may claim indemnification by the design professional if it can be proved that the design professional either breached his or her contract with the contractor, or failed to perform in accordance with applicable standards of professional practice. However, if the design professional has inadequate professional liability insurance coverage, or insufficient assets to cover the cost of the added expenses, or if the design professional is in some way safe from liability claims, the contractor is expected to compensate the client or third parties for damages resulting from the acts and omissions of the design professional.

Loss of Legal Defenses

Several key liability defenses that are available to contractors on traditionally structured projects may be unavailable to contractors engaged in Type B design/build. First, contractor cannot argue that the client has *impliedly warranted* the clarity and completeness of the design professional's drawings and specifications. In other words, the contractor cannot hold the client responsible for inadequate or incomplete drawings and specifications, as is possible on traditionally structured projects. The reason is that the design/build contractor obtains the drawings not from the client but from the design professional, who the contractor has retained in a Type B format to provide design services.

Second, the contractor may be unable to employ the *betterment rule* as a defense. This rule states that items omitted from the design documents but required on the project, such as a code-required item, must be paid for by the client. This holds true regardless of whether or not the omission was a result of the design professional's negligence.

The reasoning behind this rule, on a traditionally structured project, is that the contractor should not pay for the item since he or she is responsible only for the items listed in the plans and specifications. Neither should the design professional pay, for the following reasons: These items, which should have been included in the documents from the start, are the client's responsibility, as part of his or her overall project cost; construction law states that the client should not be unjustly enriched at the expense of the design professional; and the design professional is acting only as a consultant or advisor to the client and by exercising judgment, makes no guarantee as to the sufficiency of the design.

On a design/build project, however, the courts perceive the design professional's role as *commercial*, rather than *professional*. In Type B design/build, the design professional is responsible to the contractor. The contractor then is responsible to the client for the complete design as well as the construction of the project and, as such, must bear the costs of any items omitted from the documents. The client still derives the benefit, but because there are no factors to support unjust enrichment, the betterment rule cannot serve as a defense. For more information on the betterment rule, see Chapter 8.

Type C: Design Professional/Contractor Joint Venture as Primary Contractor

To some extent, a Type C design/build arrangement presents the contractor and the design professional with the most disliked disadvantages of both the Type A and the Type B design/build organizational forms. But unlike Type A or Type B design/build, Type C design/build establishes a new legal entity called the joint venture. Contractors may find that not only does participation in a joint venture design/build project involve them in difficult issues of management and control, but they may be jointly and severally responsible for the acts and omissions of the design professional, and without certain legal defenses. These issues are discussed in further detail in the following sections.

Difficult Issues of Management and Control

A variety of legal and business issues must be addressed in connection with the management and structure of a joint venture. Will it be a substantive joint venture, or will it be a shell organization, subcontracting all services to other construction professionals? How will the joint venture be managed? Will one party dominate, or will there be equal representation in all decision-making activities? Will the joint venture have its own employees, or will all management and administrative services required to run the joint venture be supplied by one or both of the joint venture members? How will the financial affairs of the joint venture be conducted? Who controls the joint venture bank accounts? Who keeps the books? Who audits the records and prepares the tax returns? Who is authorized to represent and contractually obligate the joint venture to clients and third parties? How are liability and insurance matters handled in a joint venture? How are disputes between the joint venture parties resolved? These are just a few of the issues that construction professionals must address in establishing a joint venture organization.

Additionally, it is possible that neither the design professional nor the contractor will enjoy that same level of control in a Type C design/build organization that they had in types A or B respectively. Contractors and design professionals in a Type C project share responsibility and liability with respect to the client, and possibly to third parties. Both are likely to want control over all the activities of the joint venture to assure themselves that such exposure is limited. Each will certainly want control over his or her own activities.

Structuring the management and administration of the joint venture can sometimes be a difficult and lengthy process. Rather than one party determining when and how the joint venture will act, each party may have the ability to veto a decision by the other. A consensus may be required to make progress at all. This can be awkward, or even debilitating. It is imperative that each joint venture member have confidence in the abilities and judgment of the other.

Joint and Several Responsibility for the Acts and Omissions of the Design Professional

Probably the single greatest disadvantage of Type C design/build is the joint and several responsibility that the contractor and the design professional assume for the acts and omissions of their joint venture associate. What this means is that a Type C contractor may be liable for the acts and omissions of the design professional under joint venture partnership law. The problem may be exacerbated if the design professional has inadequate liability insurance. The contractor may, through indemnification, shift responsibility on the design professional's shoulders, but if that design professional does not have sufficient financial protection, the contractor may not be reimbursed for the damages he or she has already paid as a result of the design professional's mistakes.

Loss of Legal Defenses

There may be certain legal defenses that are no longer available to the contractor engaged in Type C design/build. These defenses are the same as those lost by contractors in Type B design/build and include briefly, 1) the inability of a contractor to argue that the client has impliedly warranted the sufficiency of the design professional's drawings and specifications; and 2) restricted use of the betterment rule.

Loss of these legal defenses that, under traditionally structured projects, operate to shift the burden of loss to another, may be unavailable to joint venture participants. Shifting the burden from one joint venture member to another is usually accomplished by contract, in accordance with the joint venture agreement between the contractor and the design professional. If no provision for indemnification is made in the joint venture agreement, the contractor may have little recourse.

Type D: Design/Build Organization as Primary Contractor

There are disadvantages to the contractor of Type D design/build. The two cited most often are the difficulty establishing the design/build organization, and the loss of indemnification and isolation of responsibility for all project design and construction activity within the organization.

Difficulty Establishing a Type D Organization

A Type D design/build organization usually takes the greatest amount of time to establish since it is created not merely by two or more parties contractually agreeing to pursue a common enterprise, but through the creation of a separate business organization, typically a corporation. Design professionals and contractors contemplating Type D design/build often must address very difficult issues. These issues include accepting the loss of the design professional's and contractor's separate identities, since individuals no longer exist as legally distinct elements within a Type D design/build organization.

Other issues involve the appropriate philosophical weight given to design and construction decisions during start-up and throughout the life of the organization. Additionally, since it is likely that a Type D design/build organization is intended by its founders to continue to exist beyond a single project, issues of ownership, management, transition, and termination of the organization are critical and are likely to require more time and thought by the parties who establish it.

Loss of Indemnification

Of the four types of design/build arrangements, a Type D firm isolates in one organization responsibility and liability for all design and construction errors, omissions, or failure to comply with codes or contractual requirements. In each of the other three types of design/build, while the primary contractor was responsible to the client and possibly to the public for the acts or omissions of his or her associates, there was the possibility that the primary contractor could shift all or a portion of that responsibility to another party if he or she could demonstrate that it was indeed the other party who caused or performed the offending act. This is not possible in Type D design/build, however, since the design/build organization does not recognize individuals within the organization. The buck stops literally at the design/build firm for responsibility and liability with respect to all services performed by the design/build organization. Responsibility cannot be passed on to another party since, in theory, that other party does not exist.

Figure 4.2 is a summary of the disadvantages to the contractor of the design/build method.

Disadvantages to the Contractor of the Design/Build Method

Disadvantages	Type A	Type B	Type C	Type D
Gaps In Insurance Coverage		✓	✓	✓
Increased Risk of Nonpayment	✓			
Decreased Authority and Credibility with the Client	✓			
Responsibility for the Acts and Omissions of the Design Professional		✓	✓	✓
Loss of Certain Legal Defenses		✓	✓	✓
Difficult Issues of Management and Control			✓	✓
Joint and Several Responsibility			✓	
Complex and Time-Consuming to Establish			✓	✓

Figure 4.2

Summary

There are advantages and disadvantages to contractors engaged in the design/build method of project delivery. These may vary depending on the specific design/build arrangement, the individual client, the size and scale of the project, and the experience level of the participants. The reasons cited most often by contractors for involvement in design/build are: greater control over the project, an increased level of job satisfaction, minimized risk and project uncertainty, improved communication with the design professional, and greater profitability. A contractor's profit margin increases in design/build projects because the contractor can select the most economical construction methods, design- and construction-related activities are reduced, and the design/build firm responds more efficiently to unanticipated changes.

There are advantages to each design/build arrangement as well. In Type A, the contractor enjoys an increased level of communication with the design professional. In Type B design/build, the contractor as primary contractor may have the greatest degree of control over all aspects of a project, including selection of the most appropriate design professional and control over the size of the in-house staff. In Type C design/build, the contractor's marketing strength may be enhanced by the inclusion of design services provided by the design professional. This same contractor shares control over all aspects of the project. The Type D design/build firm may foster team spirit, since the design professional and contractor are partners in the same organization. The nature of this organization may facilitate more efficient evaluation of cost, schedule, and quality issues.

There are disadvantages to the design/build method of project delivery of which contractors should be aware. These include responsibility for the acts and omissions of the design professional, difficulty obtaining adequate insurance coverage, or gaps in existing coverage.

There are disadvantages to the contractor that are unique to each design/build arrangement. In Type A design/build, the contractor may face an increased risk of nonpayment by the design professional, and a decrease in authority and credibility with the client. In Type B design/build, the contractor assumes liability for the acts and omissions of the design professional, but without the benefit of certain legal defenses. In Type C design/build, the contractor may face, in addition to liability and defense concerns, difficult management and control issues in the establishment and operation of the joint venture. And in Type D design/build, indemnification is not possible. The contractor may be unable to shift the burden of responsibility to the source of the error since individuals are not recognized and responsibility rests with the organization as a whole. This, in addition to the difficulty typically encountered establishing a Type D design/build organization, should make contractors consider carefully their choice of project delivery methods.

Chapter 5 examines the advantages and disadvantages experienced by design professionals engaged in the design/build method of project delivery.

Chapter Five

The Design Professional

Construction professionals who are contemplating involvement in a design/build project should understand the implications of this relatively new method of project delivery, how it compares to other more traditional methods, and the differences between the four basic design/build arrangements. This chapter examines these issues from the perspective of the design professional.

Advantages to the Design Professional

There are many reasons why various design professionals choose to engage in the design/build process. The following paragraphs describe the most common reasons design professionals give for venturing into design/build.

Greater Control Over Project Quality

Control over the quality of the completed project is the single most important reason design professionals give for engaging in the design/build method. From the design professional's perspective, the design/build method provides the opportunity to participate in, and not merely observe, all aspects of the design and construction process.

The design/build process permits greater opportunity for on-site design decisions or design changes during construction. Traditionally structured projects typically require that all decisions first be documented by the design professional and then communicated through the contractor to the subcontractors actually performing the work. Obviously, this process can be time consuming. Often design decisions or changes that might otherwise enhance the project may not be pursued because of the time it takes to document and communicate the changes.

Using the design/build method, however, direct communication between the design professional and the contractor not only enhances the design professional's knowledge of construction matters in general, but speeds the decision-making process. This feature of design/build is especially valuable in remodeling projects where there may be hidden factors that are not known or fully appreciated until the construction crew begins work. In such cases, many design decisions cannot be made until work is in progress. If the design professional is in close contact with the contractor, these decisions may be made quickly, and with a greater emphasis on design quality than cost or time constraints.

Cost-Versus-Quality Decisions

Design professionals practicing design/build may have greater control over cost-versus-quality decisions than would be possible in traditional construction methods. Virtually all decisions concerning a project's quality have a cost impact. The relative merits of each decision can often be weighed more accurately using the design/build approach, where such changes are suggested and implemented by the same party, than in traditional methods of project delivery, where separate parties make decisions based on their individual assessments. Consequently, a design/build firm may be better able to assess the relative merits and trade-offs between quality and cost. For example, a design professional engaged in design/build is likely to know the purchase and installation costs of a given building component. As a result, he or she is in a better position to recommend the appropriate level of quality for the building's components, based on the client's budget.

Increased Level of Job Satisfaction

A design professional may experience an increased level of job satisfaction through participation in a design/build project, no doubt a result of the greater control he or she may have over project quality. This is a significant motivating factor for those design professionals who have struggled to realize their visions through the efforts of the contractor in a traditional project.

Opportunity to Increase Profits

The design professional engaged in the design/build method of project delivery may increase profitability in the following ways:

- Reducing design services
- Assuming an equity interest in the project
- Protecting against market fluctuations
- Increasing marketability and expanding the firm's client base

Reducing Design Services

A design professional using the design/build method can increase profits in much the same way a contractor increases profits—by reducing services. To a large extent, the party controlling the design/build firm determines who benefits from the cost savings. Nevertheless, both the design professional and the contractor can profit from the savings to the extent that they are able to reduce the services they provide.

For instance, the design professional may find that conceptual drawings alone will assure the client that his or her programmatic goals are being realized. Furthermore, if the design professional is in close communication with the design/build contractor, detailed plans may not be necessary. The drawings need only provide essential information to the contractor about the requirements of the project. All other design decisions can be made by the design professional and communicated to the contractor through less formal means. The design professional's direct involvement in and control over the construction process will provide ample opportunity to make such decisions and enforce their adherence.

Assuming an Equity Interest in the Project

A design/build design professional may increase profits by assuming an *equity interest* in the project, that is, by trading design services for partial ownership of the completed project, and then watching that share increase in value over time. This approach is often taken on condominium projects, since these units are easily identifiable and segregated elements, and their market value is relatively easy to determine at any point in time.

Many projects often start out on uncertain financial ground, with clients looking for ways to reduce their initial or up-front costs while information is gathered to determine the project's economic viability. Most design professionals practicing in the traditional manner find it difficult to provide services during the early stages of more than one or two such projects without assurance that they will be paid for their services. Design professionals are generally not in the financing or risk-taking business.

Although a design professional's fees are relatively small compared to total project costs, they often represent for the client the single largest initial expense during the early, feasibility stage of project development. If it is determined that a project is not feasible, significant design costs will still have been incurred by the client. For this reason, clients may be willing to incur a greater expense at a later stage in the project, in return for a reduction in costs at the initial stages.

A design/build firm may be better able to accommodate this client's needs, since income generated by its design services (as compared to construction services) is a relatively small proportion of its total annual income. The design/build firm is better able to absorb uncompensated design services than the traditional design professional, who depends on the fees generated by design services as a sole source of income.

By assuming an equity interest, the design/builder is literally investing in the project in an amount equal to the value of the design services. This expense may be high in the early stages of the project when such services are absolutely critical to the project's success. However, in return for this "investment," the design/build firm is granted either an equity or ownership interest in the completed project, or higher fees for the balance of the project.

Protecting Against Market Fluctuations

Design professionals are directly affected by cyclical fluctuations and changes in market demand for their services. When the economy is depressed, the demand for design services decreases, and a design professional's profits decrease proportionately. A contractor's profits may also decline, but it takes far fewer construction projects, perhaps only a single project, to generate the same number of dollars as earned by many design projects. This is because construction costs constitute the largest percentage of the total project budget. A design professional who practices design/build may protect against market fluctuations by generating income from construction operations to cover the reduction in design activities. This protection is of particular importance to those design/build firms that are controlled by design professionals. Such an arrangement allows them to continue providing design services during recessionary periods by allocating construction profits to cover the design portion of the business.

Increasing Marketability and Expanding the Client Base

Design professionals engaged in design/build projects may increase their profit potential by increasing their marketability. The design/build process enables the design professional to offer a prospective client both design and construction services, rather than design services alone.

The design/build method also enables the design professional to expand his or her client base. When a design professional and a contractor join forces to form a design/build firm, the existing client bases of these two individuals are combined to become part of the design/build firm's client base. For example, if the design professional and the contractor each bring the names of ten potential clients to the design/build firm, the firm will have twenty potential clients as its existing base—twice the number that each party possesses individually.

Field Experience

Many young design professionals working in traditionally structured organizations spend years on a variety of in-house tasks (such as model-making and preparation of presentation drawings, then design and working drawings) before having an opportunity to gain field experience during the construction phase of projects.

Contractors frequently complain that design professionals who have creative design ideas lack the fundamental construction knowledge necessary to translate their ideas into reality. The opportunity to work at the contractor's side during construction of the project, to see first-hand the actual construction tasks that must be performed, and to hear the questions and concerns raised by the contractor on a variety of matters, including the information contained in the drawings and specifications, can be an invaluable experience. The design professional often discovers simpler, more "constructible" and, occasionally, less expensive ways to build, and develops a keener understanding of the construction industry. Design professionals may also learn how design decisions impact the project's success, and may develop construction knowledge and appreciation earlier in their careers than their traditionally trained counterparts.

When the design professional in a design/build firm controls the construction activity, he or she rapidly develops an understanding not only of construction techniques, but construction management and construction law as well. Design/build design professionals may find themselves immersed in construction issues to an extent that few traditional design professionals, seasoned or novice, ever find themselves. Securing bids, construction permits, and performance, labor, and materials bonds; negotiating with subcontractors and material suppliers; dealing with labor organizations; scheduling and managing labor and procurement activities; estimating construction costs; as well as providing workers' compensation and other insurance protections, is an invaluable educational experience and fosters in the design professional an understanding of how each issue relates to the project as a whole.

Greater Credibility with Clients

Design professionals engaged in design/build may develop a higher level of credibility with clients than traditional design professionals. Clients are likely to perceive the design/build design professional as an individual who is not only proficient in the art and skill of design, but equally knowledgeable in the craft and science of construction. Design/build clients may side more often with the design professional's decisions, believing that these decisions have been made based on what is most feasible from a programmatic, budgetary, and constructability point of view. Clients may not feel the need to test the design professional's ideas against the realities of the construction marketplace, as is often the case in traditionally structured projects.

Furthermore, when the design professional's credibility is enhanced, a client's anxiety level may be reduced. The design professional may be permitted to perform his or her services more efficiently, to the advantage of not only the design professional, but the design/build firm and the client as well.

Reducing the Incidence of Claims by Contractors

In recent years, the number of claims by contractors against design professionals in traditionally structured projects has skyrocketed. Unfortunately, even the most diligent design professional runs the risk of a lawsuit by the contractor.

The bond that develops between the design professional and the contractor in a design/build firm, however, is likely to be far stronger than that in traditionally structured projects. The somewhat adversarial relationship that occasionally exists in traditional projects is replaced in design/build by a greater sense of cooperation. Legally, claims are still possible by contractors against design professionals under the types A, B, and C design/build (see Chapter 2 for a detailed explanation of design/build structures). In fact, there may be sources of potential conflict in these relationships which do not exist in traditionally structured projects. However, the circumstances underlying most claims, such as mistrust, lack of communication, and the desire for retribution, are substantially reduced when the parties perceive themselves as working for common goals and pursuing common interests. Particularly in design/build firms that have a continuing existence beyond a single project, the likelihood of claims by contractors against design professionals is reduced.

Advantages of Each Arrangement

The design professional who is considering participation in a design/build project should understand the advantages of each of the four basic design/build arrangements. Each of the following four sections describes the advantages to the design professional of types A, B, C, and D design/build. See Chapter 2 for extensive coverage of these four formats.

Type A: Design Professional as Primary Contractor

The advantages that a design professional gains from a Type A design/build project pertain to his or her primary contractual relationship with the client. One benefit is the influence he or she may have over the quality of the completed project. A second advantage is the opportunity to select the most qualified contractor for the project. Finally, Type A design/build may provide a vehicle for expanding the design professional's client base and increasing his or her credibility with the client.

Greatest Level of Control Over Project Quality

Even though the design professional is not contractually bound to the contractor in a traditionally structured project, and can exercise his or her professional judgment free from any conflicts of interest, the design professional typically cannot make design or cost-versus-quality decisions without the client's involvement, since those decisions may have a significant impact on the contractual relationship that exists between the client and contractor.

In Type A design/build, however, there is no contractual relationship between the client and the contractor. The design professional therefore has the freedom to make these design and cost-versus-quality decisions, in some instances without client involvement.

Having greater control over the quality of the project (the ability to make decisions without input from the client) could present a conflict of interest because the design professional may have to choose between the interests of the client and those of the design/build firm. But the design professional can avoid such conflict if he or she is aware of this possibility.

Selection of the Most Qualified Contractor

In Type A design/build, the design professional chooses the contractor whose qualifications and experience are best suited to the project. This control may give the design professional a marketing edge over other design/build arrangements that are less flexible in their ability to match project requirements with the most suitable contractor.

Expanding the Client Base and Increasing Credibility with Clients

Design professionals who provide full design/build services, as in Type A design/build, may be an attractive alternative for clients who are concerned about the design quality of their project. As the primary client contact, Type A design professionals can assure clients that design issues will not assume a secondary role to construction-related issues. The design professional can include in his or her potential client base those prospective clients who want to venture into design/build but feel uncomfortable about losing direct contact with the design element of the project.

A design professional's level of credibility with the client may also be enhanced in Type A design/build for the following reasons. The design professional has a direct contractual relationship with the client, is able to work more closely with the contractor from the project's inception, yet acts as the filter for communication between the contractor and the client. In essence, project-related decisions, whether design or construction, become the province of the design professional.

Type B: Contractor as Primary Contractor

The Type B design/build arrangement is viewed least favorably by design professionals. In this method of project delivery, the design/build firm is controlled by the contractor. However, there are advantages of which design professionals should be aware, including a reduction in risk.

"Least Effort/Least Risk" Project Delivery

For those design professionals who have never engaged in design/build project delivery, the Type B arrangement may be attractive, as it involves the least risk to the design professional of the four design/build arrangements. In this approach, the design professional has no contractual responsibility to the client. Since no new legal entity is established in Type B, all that is required to create this type of design/build firm is a properly drafted contractual agreement establishing the terms and conditions between the contractor and the design professional. Unlike the other three design/build arrangements, only Type B limits the design professional's contractual responsibility to ensuring sufficient design services and advising on matters within the design professional's expertise only. The design professional is not responsible to the client or to third parties for the activities of the contractor, nor to the client, the contractor, or third parties for construction-related issues.

Type C: Design Professional/Contractor Joint Venture as Primary Contractor

There are advantages to the design professional in Type C design/build. The internal structure of the Type C joint venture is such that both design professionals and contractors share control over and enjoy an equal status within the organization. Design professionals who engage in this type of design/build may also increase their marketability.

Sharing Control Over the Project

Type C design professionals share control with contractors over all aspects of the project, including those areas in which they normally do not participate. The design professional is in a better position to influence construction decisions in Type C design/build than in traditional methods of project delivery. Depending on the language of the contract between the joint venture members, decisions may be made by a board of policy makers composed of individuals from both the design and contracting disciplines. For the design professional, this approach ensures that the design issues are given equal weight and that decisions during the construction phase are not made without regard to the project's original design intent.

Increasing Marketability

Design professionals may find that their marketability is enhanced by participation in a Type C project. Many design/build clients prefer the joint venture structure to other arrangements because it represents most clearly the concept underlying design/build, which is the provision of both design and construction services by one organization. The Type C joint venture may also appear more stable than types A or B (typically formed for the purposes of a single project), and more flexible than the Type D organization.

Type D: Design/Build Organization as Primary Contractor

The primary advantage to design professionals engaged in Type D design/build is the team spirit that is fostered through development of a close working relationship with the contractor. The reasons for and benefits of the Type D team approach are outlined below.

Fostering Team Spirit

Type D design/build facilitates a close working relationship between the design professional and the contractor. The design and construction staffs within this organization are employees of the same company, and must comply with a single management policy which sets goals and priorities both for the company and for its projects. Awareness of goals and priorities by the company staff and a close working relationship between its members fosters the team spirit which is so critical to the success of any project.

Team spirit is not as easily achieved in traditionally structured projects, in which each of the separate design and construction elements has different, sometimes divergent, business, professional, or commercial goals or priorities. Conflicts which sometimes arise between those separately involved in design and construction are resolved quickly in Type D design/build, since management and staff share common goals.

Figure 5.1 is a summary of the advantages that design/build offers to the design professional.

Disadvantages to the Design Professional

Design professionals who are considering the design/build method should be aware of potential disadvantages. First, liability issues can be complex. In some design/build arrangements, the design professional could be held responsible for the acts and omissions of the contractor, but may lack adequate insurance coverage to pay for resulting damages or costs of additional work. Second, design/build firms can also be an expensive venture for design professionals with modest human, material, and financial resources. A third consideration depends, in part, on the particular arrangement of the design/build firm. This is the change in both the role and status of the design professionals working in design/build construction. Each of these three problem areas is explored in the following sections.

Responsibility for the Acts and Omissions of the Contractor

In traditionally structured projects, design professionals are generally liable only for their own acts and omissions. They are not normally responsible for the acts and omissions of the contractor. In certain design/build arrangements, however, the design professional may be liable to the client and the public, not only for his or her own errors and omissions, but also for the contractor's failure to build with good practice and in accordance with the requirements of the construction documents. Unfortunately, in some instances, the design professional's insurance may not cover the added risk.

Advantages to the Design Professional of the Design/Build Method

Advantages	Type A	Type B	Type C	Type D
Greater Control Over Project Quality	✓		✓	✓
Increased Level of Job Satisfaction	✓		✓	✓
Opportunity to Increase Profits	✓	✓	✓	✓
Field Experience	✓		✓	✓
Greater Credibility with Clients	✓		✓	✓
Reducing the Incidence of Claims by Contractors	✓	✓	✓	✓
Selection of the Most Qualified Contractor	✓			
"Least Effort/Least Risk"		✓		
Sharing Control Over the Project			✓	✓
Increased Marketability	✓		✓	✓
Fostering Team Spirit				✓

Figure 5.1

Gaps in Insurance Coverage

Design professionals engaged in design/build should be certain that there are no gaps in their insurance coverage. Some insurance carriers cover only the acts and omissions of the design professional, and may refuse coverage for negligence in any of the activities outside the design professional's traditional role as designer. The design professional who is responsible or shares responsibility for both design and construction, may find that he or she is insured for design activities only. Furthermore, even though individual contract language may define the responsibilities and rights of the design/build members, it is possible that one party will be unable to pay for its mistakes, with the balance of the claim falling due on the other design/build members. Because of the coverage limitations afforded to those engaged in design/build, each party should require that the other carry appropriate and adequate amounts of coverage, and provide proof of such coverage.

Large Start-up Costs

Design professionals attempting to establish a design/build organization may be faced with substantial start-up costs. Starting a business requires capital. Physical space, equipment, and supplies must be acquired, and labor lined up to operate the business and meet professional objectives.

An entrepreneur must spend money to make money. These principles are no different for those who wish to engage in design/build activities. Depending on the organizational form chosen to structure the design/build firm, a design professional's initial investment requirements can be substantial, perhaps significantly greater than for design professionals structuring their business relationships along more traditional lines. For instance, in some design/build arrangements, the design professional may be faced with the problem of how to establish *bonding capacity* so that he or she can provide the security (in the form of payment and performance bonds) on which clients will insist prior to construction. (See Chapter 10 for more information on insurance and bonding.)

The labor and equipment requirements of a design firm are typically smaller than those of a construction company. The construction company's physical plant is also likely to be much larger than the facilities of the typical design firm. A design professional going into the design/build business may suddenly be responsible for providing substantial office space and labor forces, and accommodating intensive equipment demands.

Design professionals contemplating design/build should carefully investigate the business aspects of each particular design/build arrangement, and each party's role in these organizations. The more foreign these business activities are to the interest, skills, and experience of the design professional, the more expensive and time consuming it will be to conduct business, at least initially.

Decline in Status

Many design professionals engaged in design/build projects fear that this new role may diminish their status in the eyes of the client and the public. There is little doubt that a party independently retained to provide professional advice will be viewed quite differently than one who is merely a component of a larger organization. Their fears may be exacerbated if the client appears interested more in the project's budgetary or scheduling constraints, for instance, than in issues of design and quality, and looks to the contractor as the authority.

The design professional's traditional image of upholding public trust and confidence may also seem threatened by the design/build arrangement. This is because having a financial interest in the design/build firm prevents the design professional from fulfilling its customary obligations to the public. Many believe that the design professional's decision-making ability is affected by this direct economic interest in the project. If the design professional is no longer perceived as acting solely in the best interests of the client, the party with whom the design professional traditionally has had the closest relationship, then how can that design professional act in the best interests of the public, with whom the design professional has had a far more attenuated relationship? The specific problem areas encountered by the design professional in the four types of design/build formats are described in the following section.

Disadvantages of Each Arrangement

Each of the four design/build arrangements contains elements that may pose problems to the design professional. Reviewing the drawbacks inherent in each method enables the design professional to choose the arrangement best suited to his or her needs and experience. (See Chapter 2 for a detailed discussion of the four basic design/build formats.)

Type A: Design Professional as Primary Contractor

In Type A design/build, the design professional assumes an increased risk of liability for the acts and omissions of the contractor, and the burden of construction management. These are significant factors in the decision to engage in Type A design/build.

Responsibility for the Acts and Omissions of the Contractor

Probably the biggest disadvantage to the design professional in Type A design/build is liability for the contractor's work. The design professional is responsible for construction-related matters in addition to project design. He or she is liable if the contractor fails to use good building practices or to build in accordance with the information contained in the design professional's drawings and specifications, or with the other requirements of the construction documents. The design professional's risk of liability increases in direct proportion to his or her level of responsibility.

Assuming the Burden of Construction Management

In Type A design/build, the design professional is the primary contractor, responsible for both the design and construction of the project. In addition to the traditional role of administering the construction contract, the design professional must also serve as construction manager to the client.

The design professional in Type A design/build is responsible for construction scheduling, expediting, materials procurement, cost estimating, value engineering, and construction superintending. A design professional in Type A must be prepared to step in and take corrective action when problems arise. The Type A design professional must also maintain good labor relations between tradesmen and contractors, subcontractors, and materials suppliers. Unrest or disputes between management and labor can have a drastic financial impact on the project. The design professional is not only responsible for the outcome of the project, but has a direct economic interest in it. Design professionals must learn quickly how to negotiate effectively with labor and trade unions on Type A design/build projects.

Unless the design professional has a thorough understanding of construction management, he or she may come to rely on the contractor to see that all such matters are handled properly. It is, however, risky for design professionals to forfeit control in this way because there is so much at stake personally, professionally, and financially. Depending on the project's size and complexity, design professionals may choose to engage the services of a properly qualified construction manager instead to act as his or her independent professional consultant.

Type B: Contractor as Primary Contractor

Type B design/build is least attractive to design professionals. In this arrangement, the design professional is retained by the contractor and has no contractual relationship with the client. As a result, the design professional is likely to have less control over the quality of the completed project, or over cost-versus-quality decisions made during the course of the project. The extent of design services may be reduced on a Type B project, and the design professional may be insulated from the client by the contractor. Type B design professionals may feel torn between the traditional sense of loyalty to the client, and their business obligation to the contractor. These factors are explored in detail in the following paragraphs.

Reducing the Scope of Design Services

Services that are traditionally required of the design professional may not be necessary on a design/build project. First, the design professional may not need to describe the design intent to the client and the project's prospective bidders, since contractors may be hired through negotiation rather than traditional competitive bidding. In design/build, the contractor and design professional usually work closely from the start to define the project's scope, quality, and choice of materials and systems.

In a Type A design/build organization, the design professional can determine the appropriate design and specification of detail to be included in the construction documents. However, in Type B design/build, the contractor has a much more influential role in determining what the design professional will design and how it will be documented. This reduced influence may leave the design professional dissatisfied with the extent of his or her involvement on the project.

If the contractor in Type B design/build makes clear from the start exactly what is expected of the design professional, the design professional can elect whether or not to enter into this particular design/build arrangement. Unfortunately, the contractor may not always be sure, or may not take the time to articulate those expectations to the design professional.

Isolation From the Client

The design professional may be isolated from the client in Type B design/build, since communication between the client and the design professional is filtered through the contractor. In some instances there may be no direct communication between the client and the design professional at all. Insulation from the decision-making process in Type B design/build may effectively limit the design professional's influence over design issues.

Conflicting Obligations

The Type B design professional, while retained by the contractor, may nevertheless feel that this responsibility is secondary to the traditional loyalty to the client. This feeling may, in fact, be shared by the contractor and perhaps even by the client. Sometimes the design professional ends up spending a great deal of time trying to resolve matters in the best interests of both the client and the contractor. While admirable, this approach can make a project much more difficult for the design professional.

Type C: Design Professional/Contractor Joint Venture as Primary Contractor

The disadvantages of Type C design/build are essentially the same for both contractors and design professionals since, as members of a joint venture, they share both control over and responsibility for the project, and maintain an equal status within the design/build firm.

Difficulty Establishing Management and Control

Design professionals engaged in Type C design/build face a multitude of legal and business issues concerning the internal structure of the joint venture. For this reason, Type C joint ventures may take longer to establish. Because all decisions affect the joint venture participants equally, a consensus must usually be reached before the project can resume. If there is no policy board representing the interests of the design and construction components of the firm, the decision-making process may be tedious and time consuming.

Joint and Several Responsibility for the Acts and Omissions of the Contractor

In Type C design/build, the design professional may be exposed to an increased risk of liability resulting from the acts and omissions of its joint venture associate—the contractor. Design professionals in Type C may be held jointly and severally responsible for errors made by the contractor in the construction of the project. If the contractor cannot pay for damages that result from his or her errors, the design professional may bear the brunt of the penalty imposed as a result of that error. Design professionals should be certain that their joint venture associates carry adequate insurance, and that their own insurance carriers will cover them for the work they perform in a joint venture arrangement.

Type D: Design/Build Organization as Primary Contractor

Design professionals who are contemplating involvement in Type D design/build should be aware of potential disadvantages. The greatest drawback of this arrangement is the difficulty establishing this kind of organization.

Difficulty Establishing a Type D Organization

Type D design/build firms take longer to establish than other design/build firms because the process involves more than just a contractual agreement between two or more construction professionals. In fact, it may not be accurate to speak about design professionals and contractors as individuals in a Type D organization, since individuals are not recognized in this design/build arrangement.

There are a multitude of legal and business issues to address in a Type D firm, including questions of ownership, management, transition, and, eventually, termination. In addition, decisions must be made concerning the proper weight to give design and construction issues, not only during the course of a project, but throughout the life of the organization.

Figure 5.2 is a summary of the disadvantages that the design/build method presents to the design professional.

Summary

There are many reasons why design professionals choose to engage in the design/build method of project delivery. Depending on the structure of the design/build firm, design professionals may enjoy greater control over project quality, and may influence cost-versus- quality decisions. This extra measure of control may lead to greater job satisfaction. Another benefit is the opportunity to acquire practical field experience earlier in their careers. In addition, design professionals engaged in design/build may enjoy greater profitability by reducing the extent of design services, assuming an equity interest in the project, protecting against market fluctuations, increasing their marketability and credibility, and expanding their client base. Finally, the incidence of claims filed by contractors against design professionals may be less in a design/built context.

Disadvantages to the Design Professional of the Design/Build Method

Disadvantages	Type A	Type B	Type C	Type D
Responsibility for the Acts and Omissions of the Contractor	✓		✓	
Gaps in Insurance Coverage	✓		✓	
Large Start-up Costs	✓			✓
Decline in Status	✓	✓	✓	✓
Assuming the Burden of Construction Management	✓			
Reducing the Scope of Design Services		✓		
Isolation from the Client		✓		
Conflicting Obligations		✓	✓	
Difficulty Establishing Management and Control			✓	
Joint and Several Responsibility			✓	
Difficulty Establishing the Design/Build Organization				✓

Figure 5.2

Some specific advantages offered by the four types of design/build arrangements can be summed up as follows. In Type A design/build, design professionals as primary contractors enjoy the greatest control over project quality, with the authority to select the construction components for the project. They also have the opportunity to expand their client base and improve their credibility by offering construction services. Perhaps the only advantage Type B affords the design professional is the opportunity to become involved in projects with the least degree of risk. Of course, this also means that the design professional has the least amount of control. On Type C projects, design professionals may share control over the project and increase their marketability. Finally, in Type D design/build, design professionals enjoy team spirit fostered by a close working relationship with their partner, the contractor.

Design professionals engaged in design/build should also be aware of potential drawbacks. Certain design/build arrangements involve very large start-up costs that are particularly difficult to meet for the typical design professional with few liquid assets. In addition, the design professional, depending on the design/build arrangement, may assume a less prominent or influential role than in traditionally structured projects. The design professional is often placed in a precarious legal position regarding liability issues. In some design/build arrangements, he or she is responsible not only for design services, but for construction services as well. Gaps in insurance coverage could place the design professional in serious financial risk.

There are also specific disadvantages to the design professional of each method of design/build. The Type A design professional is directly responsible for the acts and omissions of the contractor and may also assume the burden of construction management. With an increase in responsibility comes a risk of liability. In Type B, the design professional may find that the scope of design services required for the project has been reduced. The design professional may be isolated from the client in this situation, yet may feel a conflicting sense of loyalty to both the client and the contractor. In Type C design/build, the design professional may experience difficulty establishing management and control, and may be held jointly and severally responsible for the acts and omissions of its joint venture associate. Finally, in Type D design/build the design professional may again experience difficulty in establishing this most complicated design/build arrangement.

Clients, contractors, and design professionals interested in the design/build method should learn as much as possible about the advantages and disadvantages of this method of project delivery. All should consider the type of project, experience level of the participants, and the political and economic climate before assuming a role in a design/build project. Potential participants are urged to seek professional advice concerning the risks and rewards of delivering a project in this manner. Once participants understand the implications of the design/build method, and choose and establish the appropriate arrangement for their firm, construction projects can begin. Part III discusses the ways in which design/build services are procured. Chapter 6 begins by introducing the public- and private-sector clients who procure these services.

Part Three

Procuring Design/Build Services

An increasing number of clients today are choosing the design/build method to construct their projects—projects ranging from playhouses to prisons. But who is the design/build client, and how does this client procure the services of a design/build team? Part III answers these questions. Chapter 6 begins by examining private- and public-sector clients.

Chapter Six

Private- and Public-Sector Clients

The design/build method of project delivery accounts for a growing proportion of the activity in the construction industry today. The Bureau of Building Marketing Research estimated that in 1983, approximately fourteen percent of all construction in the United States employed the design/build method, and many feel this percentage is increasing.

We know that clients, contractors, and design professionals are the three primary participants in design/build projects. We also know that there are many reasons why each participant may choose to engage in design/build. This chapter focuses on the types of clients (both individuals and entities) that secure the services of the design/build firm, and the private and public arenas in which they operate.

The Private Sector

The *private sector* is that which is neither owned nor controlled by the government. To date the private sector has been the most fertile ground for design/build projects. Private-sector clients fall under two categories: 1) inexperienced clients, and 2) sophisticated clients.

Inexperienced Clients

"Inexperienced" clients may be reasonably aware of the level of responsibility required in a traditionally structured project and may wish to avoid many of the concerns connected with this method of construction. Unlike the naive client, who is simply not aware of his or her options, the inexperienced client understands that there are differences among the methods of project delivery and is able to choose one method over others.

Inexperienced design/build clients can generally be classified in the following three categories:

- Clients unfamiliar with construction practices
- Clients unfamiliar with the building type
- Clients lacking in-house project management capability

Clients Unfamiliar with Construction Practices

Clients who are unfamiliar with construction practices very often are only vaguely familiar with the distinction between the services traditionally offered by the design professional and those provided by the contractor. Design/build simplifies the process for this client by providing a single point of responsibility and, more importantly, by reducing the number of parties involved in the construction process. A client using design/build will not have to deal with more than one party in order to make project-related decisions.

Homeowners and small business owners are examples of this type of client. When building or remodeling their homes or facilities, they may feel that their projects are simple or small enough that they do not need the services of an independent design professional. These clients may not understand the important role that the traditional independent design professional plays, or may not believe that the value of the services provided by the design professional offsets the inconvenience of having to deal with more than one construction professional. This type of client may find the design/build method an attractive method of project delivery.

Clients Unfamiliar with the Building Type

A client may be familiar with construction practices in general, but may be unfamiliar with a particular building type. This client will be uncertain about how best to proceed with the design and construction of the project. The construction of new facilities to house a business, after all, is not a frequent occurrence, and although the owner of the small business knows the business, he or she does not necessarily know how to design and build a facility to house that business. The design/build method of project delivery may prove attractive for this type of client as well.

Clients with No In-House Project Management Capability

As projects grow in size or complexity, the demands placed on clients increase as well, especially during the construction phase of a project. In the course of a project, a client may be expected to make numerous and timely decisions, and to attend to complicated and time-consuming bookkeeping and accounting functions. These tasks become increasingly difficult as the project grows in size. The need for effective communication between the client and the principal players in the project grows in direct proportion. Clients with little or no project management experience may need to increase the size of their staff or ask that existing personnel handle these additional demands. Design/build may be the solution for this type of client, because it reduces the client's management burden and simplifies the construction process. The design/build firm performs many of the in-house construction monitoring, communication, and coordination tasks that might otherwise be the client's responsibility.

Sophisticated Clients

The second type of design/build client operating in the private sector is the "sophisticated" client. These clients usually have a general knowledge of construction. Often these clients are developers who not only know their market, but are aware of the programmatic and design criteria as well as the building systems best suited to their particular needs. Sophisticated clients include the following:

- Clients with well-defined programs
- Clients with well-defined design criteria
- Clients with in-house project management capability
- Developers

Clients with Well-Defined Programs

All projects have a program, whether simple or complex, written or unwritten. A program determines the types, sizes, uses, and relationships of required spaces in the facility. The client should understand the program for his or her projects so that the necessary information can be communicated to the appropriate parties. Independent design professionals can provide programming services, but for projects that require very little specialized design, clients may see no real value in retaining the services of an independent design professional. Warehouses and storage facilities are building types that fit this category.

The programs for other kinds of projects may be very complex, requiring a detailed knowledge of the various elements in order to successfully execute the design and construction. Medical and higher educational facilities, for instance, have some of the most complex programmatic requirements of the more common building types. Some clients of these facilities have the in-house capability to define in precise detail the programmatic criteria and building systems best suited to their needs. Certain of these clients may believe that their interests are best served by retaining a design/build firm familiar with the type and size of their project. The design/build firm not only provides design services but adapts the client-provided requirements to the site and to other unique circumstances of the project.

Clients with Well-Defined Design Criteria

Some clients are able to provide not only a project program, but all the design criteria as well. Such clients require little assistance from others beyond the adaptation of those criteria to the site and a familiarity with local building codes and permit procedures. Some clients may even have a working knowledge of code and permit procedures. Typical clients in this category include fast-food chains and other franchise stores. Due to the limited design services required for a project of this type, a design/build firm, even one without prior experience with the building type, may be the most practical solution.

Clients with In-House Project Management Capability

Often clients who have the capability to develop their own programs and design criteria in-house also possess the necessary project management capability. Such clients may not need to procure the services traditionally offered by an independent design professional. Clients in this category are generally heavily committed to construction and development activities over the long term. As a result, they have developed sufficient in-house expertise in project management and construction administration.

Developers

Developers are a special breed of sophisticated client. They often engage in design/build because of the reduction in both project cost and delivery time that can be achieved by this method of project delivery. Projects that represent simple building types, or that tend to be repetitive in nature, are attractive to developers as candidates for design/build. These kinds of projects are discussed below.

Commercial Office and Retail Facilities: The *spec* (speculative) or commercial office building or retail facility typically consists of an exterior shell and the interior core of fixed elements such as stairs, bathrooms, elevators, elevator lobbies, and public corridors, as well as vertical mechanical/electrical shafts and vents. This building type is simple, well understood by design professionals and contractors alike, and easily lends itself to the design/build process. Spec projects are relatively cost-effective ventures, catering more to market conditions than to the demands of a given user. This type of project requires less contract documentation and construction administration.

The *fit out* portions of the speculative project, such as partition design, lighting, and flooring, are based on the specific needs of the user and are typically left to complete at a later date when tenants have been located to occupy the facility. In the design of the project, the design/build team provides a *tenant package* or a set of *tenant standard specifications*. These documents describe building standard details, materials, and systems intended by the developer for use by tenants in fitting out their respective spaces. Tenants may then either hire their own design professionals and contractors to complete their spaces, (provided that they comply with building standard design and construction requirements), or they may be required to use the developer's design/build team to provide such services.

The design/build method is sometimes applied in a more limited fashion to speculative projects. For example, the mechanical and electrical portions of the project may be constructed on a design/build basis. A subcontractor may provide both the design and construction services required to install these systems, based on criteria established by the building's mechanical/electrical design professional. However, clients may be more concerned about the visible portions of the project, which have a greater effect on its marketability. In order to have more control over the finishes, floor plan, and/or structural bay spacing of the project, clients may choose to retain traditional design and construction services separately.

"Cookie Cutter" Projects: Building types that are repeated frequently and with a minimum of variation are also good candidates for the design/build process. These are sometimes referred to as *cookie cutter*-type projects because once one or two are completed, there is relatively little for the design professional to contribute except to prepare site adaptation drawings, code compliance reviews, and certain design revisions according to the particular project's energy consumption analysis. Residential single- and multi-family housing projects are examples of cookie cutter projects.

Remodeling Projects: Some remodeling, renovation, and rehabilitation projects are also good candidates for the design/build method. A series of projects involving similar construction techniques and procedures, even where a unique design may be applied to each project, is an example of a type of project that is well suited to the design/build method. Because of the repetitive nature of the work, the design/build team may develop a *modus operandi*, or method of operation, for use on a number of projects with similar characteristics.

The Public Sector

The *public sector* refers to that which is owned or controlled by the federal, state, or local government. Public-sector clients, therefore, are the federal government, state governments, and local or municipal governments. Historically, the public sector has been far less responsive than the private sector to the design/build approach to project delivery. In large measure the government's failure to use design/build has been due to licensing, registration, and ethical restrictions, and to public bidding laws. These restrictions have had a significant impact on the ability of parties to provide design/build services for government-sponsored projects.

Ethical prescriptions established by the various design professional societies have, until recently, precluded design professionals from participating commercially in projects for which they are retained to provide professional design services. Several states' licensing statutes even incorporate the substance, if not the actual wording, of certain ethical restrictions, making it illegal as well as unethical for a design professional to receive compensation for anything other than the professional services he or she rendered. Virtually all jurisdictions preclude both a design professional from functioning as a contractor, and a contractor from practicing as a design professional, unless in each case that individual is licensed or registered separately as both a design professional *and* a contractor.

Several states' anti-fraud statutes have also made it difficult to provide design/build services. These statutes assume that during the course of a design/build project, the client and the public will be misled regarding who is providing the required professional design services, thus destroying, or at least confusing, the fiduciary responsibility that the design professional is considered to owe the client, and the trust and confidence that is supposed to exist between the parties.

Public bidding statutes have traditionally required competitive bidding by contractors based on a single set of plans and specifications sufficiently detailed to ensure that the bidding is indeed competitive. The problem with applying these statutes to design/build is that each competing design/build firm prepares its own plans and specifications. There can be no true comparison of the various bids, therefore, since they do not follow the same set of standards. Not only does each competitor have a different set of standards, but those standards may be difficult to interpret since the plans and specifications may be documented in far less detail than a traditionally prepared set of "bid" documents. Some public bidding statutes may attempt to avoid potential conflicts of interest between design professionals and contractors by forbidding either party from having an interest, economic or otherwise, in the other party's activities on a given project.

In recent years, federal, state, and local governments have become more flexible in their approach to design/build contracting. This flexibility is often limited, however, to certain types of projects in certain well-defined situations, or by particular departments or government agencies. There are a number of reasons for this new outlook on design/build, not the least of which is project economics. The result is a growing interest in finding ways to permit the practice of design/build in the public sector.

Federal Government Design/Build Activity

At the federal level, several departments or agencies are currently, or are considering, contracting on a design/build basis for required design and construction services. This is a significant development in light of the influence federal construction contracting activity has had on both the private sector and on local and state government construction sectors. The following federal departments or agencies have employed design/build strategies on their projects or have indicated interest in future design/build projects.

Department of State

As part of its worldwide program to construct or upgrade its existing embassies and diplomatic facilities, the United States Department of State is constructing a new 60,000-square-foot, 50 million-dollar embassy facility in San'a, the capital of the Yemen Arab Republic. The design/build approach has been chosen for this ambitious project. The design/build firm's ability to complete construction more quickly than traditional project delivery methods was apparently a significant factor in the State Department's decision, as a pressing project occupancy date had to be met. The State Department anticipates future use of design/build in connection with similar projects during the next three to five years, with an estimated annual construction dollar volume of approximately 70 million dollars.

Department of Defense

The Department of Defense has also engaged in design/build using the following two-step procurement process. First, the competing design/build teams submit technical proposals in response to the department's performance specifications. Each submittal is then evaluated, and for those found acceptable, the department invites sealed bids. The project is usually awarded to the lowest bidder.

A variation on this approach is sometimes used when, for security reasons, the project's technical requirements cannot be described in detail to potential bidders. In this case, each design/build team's proposal is evaluated by a technical review board which ranks each proposal in terms of their compliance with the performance specifications. A separate review board then ranks the proposals overall, taking into consideration not only the technical review ranking, but price and other factors. The final selection represents the best combination of these factors. When this approach is used, the lowest bidder may not necessarily be awarded the contract.

In 1986, Congress authorized each branch of the military (the Army, Navy, and Air Force) to use one-step fixed-price design/build methods of project delivery on three projects per fiscal year until October 1, 1990. Each branch of the military determines which of its projects are appropriate for this method of project delivery. The department provides its contractual and technical requirements to each bidder. This information includes floor plan layouts, site plans, and site data relative to existing conditions, together with fairly detailed performance specifications. The project is awarded to the most qualified design/build team based on predetermined evaluation criteria, including price. Congress' authorization of design/build projects will likely depend on the success of these test projects.

Since 1973, the Army Corps of Engineers has often used the one-step design/build procurement process in connection with military family housing construction. Following the congressional authorization, the corps also awarded design/build contracts for an 18 million-dollar medical clinic at Kirkland Air Force Base in Albuquerque, New Mexico, and a 13 million-dollar alternate communications facility for the Department of State. Various physical fitness centers, commissaries, fire stations, instruction buildings, warehouses, and administration building projects are currently under consideration.

The Navy is contemplating using this congressional design/build authorization to build child care centers, medical centers, and other facilities that are typically procured on a design/build basis in the private sector. The Air Force has acted on the congressional authorization to award, among other facilities, a 19 million-dollar office building at Scott Air Force Base in Illinois and an 800 thousand-dollar munitions equipment storage facility at Dyess Air Force Base in Texas.

Government Services Administration

After two demonstration design/build projects in the early 1980s involving border stations in California and Arizona, the Government Services Administration (GSA), one of the largest federal procurement agencies, has indicated its willingness to continue using this method of project delivery on selected projects by issuing (in March of 1987) its standard form of contract for procurement of design/build services. On behalf of the Department of Justice, the GSA is proceeding on a design/build basis with a new three million-square-foot, multi-use International Cultural and Trade Center in Washington, D.C., with an expected initial occupancy date of late 1992 or early 1993, and full occupancy by 1996.

Veterans Administration

The Veterans Administration has not yet engaged in design/build procurement activities, but has indicated that it may do so in the future on selected office building and warehouse projects with an annual construction dollar volume of approximately 10 million dollars. The Veterans Administration is currently contemplating the award of a design/build contract for a 2 million-dollar magnetic resonance imaging facility in Milwaukee, Wisconsin.

Postal Service

The United States Postal Service recently completed its first design/build project, a 700,000-square-foot, 82 million-dollar general mail facility in Washington, D.C. Indications are that the Postal Service intends to continue employing this method of project delivery on selected general mail facility projects of at least 10 million dollars, with an annual construction dollar volume of approximately 60 million dollars.

Forest Service

The Forest Service, part of the United States Department of Agriculture, has, in the past, engaged design/build teams for selected construction projects, and expects to continue to do so. The Owl Creek Road project in Colorado, consisting of 6.4 miles of relocated roadway, was recently completed on a design/build basis for a contract price of approximately $650,000. The Forest Service has also employed this method of project delivery on a research laboratory and several residences and seasonal crew quarters.

State Government Design/Build Activity

Design/build activity is also increasing at the state level. Agencies in many states are finding ways to structure procurement practices to allow a number of nontraditional methods of project delivery, one of which is design/build. For instance, facing court pressure to expand prison housing, and citing the expected time saved, the Division of Capitol Planning and Operations in the Commonwealth of Massachusetts has indicated that it expects to allocate approximately 450 million dollars, or twenty percent of its construction budget through 1995, to design/build projects. In Massachusetts and Washington, D.C., design/build contracts have already been awarded for prison projects entailing both new and renovation construction.

Municipal Government Design/Build Activity

At the local level, there is tremendous interest in design/build in response to growing pressures to improve on traditional methods of public procurement of design and construction services. In the late 1960s and early 1970s, a number of local communities in Indiana and Colorado began to award design/build contracts for the construction of schools. The success of these programs spread, and school districts in a number of other states have embarked on their own construction programs using the design/build method. Since then, many other municipalities have chosen design/build for construction of their projects. Perhaps one of the most celebrated and controversial municipal design/build projects is the recently completed Portland, Oregon Public Services Building which was awarded to a design/build team in a national competition. The structure has received various awards and has been reviewed extensively in professional design journals.

Clients Who Purchase From Sole-Source Suppliers

Certain types of public- and private-sector clients are compelled to purchase both design and construction services from a single source. Such clients tend to be involved in either highly specialized activity, such as manufacturing or industry, or with specific types of facilities such as processing plants. Other clients in this category include public utilities that are involved in very large civil engineering projects. Often, the very specific and detailed design and construction knowledge required to successfully complete such projects exists only in highly specialized firms engaged in those fields of expertise. In many cases the building, as such, is little more than a shell or skin for the enormously complex and technologically sophisticated operations that take place inside.

Many times, the forms of the buildings themselves are an integral part of the technology of the operations. Nuclear power plants, hydroelectric generating stations, sewage treatment plants, highly automated assembly lines and food processing facilities, are examples of the types of facilities that might be designed and constructed, indeed could perhaps only be designed and constructed, by firms having the in-house capability to do both.

Summary

Clients procuring design/build services today can be categorized as private-sector (non-government-regulated) clients, and public-sector (government-owned-and-operated) clients. Private-sector clients who employ the design/build method can be generally divided into two groups: inexperienced and sophisticated. Inexperienced clients may be unfamiliar with construction practices or with a particular building type, or they may have no project management capability. These clients find design/build's single source of responsibility a manageable, and therefore appealing, method of project delivery. Sophisticated clients, on the other hand, have more experience and resources. They may be capable of providing well-defined programs and design criteria, and even in-house project management. These clients choose design/build for the time and money that it saves them.

Public-sector clients include federal, state, and local governments. They choose the design/build method for its efficiency and cost effectiveness. On the federal level, the departments of State and Defense, Government Services Administration, Veterans Administration, Postal Service, and Forest Service have used or are considering using the design/build method for projects. Design/build activity on both the state and local levels is also increasing on projects ranging from prisons to schools.

Clients, in both the public and private sector, who require detailed design and construction knowledge for their highly specialized projects, necessarily purchase these services from a single source, such as a design/build firm. Examples of these kinds of projects include nuclear power plants, sewage treatment plants, and food processing facilities. Chapter 7 introduces the three fundamental methods by which clients, in both the private and public sector, procure design/build services.

Chapter Seven

Procurement Methods

Clients who are interested in the design/build method to deliver their projects have three major issues to consider. First, the client should determine if the design/build process itself is more likely to meet his or her needs than other methods of project delivery. If this is so, the client then must select the design/build arrangement best suited to the project. Finally, after one or more potential design/build organizations have been identified, the client must procure design/build services from one of these organizations. This chapter discusses the methods by which design/build services are procured.

The Prequalification Process

Procurement methods may vary from client to client, and from project to project. Procurement typically involves a *prequalification process* in which prospective design/build teams submit their credentials for the client's evaluation. If accepted, the design/build team is then qualified to participate in the selection or competition process.

Clients of design/build projects often request *solicitations of interest* and a *Statement of Qualification* from parties interested in participating in the project. On private-sector projects, clients typically issue a *Request for Proposal* to parties whom the client suspects, whether from past association or through investigation, may be interested in submitting a proposal for the project. The *Request for Proposal* typically contains information about the size, scope, and complexity of the project, the client's requirements and budgetary considerations, selection criteria and method of evaluation, and the requested form and content of the party's proposal.

For public-sector projects, an *Advertisement for Bid* is usually required by law to be published in designated newspapers as official notice of the governmental agency's search for qualified bidders. The notice usually is required to include certain information about the project and to provide the public with a contact name for information about the solicitation, rules for submission of bids, and awarding of the contract.

The objectives of the prequalifying process are to identify those parties possessing the requisite capability, experience, quality and performance standards, interest, and financial means to successfully provide the services within the client's time and budgetary constraints. A typical qualifications statement submitted by the design/build team describes:

- The team's experience on prior projects, especially design/build projects
- Proof of adequate financial capacity
- Lists of key people who will be involved in the project, and their experience in general and with design/build projects in particular
- Current and projected work loads
- Ability to secure required performance, labor, and material bonds
- Design and construction quality of prior projects including design/build projects
- Ability to complete prior design/build projects within schedule and budgetary constraints

Standard forms, such as the American Institute of Architects' Document A305, Contractor's Qualification Statement, and the United States General Services Administration's standard forms SF 254 and 255, are used by clients in soliciting prequalifying information from contractors and design professionals.

Following receipt of these forms from one or more firms, the client then evaluates the information to identify those design/build teams that meet the minimum qualifications required for the project. All design/build teams should be notified promptly of their prequalification or failure to prequalify.

Methods of Selection

There are three principal methods through which clients procure design/build services:

- Negotiation
- Bidding
- Design Competition

Negotiation

In the *negotiation method*, the client evaluates the qualifications of various design/build teams and makes a selection based on interviews or negotiations with representatives of the teams. There are two principal approaches to negotiation: *direct selection* and *comparative selection*. Both are primarily *qualifications-based*, that is, both methods require that interested design/build teams meet basic project prequalification criteria. Neither direct selection nor comparative selection introduces the design/build team's compensation (cost of services) as a factor in the initial selection of the team by the client. Each selection method ranks the various prequalified design/build teams on interviews by the client with key personnel from each of the teams. This gives the client an opportunity to assess each team's experience, their interest in the project, design philosophy, approach to design and construction, approach to management, and the compatibility of the team's key personnel with the client's philosophy and the client's key personnel.

Direct Selection

In this approach, the client selects the highest ranking design/build team directly from those who have prequalified. In the client's judgment, this design/build firm is the most qualified to complete the project in conformance with project requirements and the client's cost and schedule constraints. The client and the design/build team review the services required of the design/build team, the design/build team's approach to the design and construction of the project, and the terms and conditions of the proposed agreement between the client and the design/build team. They then attempt to arrive at mutually satisfying compensation arrangements. If the parties cannot agree, then negotiations with the design/build team are terminated and the client begins negotiations with the next highest ranked design/build team. This process continues until mutually acceptable arrangements have been made between the client and a design/build team.

This purely qualifications-based approach is believed by many, particularly design professionals, to be the most appropriate selection method because it allows the client to secure the services of the most qualified design/build team for a fair and reasonable price. Some argue that the design and construction of each project is the product of a unique blend of client requirements, project constraints, and the design/build team's own design and construction experience, qualifications, and capabilities. The assessment of these factors, although difficult to make, is the most important qualitative judgment a client will make on a project. As such, a client's decision should not be influenced by relatively simplistic and quantitative price concerns.

One of the drawbacks of direct selection negotiation, however, is that the client is committed to a design/build team without first being given the opportunity to evaluate the design/build team's design concept for the project. To address this concern, the following alternative method of negotiating for design/build services is often employed.

Comparative Selection

Using this approach, the client selects the top three to five prequalified design/build teams and invites them to submit design concept proposals for the client's evaluation. This allows the client to evaluate each team's design concept in addition to all of the other evaluation criteria of the direct selection method.

The expected level of development of each design concept proposal may vary from client to client and depend on the project's complexity, unique characteristics, political factors such as local public and government approval, the client's philosophical attitudes, or the degree to which the design concept advances the client's public image or marketing goals. Although the design concept must be sufficiently developed for the client to make a reasonable assessment of its merits, a client requiring too much detail (what would traditionally be considered schematic design documents) might just as well use one of the other procurement methods, such as design competition, described later in this chapter.

Generating design concepts by comparative selection assures the client that the design/build team's approach to the design of the project is appropriate in light of client goals and project requirements. This method is not intended to present the client with a selection of detailed designs from which to choose. Rather, the client selects a design/build team based primarily on its qualifications and, by evaluating its design concept proposal, on its ability to meet the client's goals and the project's requirements. The client is not actually selecting a design for the project per se.

This qualifications-based approach may be appropriate for clients who are wary of being locked into a project with a particular design/build team before they know what the project will look like. After all, under traditional methods of project delivery, the project's design is subject to client approval at numerous stages during the project's design development. The client in the traditional method is not committed to any particular contractor, or even the construction of the project, until after the design professional has completed construction drawings, the project has been bid, and a construction contract awarded. In this way, the client has the opportunity to evaluate the principal features of the project's design.

The comparative selection negotiation method presupposes the client's ability to evaluate each design/build team's design concepts. However, not all clients are sufficiently knowledgeable about design and the different building types to know whether the design concept proposals address the programmatic, technical, and legal (zoning, building code, etc.) issues inherent in the project. A client generally needs to understand more than what he or she sees in the sketches accompanying the design concepts if the design proposal is to be of any real value to the client in the selection process. Some clients have in-house staff architects and engineers, while others retain a qualified design professional at this early stage to help the client choose the best design/build firm. Most clients, however, have neither in-house nor retained capabilities.

Bidding

In the *bidding method*, the client selects a design/build team based on the submission of competitive cost proposals. Bidding is the traditional method of selecting contractors to build projects. Contractors submit cost proposals, or bids, based on a complete set of working drawings and specifications prepared by the design professional. All the information the contractor needs concerning the project's requirements and building conditions is, theoretically, contained in those construction documents. The contractor is able to prepare an informed and accurate bid based on those documents.

Design/build bidding works essentially like the comparative selection negotiation approach, with one important difference: In the bidding approach, the design/build teams are required to submit *cost proposals* with their design concept submission. Although many in the design/build field advise against using price as a selection criteria, price or cost proposals are commonly used nonetheless. This may be because price is the one factor which can be quantitatively and objectively compared, and perhaps most easily justified to others.

Lump Sum Bidding

In *lump sum bidding*, clients typically require design/build teams to "propose their compensation" (place their bid) in the form of a lump sum for all services, costs, and expenses incurred in the design and construction of the project. It is imperative, using this form of bidding, that the client's requirements and the design/build team's proposed solution be described clearly to avoid confusion and misunderstanding. For instance, the contractor may misinterpret client requirements that are unclear, and discover later that the amount of work required is substantially more than what was initially understood. A client may wind up paying for a design proposal that, while seemingly complying with project requirements, falls short of the client's initial expectations for the completed project.

Much of the federal government's design/build procurement activity uses variations on this approach. Typically, the federal agency prepares very detailed technical requirements for a fixed price or lump sum bid, consisting of performance specifications, site data and, for certain facilities, even floor plans. Design/build teams who wish to participate are then required to prepare technical proposals and a cost proposal in response to this information. Selection of a design/build team is then made based not just on price but on an evaluation of all factors.

Bidding creates a heavy administrative burden for the agency and is a fairly costly endeavor for the design/build teams, since it usually takes a good deal of work to solicit, prepare, and evaluate the technical proposals. The various governmental agencies, however, require assurance that the final design and construction of the project will meet the agency's needs. It is believed that the heavy time commitment at the beginning of the project will be rewarded in the end.

Cost-Plus Bidding

An alternative to the lump sum method of bidding is the *cost plus method*. In cost-plus bidding, the client pays the design/build team for the actual costs incurred in connection with the project, plus a fee. The fee may be calculated as a fixed lump amount or a percentage of actual costs. Through negotiation with the client, the design/build team is assured of receiving a fair fee, or profit, for its services, while being covered for costs incurred in the performance of those services. The client pays only for those services and materials performed on behalf of or incorporated into the project. The design/build team is not required to establish, and the client does not have to pay for, design and construction contingencies that might never be utilized.

A client may be uncertain initially about the total cost of the project. This uncertainty makes economic planning extremely difficult for a client. Most projects require a degree of certainty regarding the impact the project will have on the client's financial resources so that the client can raise and allocate those resources to pay for the project's costs. This is especially critical to clients seeking construction financing from third parties. Lenders must evaluate the probable value of the project against the amount to be loaned to the client. If construction costs are not fixed, lending institutions become wary.

Guaranteed Maximum Price

A third type of bid often used on design/build projects is the establishment of a *guaranteed maximum price* for the design and construction of the project. This approach reduces the risk of runaway costs to clients and lenders alike. The design/build team is compensated, as it would be on a cost plus project, for the actual costs incurred in connection with the design and construction of the project, plus a fee. This compensation is subject, however, to a ceiling, or guaranteed maximum price, beyond which the client is not obligated to pay. If the actual costs plus the fee is greater than the guaranteed maximum price, the contractor is not entitled to any additional compensation beyond the guaranteed maximum price. If the fee is less than the guaranteed maximum price, the difference may either be retained by the client, or shared proportionally by the client and the design/build team.

A drawback common to each of these compensation or bid arrangements is the difficulty the client encounters in comparing cost proposals. On traditional projects, all bidders are submitting their bids based on the same set of construction documents. In design/build bidding, the design proposals on which each cost proposal is based will usually vary significantly, since each design/build team submits its own design scheme based on the client's requirements. Each design/build bid is based on a different design proposal. Design/build clients must therefore have a keen understanding of the material similarities and differences of each design proposal in order for the competitive bidding approach to be of any value.

Design Competition

A third method of procuring design/build services is by conducting a *design competition*. In a design competition, design/build teams submit detailed design proposals to the client, who selects the team based on the ability of their proposal to meet the requirements of the project. The "winner" of the competition is awarded the contract to complete the design and construct the project. This approach is similar to both the negotiation and bidding methods of procurement.

If a cost proposal is part of the submission requirement, the design competition approach takes on characteristics of the bidding approach. The only difference is that the design in the design competition is far more detailed than in the bidding method. For the most part, the more detailed the design, the easier it is for the client to assess the appropriateness of the design/build team. But this may not always be true. For instance, complex design submissions that are technical in nature and not visually apparent may confuse the client. Many clients, therefore, seek the assistance of an independent design consultant to evaluate and choose the winning design.

When no cost proposal is required as part of the submission documents, the design competition is very similar to the comparative selection negotiation approach. Again, the difference is that the design submission in a competition is typically far more developed than the more conceptual design proposal in the negotiation approach.

The level of detail required in a design competition is often based on the client's desires, the level of complexity of the project, and the project's and/or client's prestige in the eyes of design professionals. Very prestigious projects often attract many design professionals. Clients should keep this in mind when deciding who should be invited to compete, the level of detail which can reasonably be expected of the competing design/build teams, and whether or not compensation should be paid to the competitors who are not chosen.

The submissions in design competition often constitute what would normally be considered schematic designs on a traditionally structured project. A significant amount of work is involved in preparing schematic designs. It is unusual to ask design professionals to spend that kind of time on what is, essentially, a contest entry. In many design competitions, clients reimburse or pay *honoraria* to the unchosen design/build teams to help defray their costs. From the design/build team's perspective, however, the honorarium seldom covers the full cost of their efforts. For a relatively nominal cost, the client conducting a design competition may receive a number of schematic design solutions from qualified and experienced design/build teams without having to pay anywhere near what it would cost to solicit individually the same number of design/build teams.

Design/build competitions may be open to all who prequalify and wish to compete, or they may be closed or limited to only those parties invited by the client to participate. Limited competitions, especially if the project is unique or exciting, are likely to attract a higher level of design effort than open competitions, since only the best design professionals are invited to enter, and since the chances of any one team's success in winning the award are increased substantially. This is important considering the high cost of entering a design competition. Except for academic or publicity reasons, there may be little incentive for a design/build team to participate when the chances of winning are small.

Some argue that out of the various procurement methods, the design competition approach is most likely to increase overall design quality of the project. Others believe, however, that design competition may repel some qualified competitors who refuse to participate in competitions for professional and commercial reasons. Similarly, since the quality of the design is judged subjectively by the client and the client's professional consultant, the design submissions may be conceived and developed as "sales tools" of the design/build team, and not necessarily with the thought warranted by the project and program issues.

Summary

Clients who have determined that the design/build method suits their specific project needs, and have chosen the design/build arrangement to deliver their project, are ready to select a design/build team. But first, design/build teams must prequalify for participation in this selection process by submitting their credentials for the client's perusal.

There are three methods by which clients procure design/build services from prequalified design/build teams: negotiation, bidding, and design competition. In the negotiation method, the client interviews one or more design/build teams to assess the team's interest, experience, and qualifications. Design/build teams may be chosen directly, purely on qualifications, or they may be chosen by comparison with several teams based on qualifications as well as on a preliminary design proposal.

In the bidding method, the client selects the design/build team based on cost proposals or bids submitted by a number of design/build teams. Design/build bidding is similar to traditional competitive bidding, except that design/build clients require that design concept drawings be submitted along with cost proposals. The design/build teams estimate the amount they will charge for their services. Compensation is proposed as either a lump sum, cost plus, or a guaranteed maximum price. The extent of detail required in design proposals is greater in the bidding method since design/build teams will need to justify, document, and ensure the accuracy of the estimate. Clients will need some understanding of design concepts to make the most of this method.

In a design competition, the client awards the contract to the "winning" design/build team chosen from a number of design contestants. In this method, design proposals are highly developed and complex. Clients may enlist the help of a design consultant to assist in evaluating the complex design entries. Because of the extensive design work involved in preparing a competitive proposal, some clients grant honoraria to the design/build teams not chosen to help defray their expenses, although this amount is generally small compared to what it costs to solicit the same number of design submissions from individuals.

Once a design/build team is secured, work can begin. However, this is not always without incident. Part IV examines principles of liability in the construction industry today. Chapter 8 begins by exploring common theories of liability and their application to design/build.

Part Four

Liability

The concept of liability, or legal responsibility, for loss or injury in connection with construction is rooted in antiquity, when the master builder was held accountable for both the design and the assembly of the structures he created. With the divergence in roles came a differentiation in responsibility for errors and omissions in design and construction. Theories of liability and the manner in which they are imposed have evolved over the centuries. Today we have a system of laws in this country in which construction professionals practicing in traditionally structured projects are typically liable only for their own actions or failure to act, based on three traditional theories of liability: breach of contract, negligence, and statutory violations.

This concept changes in design/build, however. Depending on the design/build arrangement, construction professionals may be liable for the errors and omissions of their associates as well as their own. Furthermore, there are additional theories of liability that are more apt to be applied specifically to design/build projects, and against which design/build participants may have few defenses. There are also a multitude of legal issues surrounding the imposition of liability that may have an impact on parties involved in actions. Part IV examines the concept of liability in the construction industry today. Chapter 8 begins with a discussion of the individual theories of liability and their significance in design/build.

Chapter Eight

Theories of Liability in Design/Build

Design/build is a time-honored practice rooted in antiquity. So is the concept of liability, or legal responsibility, for loss or injury sustained in connection with the design and construction of buildings. The master builder of the ancient world was responsible for both design and construction. In ancient Babylonia, for example, the *Code of Hammurabi* imposed absolute and unconditional liability on the master builder for all design and construction errors. The following is an excerpt from the code.

> *If a builder has built a house for a man, and his work is not strong, and if the house he has built falls in and kills the house-holder, that builder shall be slain.*
>
> *If the goods have been destroyed, he shall replace all that has been destroyed; and because the house that he built was not made, and it has been fallen in, he shall restore the fallen house out of his personal property.*
>
> *If a builder has built a house for a man and his work is not done properly, and a wall shifts, then that builder shall make that wall good with his own silver.*

It was not necessary to demonstrate that the master builder was at fault in order to impose liability. If an injury was sustained, the master builder was subject to the penalties imposed by the code. We might well wonder how many master builders lived long enough to retire!

During the Renaissance, a divergence appeared between design and construction tasks, and the words used to describe the individuals who performed those tasks. The term "architect" was used to describe the party who designed the project, while the term "master builder," or "builder," referred to the party who constructed the project. With this divergence in roles began the process of differentiating responsibility for design- and construction-related matters.

This process was slow in evolving. Even in 18th century France, the architect was still responsible for construction errors, as the following excerpt from Code Napoleon, Article 1792, indicates:

> *If a building, which an architect or other workman has undertaken to make by the job, should fall to ruin, either in whole or in part, on account of the badness of the workmanship, or even because of the badness of the soil, the architect and the undertaker shall bear the loss, if the building falls to ruin in ten years.*

What is interesting to note in this excerpt is that the phrase "architect or other workman" implies that the architect and the builder were considered equals, to a far greater extent than is true today. This excerpt also introduces the notion of a *statute of limitations*, or a time limit within which action must be taken against the architect for errors in his work. The phrase, "If the building falls to ruin in ten years" implies that the architect is responsible for his work for at least ten years after the building has been completed.

Today, American *jurisprudence*, or system of laws, dictates that, unless stated otherwise in a contract, the design professional who performs design services exclusively will be liable only for the design of the project. The contractor, when acting exclusively in that capacity, will be liable only for the construction of the project. **These basic principles may change, however, if either or both the design professional and the contractor provide services outside of their respective traditional disciplines.**

Contractors and design professionals venturing into the design/build field should therefore have a general understanding of the basic legal theories employed to impose liability on construction professionals for errors, omissions, or other improper actions. While legal theories used to impose liability in traditionally structured projects are also applicable in a design/build context, there are additional theories that may have special application to design/build. This chapter will explore these theories, first by giving a brief overview of the history of the concept of liability, next by defining each theory of liability and, finally, by exploring those theories that have particular relevance to design/build.

Historical Overview

The imposition of liability for injury sustained in connection with design and construction is as ancient as the master builder. These concepts have evolved over time in response to changes in the nature and extent of both design/build practice and society's attitudes concerning the assumption of responsibility for one's actions.

Under the Code of Hammurabi, absolute and unconditional liability was imposed on the master builder, independent of the notion of fault. The code did not require, as a prerequisite to the imposition of liability, any special or contractual relationship between the master builder and the injured party, although such a relationship may have been implied. It was not until the rise of the Roman Empire that the notion of *privity*, (or, more precisely, the *absence of privity*) between the master builder and the injured party, was introduced into law to limit claims by remote parties against the master builder. Privity refers to the relationship that exists between two or more contracting parties. Privity does not exist between parties who do not share a contractual relationship. While limiting the number of parties who could make claims against the master builder, it provided no relief to the master builder from liability to the party that hired him.

Nineteenth-century English law required both the Roman concept of privity between the parties, referred to here as *privity of contract*, and evidence of *negligence*. Negligence is a breach of a duty that the law imposes on one party by virtue of its special relationship to the injured party. The privity of contract theory espoused by the English courts in *Winterbottom v. Wright* (1842) argued that permitting parties other than the contracting parties a right of recovery for injuries sustained would impose liability on the parties beyond that for which they had contracted, and that without such a limitation, excessive and unlimited liability would result.

The second requirement, negligence, required that the *plaintiff* (the party who brings a lawsuit against another) also had to prove that the *defendant* (the party against whom the plaintiff has brought a lawsuit) was negligent—that he failed to exercise the degree of skill, care, and diligence that would have been exercised in the same or similar circumstances by practitioners of that same profession. In the absence of both privity of contract and negligence, liability could not be imposed on the *defendant*.

American courts followed English law closely until the early twentieth century, when the first exceptions to the privity defense were successfully argued. In a case entitled *MacPherson v. Buick Motor Company* (1916), an automobile manufacturer was held liable for injuries sustained by parties who had no contractual relationship with the manufacturer. Exceptions to the privity defense have eclipsed the rule to such an extent that today, in virtually all jurisdictions and in both situations involving personal injury and economic loss, the absence of privity is no longer a viable defense. Proof of negligence alone is usually sufficient to impose liability on a party for errors, omissions, and other improper actions.

Defining Liability

Liability refers to a situation in which one party is legally obligated to assume responsibility for another party's loss or burden. Liability is created when the law recognizes two elements:

- The existence of an enforceable legal duty to be performed by one party for the benefit of another
- The failure to perform the duty in accordance with applicable legal standards

Sources of Duty

A *duty* is an obligation or standard of conduct. The concept of duty is inseparable from the concept of liability. There is no liability in the absence of a legally enforceable duty. Legally enforceable duties are those duties that the law recognizes as existing between and legally binding the parties.

There are three sources of legally recognized and enforceable duties. They are:

- Contracts
- Common Law
- Statutes and Regulations

Liability may be imposed based on a violation of one or more of these three sources of duty.

Contracts

The first source of duty is the *contract*. A contract is an agreement between two or more parties consisting of one or more legally enforceable promises that the law recognizes as a duty to be performed by one of the parties. For example, a design professional or contractor may promise to perform specific services within a certain period of time. The client may promise to pay the design professional or the contractor for the performance of those services, and to make the payments within a prescribed time frame.

Contracts may also contain promises that are only marginally related to the main purpose of the agreement. For example, a contract may contain a promise by the construction professional to refrain from performing similar services for other projects that compete with the client's project. Or, the client may promise in his or her contract to refrain from using documents prepared by the design professional for other projects by the design professional. A large number of legally enforceable duties like these are created through the vehicle of the contract.

A valid and legally enforceable contract consists of four elements:

- Mutual Consent
- Consideration
- Legal Capacity
- The Contract Must Not Be Void by Statute or by Rule of Common Law

Mutual Consent: Parties must, with a reasonable degree of certainty, agree on the same thing, at the same time, and on the same terms.

Consideration: Each party's promise must be supported by or given in return for a legally sufficient consideration. Consideration is that which is bargained for in return for the performance of some act, a forbearance from performing some act, or a promise. Consideration itself may be an act, a forbearance from performing some act, or a return promise. In design and construction contracts, consideration may be the client's promise to pay money for the services to be performed by the design professional or the contractor, or the design professional's or contractor's promise to perform such services. In order for consideration to be legally sufficient, it must benefit the promisee or be detrimental to the promisor.

Consideration is measured in legal, not economic, terms. Benefits to the promisee are not things for which the promisee is otherwise legally entitled to receive from the promisor. On the other hand, if the promisor has obligated itself in some way, or has promised something for which he or she was not previously legally obligated, then the promisor has suffered a legal detriment sufficient to serve as consideration for the original promise of the promisee.

Legal Capacity: Each party to the contract must have the legal capacity to enter into a binding arrangement with another party. Contracts that are entered into with parties who do not have the legal capacity to do so may be void. For instance, corporations may be limited by their charter, articles of organization, or by statute, from entering into certain types of contractual arrangements. A contract attempted by such a corporation may be invalid and unenforceable.

Contract Must Not Be Void by Statute or by Rule of Common Law: Contracts that are illegal are void and unenforceable. Contracts may be declared illegal by statute or by the courts if the contract violates public policy. An example of an illegal contract is one that defrauds the public or restrains trade. Some contracts may be unenforceable if they are not in writing. Most jurisdictions have a so-called "Statute of Frauds" which, among other requirements, states that contracts that cannot be performed within one year from the date of execution must be in writing to be enforced by the courts. There may be exceptions to this rule, however, depending on the particular facts and the language of the applicable statute. For instance, if a party has performed a considerable amount of work under an oral contract, courts may rule that it is unjust to permit the other party to use the purely legal formality of the writing requirement to avoid its obligations.

Common Law

A second source of duty is *common law*. Common law comprises principles of conduct based on usage, custom, or commonly held beliefs as interpreted by the courts on a case-by-case basis. Common law is not founded on the will of legislative or rule-making bodies, but on accepted standards of conduct. Common law is under a constant state of redefinition, as courts attempt to reflect in their decisions their understanding of the current values of society, and to maintain the delicate balance between freedom and responsibility.

Professional Standard of Care: Common law has developed a set of general standards that apply to all members of society, including clients, design professionals, and contractors. Common law has developed a more particular set of standards to apply to design professionals which, theoretically, reflect the expectations held generally by society regarding the level of training, skill, care, and competence that a design professional should possess. These expectations have been and continue to be molded by the courts through case-by-case interpretations of normal conduct based on duties that the design professional is obligated to perform. These duties are normally referred to as the *professional standard of care*.

What is this standard of care to which the law requires design professionals to conform their conduct? Precedents have been established in the development of common law which state that a design professional has a duty to possess a degree of learning and skill ordinarily possessed by design professionals in good standing in the same locality under similar circumstances in that profession. It is the design professional's further duty to use that same level of care ordinarily exercised by reputable members of that design profession practicing in the same locality under similar circumstances. By practicing that profession, the individual declares that he does indeed possess a level of competence and expertise. A design professional is expected to uphold that standard level of care through diligence and the exercise of good judgment.

This professional standard of care does not, however, require that the design professional be free from error in judgment, or to guarantee, warrant, or ensure the occurrence of a specific result. Design professionals, like doctors, attorneys, and other professionals who practice somewhat inexact sciences, are required to exercise their skilled judgment in order to anticipate and provide for random factors that cannot be measured precisely. The indeterminate nature of these factors makes it impossible to gauge them with complete accuracy. Because of the possibility of error in the exercise of this judgment under a given set of circumstances, the law has traditionally allowed for imperfect results as long as the design professional exercises that level of skill expected from a similarly situated design professional. Courts feel that until the random element is eliminated in these professions, it is only fair for the party retaining the professional's services to bear the risk of unforeseeable difficulties. It is just as important to recognize that it is the standard of care existing at the time professional services are performed that is relevant, not future modifications to that standard. There will undoubtedly be modifications to any standard based on advances in technology or methods of service.

Statutes and Regulations

The third source of duty is established through acts, statutes, ordinances, rules, regulations, and other enactments of the various federal, state, and local rule-making bodies. Congress, state legislatures, local planning and zoning boards, as well as an infinite array of administrative and regulatory bodies continue to develop laws and regulations prescribing acceptable behavior in our society. Unlike common law which establishes standards through custom, or contracts which delineate lines of responsibility through verbal or oral agreements, statutes and regulations are legal rules or laws that prescribe or prohibit conduct.

Traditional Liability Theories

There are three traditional theories of liability applicable to the construction industry today. Each theory is imposed based on the violation of one or more sources of duty: contracts, common law, and statutes or regulations. These three theories are:

- Breach of Contract
- Tort of Negligence
- Statutory Violations

These three theories, breach of contract, negligence, and statutory violations, may apply to participants of both traditionally structured projects as well as design/build projects. This section will examine each theory of liability, identify its source(s) of duty, describe the elements necessary to impose liability, and comment on the applicability of traditional theories of liability to design/build projects.

Breach of Contract

A party may be held liable based on a *breach of contract*. A breach of contract is the failure by one party to a contract to properly perform some contractually described obligation in accordance with the terms of the contract. As expected, the source of duty for a breach of contract action is the contract itself.

In order for a defendant to be held contractually liable for damages, a plaintiff must demonstrate the following conditions:

- There exists a valid written or oral, legally enforceable contract between the plaintiff and the defendant
- The defendant must have materially failed to perform one or more duties defined in the contract as his or her responsibility
- The plaintiff must have suffered damages as a result of the defendant's material failure to perform the duties

If all of these conditions are present, than a cause of action against the defaulting party may be established by the plaintiff.

The contract may be more or less clear in defining the obligations and the criteria employed to judge proper performance of that obligation. There may be legal rules of construction available to help clarify ambiguities in the contract. Nonetheless, in a breach of contract action, the parties essentially look to the contract to determine the existence and scope of the obligations or duties.

Tort of Negligence

A party may be held liable based on a *tort of negligence*. In order to discuss the concept of negligence we first must understand the concept of *tort liability*.

Tort Liability

Tort liability is based not on a failure to fulfill a contractual obligation, but in the breach of a legally imposed duty owed by one party to another. While the contract is the source of contractually imposed obligations, common law is the principal source of duties, the breach of which is considered a *tort*.

It is not possible to arrive at a really good definition of a tort. Basically, a tort is a private, civil wrong committed by one party against another. It is not a breach of contract. It is not a criminal offense. It arises by operation of law based on some breach of a legally imposed duty owed by the defendant to the plaintiff. The duties imposed are generally those defined by common law, although breaches of contractually or statutorily created duties may also, under certain circumstances, constitute a tort.

There are many types of torts. There are *intentional torts*, such as civil assault, civil battery, trespass, conversion (illegally assuming ownership of another's personal property), infliction of mental or emotional stress, and loss of consortium (the right to aid and affection from a lawful spouse). These torts require the defendant to perform an act which both intends to cause harm and which results in harm. Intent and result are both prerequisite to the existence of intentional torts. There are also a limited number of intentional torts which, while the act may have been intentional, the harm that resulted was not. The liability resulting from this type of tort is often referred to as *strict liability* and will be discussed in greater detail later in this chapter.

Unintentional torts result not from an intention to cause harm or to perform some harmful act, but are acts which result in harm to another because the defendant did not conform his or her conduct to the standard of care required by common law. This is referred to as *negligence* and has been of most concern, historically, to design professionals and contractors.

Four conditions must be demonstrated in order to establish a tort of negligence and impose liability on a defendant.

- The defendant must owe a duty or be under an obligation to another to conform his or her conduct to the applicable standard of care required by the law
- The defendant must fail to conform his or her conduct to such standard of care
- There must be a legally sufficient causal connection between the breach of duty owed by the standard of care and the injury suffered by the party to whom the duty was owed. (This causal connection is often referred to as *proximate cause*.)
- Actual damages must have resulted to the party to whom the duty was owed

Traditionally, the absence of any one of these elements is sufficient to bar the imposition of tort liability on a defendant.

Statutory Violations

Liability may be imposed based on violations of acts, statutes, ordinances, rules, regulations, and other requirements of the various federal, state, and local rule-making bodies. Recall that in a tort of negligence, the defendant owes a duty or is under an obligation to another party to conform his or her conduct to an applicable standard of care required by law. That duty or obligation, however, may be established by statutes and regulations. Violation of one or more duties mandated by statutes or regulations may constitute *negligence per se*.

In order to impose liability based on statutory violations, the following elements must be demonstrated:

- The existence of a duty mandated by an act, statute, ordinance, rule, regulation, or other requirement of the various federal, state, or local rule-making bodies
- A violation of such regulatory requirements
- A sufficiently close causal connection between the violation and some damage or injury to persons or property
- The regulatory requirement must be determined to have been enacted, at least in part, to prevent such damage or injury from occurring
- The person or property suffering such damage or injury must be determined to be of the class of persons or property for whose protection the regulatory requirement was adopted

In a number of jurisdictions, if all of these requirements are met, then a *presumption* of negligence is said to exist. This presumption may be overcome only if substantial evidence can be produced which demonstrates that the defendant acted reasonably under the circumstances. If evidence cannot be produced, then liability will be imposed on the defendant.

In other jurisdictions, the violation of statutes or regulations is seen merely as *evidence* of negligence, as opposed to a presumption of negligence, and left, like all other evidence, to the judge and jury to weigh.

The reasoning behind the presumption of negligence in the face of statutory violations is that regulatory requirements establish minimum standards of conduct and are intended to secure the health, safety, and welfare of the parties covered by the requirement.

Traditional Liability Theories in Design/Build

The three traditional liability theories—breach of contract, tort of negligence, and statutory violations—have been applied primarily in traditional projects, but may be applicable in design/build projects as well. Liability is imposed based on a breach of duty. In order to establish a breach of duty, all of the conditions or elements listed under each theory must be present. The absence of even one element is sufficient cause for dismissal of the claim. Once a breach of duty has been established, responsibility or liability for the breach may be imposed. Responsibility may vary, however, depending on the method of project delivery or, in the case of design/build, depending on the design/build arrangement. Refer to Chapter 2 for a discussion of the lines of responsibility in each design/build arrangement.

Additional Liability Concepts

Contractors and design professionals engaged in traditional methods of project delivery have typically faced risks of liability from the three sources of duty previously described: contracts, common law, and regulatory pronouncements. What happens, however, when contractors and design professionals arrange themselves contractually so that each provides those services traditionally provided by the other, or associate themselves in such a manner that all design and construction services are provided by a single entity? **Are there additional or increased liability implications for contractors or design professionals participating in design/build methods of project delivery?**

There are indeed several liability concepts that, while having some application under traditional methods of project delivery, have substantially greater application to contractors and design professionals participating in design/build. These additional liability concepts include:

- Breach of Warranty
- Strict Liability

Breach of Warranty

A *warranty* is a promise that a statement about some fact is true and that it will continue to be true. Liability may be imposed based on a *breach of warranty*. If for any reason the statement is proven false, the individual making the statement or promise (called the "promisor") may be liable to the person to whom the promise was made (the "promisee") for damages incurred by the promisee.

Warranties are typically found in contracts. However, contract language may be deleted, or more appropriate and properly qualified language may be substituted to limit the extent of coverage guaranteed in the contract. In this regard it is important that construction professionals recognize what language is insurable under standard professional liability insurance policies and what language is typically excluded from coverage. Policies typically exclude coverage for warranties, since the terms of the policy provide coverage only for negligence in providing or failing to provide professional services.

There are two types of warranties applicable to design/build projects:

- Express Warranties
- Implied Warranties

Express Warranties

An *express warranty* is a promise or guarantee made by one party to another that is clearly stated, either orally or in writing. Most express warranties are in writing, since oral express warranties are usually more difficult to prove in a court of law.

The nature of the client-design/build relationship is different from the relationship that exists in traditionally structured projects—different in some very important ways. The existence of a single point of responsibility in the design/build firm for all design and construction activities makes the inclusion of express warranties in the parties' written agreements far more likely. One reason for this is that the design/build firm may feel that by having greater control over the project, it must accept the obligations imposed by warranties as part of the consequences associated with being that single source of responsibility.

Warranties concerning the quality, completeness, and conformance to regulatory requirements of the drawings and specifications prepared by the design/build firm, as well as warranties concerning adherence to design and construction schedules and conformance to construction cost budgets or other limitations, are among the types of warranties found more often in design/build agreements than in traditional agreements. Again, this may be due to the belief often held by design/build professionals that they have greater control over the design and construction of design/build projects and that, as such, they are in a better position than on traditionally structured projects to control the outcome of the project. This belief provides a measure of assurance to the design professional and the contractor that the goals represented by the warranties are achievable and that their realization is directly affected by their acts. This assurance simply is not possible on traditionally structured projects.

Additionally, on traditionally structured projects, the design professional and contractor may be uncertain about the capabilities of the other party. This could be a significant deterrent for these parties to commit themselves to a warranty whose existence is dependent, at least in part, on the performance of the other party. On a design/build project, however, especially on those for which the design professional and the contractor have worked together before, that uncertainty is reduced or eliminated.

A breach of an express warranty is typically viewed these days to constitute a breach of contract. What distinguishes it from a normal breach of contract action is that in a breach of an express warranty, there is no requirement to establish fault on the part of the breaching party. A typical breach of contract action must establish a substantial breach of a material contract obligation, that is, more than merely a minor or insubstantial failure to conform to an important provision of the contract, or even a substantial breach of an unimportant contract requirement. Since it is considered a breach of contract action, the consequences to the parties of a breach of warranty action, therefore, are similar to those of a breach of contract.

Implied Warranties

An *implied warranty* is created not from the explicit oral or written statements made by one party to another, but through a promise or guarantee that is *inferred* under the law by virtue of the transaction or the circumstances between the parties, or by the relative position one party holds with respect to another.

Typically, implied warranties exist in situations in which parties have entered into some form of contractual relationship with each other, whether a purchase or sale agreement, a lease or rental agreement, or an agreement for the provision of payment for services. Any product or service that is covered under an implied warranty is said in legal terms to be *impliedly warranted*. The source of duty in implied warranties may come from contracts or common law. The breach of an implied warranty may constitute a breach of contract or negligence, depending on the nature of the contract and the standard of care with which the work was to be performed

Most jurisdictions have ruled that design professionals practicing in traditional roles are not generally considered to have made implied warranties. In addition to normal breach of contract theories, the standard of care applicable to design professionals in connection with negligence is typically held by the courts to be sufficient to determine whether or not to impose liability. A contractor engaged in traditional project delivery, on the other hand, is generally held to have impliedly warranted that his of her work will be performed in a reasonably skillful and workmanlike manner.

Furthermore, in traditionally structured projects, the client is normally viewed to have impliedly warranted to the contractor that the drawings and specifications prepared by the design professional and provided to the contractor by the client are reasonably complete, detailed, coordinated, and sufficiently clear to permit contractors generally experienced with that type of project to construct the project with no more than the usual clarification and interpretation typically required on such projects. If a client fails to provide the contractor with sufficient drawings and specifications, the client would likely be liable for the extra costs incurred by the contractor because the drawings and specifications failed to conform to the standards expressed in the implied warranty. This implied warranty is based, of course, on certain assumptions concerning what a contractor should reasonably be entitled to rely on with respect to the documents furnished by the client, as well as the different roles of the design professional and contractor and each of their separate and distinct relationships with the client on a traditionally structured project.

However, when design professionals and contractors provide design/build services, courts are increasingly inferring the existence of certain types of implied warranties on the part of the design/build firm and the elimination of certain implied warranties on the part of the client.

On a design/build project, the client is certainly not concerned with the creation and maintenance of separate roles for the design professional and the contractor. After all, the client chose design/build for its single point of responsibility and accountability. And although design/build design professionals and contractors may, for some reason, wish to maintain the appearance of separate entities, legally either the design professional or the contractor or some combination of the two have assumed full responsibility to the client for all design and construction activities in connection with the project. Courts have generally acknowledged these intentions on the part of design/build participants and have held that one consequence of this is that no implied warranty is deemed to exist on the part of the client with respect to providing sufficient drawings to the contractor. To do otherwise would permit the design/build firm to escape responsibility for preparation of such documents and shift the responsibility to the client.

Courts have traditionally distinguished between the provision of services and the manufacturing of products. In the construction industry, courts normally recognize that the design professional's drawings and specifications are the means through which he or she communicates the design intent to the contractor, and that such documents are not products intended for use by third parties or the general public. However, if the design professional engages in nontraditional methods of project delivery such as design/build, he or she runs the risk that a court could change its position. The court could conclude that the traditional distinctions between the design professional and the contractor do not exist. Rather than focusing on the design professional in isolation, the court may focus on the design/build firm as a whole and conclude that the design/build firm is no different conceptually than manufacturers of consumer products that are both designed and built by the manufacturer. These courts are becoming much more aggressive in inferring implied warranties of habitability and fitness on structures designed and constructed by design/build entities.

Courts have tended to focus on design/builders who also act as vendors. A typical example that has generated a fair amount of litigation is the design/builder/vendor of mass-produced housing. Based on the regulations of the *Uniform Commercial Code*, or *UCC*, (a body of laws that govern consumer transactions), and generally more consumer-oriented legislation by Congress and state legislatures in recent years, courts are considering that these individuals have impliedly warranted that the homes they are selling, as well as the various components comprising those homes, are habitable and fit for their intended purpose for use as homes. This argument is based on the notion that such homes are products in much the same way other items purchased by consumers are products. They are normally sold to unsophisticated purchasers who lack the expertise to evaluate the soundness or fitness of the product before purchase, while the design/builder/vendor, on the other hand, has had ample opportunity as well as the expertise to evaluate the fitness of the home prior to sale. To protect the reasonable expectations of the home buyer, the law implies warranties of habitability and fitness, the violation or breach of which subjects the design/builder/vendor to liability for damages.

The imposition of these implied warranties is not limited to mass produced projects. Courts are extending this rationale to include one-of-a-kind projects as well. Here the argument is that clients are not sufficiently capable of determining, prior to the extended use of their new facilities, the appropriateness or fitness of the facilities to the specific purposes for which they are intended and that instead, clients are relying on the design/build organization's expertise to deliver a structure that fulfills the needs and expectations of the client.

Tests to Determine the Nature of a Transaction: If the underlying nature of the contract between the client and the design/build firm is one in which the design/build firm is providing services to the client, then the design professional will be judged in accordance with traditional theories of liability. On the other hand, if the underlying nature of the relationship between the client and the design/build firm is one in which the design/build firm is supplying a product to the client, the design/build firm will be judged in accordance with both traditional as well as consumer-oriented theories of liability.

Courts have developed a number of tests or ways of analyzing the underlying nature of a transaction to determine if it is product- or service-oriented, and how and to what extent to apply the Uniform Commercial Code to a given situation. One test looks to the *predominant purpose of the activities* of the design/build firm. This analysis attempts to determine which aspects of the relationship between the design/build firm and the client predominate. If the predominant purpose of the transaction is to provide a service, then the UCC does not apply. However, if the predominant purpose of the transaction is to effect the sale of a product, then the UCC and its implied warranties are likely to apply.

Another approach to determining this matter is to *apply the UCC to the "sales" portion of the transaction only*. This approach avoids the application of one characterization to a transaction that can be characterized in more than one way.

A third approach used to determine the applicability of the UCC is to *determine the "essence" of the transaction*. Here the court attempts to best characterize the underlying nature of the contractual relationship between the design/build firm and the client, rather than attempting to determine which aspect of the transaction is a service and which is a product. Theoretically, while the extent of services provided by the design/build firm may be small in comparison to the sales, under the essence approach the court may conclude that the purpose of the contract was to retain services from a specially qualified entity, not purchase a product.

Design/build participants should also realize that jurisdictions vary in their willingness to determine the existence of such implied warranties, and the particular nature of the design/build firm may be of significance in shaping the court's decision. For instance, a design/build firm that is merely a contractor offering minimum design services may be treated differently than a firm offering full professional design services.

In negotiating and drafting contracts, design/build participants should state their intentions clearly to avoid any question regarding the nature of their transaction. In this way, each participant can protect its rights and fulfill its responsibilities.

Strict Liability

In *strict liability*, the law goes one step further and imposes liability for physical harm (but generally not for economic loss) caused by defects or deficiencies in products. What distinguishes this theory from other theories of liability is that liability is imposed regardless of fault or negligence on the part of the seller of the product, and regardless of whether a contract exists between the seller and the injured party. In express and implied warranties, a contractual relationship exists between the defendant and the plaintiff and acts as the underlying legal structure supporting imposition of the warranty. In strict liability, a contractual relationship is not a prerequisite to the imposition of liability.

The strict liability theory evolved in the late 1800s from cases in which injury was sustained by one party as a result of hazardous or unusually dangerous conditions created by another party. In the past 50 years, strict liability has been used increasingly as the basis for consumer protection liability legislation. The application of this theory requires that the rights of one party to conduct its activities in a reasonable manner be weighed against the rights of another party to be free from injury or harm caused by such activities. Under this theory, courts and legislatures have determined that in the absence of fault, liability will be imposed on the party who is in either the best position to control the activity or in the best position to bear the economic loss.

Contemporary consumer protection laws impose liability on a party if that party sells a product in a condition such that it is unreasonably dangerous to any user of that product, regardless of whether or not that user is the original purchaser. The seller of that product is liable for injuries and property damage sustained by the user, provided the seller of the product is in the business of selling the product, and it was or should have been expected by the seller that the product would ultimately find its way to the injured party substantially unaltered from the condition in which it was originally sold. (Strict liability is not usually found to exist for parties further down the line from the seller. More traditional contract or negligence theories must be relied on in order to impose liability.) There is no requirement of fault, negligence, or breach of contract on the part of the seller for liability to be imposed. **Strict liability, like implied warranties, may be particularly applicable to design/build entities in those jurisdictions in which design/build activity is considered to be the manufacturing of a product.**

The criteria typically applied by the courts to determine strict liability include:

- The magnitude of harm that may occur as a result of a particular activity
- The likelihood that such harm may occur as a result of the activity
- The inability of the injured party to know or to be able to reduce the risk of harm resulting from the activity
- The unusualness or inappropriateness of the activity to the location in which it is conducted
- The value to the community resulting from such activity
- The extent to which such activity is a matter of common occurrence

Multiple Liability Theories

Although each of the various liability theories discussed above have been examined essentially in isolation from one another, often more than one theory may be applicable to each of the parties, or different theories may be applicable to different parties, depending on the design/build arrangement chosen to deliver the project.

For instance, the primary contractor on a design/build project may be held liable by the client based on a breach of contract. However, if the subcontractor failed to provide services with the requisite standard of care, resulting, ultimately, in schedule delays, he or she may be held liable based on negligence. This is assuming, of course, that all of the conditions are present for each theory.

The imposition of multiple liability theories is more likely on design/build projects than on traditionally structured projects because the nature of design/build is such that both the traditional theories of liability as well as the additional theories of breach of warranty and strict liability apply. Individuals contemplating involvement in a design/build project should consult with a legal expert before committing to participation.

Defenses Unavailable in Design/Build

The nature of design/build may preclude certain liability defenses normally employed by clients, contractors, and design professionals in traditional projects. Loss of these defenses should be considered when weighing the risks of design/build project delivery.

The Betterment Rule

One liability defense that may not be available to design/build participants is the *betterment rule*. The betterment rule states that if one party fails to perform a duty that results in extra expense incurred by a second party, the first party will not be liable for that cost or expense if the second party would have incurred the expense, anyway, whether or not the first party failed in the performance of its duty.

For example, projects must satisfy requirements contained in building codes, even if they are not shown on the drawings and specifications. The contractor is not required to pay for omitted items since the contractor is typically required to include in the project only those items called out in the drawings and specifications. But the design professional is also not generally required to pay for them because had they been included in the drawings and specifications originally, the client would have had to pay for them. To require the design professional to pay for them results in a windfall for the client. The law has ruled that the client should not be unjustly enriched at the expense of the design professional.

On design/build projects, however, this defense may not be available to the design professional or the contractor. There are several reasons for this. First, on design/build projects, the contract between the primary contractor and the client in each type of design/build firm is likely to include a statement concerning compliance of the completed facility with applicable codes. Any variation from applicable codes will subject the design/build firm to liability for breach of warranty, and the design/build firm then must bear the cost of bringing the structure up to code. The design/build firm cannot invoke the betterment rule to protect it from a breach of warranty. Second, the design/build firm may typically be seen as selling a product subject to implied warranties, the breach of which requires the guilty party to pay for the mistake—in this case, reimbursement for the omitted item.

Responsibility for the Accuracy of the Design Professional's Drawings and Specifications

Design professionals and contractors practicing design/build may lose the protection afforded them through warranties implied by the client concerning the accuracy and completeness of the drawings. On traditionally structured projects, clients impliedly warrant that the drawings and specifications prepared by design professionals and furnished to the contractor are sufficiently coordinated, complete, and suitable for use by contractors familiar with the construction of similar projects, and that the documents need no more than the usual amount of clarification typical of documents normally prepared by design professionals for projects of this type. Contractors necessarily rely on this implied warranty. Otherwise, they would either become insurers of the adequacy of the design professional's documentation, or they would have to design the project themselves in order to confirm the adequacy of the documentation. If the documents fail to meet this adequacy standard, the contractor may be entitled to recover from the client reasonable extra costs incurred by the contractor as a result of the failure.

On a design/build project, however, the design/build firm prepares the drawings, not an independent design professional retained by the client. The design/build firm, therefore, is responsible for the accuracy and completeness of the documents. While the contracting component of a design/build firm may have a cause of action against the design professional, neither the design/build firm itself, nor the contractor component thereof, will have a cause of action against the client for inadequate contract documents.

Responsibility for Site Safety

Traditionally structured projects are clearly organized in such a manner that responsibility for job site safety and compliance with federal, state, and local health and safety rules and regulations, including OSHA construction safety standards, rests solely with the contractor. The contractor is traditionally viewed as solely responsible for all construction activity and in the best position to provide adequately for and to monitor and maintain the safety of the job site for the contractor's and subcontractor's construction workers. This allocation of responsibility can be modified by contract, of course, but most traditionally structured projects maintain this distinction and, indeed, most standard form client-design professional and client-contractor contracts recognize this distinction in their preprinted text.

In some design/build arrangements, this distinction becomes blurred or nonexistent. In Types A and C design/build, the design professional either solely or partially constitutes the primary contractor who contracts with the client for all design and construction services. The Type A or C design professional assumes primary responsibility to the client and to third parties for all construction-related matters. In these two types of design/build entities, therefore, the design professional assumes partial or sole responsibility for a reasonably safe site that complies with federal (including OSHA), state, and local health and safety rules and regulations.

Summary

In the ancient world, the master builder was liable for both the design and assembly of the structures he created. With the divergence in roles, however, came a rethinking in the way liability was imposed for loss or injury in connection with construction. Today, American jurisprudence provides that design professionals will be liable solely for errors and omissions in the design of a structure, and contractors will be liable for construction alone. These principles may change, however, if either or both of the parties provide services outside of their respective traditional disciplines.

Liability is imposed based on the breach of one or more of three sources of duty: contracts, common law, and statutes and regulations. Traditional liability theories are those theories that have historically been applied to traditional projects, but which also may be applied to design/build projects. These include breach of contract, the tort of negligence, and statutory violations. In order for liability to be imposed, there are certain conditions that must be established. In the absence of these conditions, claims of liability will be dismissed.

There are two additional theories of liability that have special application to design/build projects. These include breaches of warranty (both express and implied warranties), and strict liability. Warranties are more likely to exist in design/build projects because the nature of the firm is such that design/build professionals are perhaps more willing to make promises or guarantees regarding their work in projects over which they feel they have a significant degree of control. Implied warranties and strict liability are imposed on manufacturers and sellers of defective products. Implied warranties and strict liability are more likely to be imposed in design/build projects because some courts view design/build activity as the manufacture or sale of products, rather than the provision of services.

If these additional liability theories are not sufficient to warn potential design/build participants, there are other legal pitfalls associated with this relatively new method of project delivery. The incidence of multiple liability theories applied to a single project is likely to be greater in design/build. There are also traditional legal defenses unavailable to participants of some design/build arrangements. These include the betterment rule, and the client's implied warranty guaranteeing the accuracy of the design documents. In addition, the design professional may be held responsible for site safety in certain design/build arrangements.

There are other legal issues directly associated with liability. These include the way in which clients and construction professionals file their claims, the legal devices available to protect their interests, ways in which they can reallocate risk, and resolve their disputes, and what they can expect in terms of compensation. These issues are discussed in Chapter 9.

Chapter Nine

Additional Legal Issues

There are additional issues surrounding the imposition of liability of which design professionals, contractors, and clients should be aware. Some of these issues may apply differently to participants of design/build than to participants of traditional projects. The five major issues are:

- Time Limitations for Filing Claims
- Damages
- Mechanic's Liens
- Indemnification
- Dispute Resolution

Time Limitations for Filing Claims

All of the theories that can be employed to impose liability on clients, contractors, and design professionals are useless if the claim is not filed within the period of time prescribed by law. Every jurisdiction prescribes time limitations within which certain claims must be filed. Time limitations may vary depending on the the legal theory underlying the claim, and the jurisdiction in which the claim is filed.

Statutes defining the period of time within which claims must be brought are established for two reasons. First, adherence to these statutes reduces the likelihood that a witness will have forgotten relevant events, that the witness will have died or otherwise be unable to be located, or that pertinent documents will have been lost or destroyed. Second, the existence of statutes provides a measure of assurance to citizens that claims that are not brought within the statutory period are forever barred. If a limitations period were not established, the accumulated experiences of an individual's lifetime could threaten their financial security and reduce their willingness to assume the normal risk-taking activities required to function in our society.

There are two types of statutes which prescribe the applicable period of time within which to file a claim:

- Statutes of Limitations
- Statutes of Repose

Statutes of Limitations

A *statute of limitations* states that no claim can be maintained against a party unless that claim is brought within a specific period of time. The right to bring a claim occurs at some "trigger point" stated in the statute. Sometimes the trigger is that point in time when the defendant actually breached his or her duty to the plaintiff. Often the trigger is the point at which the plaintiff knew or should have known that the defendant failed to perform the duty. Or, the trigger may occur at a later point in time.

The actual period of limitation varies depending on the jurisdiction in which the claim is filed, and the liability theory underlying the claim. For instance, the statute of limitations in Massachusetts is three years after the error or omission is discovered for torts of negligence and actions of contract to recover for personal injuries, and six years after the discovery of the error for actions of contract other than those to recover for personal injuries. If the agreement between the client and the design/build entity constitutes a contract for the sale of products or goods under Massachusetts' version of the Uniform Commercial Code, then the statute of limitations is likely to be four years after the discovery of the error. Because statutes of limitation vary, it is crucial that the plaintiff avoid delay in filing a claim.

Sometimes a plaintiff may have more than one legal theory with which to impose liability on a defendant. The plaintiff may choose that theory whose elements are easiest to establish, but the choice must be made in light of the statute of limitations for that particular liability theory. If the limitations period has already expired, another theory must be selected whose limitations period has not yet expired.

Design/build entities may be at a fundamental disadvantage when it comes to statutes of limitation. For example, courts may conclude that the applicable period of time within which to file a negligence claim for faulty design against a design/build entity begins from the date that the project was substantially completed, and not from the date that the error or omission in design was discovered, or should have been discovered, by the client. This may extend the period of time within which the claim can be brought against the design/build entity beyond that which typically applies to traditionally structured projects.

In this case, the court is focusing on the distinction between design/build services on the one hand, and merely design services on the other. Design professionals are retained by clients essentially to provide design services for the project, whereas a design/build entity is retained to provide both design and construction services. Courts are likely to reason that on a design/build project, the design/build entity's services (both design and construction) are not considered complete until construction is substantially completed. As such, the limitations period will commence upon completion of all the services, not just the design portion.

Clients, contractors, and design professionals who intend to bring a claim against another party must be aware of not only the elements required to establish the particular theory of liability, but of the time limitation of each theory established by statute within which a claim may be filed.

Statutes of Repose

Unlike a statute of limitations, which commences on or after the point at which a breach of a duty has occurred, a statute of repose begins at a point established by the statute, regardless of whether or not a breach of a duty has occurred. Since a plaintiff cannot bring a claim against another party until there has first been a breach of a duty, a statute of repose can effectively extinguish any opportunity to bring that claim if the breach occurs after the period of time prescribed by the statute has passed. Below is an example of a statue of repose:

> *Action of tort for damages arising out of any deficiency or neglect in the design, planning, construction, or general administration of an improvement to real property, other than that of a public agency...shall be commenced only within three years next after the cause of action accrues; provided, however, that in no event shall such actions be commenced more than six years after the earlier of the dates of:* (1) *the opening of the improvement to use;* or (2) *substantial completion of the improvement and the taking of possession for occupancy by the owner.*

What this means is that a claim can be filed within three years of the discovery of the error, as long as this is less than six years after either the opening or the completion and occupancy of the facility, whichever comes first.

Damages

Once liability has been established, the plaintiff is then entitled to recover damages from the defendant. Damages are the measure of monetary compensation that a court or arbitrator awards to a plaintiff for loss or injury suffered by the plaintiff's person, property, or other legally recognizable rights.

The three basic types of damages are:

- Compensatory Damages
- Punitive Damages
- Consequential Damages

Compensatory Damages

Compensatory damages are intended to compensate the plaintiff for loss or injury by granting the plaintiff a monetary amount equal to the loss or injury suffered, and nothing more. Compensatory damages are composed of *general* and *special damages*. General damages are those damages that the law considers to result from the defendant's wrongful conduct. They are the natural or usual result of such conduct without reference to any special circumstances concerning the plaintiff. Special damages are those damages resulting from the defendant's conduct with respect to the special circumstances of a plaintiff. Included under the category of general and special compensatory damages are *direct damages*.

Direct Damages

Direct damages are recognized by the law as the natural and usual result of wrongful conduct on the part of a defendant. Direct damages are awarded for *personal injury*, *wrongful death*, or *destruction of property*.

Damages Awarded for Personal Injury: Damages for personal injury are normally awarded when physical injury is inflicted on persons, although courts or statutes may give the term a wider meaning to include invasion of various personal rights, such as the invasion of privacy, that do not involve physical injury. Damages awarded for personal injury in the construction industry are usually, but not exclusively, sought in connection with negligence involving physical injury and workers' compensation claims. Design professionals and contractors are the likely targets of personal injury claims from workers who are injured on the project site and from users of the facility who are injured on the facility after it is constructed. Damages for personal injury include the following:

- Reasonable medical expenses incurred from the date of the accident or injury to the date of settlement or trial, plus a reasonable estimate of medical expenses to be incurred in the future as a result of the accident or injury.
- Loss of or reduction in earnings from the date of accident or injury to the date of settlement or trial, plus a reasonable estimate of future lost or reduced earnings.
- A reasonable amount for pain and suffering incurred prior to the date of settlement or trial, plus a reasonable amount for future pain and suffering, if any.
- All special damages which can reasonably be proven at trial.

Damages Awarded for Wrongful Death: Damages may be awarded for wrongful death when a worker is killed on the project site or a user of the facility dies while using the facility after it is constructed. In many jurisdictions, wrongful death actions are regulated by statutes that prescribe who is entitled to bring a wrongful death action and establish limits on the amount recoverable by a plaintiff from the defendant. All states have some form of workers' compensation statute that mandates the amount an employer must pay on account of injury to or death of an employee during the course of employment. In return for this guaranteed payment, the employee is precluded from seeking further recovery against the employer. Recovery from others who may be wholly or partially at fault, however, is not normally barred.

Depending on the age and marital status of the decedent, four principal categories of damages are recoverable in the event of wrongful death:

- Recovery to the date of the decedent's death for the damages connected with personal injury including medical expenses, loss of earnings, and pain and suffering, as well as special damages awarded for reasonable funeral and burial expenses.
- A reasonable monetary value paid to the surviving spouse, if any, for the lost comfort, society, and protection the law assumes one spouse affords the other; for the loss of consortium or sexual relations; and recovery for the decedent's probable future earnings less a reasonable estimate of the cost of the decedent's personal maintenance expenses.
- Reasonable monetary value paid to the decedent's children, if any, for the lost comfort, society, and protection that the law assumes the decedent affords his or her children, and recovery for the reasonable amount the deceased would have contributed to their care, support, and maintenance, including educational expenses, had they each lived to their normal life expectancy.
- If the decedent was a minor and under the legal custody of his or her parents at the time of death, or at the time of the accident or injury leading to the decedent's death, whether or not the decendent was temporarily living away from home at the time of death or accident or injury leading to the decentent's death, recovery by the parents for the reasonable monetary value of the loss of enjoyment and society in rearing children.

Damages Awarded for the Destruction of Property: Damages may be awarded for physical injury to or destruction of another's property, and may be sought in claims based on any of the liability theories already discussed.

There are two principal approaches to determine the amount of the damages. The first approach is used most often in breach of contract or breach of warranty actions based on violation of a contractual agreement, and is typically referred to as the *benefit-of-the-bargain* approach. This method of damage assessment attempts to place the plaintiff in a position as though the defendant had fully performed his or her contractual obligations.

The second approach is referred to as the *out-of-pocket* approach and is typically used in connection with a tort of negligence or strict liability—claims that are not based on contractual agreements. This approach attempts to place the plaintiff in the same position he or she was in immediately prior to the negligent conduct of the defendant.

There are two principal methods used in construction litigation cases to determine the amount of out-of-pocket damages. The first determines the costs required to reconstruct that portion of the facility that was improperly constructed. The second determines the decrease in market value of the improperly constructed facility compared to what its market value would be had it been constructed properly. This method is often used when the costs to reconstruct the facility are far greater than the benefits achieved from the corrections.

Punitive Damages

Punitive, or *exemplary*, *damages* are another form of compensation that may be awarded to a plaintiff for loss or injury suffered as a result of the defendant's wrongful conduct. These damages are awarded not merely to compensate the plaintiff for losses incurred, but are awarded when the circumstances surrounding the defendant's conduct are aggravated by violence, malice, or fraud. Punitive damages are intended to punish the defendant for wrongful conduct and to use the plight of the defendant as an example to potential wrongdoers.

Punitive damages are most often awarded in cases of fraud. In the construction industry, punitive damages may be imposed on design professionals in traditionally structured projects where the special fiduciary relationship of trust and confidence between the design professional and the client and the public at large is breached. On design/build projects, however, the design professional has a commercial stake in the project. It is therefore not possible for the design professional to represent the client's interests without affecting his or her own financial interests. If fraud is to continue to be used as a basis for imposing punitive damages on design/build entities, breaches other than that of the fiduciary relationship between the client and design professional will have to be used as the basis for the fraud.

There is a tendency by courts in some jurisdictions to treat the activities of design/build firms less like the provision of services and more like consumer transactions for the sale of goods. (See Chapter 8.) Plaintiffs in certain circumstances may take advantage of state consumer protection statutes which provide for an increase in the amount of damage awards to the plaintiff if it can be shown that the defendant fraudulently misrepresented some material fact or used unfair or deceptive acts or practices in the conduct of its business. Some states, such as Massachusetts, permit a plaintiff to recover double or triple the amount of damages, plus attorneys' fees and costs.

Consequential Damages

A third type of damages is *consequential damages*. Consequential damages refer to compensation for loss or injuries which are not directly attributable to some wrongful act on the part of the defendant, but are the result of one or more of the consequences of that act. They are damages awarded as the result of the intervention of special, often unpredictable circumstances, or circumstances that are not ordinarily the natural and usual result of the defendant's act.

Consequential damages often involve claims for extra costs incurred by the plaintiff due to delays in completion of construction, allegedly due to some fault on the part of the construction professional. Claims for consequential damages may be filed against design/build entities as well as traditional contractors and design professionals. In actions by a client against a design/build entity retained to design and construct an office building, for example, the client may claim consequential damages for loss of rental income from the facility and extra finance charges incurred during the period of the delay. Prospective tenants may claim damages from the design/build entity for loss of use of the facility during the period of the delay, and for extra costs incurred in having to make alternative arrangements to house the tenant's operations during the period in which the facility was not available for use. Both the client and the prospective tenant may claim damages for profits lost on account of the delay, but neither party would be permitted to recover for both lost profits and loss of use, since each loss is considered to be included in the other. All claims for consequential damages must be reasonably calculated and not unduly speculative.

Mechanic's Liens

A *mechanic's lien law* is a legislative attempt to provide a measure of financial leverage to help secure payments owed to parties whose work results in an improvement to real property. All jurisdictions have some form of a mechanic's lien law, although the law may vary significantly from one jurisdiction to another, depending on the classes of parties afforded protection as well as the specific procedures used to *perfect*, or enforce, the lien. Essentially, parties providing labor, materials, or services in connection with a project, whether or not they have a contract with the owner of the project, may file a *lien*. The lien acts as an encumbrance on the real property of the owner for the work that is performed. It is not a personal debt of the owner or of any other party, nor is it an encumbrance on any of the owner's property other than the buildings and land on which the work took place.

A lien is usually enforced through *foreclosure* (the forced sale of property). The lien holder's payment priority from the proceeds of the sale typically follows other encumbrances against the property which may have been established previously by other parties. Lien laws can be rather complex. Parties contemplating perfecting a lien should consult with a qualified professional about the lien laws of the jurisdiction in which the project is located.

Contractors, subcontractors, and material suppliers have traditionally been afforded the most extensive protection under lien law statutes. Design professionals historically have not been afforded the same protection. This is due, in large measure, to the belief that some form of visible activity in connection with the improvement to the owner's real property was required to notify the property owner, as well as the owner's creditors, that others may be performing activities for which a lien may be filed. But a design professional's activities are not readily apparent at the project site, even though they may be seen observing construction activity, performing construction administration, or performing services in connection with the project. Moreover, many states do not consider this type of activity to be the kind of construction activity eligible for the protection under the state's lien laws.

Some states do consider design and construction administration activity and, more importantly, the pre-construction design activity of the design professional, eligible for protection under the lien law. Other states require that the design professional actually supervise construction of the project and control the means and methods of construction and the manner in which material is incorporated into the construction, in order to qualify for lien law protection. This, of course, is not the traditional role of the design professional, and is stated as such in many standard form agreements between design professionals and clients, most notably in those of the American Institute of Architects. In this case, an express disclaimer of responsibility for the means, methods, techniques, and procedures of construction is included in each design professional's agreement with the client. Design professionals who attempt to qualify for protection under a given jurisdiction's lien law by claiming responsibility for the supervisory or superintendence services required under the lien law, may unwittingly open the floodgates to claims by others for liability for a broad range of activities.

Design professionals engaged in design/build fare considerably better than traditional design professionals in those jurisdictions that require the design professional to have some "supervisory" role during the construction phase in order to establish a valid lien. This is because the design professional in a design/build entity possesses the two "triggers" most often associated with protection under lien statues: a financial interest in the outcome of the project, and a supervisory role over the construction of the project. (This is true for all but Type B design/build, where the design professional is subcontracted to the contractor.) There may be some question, however, as to whether or not pre-construction design services can be protected by a lien, even when the design professional's construction services are entitled to lien protection.

Indemnification

Indemnification is the process by which one party is protected from loss or damage resulting from acts committed by another. An *indemnitee* is the party who is to be protected; the *indemnitor* is the party who is legally bound to protect or indemnify the indemnitee. Indemnification is created by an express written or oral agreement between the parties (however, indemnity in oral contracts may be difficult to prove). Indemnification may exist even in the absence of an express written or oral agreement, based on the particular relationship between the parties and considerations of justice and equity. This is sometimes referred to as a *quasi-contractual* or *common law indemnification* and is a legal fiction or assumption invented by common law to permit recovery by one party from another in the absence of a contract, but where the nature of the relationship between the parties is such that justice warrants a recovery as though a contract existed.

Most clients choose the design/build method of project delivery for its single point of responsibility for all design and construction activities. These clients usually include in their contracts with design/build entities some form of an express indemnification agreement. Design/build entities often feel compelled to agree to some form of an indemnification provision because they feel that their refusal to do so might be viewed as an attempt to shirk their responsibilities. Since most of the "finger pointing" which takes place between the design professional and the contractor on traditionally structured projects is avoided in design/build, and since many of the liability defenses available to the traditional design professional and contractor are not available to design/build participants, the design/build team may feel that if something does go wrong on the project, they must necessarily be liable for the ensuing damages. This thinking, of course, does not take into account the fact that each theory of liability has certain prerequisite elements which first must be established before liability is imposed and that, although more limited in number, there may still be certain legal defenses available to the imposition of liability. Design/build entities operating under this belief, therefore, may contract to indemnify the client for damages beyond that for which they might otherwise be liable.

Contracting parties should pay particular attention to the indemnification provisions in their agreements, not only in terms of scope, but in terms of enforceability and insurability. Many states limit the scope and enforceability of certain types of indemnification agreements and may even place restrictions on the types of parties who can be indemnified.

Because of the potentially significant financial impact an indemnification obligation may have on both the indemnitor and the indemnitee, its insurability is usually of critical importance. Indemnification for certain types of losses may not be insurable, or may be insurable at a prohibitive rate. For instance, standard professional liability insurance policies available to design professionals generally afford protection against liability arising out of negligent acts, errors, mistakes, or omissions in the performance of professional services. They do not afford protection against contractually assumed obligations such as an indemnification clause, because in the absence of the provision, the design professional would not otherwise be liable. Any proposed form of indemnification agreement should be reviewed by a qualified professional to determine the extent, enforceability, and insurability of the obligation. Inadequate protection will be an unwelcome surprise to everyone in the wake of an accident.

Design professionals and contractors, when acting either as primary contractors (Types A and B design/build), or who are members of a joint venture (Type C design/build), who obligate themselves to indemnify the client or other third parties on account of the activities of their associates, should ensure that they, in turn, receive an enforceable and insurable indemnification agreement from their associates. Without indemnification, the primary contractors in the design/build entity may be liable to the client and be without recourse for the errors and omissions of their associates.

Dispute Resolution

Disputes arise on virtually all construction projects. Design/build projects are no exception. Fortunately, most disputes are solved amicably by the parties themselves. Occasionally, some are not. The individuals involved must then turn to a third party to help them resolve their disputes. These individuals may agree, either in their contract or at the time of the dispute, to resolve their differences through *binding arbitration*. Binding arbitration is the process by which feuding parties submit the matter to a "disinterested" party (an *arbitrator*) for objective judgment and resolution, using arbitration procedures mutually selected and agreed on by the parties. However, if at least one party is unwilling to arbitrate the dispute, a legal proceeding through the court system, called *litigation*, is usually the only other way to resolve the matter.

Given the increasing time and cost involved in arbitration and litigation, there is a growing interest in finding alternative dispute resolution procedures. The American Arbitration Association's arbitration rules and mediation procedures offer clients, contractors, and design professionals two alternatives to reduce the time and cost of dispute resolution. The first alternative involves streamlining the procedures used during the course of an arbitration hearing. The second provides for nonbinding mediation by a qualified mediator who does not impose a decision upon the parties but, rather, assists the parties in arriving at their own resolution. Of course, parties are free to select virtually any method they feel is best suited to their particular circumstances, as long as it is legally permissible. Agreeing on procedures before disputes arise is generally the best approach, since it can be done more objectively during contract negotiation, when parties are not driven by suspicion and self interest.

An alternative often chosen by parties on traditionally structured projects is one in which disputes between the client and contractor over the interpretation of the contract documents or the execution or progress of the work are initially submitted to the design professional for deliberation. Courts have long recognized the role of the design professional as interpreter, judge, and arbitrator in this context, focusing on the professional rather than the commercial nature of the traditional design professional's obligations to the project and to the public that require impartiality and objectivity over self interest. But in some instances, the design professional's decision may be unacceptable to the client or the contractor. The design professional's decision itself may then be subject to arbitration if a demand (petition) is filed by one of the disputing parties within the period of time prescribed in the client-contractor agreement (typically thirty days). If the design professional's decision is uncontested, or if the petition is denied, the decision becomes binding. Often, the parties will agree that any decision that the design professional makes regarding artistic effect is binding in and of itself, without any recourse to arbitration by the client or contractor. In either of these roles, the design professional is required to be impartial and to favor neither the client nor the contractor.

On design/build projects, however, the design professional's financial interest, either in the project or in the financial arrangements between the client and the contractor, undermines his or her objectivity. Nevertheless, on many design/build projects, particularly Type B projects (where the contractor is the primary contractor), the client and contractor insist that the design professional assumes the traditional role as judge or arbitrator of disputes between the client and contractor. In reality, this places the design professional in a position of irreconcilable conflict, torn between his or her contract obligations to the contractor, financial stake in the project, and traditional loyalty toward the client. It is virtually impossible, under these circumstances, for the design professional to make impartial decisions.

It might be useful for design/build participants to consider alternative approaches to resolving the minor disputes that occasionally arise between the client and the contractor. One method is for the client and the contractor to agree in their contract to appoint an independent party to serve as an *on-call arbitrator or mediator*. This method is usually attractive, since the parties have an obvious interest in resolving their disputes quickly and may only need the experienced guidance of a qualified mediator. If mediation is unsuccessful, the American Arbitration Association's expedited arbitration procedures may be appropriate for certain types of disputes, or for disputes involving limited sums. For more serious disputes, the regular arbitration procedures of the American Arbitration Association may be appropriate. However, what is important for design/build participants to recognize when choosing a method of arbitration is that the design professional is not in a position to provide to the parties the independent judgment it normally provides on traditionally structured projects.

Summary

There are additional legal issues surrounding the imposition of liability of which the design professional and contractor should be aware. First, there are time limitations that regulate the filing of claims, although they may vary depending on the liability theory underlying the claim, and the jurisdiction in which the claim is filed. Statutes of limitations prescribe the period of time within which claims must be filed. Claims cannot be filed after the statute of limitations has expired. Statutes of limitations help ensure that witnesses and evidence will be available at the time of trial, and that individuals will not be held responsible for the accumulated acts and experiences of their lifetime. Statutes of repose serve to limit the period of time within which claims can be filed by stating at the outset the period of time after which claims will not be considered.

An individual or entity who is found liable may be required to pay damages. Damages are monetary compensation that is paid as a result of harm, injury, or destruction to property. There are three kinds of damages: compensatory, punitive, and consequential. Compensatory damages are equal to the amount of injury and damage suffered. Direct damages are a type of compensatory damages owed as a direct result of an act. They may be awarded for personal injury, wrongful death, or destruction of property. Punitive damages, unlike compensatory damages, are imposed to punish an individual and make an example of that individual to others. Finally, consequential damages are awarded to individuals or entities who suffer loss not from a deliberate action on the part of another, but as a consequence of that act.

There are protections to individuals who perform services for others. Mechanic's liens were instituted as a legislative attempt to provide financial leverage to secure payments for work that is done to improve property. Design professionals and contractors may resort to enforcing or protecting their lien rights when faced with a risk of nonpayment for work that has already been completed.

Indemnification refers to the process by which individuals are protected from loss or damage that results from the acts committed by another. Indemnification is created through the express oral or written agreements between parties, but may also be established based on considerations of justice and equity.

When conflicts arise, as they invariably do on construction projects, there are methods that construction professionals can use to resolve disputes before they escalate into legal battles. Because of the increasing costs of arbitration and litigation, a number of alternatives have been developed to hasten the dispute resolution process. Dispute resolution procedures may be streamlined, and mediators may be called in to assist the parties in reaching an agreement. Design/build participants should not, however, depend on the design professional to act as arbitrator in disputes on a design/build project.

Design professionals and contractors should familiarize themselves with these legal issues before entering into non-traditional methods of project delivery like design/build, which may involve a greater risk of liability. The construction professional who understands the legal issues surrounding design/build is ready to participate. Part V examines the administrative issues that design/build participants face as they prepare for involvement on design/build projects. Chapter 10 begins with insurance and bonds.

Part Five

Administration

Understanding the theories of liability and the legal issues surrounding its imposition is a significant achievement for clients, contractors, and design professionals contemplating involvement in this relatively new method of project delivery. But there are several other issues that could conceivably inhibit a party's ability to engage in design/build.

The design/build method establishes a fundamentally different set of relationships among the project's participants. Depending on the design/build arrangement and the jurisdiction in which the project is located, design/build participants may be faced with gaps or exclusions in insurance coverage as well as additional licensing requirements. Fortunately, the three largest national construction organizations publish a series of standard form design/build contract agreements to define and structure these unconventional relationships. But there may be restrictions in their use and issues that are not addressed in these documents. Part V discusses those business and administrative issues that all clients and construction professionals on both traditional and nontraditional projects face, but that may raise important questions for design/build participants—insurance and bonding; licensing, registration, and codes of ethics; and standard form design/build contract agreements. Chapter 10 begins with insurance and bonding.

Chapter Ten

Insurance and Bonds

Design/build projects, like all other construction projects, require that their participants be insured and bonded. *Insurance and bonds* not only provide a measure of protection to clients, contractors, and design professionals against certain types of losses in connection with the project—protection that these parties could not otherwise provide for themselves—they are also an integral part of negotiating the allocation of risk among the parties of incurring such losses.

To determine how best to allocate that risk, the parties typically look to see which party is in the best position to reduce the risk of loss from occurring, who is in the best position to bear the loss should it occur, and who is best able to spread the risk of loss to others. An individual may allocate or share the risk with others by bonding or purchasing insurance. An insurance or bonding company agrees, for a fee, to assume a portion of the risk and, in doing so, indemnifies the individual against such risks.

Throughout its history, the insurance and bonding industry has been structured in a manner responsive to traditional methods of project delivery. Design/build participants, as a result, may have difficulty obtaining adequate coverage since, depending on the particular arrangement of the design/build entity, the design professional and the contractor may place themselves in nontraditional roles, legally responsible for aspects of a project over which they traditionally would not have control, and involved in activities for which the insurance or surety companies traditionally do not provide protection.

Questions may arise concerning the availability and extent of coverage afforded the design/build participants for certain types of losses—questions not frequently encountered on traditionally structured projects. Prospective design/build participants should be aware of the limitations of traditional forms of insurance and bonding, and should discuss with their respective insurance and legal advisors ways to protect themselves. This should be done before entering into a design/build relationship, since these issues may influence contract negotiations over the allocation of risks and the costs to the parties to bear those risks.

Insurance and bonding is a complex topic. Unfortunately, a detailed discussion is beyond the scope of this book. This chapter, however, will introduce the basic types of insurance policies and bonds available to construction professionals, and the gaps and limitations in coverage that clients and construction professionals may face when they engage in design/build. Suggestions will also be made concerning ways in which design/build participants can protect themselves from risks of loss by improving their insurance coverage and bonding capacity.

Types of Insurance

There are several principal types of insurance coverage providing protection to clients, contractors, and design professionals. Keep in mind, however, that no single type of insurance coverage is intended to provide protection to all parties. Each type is structured to provide some measure of protection against a specific kind of loss. The four most common types of insurance coverage are:

- Workers' Compensation Insurance
- Comprehensive General Liability Insurance
- Property (Builder's Risk) Insurance
- Professional Liability Insurance

Workers' Compensation Insurance

Employers in every state are statutorily required to carry *Workers' Compensation Insurance*. Workers' Compensation Insurance *provides payments to employees* who are injured while performing their jobs. It is not necessary for the employee to demonstrate that the employer was negligent or otherwise responsible for the injury in order to be compensated. The injured employee is guaranteed the amount of the benefit specified in the statute as compensation for the injury, regardless of negligence. In return for this guarantee, the employee forfeits the right to sue the employer for damages that exceed the amount of the benefit. The amount of the benefits payable for each type of injury is usually stated very specifically in the statute, although the extent of coverage may vary from state to state.

In some states, employers with fewer than a certain number of employees are not required to carry Workers' Compensation Insurance. In certain states, employees may waive, in advance of injury, the protection afforded to them by the employer's policy. This occurs most often in those states in which the benefits that are paid to the injured employee are considerably lower than the probable cost of the injury itself. Employees may prefer to take their chances suing the employer, rather than collecting the mandatory, but often times insufficient, benefit. In still other states, spouses or other relatives of the injured employee may be eligible to sue the employer for certain losses that they incur as a result of the injury sustained by the employee. An example of this is the loss of consortium (aid and affection) of an injured employee's spouse.

On construction projects, every employer with a requisite number of employees is required to carry Workers' Compensation Insurance; but an employer is never required to carry it for another employer's workers. On traditional projects as well as types A, B, and C design/build, the design professional is the employer of the design personnel on his or her staff, the contractor is the employer of the construction personnel on his or her staff, and each of the separate subcontractors are the employers of the construction personnel on their respective staffs. Neither the design professional nor the contractor is responsible for providing Workers' Compensation Insurance for the employees of the other. Nor is the design professional or the contractor responsible for providing Workers' Compensation Insurance for the other, regardless of any contractual relationship that may exist between them.

In Type D design/build, however, the design/build firm is the employer and, as such, is responsible for carrying Workers' Compensation Insurance for all of its employees, regardless of their specific role (design or construction) on an individual projects.

To protect an employer from the potentially costly situations that may result from employee injury on the job, employers can obtain *Employers' Liability Insurance*, often as an *endorsement* or supplement to the Workers' Compensation Insurance package, and sometimes as a separate policy.

Comprehensive General Liability Insurance

Comprehensive General Liability Insurance is a *broad form policy*, which means that it includes many types of coverage that can be tailored to suit the specific requirements of the *insured* (the party protected by the insurance). It is structured to *provide protection to the client and contractor* against claims for both bodily injury and property damage.

On both traditionally structured projects and design/build projects, the contractor typically procures and pays for the insurance, either as a reimbursable cost item or as part of its lump sum fee. If the insurance is part of a lump sum fee, the contractor will simply increase its price to cover the cost of the insurance. On some projects, especially for sophisticated clients, the client may, either at the beginning of the project or at some point during its construction, procure and pay for so-called *wrap-up insurance*, which bundles all sorts of coverages normally separately provided by the client or the contractor. If the contractor's price had included payment for insurance that was later included in the wrap-up insurance, then the contractor's price is typically adjusted downward by that amount, or by some prorated amount if it has already paid a portion of the premiums for the coverage.

In some design/build projects, the design professional is responsible for the work traditionally performed by the contractor. A design professional who is also functioning as a contractor, as in Type A design/build, should try to obtain the types of coverage that a general contractor would normally carry. Design professionals can purchase Comprehensive General Liability Insurance, subject to the same underwriting requirements as contractors. In fact, most design professionals do have a Comprehensive General Liability policy of one kind or another. The following types of coverage are typically included under Comprehensive General Liability Insurance:

- Owners', Landlords', and Tenants' Liability Insurance
- Manufacturers' and Contractors' Liability Insurance
- Protective Liability Insurance
- Products and Completed Operations Insurance
- Explosion, Collapse, and Underground (XCU) Coverage
- Broad Form Endorsement

Owners', Landlords', and Tenants' Liability Insurance

This type of coverage provides protection against liability arising out of the insured's (the client's) ownership, use, or maintenance of its premises, and against off-premises liability arising out of the insured's business operations.

Manufacturers' and Contractors' Liability Insurance

This type of coverage provides protection against liability arising out of claims by third parties who are injured at the insured's place of business (or job site, if the insured is the contractor), or injured as a result of the insured's business operations (or construction activities), wherever those operations may be conducted.

Protective Liability Insurance

This type of coverage protects the insured from claims brought as a result of the activities of the insured's subcontractors or subconsultants. Protective Liability Insurance is typically not available to design professionals providing professional design services. Unlike Professional Liability Insurance, which provides coverage for negligent design errors or omissions, this type of insurance provides coverage for construction-related activities only.

Products and Completed Operations Liability Insurance

This type of coverage is intended to protect the insured (the contractor) after the project has been completed. It also includes coverage for claims by third parties for damages caused by the insured's products (the materials or systems incorporated into the project).

Explosion, Collapse, and Underground (XCU) Coverage

This type of coverage provides protection against certain types of damage resulting from explosions (blasting), collapse (damage to property as a result of the collapse of the work, but not including damage to the work itself), and interference with underground utilities during the course of excavation or in connection with site work preparation. These are operations performed on many construction projects, but are typically excluded from coverage under a Comprehensive General Liability policy. Coverage for these events must be specifically endorsed onto the policy.

Broad Form Endorsement

Coverage afforded under this endorsement may include: contractual liability (the liability assumed by the insured based on its contract with another party); personal injury liability; and broad form property damage, which includes protection for certain portions of the project which would not normally be covered, since property damage coverage does not extend to property that is in the care, custody, and control of the contractor.

Gaps in Comprehensive General Liability Coverage

Through Comprehensive General Liability Insurance and certain available endorsements, contractors and clients are able to protect themselves against most losses incident to the construction of the project. Comprehensive General Liability policies, however, limit their coverage to bodily injury or physical damage to persons or property caused by the work or the operations of the contractor. Actual damage to the work itself which caused the injury to others or damage to other property is not covered by these policies.

Defective materials incorporated into the project and poor workmanship in constructing the project are also not covered by this policy. Not only would damage to the defective part of the project itself be excluded, but the cost to repair the same defective condition in other parts of the project, or on other projects, is also excluded.

Additionally, an insured who is aware of a defective or dangerous condition that might result in injury or damage to others, and who does nothing to prevent it from occurring, is also excluded from protection.

Property Insurance

Property Insurance, often referred to as *Builders' Risk Insurance*, is typically purchased by the client and *protects the client, the contractor, and subcontractors* from fire and other named losses that may occur during construction. An "all risk" endorsement to this policy significantly increases the number and types of perils included within the scope of the policy's coverage and should be considered by the parties, depending on the circumstances of their individual projects. Again, in some design/build arrangements, the design professional is the primary contractor responsible for both design and construction. Type A and C design professionals can purchase this form of insurance and will be covered as long as they are listed in the policy as the insured.

Property Insurance typically does not include coverage for material in transit or material stored off site. This kind of coverage must be obtained through an endorsement to the Property Insurance policy or through purchase of a separate policy. Under a Property Insurance policy, protection is typically afforded not only for the structure itself, but for all permanent attachments and fixtures, for all temporary structures necessary in the course of construction, and for all equipment, materials, and supplies used in connection with the project's construction.

Professional Liability Insurance

Many design professionals carry *Professional Liability Insurance* as their principal source of protection against liability. Professional Liability Insurance *protects the design professional*, in the amount stated in the policy, from damages and expenses (such as attorneys' fees and court costs) resulting from the negligent acts, errors, or omissions of the design professional, the design professional's employees, or others for whom the design professional is legally responsible. Protection is limited to the design professional's negligent performance or failure to perform services in accordance with applicable standards of professional skill, care, and judgment. (See Chapter 8 for a discussion of these standards.) This insurance coverage provides protection to the design professional when, through negligence, he or she fails to meet the required standard of care, and that failure results in damage to another.

Workers' Compensation Insurance, Comprehensive General Liability Insurance, and Property or Builders' Risk Insurance are written on an *occurrence basis*. An occurrence-based policy affords protection to the insured against any event described in the policy that occurs during the policy period, regardless of how long after expiration of the policy period the claim is filed. Professional Liability Insurance, on the other hand, is typically written on a *claims-made basis*. A claims-made policy affords coverage only if the policy is in effect at the time the claim is made. Coverage under standard Professional Liability policies is provided on a *per-claim* and *in-the-aggregate* basis. In other words, once the claims filed in any one policy year exceed the available coverage, all subsequent claims are not covered.

For instance, if a design professional has a $1,000,000 policy and incurs a claim for $900,000 within the policy year, a second claim filed within that policy year would be afforded coverage for no more than the remaining

$100,000 on the policy. If the second claim exceeds that figure, the excess amount would not be covered by the policy, nor would the balance be carried over to the next year's policy. Professional Liability claims are paid on a first-come, first-served basis.

Professional Liability Insurance claims are structured on a claims-made basis because the nature of a claim against a design professional is different than claims for other types of losses. For claims arising from other losses, the fact of the loss is the basis for the claim. For instance, a fire that results in damage to property is the cause of the loss and the basis for the claim. The loss, though not necessarily the monetary value of the loss, is known at or shortly after the fire.

Claims against design professionals, on the other hand, typically arise long after the event giving rise to the loss occurs. This is because the immediate event (the fire) which gives rise to the loss is not the basis of the loss itself; rather, it is the design professional's error which resulted in the loss. The design professional's error may have occurred well before, perhaps even years before, the error was discovered or the loss occurred. Often the error isn't discovered unless and until there is a loss such as that which results from a fire. Insurance companies would have difficulty underwriting risks on an occurrence basis because it would mean offering coverage for an indefinite period of time.

Some Professional Liability Insurance companies do write a type of occurrence-based policy called a *project policy*. A project policy affords protection to design professionals for their professional activities in connection with a single project. This policy is written to cover claims that may arise during the course of the project, and for a stated period of time following substantial completion of that project. The premiums for this type of policy are quite expensive. However, the coverage it affords is not subject to reduction or elimination on account of claims that arise out of errors and omissions on other projects, as is the case under standard Professional Liability Insurance policies. In effect, this policy creates a guaranteed pool of reserves in the event of a claim.

Soaring premium costs in recent years have forced some design professionals to forgo Professional Liability coverage, or to reduce or drop coverage that they may have carried in the past. The design professions and the insurance industry have been exploring alternatives to the protection traditional Professional Liability Insurance affords design professionals. *Self-insurance* is one possibility, but is not economically feasible for most design professionals. It requires the design professional to make cash or other assets available in the event of a claim. The amount to be set aside, if it is to provide any real protection, is usually more than the typical design professional can afford.

Due to recent changes in federal legislation, some design professionals have created *risk retention groups* which, in effect, permit groups of design professionals to pool their resources to cover potential losses by members of the group, with the understanding that additional capital may be needed in certain situations in the future. Once again, however, the capital contribution requirements of risk retention groups are usually beyond the means of most design professionals.

Professional Liability Insurance Exclusions

Professional Liability Insurance policies are intended to provide coverage in connection with the professional activities of the design professional only. Since clients and contractors do not perform professional activities of the sort contemplated by these policies, **clients and contractors cannot obtain Professional Liability Insurance, nor can they be named as additional insureds on the design professional's Professional Liability policy**. What this means for participants of design/build projects is that contractors engaged in those design/build arrangements in which they are responsible for providing design services to the client, will not be insured against errors or omissions by the design professional they retain to perform the actual design work.

Similarly, breaches of contract arising out of contractually assumed obligations which extend the design professional's liability beyond that for which the design professional would be legally responsible in the absence of such obligations, are also excluded from coverage under Professional Liability Insurance. This is critical to the design/build design professional who is acting as primary contractor for the project. A Type A design professional is legally responsible for both design and construction services, but is only insured for errors and omissions in the design of the project under its Professional Liability Insurance policy. The Type A design professional may not be insured against the acts and omissions of the contractor, who is hired by the design professional to perform the actual construction for the project. However, the design professional can insist that the contractor carry insurance for his or her own acts or omissions (Comprehensive General Liability Insurance), and to show proof as such.

There are several other exclusions to Professional Liability Insurance coverage, some of which may have a significant bearing on design/build projects and their participants. Professional Liability Insurance policies normally do not provide coverage for claims arising out of the following:

- **Intentional acts of the design professional**
- **Schedule delays**, unless the delay is the result of the design professional's negligence
- **Inaccurate cost estimates or cost estimates that are exceeded**, regardless of whether or not they were negligently prepared

  The schedule delay and inaccurate cost estimate exclusions of a standard Professional Liability Insurance policy are important to a design professional in a Type A or C design/build entity because, as primary contractor, the design professional will be providing schedule and cost information to the client as part of its normal design/build services. The scheduling and cost information that a Type A or C design professional provides is typically provided by the contractor on traditional projects (including any agreement to a fixed limit or upset limit of construction cost). Design professionals functioning in traditional roles, which is essentially what a design professional is doing in a Type B design/build entity, typically do not provide these services, nor are they capable of doing so themselves.
- **Breaches of express or implied warranties.** This can be particularly troublesome on design/build projects, where express or implied warranties are more likely to be found. The pressure to provide warranties or guarantees with respect to code conformance, client-imposed performance standards, budgetary constraints, and other matters is more acute in design/build than on traditionally structured projects. Breaches of express warranties are not covered under this type of insurance because they are obligations contractually assumed by the design professional for which the design professional would not otherwise be responsible under applicable standards of professional care.

Breaches of implied warranties are not protected since they too typically go beyond the standard of care to which the design professional is normally held. Since the standard of care essentially obligates the design professional to avoid negligence, any obligation that imposes liability on the design professional in the absence of negligence is not insured.

- **Imposition of strict liability in connection with activities of the design professional.** Application of the doctrine of strict liability does not require the design professional to be negligent in order to be liable for some activity. Since Professional Liability Insurance only affords protection to the design professional for his or her negligent activities, the policy affords no protection to the design professional for liability arising out of the imposition of strict liability.

  This might be particularly troublesome to design professionals where the nature of the design/build entity's services as a whole are viewed as the manufacturing of a product rather than the rendering of a service. As such, consumer protection laws regarding the allocation of loss to those parties best able to spread or to control the loss, regardless of fault, may find the design professional liable for a defective design even though the design professional was not negligent in its design.

- **The design professional's participation in a joint venture**, such as in a Type C design/build arrangement, unless such participation is specifically endorsed in the policy, and then only for those professional services performed by the design professional on behalf of the joint venture. This limitation holds true regardless of whether the other joint venture member(s) is a design professional or a contractor, since the policy is intended to provide protection for the named insured only, not other members of the joint venture.

- **Projects in which the design professional holds an equity interest.** Professional Liability Insurance normally excludes protection to design professionals who hold an equity interest in a project, unless specifically endorsed to the policy, and then only to the extent necessary to rectify the error, mistake, or omission. The policy does not include lost profits, fees, income, or any other consequential or indirect losses, costs, or expenses. The extent of coverage is inversely proportional to the design professional's ownership interest in the entity, provided it does not exceed fifty percent. No coverage is provided if the design professional's ownership interest exceeds fifty percent.

  This exclusion may affect design/build design professionals more often than traditional design professionals, since design/build design professionals are more likely to hold an equity interest in their projects. The fiduciary relationship or loyalty and trust that exists between the design professional and client in a traditionally structured project prevents the design professional from having a financial stake in the project and is therefore not affected by this exclusion.

The effect that each of these exclusions has on design/build participants may depend on the design/build arrangement. For example, design professionals are most often affected by these exclusions when practicing in either Type A or Type C design/build, where the design professional either alone or in a joint venture with the contractor, has a contractual agreement with the client and is obligated to provide both design and construction services for the project.

Type B design professionals are less affected by these exclusions, since the design professional provides essentially traditional services on the project, albeit to the contractor, and is in no way responsible for construction activities. Most of the exclusions described above have little or no bearing on the Type B design professional except for the pressure the contractor might exert on the design professional to provide warranties or guaranties with respect to the project's design.

However, in either Type B or Type C design/build, where the contractor is liable to the client for the design services performed on the project, the design professional's Professional Liability policy affords the contractor no protection, and the standard contractor insurance policies described earlier in this chapter do not consider errors or omissions in the design of the project to be within the range of perils for which contractors should be insured.

Finally, participants in Type D design/build must work closely with their insurance advisors to tailor a Professional Liability Insurance policy covering the design/build organization's professional design services only, since there is no separate design component in a Type D design/build firm as there is in each of the other three design/build structures.

Types of Bonds

A *bond* is a guarantee against failure to perform. In the construction industry, bonds are purchased by the contractor, at the client's request, to provide a measure of protection to the client from the risks of default during the various stages of construction. There are three types of bonds commonly required on construction projects:

- Bid Bonds
- Performance Bonds
- Labor and Material Payment Bonds

Bid Bonds

A *bid bond*, sometimes referred to as a *proposal bond*, is a form of bid security that guarantees that the bidder (the contractor) will enter into a contract with the client within a specified period of time, and furnish any required performance bonds and labor and material payment bonds. If the contractor fails to enter into a contract for the amount of the bid or proposal, the bonding or surety company pays the difference between the amount of the selected contractor's bid or price proposal and the cost to the client to award the contract to the next qualified contractor. The bond's stated limit is referred to as the *penal sum*, or the bond's penalty, and is the limit of the insurer's liability under the bond.

Assume, for example, that a contractor is awarded a project based on the figures in his or her bid proposal, and provides a bid bond for the amount of the project: $100,000. If that contractor then fails to enter into a contract with the client based on that bid, and the next qualified contractor's bid is $150,000, the bonding or surety company would pay the client the sum of $50,000, to award the job to the next highest bidder at no additional expense to the client.

However, if the difference between the first and second bids is $150,000, the bonding company is only liable for the penal sum of $100,000, which is the face value of the bond. The client would bear the additional $50,000. The client could seek recovery of that amount from the defaulting contractor, but that approach is usually futile.

Clients do not always require contractors to furnish bid bonds. Those who do, typically require that the amount of the bond be based on the probable range of bid prices from the various contractors, so that anticipated differences in bids will be covered. A bid bond is typically five percent of the amount of the contractor's bid or proposal.

Performance Bonds

Through a *performance bond*, the bonding or surety company guarantees the client that if the contractor fails to complete the project in accordance with the terms of the construction contract, the bonding company will either complete the contract itself or arrange for a client-approved contractor to complete the contract and pay that contractor the amount required to finish the work, minus the unpaid amount under the original contract. The bonding company will not have to pay more than the penal sum or limit of liability stated in the bond. In short, the bonding company will provide whatever money is necessary to finish the project beyond the unpaid amount of the original contract, to the extent of the value of the bond.

Many clients require that their contractors provide performance bonds, since the consequences of a contractor's failure to perform are likely to be disastrous for the client. Additionally, most lending institutions require that the contractor furnish a performance bond as a precondition to financing. The amount of the performance bond may vary, but is usually equal to one hundred percent of the contract amount. It is simply too risky for a client or lending institution to require less. Providing more is typically not necessary.

For example, if the amount stated in the client-contractor agreement is $1,000,000, the client is likely to require a performance bond for the same amount. If the contractor walks off the project (through bankruptcy, perhaps) after having already been paid $700,000, the client would have to pay the $300,000 remaining in his or her contract with the contractor to the bonding company or to a second contractor to complete the project, but the bonding company will cover all costs that exceed the $1,000,000 cost in the original agreement, up to $1,000,000. Even if the cost to complete the project exceeds what it would have cost if the first contractor had not defaulted, there should be ample funds available to complete the project.

The most significant costs incurred in hiring a second party to complete the project are: 1) inflation, since a default by a contractor inevitably results in delays until a new contractor can be found to resume work and complete the project; and 2) the start-up costs a new party must spend to become familiar with the condition of the project at the time of takeover. It may also be the case that other contractors are simply more expensive than the first contractor. Or, the first contractor may have underbid the project in order to receive the bid, and was unable to continue in the face of financial loss. If the cost incurred by having the second contractor complete the project exceeds the balance of the original contract amount plus the amount of the performance bond, the client is responsible for the difference. Of course, the client could try to recover that difference from the initial contractor, but unless that contractor's financial position has improved since leaving the project, there would be little point in pursuing it.

Labor and Material Payment Bonds

Labor and material payment bonds are typically issued with the performance bond and obligate the bonding company to pay subcontractors, laborers, and material suppliers amounts due to them for their materials and services under the terms of their contractual arrangements with the contractor, should the contractor default in his payment obligations to them. Since it usually takes some time after the default to arrange for a second contractor to take over the project, the labor and material payment bond speeds up payment to these parties prior to the commencement of work by the second contractor.

Clients are well advised to require a labor and material payment bond as well as a performance bond in an amount equal to one hundred percent of the contract amount. If the contractor defaults, this bond covers any claims up to the amount of the bond for labor and material already furnished to the project but not yet paid for by the contractor, even if the client has already paid the contractor for the labor and material. For instance, if a contractor receives $100,000 from the client for payment of subcontractors and materials, and the contractor, for some reason, does not pay these parties, then the bonding company is required to pay these parties amounts due to them up to the face value of the bond.

Bonding Issues in Design/Build

Limited Bonding Capacity of the Design Professional

A design professional can purchase performance bonds related to his or her design services. Design professionals in some design/build arrangements, however, may have difficulty obtaining proper bonding for construction activities for which they are now responsible. In Type A design/build, for example, the design professional is likely to have a limited *bonding capacity*, if any. Bonding capacity is the amount that a bonding or surety company is prepared to put at risk in the bonds that it writes for the construction professional. A construction professional's bonding capacity is based on the amount of liquid assets held by the insured, or the amount of assets which can be readily liquidated. It is also based on the experience and track record of the individual. The design/build design professional usually fares poorly on both accounts. A design professional typically has few assets compared to the size of the required bonds and, until he or she has been in practice for awhile, may have little construction experience on which the surety can base its review.

The Type A design professional often must rely on the bonding capacity of the contractor, whom the design professional retains to perform required construction on the project. A contractor in Type A or C design/build can provide a performance bond in favor of the client, and perhaps also in favor of the design professional. But first, use of the bonding capacity of the contractor needs to be discussed and negotiated with the client before the contract is signed to ensure that the arrangement is acceptable to the project's lenders.

While this may solve the design professional's immediate problem, another may be created in that the contractor is given greater leverage in his or her bargaining position with the design professional than the design professional might like. The design professional may have to forfeit a certain measure of control over the contractor in return for use of the contractor's bonding capacity.

The Surety Company's Predicament

When deciding whether or not to provide a performance bond to a contractor, the surety traditionally tries to determine the scope and the cost of the work that the contractor is obligated to perform under the construction contract. If either the cost or the scope of the work cannot be determined, the surety is faced with two problems. First, it doesn't know the amount in which to provide the bond. Second, the conditions of contractor nonperformance that the bond will be required to cover are unclear. That is, it may be difficult to distinguish between those services performed by the design professional and those performed by the contractor on a design/build project.

In a Type B design/build firm, for example, the client contracts with the contractor for all required design and construction. The contractor then subcontracts design services to a design professional. If the contractor chooses to perform some of the design services typically performed by design professionals, do those services now constitute construction services the performance of which the surety is obligated to guarantee? Or, are they still considered design services (although performed by the contractor) for which the bonding company is not responsible?

Often the documents for which a surety company is asked to provide a bond are not nearly as complete on design/build projects as on traditionally structured projects, and the more frequent use of fast track construction in design/build projects than in other methods of construction makes this a particularly troublesome issue. An improper bond amount may result in either too little protection for the client or too high a premium payment by the contractor. The surety's risks are also increased in that if it elects, under the performance bond, to complete construction of the project after the contractor has defaulted, the actual cost to complete construction may exceed the amount on which the performance bond premium was based. Given these uncertainties, sureties are likely to raise their premiums to cover their increased risks.

Added to the sometimes uncertain scope of the construction work is the uncertain scope of the design services. It is possible to determine the allocation of design and construction services through the subcontract amount assigned to the contractor in Type A design/build, and the subcontract amount assigned to the design professional in Type B design/build. But it is often not clear what the parties intend to allocate between design and construction services in a Type C joint venture (although the parties could have, but don't necessarily require, subcontracts with the joint venture that allocate design and construction costs). Furthermore, in a Type D design/build organization there is no differentiation in cost between design and construction services. It is not always clear which part of the design/build entity's compensation is properly allocated to bondable construction work, and which is attributed to professional services that are insurable under Professional Liability Insurance policies.

In the typical monthly certification for payment that the design professional furnishes to the client on traditionally structured projects, the bonding company is fairly secure knowing that the design professional is observing the contractor's conformance to the contract documents, and that the design professional's recommendations for payment to the contractor are based on these observations. Under this scrutiny it is unlikely that the contractor will be overpaid at any point in time. The bonding company's risk of having to pay for work that was not completed by the contractor, but for which the contractor has already been paid, is substantially reduced.

On all but Type A design/build projects, however, it is unlikely that the design professional will be observing the contractor's performance and making recommendations for payment. (If the design/build design professional does perform these duties, a potential conflict of interest exists because in all but Type A design/build, the contractor is either the design professional's employer or partner.) Rather, requests for payment are typically made by the contractor directly to the client. The risk of overpaying a contractor is therefore greater, and so is the surety's risk under its performance bond. If the contractor defaults after having been paid a substantial amount under its contract, and the surety elects to complete construction, the amount required to complete the project may be more than the remaining unpaid balance of the contract amount plus the amount of the bond. But since the surety has elected to complete construction itself, the penal amount of the bond is inapplicable.

If the contractor defaults early and has been overpaid, and the surety elects to have the client complete the project using a second contractor, the surety's payment obligations under the performance bond, though subject to the penal amount of the bond, are likely to be higher than if the contractor had not been overpaid. The absence of an independent design professional is a significant risk to both the client and the surety in this regard. Some bonding companies, therefore, may require an independent design professional for this purpose, thus adding to the costs of the project.

Summary

All construction projects, both traditional and nontraditional, require that their participants be insured and bonded. Insurance and bonding provides protection from loss to clients, contractors, and design professionals—protection they would otherwise be unable to provide for themselves—and is an important part of negotiating the allocation of risk of incurring loss. There are four basic types of insurance typically used on construction projects: Workers' Compensation Insurance, Comprehensive General Liability Insurance, Property Insurance, and Professional Liability Insurance.

Unfortunately for design/build participants, the insurance industry is organized to meet the needs of traditionally structured projects. As a result, construction professionals who step outside their traditional roles may, in some instances, face gaps or exclusions in available coverage, or be required to carry additional insurance or bonding. For instance, design professionals who are contractually responsible for the construction of a project should carry the same kinds of insurance that a contractor would need. On the other hand, it may be difficult to obtain proper coverage. For instance, clients and contractors cannot obtain professional liability insurance, nor can they be named as additional insureds on the design professional's policy. This may be problematic on those design/build projects in which the contractor is responsible for the design of the project as well as the construction.

A bond is a guarantee against failure to perform. There are three types of bonds typically required on construction projects: bid bonds, performance bonds, and labor and material payment bonds. Design professionals who are responsible for the construction of a design/build project may need to be bonded. Unfortunately the criteria that the typical surety company uses to evaluate an individual's bonding capacity may make it difficult for the design professional to obtain bonding. A design professional in this situation could depend on the bonding capacity of the contractor, but may forfeit a certain degree of project control by doing so.

Likewise, the surety company may have difficulty evaluating the bonding capacity of a party engaged in design/build, since the cost and scope of the work as well as the allocation of responsibility are often unclear. Parties who are contemplating involvement in a design/build project should seek the advice of a qualified insurance or bonding agent to ensure that they are adequately protected. Those design/build professionals who are able to obtain proper coverage may turn to other administrative issues. Chapter 11 examines licensing, registration, and professional codes of ethics in design/build.

Chapter Eleven

Licensing, Registration, and Professional Codes of Ethics

Each state has the authority to require that parties who wish to provide design or construction services in that state be properly licensed or registered by the state. This authority is founded in the inherent police powers of the state to protect and provide for the general health, safety, and welfare of the public.

Licensing and registration requirements vary from state to state. Each state has its own licensing and registration requirements for design professionals. Many states, though not all, have some form of licensing requirement for contractors. Failure to comply with these requirements may result in civil or criminal penalties, or sanctions including fines, license or registration suspension, injunctions against performing or providing such services, and even imprisonment. Failure to comply with applicable licensing and registration requirements may also be used against a construction professional in a court of law. For instance, a client may use this information as a defense when sued by a contractor or design professional for the recovery of overdue payments.

In addition to licensing and registration, design professionals who are members of national professional organizations are required to conform to codes of ethics and professional conduct adopted by those organizations. Violation of these codes may result in disciplinary action ranging from admonishment and censure, to temporary suspension or even termination of membership.

The licensing and registration requirements of each state apply to construction professionals whether they are engaged in traditionally structured projects or design/build projects. However, unlike construction professionals who provide services on traditionally structured projects, parties engaged in some design/build arrangements may face additional licensing and registration requirements or other obstacles that may hinder their ability to conform to applicable requirements and codes of ethics. This, in turn, could affect their ability to practice design/build.

This chapter explores the licensing and registration requirements and professional codes of ethics that contractors and design professionals may face when engaged in design/build practice. Construction professionals contemplating design/build should review their jurisdiction's laws and regulations with a qualified professional to assess their legal ability to provide or perform design/build services.

Contractor Licensing Requirements

Contractor licensing requirements vary from state to state. Some states require that contractors be licensed for both private and public work. Others do not require licensing. Some require licensing for certain types of construction only. Some states require contractors to be prequalified, but not necessarily licensed, in order to bid on state work. Others require both. Work on federal projects is generally exempt from licensing requirements, while local ordinances may require local registration prior to commencement of work in the particular municipality.

When licensing is required, the contractor must usually provide the following: payment of registration fees and completion of an application providing information about the nature of the contractor's business, the owners of that business and, if the business is a corporation, the officers of that corporation. A testimony to the contractor's experience, ability, character, and financial condition may also be required. In addition, proof of bonding capacity and maintenance of various bonds, and Property Damage, Workers' Compensation, and other types of insurance may be required as a precondition to licensing.

Some jurisdictions may also require a written examination intended to demonstrate a general understanding of business management, familiarity with applicable building, health, safety, and lien laws, as well as administrative and other regulations applicable to the conduct of business in general. The contractor may be required to pay business, income, sales, franchise, or other taxes and assessments in order to obtain and maintain the license. A business license may also be required, in addition to a contractor's license. If the contractor is a corporation based out of state, a certificate of authority to conduct business is also likely to be required from the secretary of state in that project's jurisdiction.

Contractors who intend to engage in design/build must understand that any license or registration granted to a contractor by the state or any local municipality in connection with the contractor's intended construction activities, does not permit the contractor to engage in or to offer to provide or perform design services of the sort regulated by applicable state laws governing the licensing of design professionals. **Contractors who wish to perform design services must be licensed or registered separately according to applicable design professional licensing laws** to the extent that design professionals are subject to such requirements.

Contractor Licensing Requirements in Design/Build

In traditionally structured projects, contractors are hired by clients to provide all construction services required for the project. These independently retained contractors are required in some states to be properly licensed in order to conduct their business. On design/build projects, however, the contractor may not always be the party contractually responsible to the client for the construction of the project. In some design/build arrangements, the design professional may be responsible for both design and construction. Design professionals who are responsible for construction services must be licensed or registered according to applicable contractor licensing laws of the state to the same extent that contractors are subject to such requirements.

The design professional engaged in either Type A design/build (where the design professional is the primary contractor), or Type C design/build (where the contractor is a member of a joint venture), must comply with contractor licensing requirements since the design professional is the party contracting with the client to perform or to provide required construction services for the project.

Of course, if the design professional is engaged in Type B design/build (where the design professional is a subconsultant to the contractor who is the primary contractor), licensing is not an issue since the design professional is neither performing nor providing construction services. In this case, the design professional is acting in the same capacity as a design professional on any traditionally structured project except that here, the design professional's employer is the contractor, not the client.

Design professionals may avoid the licensing issue by careful drafting of contract language to make clear that it will be the contractor retained by the design professional who actually *performs* the required construction services.

Design Professional Licensing Requirements

Each state licenses and registers members of most of the various design professions to practice within the boundaries of that state. Typically, architects, engineers (including structural, mechanical, electrical, plumbing, and civil engineers), and land surveyors are required to be licensed and registered. Landscape architects are usually required to be licensed. Interior designers generally are not. This could change in the next several years as pressure mounts from interior designers to establish some form of licensing requirement.

The purpose of licensing design professionals is to assure the public that only properly qualified persons will be permitted to offer their services to the public. The state assures itself that such persons are properly qualified by requiring minimum levels of education and experience and, typically, by requiring each person to pass a written, and sometimes an oral, examination. The state's concern is that the public is generally not able to determine for itself the requisite qualifications and appropriate minimum level of expertise that a design professional should possess. The public is assured, to a certain extent, that the design professional is reasonably well qualified to provide the services it offers if licensed and registered by the state.

Types of Design Professional Licensing Statutes

Licensing and registration statutes vary in the way they are worded and in their effect. There are basically three types of licensing statutes:

- Title Statutes
- Practice Statutes
- Hybrid Statutes (a combination of both)

Title Statutes

A *title statute* regulates the way in which someone describes themselves to the public. For instance, a title statute prohibits unlicensed individuals from identifying themselves to the public as design professionals through the use of such titles as "architect" or "engineer." The following is typical of the way in which an architectural title statute might be worded:

> *No person shall use the title "architect," "registered architect," "architectural designer," or display or use any words, letters, figures, title, sign, card, advertisement, or other device to indicate that such person offers to engage or engages in the practice of architecture unless that person is registered under applicable provisions of this statute.*

Not only is use of the term "architect" by improperly licensed individuals prohibited, but derivatives of the word are also prohibited. An unlicensed person using this or any other prohibited title is subject to the penalties imposed by the statute.

Practice Statutes

A *practice statute* regulates not what a person may call him or herself, but what services that person may actually perform. A typical architectural practice statute might read as follows:

> *No person shall, directly or indirectly, engage in the practice of architecture in this state unless that person is registered under applicable provisions of this statute.*

What constitutes the "practice of architecture" also varies from state to state. It is typically defined in the licensing statute, often in broad terms. The following definition is taken from Chapter 112, Section 60A of the Massachusetts General Laws:

> *...performing or agreeing to perform or holding one's self out as able to perform professional services in connection with the design, construction, enlargement, or alteration of a building including consultations, investigations, evaluations, preliminary studies, aesthetic design, the preparation of plans, specifications, and contract documents, the coordination of structural and mechanical design and site development, administration of construction contracts, and any other similar service or combination of services in connection with the design and construction of buildings....*

A person performing any of these services without a license would be subject to the penalties set forth in the statute.

Hybrid Statutes

Hybrid statutes regulate both what persons may call themselves and what services they may perform or offer to perform within the state's jurisdiction. Some courts in "title states" regulate by judicial interpretation what services persons may perform. Similarly, some courts in "practice states" regulate what persons may call themselves. But those states whose licensing statutes clearly describe both what unlicensed persons may not call themselves and what services they may not perform, generally provide the broadest scope of prohibited conduct by persons who are not properly licensed.

The following is an example of such a statute, taken from Chapter 112 of the Massachusetts General Laws, Section 60K, and combines the language of the typical title and practice statutes described above:

> 112:60K. *Unregistered Person Not to Engage in Practice of Architecture, Nor Use Title "Architect" etc.*
>
> *Section 60K. No person shall, directly or indirectly, engage in the practice of architecture in this commonwealth, except as hereinafter set forth in section sixty L, or use the title, "architect," "registered architect," "architectural designer," or display or use any words, letters, figures, title, sign, card, advertisement, or other device to indicate that such person offers to engage or engages in the practice of architecture unless he is registered under the provisions of sections sixty A to sixty O, inclusive.*

In states with hybrid design professional licensing statutes, it is clearly unlawful for an unlicensed individual to both use the title of that design profession (or one of the derivatives thereof) as well as to perform or even offer to perform the services described as those belonging to that discipline.

Design Professional Licensing Requirements in Design/Build

In a traditionally structured project, the design professional is hired by the client to provide all design services necessary for the project. This independently retained design professional is required to be licensed in order to practice his or her profession. However, in design/build project delivery, the party who is contractually responsible to the client for the design of the project is not always the design professional. In some design/build arrangements, the contractor may be responsible for both the design and the construction, and may need to comply with applicable design licensing statutes.

For instance, if the contractor is engaged in either a Type B design/build firm (where the contractor is the primary contractor), or a Type C design/build firm (where the contractor is a member of a joint venture), then compliance with design professional registration requirements may be required, since the contractor is the party contracting with the client to perform or to provide professional design services for the project.

Of course, if the contractor is engaged in Type A design/build (where the contractor is a subcontractor to the design professional who is the primary contractor), licensing and registration is not an issue since the contractor is neither performing nor providing design services. In this case, the contractor is acting in the same capacity as a contractor on any traditionally structured project, only in this case the contractor's employer is the design professional instead of the client.

Title, Practice, and Hybrid States

Participants in Types B, C, and D design/build firms should review the design professional licensing statutes and judicial and local design professional registration board interpretations in the jurisdiction in which the project will be located to determine whether the design/build firm can provide design services to the public without requiring that the contractor be licensed in design.

In a true "title state," without expansive judicial interpretation, it may be possible for the Type B, C, and D design/build firm to provide required design services on certain types of projects as long as the design/build firm does not use one of the prohibited terms to describe itself.

In a true "practice state," parties are prohibited from performing design services unless licensed as design professionals. However, some courts have drawn a distinction between those parties obligated by contract with the client to *provide* design services, which are then to be performed by properly licensed individuals subcontracted to that party, and those parties obligated by contract with the client to *perform* design services. It may be argued that the party contracting with the client was merely obligated to *arrange for the performance* of required design services by properly licensed design professionals and not to actually perform such services. Unfortunately, not all courts will be persuaded by this argument.

In a practice state whose definition of the term "practice" does not include the "offering of services" to the public, while the design/build firm could not *perform* such services itself, it may be possible for the design/build firm to *provide* services through other persons who are properly licensed. These services might be performed by subconsultants to the design/build firm. In some states it may even be possible to provide design services through licensed employees of the design/build firm itself. In pure practice states, the design/build firm may also be permitted to use the descriptive terms that are otherwise prohibited in a pure title state, such as "architect," and "engineer."

However, if the practice statute does include the "offering of services" to the public within its prohibition of activities by unlicensed individuals, then it is possible that the design/build firm itself may not be permitted to offer design services to the public, even though it may have subcontracted such services to licensed individuals or have licensed individuals on its staff. This is because it is not the licensed individual but the unlicensed design/build firm who is doing the "offering."

The scenario described above may be confusing, since it seems to permit a design/build firm to describe itself using terms otherwise prohibited in a title state, although the firm couldn't provide those services represented by the use of such terms, even if those services were to be actually performed by properly licensed individuals. In these cases, judicial interpretation may be necessary to distinguish between the terms "provide" and "perform." Careful drafting of contract language at the start of the project is critical to establish the proper role of the party contracting with the client so that it is consistent with applicable state licensing statutes.

States with hybrid statutes, especially those that include the "offering of services" to the public within their definition of the term "practice," clearly provide the greatest difficulty to design/build firms. These statutes prohibit the design/build firms from both describing themselves using one or more of the prohibited terms, and from offering the services described within the term "practice." Depending on the creativity, support, or leniency of the courts, it may be possible to provide various design services through licensed individuals in various relationships to the design/build firm, although it may not be possible to actually describe the firm using one or more of the prohibited terms.

The Design Professional's Fiduciary Role

Participants of design/build arrangements in which a party other than the licensed design professional is responsible for providing design services to the client, must be aware of design professional licensing and registration statutes and of their interpretation by the courts and local registration boards. The underlying reason behind many state registration statutes, judicial decisions, and registration board administrative actions that prohibit unlicensed firms from providing design services through licensed individuals is that use of an intermediary may mislead the client. The client may be misled into believing that he or she enjoys a fiduciary relationship (a relationship based on loyalty and trust) with the design professional actually performing the services when that relationship is compromised because of the absence of a direct contractual relationship with the client. It is felt that, traditionally, the fundamental relationship between the design professional and the client is a fiduciary relationship, that such a relationship must exist, and that unless the design professional is in direct contractual relationship with the client, such a relationship cannot exist. Use of an intermediary, licensed or not, which occurs in Type B, C, or D design/build, is thought to destroy that fiduciary relationship.

In addition to the penalties imposed by the registration statutes for the unauthorized practice of one or more of the design professions, there may also be applicable consumer protection laws that treat the provision of services by an unlicensed individual as a fraudulent misrepresentation, with penalties including, under some states' consumer protection laws, double or triple damages.

A written disclosure by the design professional (or other party contracting directly with the client) stating that a fiduciary relationship does not exist should satisfy a state's interests in protecting the legitimate expectations of its citizenry, while affording all parties the freedom to contract for such services on whatever basis they see fit. A client who has been clearly informed that a design professional neither has nor owes a fiduciary duty to the client cannot complain that he or she was misled to believe that such a relationship ever existed.

The American Institute of Architects, in its standard form owner-design/builder and design/builder-architect agreements (discussed in Chapter 12) has included a clause which clearly discloses to the client the lack of any fiduciary relationship between the architect and the client. Other standard construction industry forms of agreements currently do not include this provision, although the parties are certainly free to modify these documents to include appropriate language to this effect.

Other Licensing Restrictions

There are several other licensing-related restrictions that have been problematic for parties who wish to provide design services in a design/build arrangement. Each state's legislative, judicial, and regulatory approach to design/build matters is different. To date, most states have been quite permissive in their legislative and/or regulatory control, although several, notably Pennsylvania and New York, have not. It is important, therefore, for parties intending to engage in design/build practice to determine current legislative, judicial, and regulatory restrictions, if any, on design/build practice in the jurisdiction in which the project is located. Several restrictions are discussed below.

Corporate Licensing Exclusions

Some courts and design professional registration boards have taken the position that a corporation cannot provide or offer to provide design services because a corporation cannot be licensed. Design services can be provided by individually licensed design professionals only. In these jurisdictions, it would be illegal for a Type D design/build firm or any corporation to provide design services, even though the design services may be actually performed by properly licensed design professionals on the corporation's staff. Again, in some jurisdictions, careful drafting of contract language may be necessary to structure the relationships among the parties so that they comply with local licensing and registration laws.

Prohibitions Against Forming Partnerships with Nonprofessionals

Some jurisdictions prohibit their licensed design professionals from forming partnerships with individuals or firms unlicensed in the appropriate design discipline. Type C design/build firms (design professional-contractor joint ventures) would therefore be prohibited from practicing in these jurisdictions. Type D design/build organizations in which design professionals form partnerships with others who are not licensed as design professionals are also prohibited. Prohibitions against forming partnerships with unlicensed individuals or firms may, in some jurisdictions, extend to members from one design discipline forming partnerships with members of another design discipline, unless very strict criteria are followed. This criteria may involve the extent of the ownership interest in the partnership held by members of each discipline, the name of the partnership and how stationary, advertisements, contracts, and other documents identify the various members of each design discipline, and who is responsible for the professional activities of the partnership on a given project.

Once again, these prohibitions represent a state's effort to protect the public from being misled in its belief that a member of a given design discipline will perform required services of that discipline when such services will be performed by members of another design discipline or by unlicensed individuals. The state is also concerned that if the appropriate design professional does not prepare or supervise the preparation of the construction documents, then the design professional's stamp on those documents may be a fraudulent misrepresentation regarding who prepares those documents, and that the professional expertise required by those documents may, in fact, be missing.

Furthermore, it is felt in some jurisdictions that when a design professional does not have a sufficient ownership interest in the partnership, or when his or her judgment is subject to the authority of a superior in that organization, that design/professional's judgment may be compromised—to the detriment of the client and the public in general. In some jurisdictions, these concerns also apply to corporations formed for the purpose of providing professional design services, since the state's interest in protecting the health, safety, and welfare of its citizenry requires that professional services be provided by properly qualified individuals.

Prohibitions Against Splitting Fees with Nonprofessionals

Some jurisdictions prohibit design professionals from splitting their fees with unlicensed individuals or entities. This is particularly problematic when a corporation employs a licensed design professional where corporations are not permitted to practice design, and where the design professional is paid a salary, and not the fees received by the corporation, for the design services rendered to the client by the design professional.

A Type D design/build firm, whether a corporation or some other business arrangement, faces a similar problem. The prohibition against splitting fees with nonprofessionals is also a problem in situations where the design professional is a subconsultant to a contractor (Type B design/build), or where the design professional is in some form of partnership with a contractor (Type C design/build). If, in any of these situations, the party contracting with the client for design services pays less than one hundred percent to the design professional for all design services provided to the client by the design/build firm, then an impermissible splitting of fees may have occurred.

States which have a prohibition against splitting fees with nonprofessionals are concerned that unlicensed individuals or firms may be receiving fees for professional design services when, in fact, they performed no such services, and that to continue to receive fees for such services compromises the integrity of the licensing statute and allows unqualified individuals to provide inadequate or improper services to an unsuspecting public.

Under certain circumstances, it may be possible to bypass the prohibition by having the design fee stated separately in the written agreement between the design/build firm and the client, and then having the design/build firm agree in its contract with the design professional to pay that same amount to the design professional.

This is accomplished most easily in Type B design/build, where the design professional is a subconsultant to the contractor. It could also be done in Type C design/build if the design professional-contractor joint venture were structured as a pass-through joint venture, at least with respect to the design services for the project. The joint venture agreement with the client would, once again, state separately the design fee paid to the joint venture for required design services for the project. The joint venture would then subcontract in writing to the design professional component of that joint venture (or to any other design professional if it wishes) all of the design services required of the joint venture by its contract with the client and would pay, pursuant to that subcontract, the entire amount of design fees stated in the joint venture's contract with the client.

It might also be possible to structure a Type D design/build firm in a similar manner. However, a Type D design/build firm that intends to perform design services through staff personnel has the same problem any corporation has which intends to perform design services through its employees.

Codes of Ethics and Professional Conduct

In addition to state licensing and registration laws, the design component of a design/build firm may be required to conform its conduct to the code of ethics of that particular design professional's national professional society. While national professional societies, such as the National Society of Professional Engineers (NSPE) or the American Institute of Architects (AIA), are voluntary organizations in which membership by qualified design professionals is at the discretion of the individual design professional, there may be significant professional and commercial benefits to membership in one or more of these societies.

Membership is thought by many professionals to enhance the reputation of the design professional and his or her ability to obtain projects. Even if the design professional does not actively seek membership, several states have incorporated at least some portion of a national society's present or past code of ethics into its licensing laws, making compliance with these codes a condition of continued licensure, and noncompliance the cause for penalties or fines.

Compliance with codes of ethics today does not present the obstacles it once did to a design professional's participation in design/build activity. Before 1978, codes of ethics placed severe restrictions on a member's ability to participate in competitive bidding for professional services or to act as a contractor on a project. For instance, the code of ethics of the NSPE prior to 1978 prohibited an engineer from soliciting or submitting proposals on the basis of competitive bidding. The AIA's code of ethics at that time prohibited its members from acting as contractor on the same project for which they were also providing professional architectural design services. These ethical proscriptions effectively prevented design professionals from participating in all but a Type B design/build firm in which the design professional essentially served in its traditional capacity, but with the contractor, rather than the client or user of the facility, as his or her employer.

However, in a case entitled *National Society of Professional Engineers v. United States*, 435 U.S. 679, (1978), the United States Supreme Court determined that the NSPE's prohibition against competitive bidding by its members violated the antitrust provisions of the Sherman Act. The court was not persuaded by the NSPE's arguments that its ethical restrictions were reasonable because competition among professional engineers was contrary to the public interest, or would adversely affect the quality of engineering, or that it would be dangerous to the public health, safety, and welfare.

Later that same year, as a result of increasing pressure from its members to increase business opportunities and explore alternative approaches to participation in project delivery, (and with the NSPE case very much in mind concerning antitrust problems involved in the imposition of commercial restraints on trade arising out of a professional society's ethical restrictions), the AIA suspended for a three-year period its prohibition on member participation in projects as both architect and contractor. Due, in part, to another antitrust case entitled *Mardirosian v. The American Institute of Architects*, 474 F. Supp. 628, (D.C. Cir. 1979), which dealt with other restraints on trade, and due, partly, to the generally favorable reaction of its members to the opportunity to participate in design/build activity, the AIA permanently removed its ban on member participation as contractors on projects. In removing the ban, however, the AIA stressed its concern over the conflict of interest that is likely to exist between the client and the architect by requiring the architect to exercise impartial and independent professional judgment with respect to its professional activities on the project, and to disclose to the client in writing the existence of any conflict of interest and provide all cost data relative to the project.

In recent years, the NSPE and the AIA have revised their respective codes of ethics. Section II 4a of the current edition (January 1987) of the NSPE's *Code of Ethics*, included as Appendix A, now provides that:

> *Engineers shall disclose all known or potential conflicts of interest to their employers or clients by promptly informing them of any business association, interest, or other circumstance which could influence or appear to influence their judgment or the quality of their services.*

Also, Ethical Standard 3.2 and Rule of Conduct 3.202 of the AIA's current (1987) *Code of Ethics and Professional Conduct*, included as Appendix B, provides that:

> *E.S. 3.2 Conflict of Interest: Members should disclose to clients or owners significant circumstances that could be construed as conflicts of interest and should ensure that such conflicts do not compromise those interests.*
>
> *R. 3.202 If members have any business association, direct or indirect financial interest, or other interest which could be substantial enough to influence their judgment in connection with their performance of professional services, the members shall fully disclose to their clients or employers the nature of the business association, financial interest, or other interest, and if the clients or employers object to such association, financial interest, or other interest, the members will either terminate such association or interest or give up the commission or employment.*

The AIA's commentary to Rule of Conduct 3.202 illustrates the breadth of the AIA's position on disclosure of conflicts of interest. It states:

> *Commentary: These rules are intended to embrace the full range of situations which may present a member with a conflict between his interests and those of his client or employer. In some situations a conflict is easily discerned, as when the architect owns property adjacent to property upon which he has been asked to design a structure and is faced with design options which would affect the value of his property. Other instances are not so clear, and that is more frequently the case as new systems and procedures for the construction process, such as design-build, come into the market. In every case the architect must take adequate steps to ensure that the client is aware of any substantial interest which the architect has which might run counter to the interests of the client.*

Design professionals who are members of either the NSPE or the AIA, and who participate in types A, C, or D design/build, are subject to the disclosure requirements of their respective professional society's code of ethics. While often the client is fully aware of the potential conflict of interest that exists in the design professional's role on the project by the time the design/build contract is executed, this may not always be the case.

Many clients are truly unaware of the conflict, viewing the design/build process more in terms of an opportunity to simplify the administrative aspects of project delivery, to increase the efficiency of operations, and to reduce the cost and time required to complete the project. Not all clients appreciate the significant professional, legal, and contractual changes in the parties' relationships with one another in design/build compared to those traditionally existing between the design professional and client. Common sense alone should indicate to the design professional that in order to avoid future problems, potential conflicts of interest should be revealed at the outset. A written disclosure of any conflict of interest and of the existence, nature, and extent of the design professional's contractual relationship with the client is well advised.

Summary

Every state has the authority to require that construction professionals be licensed and registered. Licensing assures that the construction professional is reasonably well qualified to provide the services that he or she offers.

Licensing and registration statutes vary from state to state. Some states require contractors to be licensed. In design/build, however, the individual contractually responsible for construction may be the design professional. In Type A design/build, the design professional may have to comply with contractor licensing statutes in those states that require contractors to be licensed. Design professionals may avoid the licensing requirement by drafting contract language so that the licensed contractor retained by the design professional is the party actually performing the construction services.

Every state requires that design professionals be licensed, although wording of the statutes may vary from state to state. There are three types of licensing statutes that regulate the activity of design professionals: title statutes, practice statutes, and statutes which are a hybrid, or combination, of the two. In some design/build arrangements, the contractor may be contractually responsible to the client for all design services. Contractors in Type B design/build, and in some cases Type C, may need to be licensed as design professionals, depending on whether the jurisdiction in which the project is located invokes title, practice, or hybrid statutes, and whether the contractor is viewed as "providing," "performing," or "offering" to provide or perform design services.

Some states prohibit unlicensed individuals from providing design services through licensed intermediaries (as is typical in design/build projects) unless it is disclosed to the client in writing. These states have ruled that use of an intermediary violates the fiduciary relationship that traditionally exists between the client and the design professional. In some states, corporations cannot be licensed. Type D design/build firms may be unable to provide design services in these jurisdictions. Other prohibitions include forming partnerships or splitting fees with nonprofessionals.

In addition to licensing and registration requirements, design professionals may be required to conform to professional codes of ethics prescribed by that design professional's national organization. Chapter 12 examines the standard form documents published by these national organizations which are often used by clients, contractors, and design professionals to contract design/build services.

Chapter Twelve

Standard Form Design/Build Contract Agreements

Clients, contractors, and design professionals, particularly those involved in the design/build method of project delivery, are advised to use written agreements to record and describe each party's rights and responsibilities. Carefully drafted contract language may reduce or eliminate many of the legal pitfalls typically encountered on both traditional as well as design/build projects.

Whenever parties engage in activities that are not yet standard practice, the potential exists for confusion and misinterpretation, despite good intentions. If the parties fail to articulate their relationships with and obligations to one another, it may be difficult later on for a judge, jury, or arbitrator to discern what the parties' intentions were at the time they began their activities.

Drafting and negotiating a written agreement achieves two goals: It defines the relationships and obligations of each party at the start of the project, and it records their understanding and agreement of these matters for reference when conflicts arise during construction and occasionally thereafter. Often, these conflicts are resolved by the parties themselves. However, it is sometimes necessary to bring in a third party to resolve the dispute. When this happens, a written agreement can prove invaluable.

Fortunately, the parties need not invent the wheel when preparing written design/build agreements. While preprinted standard form contracts are seldom suitable "as is," with appropriate modifications, they provide the best starting point for most design/build projects.

Some large public- and private-sector clients have developed their own design/build documents. At the federal level, the General Services Administration has developed a design/build "Request for Proposal" form and an agreement form for use on selected GSA-managed projects. Similarly, a number of state and local government agencies have developed their own design/build contract documents.

Whether one is required to use a government-mandated design/build agreement form, or free to select or develop one's own, the content of the document should be reviewed, and modified if necessary, to describe as accurately as possible each party's rights, responsibilities, and relationship to other participants on the project.

Choosing Standard Form Design/Build Documents

Three sets of standard form design/build documents are currently available to design/build participants. Each set is published by one of the following national organizations: the *American Institute of Architects* (AIA), the *National Society of Professional Engineers* (NSPE), and the *Associated General Contractors of America* (AGC). Each set of documents assumes a different party as the primary contractor to the client, thus providing a set of documents for a variety of design/build arrangements.

This chapter will discuss these three sets of documents, the organizations that publish them, the basic structure and organizational framework of the individual documents, the basic relationships defined in the documents, and special considerations for users of these documents. A comparison of the documents, and an analysis of the way in which they address several key issues will also be provided. (These documents have been reprinted in appendices C, D, and E for reference purposes.) Before exploring these issues, we will first examine who chooses to use standard form design/build documents, and why.

Who Uses Standard Form Design/Build Documents?

Standard form design/build documents are used extensively in the construction industry. The documents published by the AIA, NSPE, and AGC are used most often. However, many clients, contractors, and design professionals have either drafted their own documents, or have adapted one or more of the existing standard form documents to meet their specific needs.

In the normal course of their practices, design professionals and contractors are likely to suggest that their clients use the standard form documents prepared by their respective organizations. Clients do not have the benefit of a national organization to develop standard form documents that reflect their perspective, and most design professionals and contractors do not have the necessary resources to develop their own documents. For these reasons, the documents produced by the AIA, the NSPE, and the AGC, with appropriate modifications, are those used most often by design/build participants.

Some parties do have the resources to develop their own standard form agreements. These tend to be the larger contracting and design professional organizations, large corporate or institutional clients, or government agencies. Typically, the standard form documents that these parties use are modified versions of the AIA, NSPE, and AGC documents. Of course, there are those parties whose documents have been so revised that they no longer bear any resemblance to the standard form documents published by the national organizations. These documents are usually developed by government agencies constrained by statutes and procurement rules and regulations, by land developers, and by design professionals and contractors whose primary activity is design/build.

For example, it would not be unusual for a large design/build firm to draft its own standard form design/build documents to reflect the firm's specific methods of project development or delivery. Real estate developers may also draft their own documents to represent their proven and profitable methods of project design and construction. Similarly, clients with significant financial assets may draft their own documents so that they provide more protection than standard form documents.

Why Use Standard Form Design/Build Documents?

Perhaps the single most important reason for using standard form design/build documents is that these documents are the most comprehensive, readily available source of language that deals, in a reasonably equitable manner, with most of the issues likely to arise in design/build projects. There is concern, however, that these standard design/build documents are drafted to favor the party whose organization prepared the documents. In fact, each set of documents advocates the professional organization's perception of the proper relationship and balance among the parties with respect to design, construction, financial, and legal issues. But on the whole, all parties are generally treated more fairly using standard form documents than a given party's customized documents. The clarity and comprehensiveness is simply better in standard form documents than in customized documents. Only those individuals with significant construction industry and contract drafting experience are likely to achieve similar standards of quality. Most construction professionals understand this and, through continued use, have enabled standard form documents to achieve a level of general acceptance by the industry.

Both the experienced and the novice find standard form documents useful. The less experienced parties choose these standard form documents because they deal with a myriad of issues with which the parties may be unfamiliar. More experienced parties appreciate the comprehensive nature of these documents and, while they may not use the documents as they exist, they are likely to use them as the basis for their agreements, making modifications as needed. Standard form documents are also a valuable reference for issues that the parties may confront during the course of the project.

Which Set of Standard Form Documents to Use?

The answer to this question is likely to vary among the parties. For the most part, those documents should be used which best meet the requirements of the project and the needs of its participants. A "battle of the forms" is not likely to be in anyone's best interest, since what may be gained in the battle is a measure of distrust and inflexibility by the other project participants.

This is not to suggest that the documents are interchangeable. There certainly are differences among them, as the following discussion will illustrate. One set of documents may be more appropriate than another on certain types or sizes of projects, or on projects for which the client has certain expectations. Choosing the set of documents best suited to the circumstances of the project is essential for their effectiveness. For example, an architect who is contracting directly with the client for all design and construction services probably would not choose a design/build document published by the Associated General Contractors of America to record its agreement with the client.

The AIA and NSPE documents are perhaps the most adaptable to the different design/build arrangements, since the design/builder who contracts with the client using these documents could be either an architect-contractor or engineer-contractor joint venture (Type C), or a separate and legally distinct design/build organization (Type D). These documents assume that the party contracting with the client (the design/builder) is a separate and distinct entity from the design professional and the contractor. The AGC documents are less flexible, since they only contemplate an arrangement in which the contractor contracts directly with the client for all design and construction services and then subcontracts to appropriate design professionals for the required design services (Type B). The AGC documents cannot be easily adapted for use on other design/build arrangements.

Caution must be used when combining one set of standard form documents with another, or with nonstandard forms. Each set of standard documents is a tightly knit group, intended for use with documents of its kind. Each set of documents reflects a delicate balance of the rights and responsibilities of the parties, which may not necessarily be the same in other sets. Each set also proceeds from a different set of underlying assumptions that are expressed in their own unique drafting conventions. Mixing assumptions or conventions may confuse the intentions of the parties in what are otherwise fairly explicit statements. This is not to say that selected portions of a document from one set may not be incorporated into a document from another set. However, combining documents must be done with great care by persons who are thoroughly knowledgeable with each document.

AIA Standard Form Design/Build Documents

The American Institute of Architects (AIA) is a national society of registered architects. Founded in 1857, today it is by far the single largest representative body of architects in the United States. The AIA publishes one of the most extensive sets of standard form construction industry documents of any organization in the country. Its documents, particularly the owner-architect agreements, owner-contractor agreements, and construction contract general conditions, are some of the most widely used sets of documents of their kind in the industry. They often serve as the basis for, or contribute language to, standard form documents prepared by other organizations.

Basic Structure and Organization of the Documents

The AIA publishes a family of three interrelated design/build documents. These documents are reproduced in their entirety in Appendix C. Each document contains a set of two agreements: a Part 1 agreement governing preliminary design and pre-construction matters, and a Part 2 agreement governing final design and construction. These documents are as follows:

- AIA Document A191, Standard Form of Agreements Between Owner and Design/Builder (1985 Edition)
  - Part 1 Agreement—Preliminary Design and Budgeting
  - Part 2 Agreement—Final Design and Construction
- AIA Document A491, Standard Form of Agreements Between Design/Builder and Contractor (1985 Edition)
  - Part 1 Agreement—Pre-Construction
  - Part 2 Agreement—Construction
- AIA Document B901, Standard Form of Agreements Between Design/Builder and Architect (1985 Edition)
  - Part 1 Agreement—Preliminary Design
  - Part 2 Agreement—Final Design

The two agreements within each document are intended to be used in sequence. It is anticipated that the parties will first enter into their respective Part 1 agreements. Services provided under these agreements include preliminary design, cost estimating, scheduling, and value engineering services for the project in order to determine its scope and feasibility. If the client elects to proceed with the project, the parties then enter into their respective Part 2 agreements. Part 2 agreements provide for completion of the project's design and its construction. It is important to note that the Part 1 and Part 2 agreements within each document do not break the project down into the traditional five phases (schematic design, design development, construction documents, bidding or negotiation, and construction administration) found in other AIA documents.

By executing a Part 1 agreement, the parties are not bound to execute their Part 2 agreement. The client is free to contract with other parties for remaining services on the project. It is expected, however, that prior to execution of the Part 1 agreement, the parties would have substantially agreed on the terms of their respective Part 2 agreements, and that the parties would continue their relationship through to completion of the project.

The Part 1 agreement in each of the documents is organized into ten articles. These articles include provisions related to the obligations of the participants, scheduling, terms of compensation, arbitration, and other guidelines for the early stages of the project. The Part 2 agreements in the Owner-Design/Builder document (A191) and Design/Builder-Contractor document (A491) each consist of fourteen articles that provide information on insurance requirements, changes or corrections to the work, compensation, scheduling, and other issues related to the final design and construction of the project. The Part 2 agreement in the Design/Builder-Architect document (B901) consists of ten articles, lacking only the four articles found in the previous two documents which deal with matters wholly unrelated to the architect.

These documents are intended for use as a family of documents. Each pair of agreements corresponds with the agreements between the other parties. Changes to one document, therefore, must be followed through in each of the other agreements to ensure that the documents are consistent.

Finally, each document is accompanied by an instruction sheet with general information about the purpose, use, and execution of each agreement. Cautionary comments are also provided to alert the parties that licensing, registration, and corporate practice laws vary from one jurisdiction to the next, and that consultation with appropriate legal, insurance, and management advisors is recommended to determine the extent of restrictions, if any, on the use of design/build practices in the jurisdiction in which the project is located.

Basic Relationship and Duties of the Parties

The AIA documents assume a design/build organizational structure such as that depicted in Figure 12.1. In this Type D arrangement, the client contracts with a single design/build firm for all design and construction services required for the project. This is accomplished using Document A191. The design/build firm then subcontracts separately with a contractor, using Document A491, for all required construction services, and with an architect, using Document B901, for all required design services.

These documents could also be used on projects in Type C joint ventures. In this design/build arrangement, the architect and contractor join forces to form a joint venture that provides all design and construction services for the project. A separate joint venture agreement would exist between the architect and the contractor creating the joint venture. The joint venture would essentially be a *pass-through arrangement*, in which the joint venture performs some services itself but subcontracts all other services to the architect and contractor. This arrangement is illustrated in Figure 12.2.

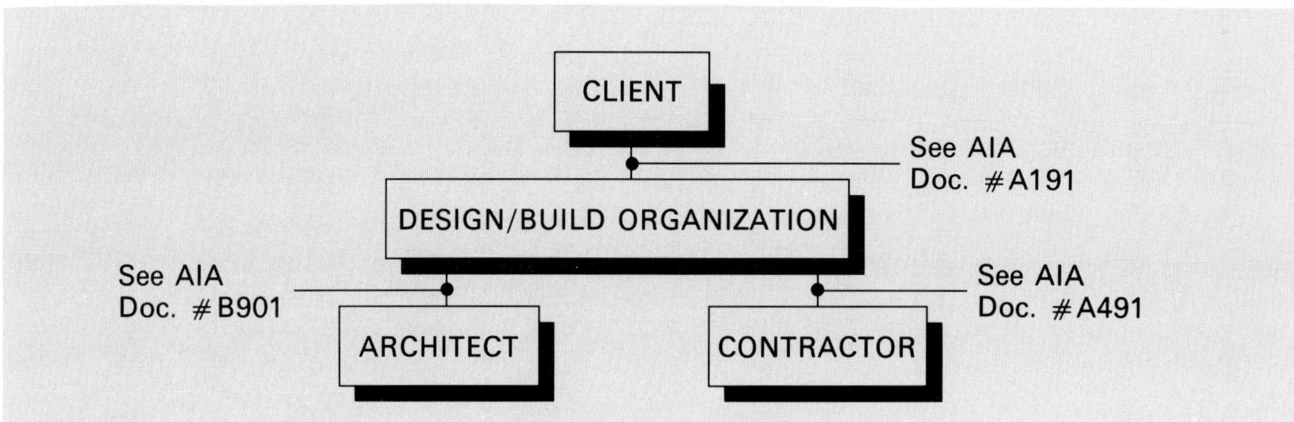

Type D Design/Build
Using AIA Standard Form Documents

Figure 12.1

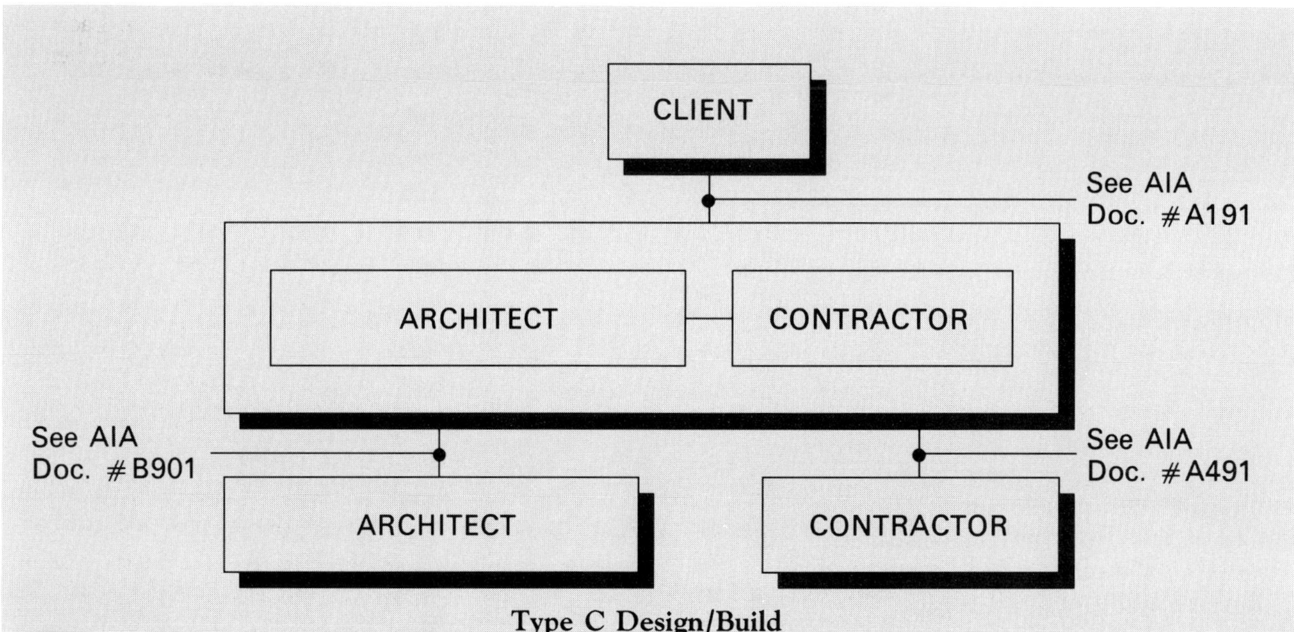

Type C Design/Build
Using AIA Standard Form Documents

Figure 12.2

AIA Document A191, Standard Form of Agreements Between Owner and Design/Builder

In the Part 1 agreement of this document, the design/builder is obligated to submit to the owner (the client) preliminary design documents prepared by qualified architects, engineers, and other professionals selected and paid by the design/builder. These preliminary design documents are to include the same type and extent of information normally found in design development documents as defined by the AIA in its traditional standard form design agreements. The design/builder is also to provide the client with a schedule and a proposed contract sum for completion of the project.

Should the client elect to proceed with the project, then under the Part 2 agreement, the design/builder is to submit to the client construction documents prepared by architects, engineers, and other design professionals selected and paid by the design/builder. This agreement has added language to make it clear that the level of information and the type of documentation to be provided in the construction documents is to be similar to that customarily required by subcontractors and approval granting authorities. Following the client's approval of the construction documents, the design/builder is to provide all labor, materials, and services required to construct the project in accordance with the construction documents.

In order to fulfill its obligations to the client, it is expected that the design/builder will contract with a contractor and an architect, using AIA Documents A491 and B901 respectively, for all of the design and construction services that the design/builder is required to provide to the client.

AIA Document A491, Standard Form of Agreements Between Design/Builder and Contractor

In the Part 1 agreement of this document, the contractor is obligated to provide the design/builder with construction cost estimates, value engineering and project scheduling services, an evaluation of program and budget requirements, and a review of alternative approaches to design and construction. If the design/builder is retained by the client to proceed with the final design and construction of the project, then under the Part 2 agreement, the contractor is obligated to provide all labor, materials, and equipment required to construct the project, and to supervise and direct the construction of the project.

It is interesting to note that Part I of the A491 design/build agreement lists a number of the same contractor services that the construction manager provides in AIA document B801 owner-construction manager agreement. However, nowhere in the Part 2 agreement of A491 is the design/build contractor obliged to "perform all the Work required by the Contract Documents" as the contractor is obligated to do under B801. Rather, the design/build contractor is obligated to "obtain the services of qualified Subcontractors and suppliers as necessary to perform the Work" and to "supervise and direct the Work."

The omission of the design/build contractor's obligation to "perform" the work in conjunction with the "construction manager" type services described in Part 1 of the A491 document make this document a bit more versatile than the B801 agreement, in that the A491 document can be used not only on projects where the contractor acts as a contractor, but also on projects where a construction manager fills the role of contractor. Unlike B801, which describes the construction manager's role in a manner that precludes it from also acting as a contractor, A491 is not as restrictive and can accommodate a party acting either as a contractor or as a construction manager/contractor. Without modification, the A491 standard form document provides a significant degree of flexibility and adaptability for use on a variety of projects.

AIA Document B901, Standard Form of Agreements Between Design/Builder and Architect

In the Part 1 agreement of this document, the architect is obligated to provide the design/builder with preliminary design documents for the project. Like the A491 agreement, the type and extent of the design documents is similar to that of design development documents required by other traditional AIA agreements. These documents consist of preliminary design drawings and outline specifications for the architectural portion of the project and for the project's structural, mechanical, and electrical systems. The preliminary design documents also include selected materials and any other project elements that may be appropriate. There is also an extensive list of services that the design/builder may ask the architect to provide, depending on the particular nature and requirements of the project.

Should the client elect to proceed with the project, then the design/builder and the architect enter into the Part 2 agreement. Under this agreement, the architect provides the design/builder with construction documents based on the preliminary design documents, and establishes in detail the requirements for the project's construction. During the construction phase, the architect is expected to visit the site to observe the project's progress and to determine if it is proceeding according to the construction documents. The architect is to provide interpretations of the construction documents and provide its opinion with respect to the project's execution or the interpretation of the construction documents. The architect is also to review and approve shop drawings submitted by the contractor. Like the Part I agreement, there is a list of services that the design/builder may ask the architect to provide, depending on the project.

Unlike traditional AIA owner-architect agreement forms, the architect is not responsible for the administration of the contractor's construction contract under the B901 design/build agreement. The architect does not act as the design/builder's representative, nor does the architect function as the conduit through which all communication with the contractor flows, as is typically the case on traditionally structured projects. In the B901 design/build agreement, the architect does not review the contractor's applications for payment, nor make recommendations or issue certificates for payment to the design/builder. Furthermore, the architect does not have authority to reject work that does not conform to the contract documents, and does not review or prepare punch lists of uncompleted work. The Part 2 agreement makes it clear, by identifying all administration duties as additional services under the agreement, that the architect is not to perform any construction contract administration duties on the project as part of its basic services provided to the design/builder. If the design/builder wants the architect to provide any of these services, they must be specifically authorized or confirmed in writing by the design/builder.

It is absolutely essential to understand that this family of AIA design/build documents creates a fundamentally different set of relationships between clients, contractors, and architects from that which exists in other AIA documents. This new set of relationships is the result, of course, of the introduction of the design/build firm into the project.

One of the practical difficulties in using this family of AIA design/build documents is getting all parties to acknowledge this new set of relationships. It is especially critical for the architect to "play by the rules" since, in design/build project delivery, the architect is no longer special advisor or representative to the client. This is stated clearly in documents A191 and B901.

In each of the Part 1 and Part 2 owner-design/builder agreements in Document A191, the following language appears:

> *Design services shall be performed by qualified architects, engineers, and other professionals selected and paid by the Design/Builder. The professional obligations of such persons shall be undertaken and performed in the interest of the Design/Builder.... Nothing contained in [Part 1 or Part 2] shall create any professional obligation or contractual relationship between such persons and the Owner.*

This express statement regarding the absence of any fiduciary, professional, or contractual relationship between the client and the architect is carried through to the design/builder's agreement with the architect in both Part 1 and Part 2 of the design/builder-architect agreements, Document B901:

> *The professional obligations of the Architect are undertaken and performed in the interest of the Design/Builder. Nothing contained in [Part 1 or Part 2] shall create any professional obligation or contractual relationship between the Architect and the Owner....*

Curiously, similar statements are not found in either the Part 1 or Part 2 agreements of the A491 document between the design/builder and the contractor. One reason for this may be the historical distinction between the fiduciary relationship of trust and confidence expected to exist between the architect and the client, and the more commercial relationship which exists between the client and the contractor on traditionally structured projects. Therefore, it is appropriate, if not required by law, to include a disclaimer in the architect's agreements, but not in the contractor's.

To the extent that local law in a given jurisdiction does not mandate a fiduciary, professional, or contractual relationship between an architect and a client, then the language quoted in these standard form documents should be sufficient to satisfy any legal disclosure requirements.

Despite the language in these agreements, however, clients often still expect the architect to represent their interests on the project. Except where mandated by applicable codes, the design/build architect is not representing the interests of the client. Clients may tend to focus on the design/build method of project delivery principally from a commercial perspective, such as speeding the total design/construction process, reducing total costs, and creating a single point of responsibility. Many clients will not acknowledge the absence of both a contractual and professional relationship between the client and the architect, and may indeed express shock, even outrage, that the architect is no longer acting in the client's interest. Some clients may even threaten expulsion from the project if the architect does not "accept responsibility" for his or her role on the project "like other architects." Architects themselves may have difficulty understanding and conforming their activities to their new role on a design/build project, feeling that by refusing to advise the client, they are somehow shirking their professional responsibilities.

Architects should be prepared to respond to client demands with cogent answers and a solid understanding of their role on design/build projects based on these AIA documents. Architects must be sensitive to the nontraditional role they play on design/build projects, and to refuse to permit the design/builder or the client to create a situation in which the architect is performing its traditional role. This only confuses the roles the parties play and increases the chances that if something does go wrong, the architect will be directly responsible to the client. Fortunately, for those design professionals using AIA documents A191 and A491, the language is stated clearly in the agreements to document and support their new role.

Through carefully drafted contract language, these AIA documents also address and clarify the issue of licensing and registration requirements. Some courts have distinguished contract language obligating an unlicensed party to "furnish" or "provide" design services from language obligating that party to "perform" the same services. These courts feel that an unlicensed party is not legally permitted to perform such services, but can furnish or provide design services if it is clear that required design services will be performed by licensed individuals subcontracted to the party obligated to provide them to the client. The obligation to provide services, the courts reason, means only that the party is obligated to "arrange for the procurement of" required design services by properly licensed individuals, not that the party is obligating itself to perform them.

The following language found in both Part 1 and Part 2 of the owner-design/builder A191 agreements makes it clear that design services will not be performed by the design/builder itself but by others properly qualified to do so:

> *Design services shall be performed by qualified architects, engineers, and other professionals selected and paid by the Design/Builder.*

Furthermore, the following language found in paragraph 7.6 of Part 1, and Paragraph 11.9 of Part 2 in Document A191, which discusses the design/builder's obligations to the client with respect to the design/builder's termination of the architect, make it unmistakably clear that the architect who is to perform required design services in the interest of the design/builder must be lawfully licensed:

> *In case of termination of the Architect, the Design/Builder shall provide the services of another lawfully licensed person or entity against whom the Owner makes no reasonable objection.*

The language in these standard form design/build agreements should be sufficient to satisfy licensing laws in those jurisdictions in which local law does not require a contractual relationship between the client and the party actually performing required design services for the project, but permits a third party to arrange for them to be performed by properly qualified and licensed persons or entities.

Special Considerations for Users of These Documents

This AIA family of design/build documents is a carefully coordinated and integrated package of agreements. It is well suited for use, with few modifications, on a substantial portion of design/build projects. There are, however, several rather technical issues that may arise regarding their use and interpretation which may have unintended and undesirable consequences for the parties. These include the absence of a set of general conditions, choice of governing law, and integration clauses.

Absence of Comprehensive General Conditions

It is important to note that neither the owner-design/builder document (A191), nor the design/builder-contractor document (A491), include a set of general conditions similar to the comprehensive conditions contained in AIA Document A201, General Conditions of the Contract for Construction. Rather, they are more like the abbreviated conditions found in AIA documents A107 and A117, abbreviated forms of agreement between owner and contractor. (General Conditions are a set of guidelines that define many of the rights, responsibilities, and limitations of authority of the owner and contractor, and include the general procedures governing the contractor's performance of the work.) The client using standard form AIA design/build documents, therefore, is not afforded the same comprehensive set of rights or checks with respect to the design/builder as a client has with respect to a contractor on a traditionally structured project using the traditional AIA documents such as the A201, General Conditions.

Likewise, the design/builder is not afforded a set of rights or checks with respect to the contractor when using standard form AIA design/build documents. This is due, in large part, to the fact that the architect does not provide construction administration services, nor does he or she act as the client's or design/builder's representative in design/build projects.

Contract's Governing Law

Matters related to contract formation, interpretation, and enforceability must be governed by the body of law of a particular jurisdiction. This is referred to as the *contract's governing law*. Governing law refers not to the applicability of building codes, but to the entire body of both *statutory* and *case law* (those laws established or interpreted by legislatures and courts, respectively) that exists in a given jurisdiction. In most instances, and within certain parameters, the parties themselves are free to choose which state's law shall govern. They usually do so by inserting a clause in their contract to that effect. If they don't, then the courts will decide which body of law will govern.

The AIA's design/build documents include provisions describing which state's laws shall govern. In fact, these documents establish three potentially different bodies of law to be applied in cases of dispute:

- The law of the place where the principal office of the design/builder is located
- The law of the place where the principal office of the architect is located
- The law of the place where the project is located

It is possible that all three locations may be different. Depending on the parties involved in the dispute, and whether the dispute pertains to either of the parties' Part 1 or Part 2 agreements, a potentially confusing and complicated situation may result in attempting to determine which body of law to apply to the underlying dispute. The design/builder could potentially contend with three different sets of laws to resolve its disputes—disputes which arose out of the same set of facts and circumstances! Since each state's laws may vary on any given issue, the design/builder may be faced with a situation in which the law is not applied uniformly to the same factual situation or legal issues involved in each dispute.

This confusion may be alleviated somewhat if the AIA dispute resolution provisions are followed. These provisions prohibit the *joinder of third parties* (the inclusion of a third party in an arbitration proceeding between two other parties) in arbitration hearings. The various claims by or against the design/builder would be handled, instead, in separate arbitration proceedings with the owner, architect, and contractor. While this may be of some help procedurally to the design/builder, there are other issues with which the design/builder must be concerned. For instance, even if the various states' laws are consistent with respect to a given legal issue, there is always the danger that they will be applied inconsistently by different panels of arbitrators.

If the arbitration provisions are stricken from each party's agreements, and the parties are left to the courts for resolution of their disputes; or if the arbitration provisions are not stricken but the parties consolidate their separate arbitration proceedings into one procedure, then a judge, jury, or arbitration panel faces a significant problem in attempting to sort out which of the state's law is to be applied to which factual and legal issues, and to which party. Although historically these problems have existed on projects using other AIA documents, they are greatly exacerbated with the introduction of a fourth party, the design/builder, into the design and construction process.

Integration Clause

A third consideration for design/build participants using these contract agreements is the effect that the *integration clause* contained in each of the party's Part 2 agreements has on their Part 1 agreements. An integration clause establishes that only the provisions actually contained in the agreement of which the integration clause is a part are to be included in the agreement between the parties. Its purpose is to prevent inclusion of, or reference to, prior negotiations, representations, or other agreements in interpreting the agreement or in determining the parties' respective rights and obligations under the agreement.

Integration clauses are found in the Part 2 agreements in each of the AIA standard form design/build agreements. An example of an integration clause is taken from Subparagraph 11.01.1 of Document A191:

> *Part 2 represents the entire agreement between the Owner and Design/Builder and supersedes Part 1 and prior negotiations, representations, or agreements. Part 2 may be amended only by written instrument signed by both Owner and Design/Builder.*

Each integration clause states specifically that the Part 2 agreement represents the entire agreement between the parties and supersedes the Part 1 agreement as well as prior negotiations, representations, or agreements between those parties. As if that weren't sufficient to invalidate the Part 1 agreements, similar integration clauses in each of the Part 1 agreements themselves provide that the Part 1 agreements can only be amended by a written instrument (legal document) signed by the parties. The Part 2 agreements certainly qualify as written instruments. Therefore, upon execution of the Part 2 agreements, the Part 1 agreements and each and every clause within them are superseded by the Part 2 agreements. This means that even the *survivorship provisions* contained in the arbitration clauses and the successors and assigns clauses in the Part 1 agreements, are no longer valid. This complete supersession of the Part 1 agreements may be of concern to the parties.

For instance, each Part 2 agreement's arbitration clause states that all disputes between the parties arising out of the Part 2 agreement shall be decided by arbitration. But the clause does not address disputes arising from the parties' Part 1 agreement. Since the Part 2 agreement supersedes the Part 1 agreement, and since the Part 2 agreement's arbitration clause says nothing about how to resolve Part 1 disputes, the parties are left with no agreement on how to resolve Part 1 disputes once the Part 2 agreement is executed.

In all jurisdictions, if the parties cannot resolve their disputes, or if they cannot agree to have their disputes settled by arbitration, then litigation may be the only alternative. It is then possible that the parties will have to litigate their Part 1 disputes, and arbitrate their Part 2 disputes—another potentially confusing situation for all parties, particularly in cases where there may be more than one governing law. It is also possible that one party may exercise some leverage over or win concessions from another, or select a forum for dispute resolution, such as its own state's courts, that is more favorable to that party's position.

Contract provisions are modified frequently by the parties during contract negotiations. As such, a danger exists in that considerable time and thought may be spent modifying portions of the Part 1 agreements, only to find that they are superseded or voided by the Part 2 agreements. For instance, the limitations established in Part I agreements concerning the design/builder's ability to use the drawings and specifications prepared by the architect may be inadvertently eliminated or made less restrictive upon execution of the Part 2 agreement.

If courts enforce the Part 2 agreement's integration clauses according to their terms and in accordance with existing legal theories applicable to those clauses, confusion may result. Appropriate modifications to these documents could, of course, reduce or eliminate the confusion.

NSPE Standard Form Design/Build Document

The National Society of Professional Engineers (NSPE) was founded in 1935. Like the AIA, the NSPE publishes an extensive set of standard form construction documents that are used throughout the industry. Among those documents is an agreement intended for use on design/build projects titled *NSPE Document 2802-1, Standard Form of Agreement Between Owner and Engineer-Contractor for Design and Construction Services* (1977 Edition). This document is reproduced in its entirety in Appendix D.

Basic Structure and Organization of the Document

Unlike the AIA documents, each of which is composed of two agreements—one for preliminary design and budgeting and a second for final design and construction—NSPE Document 2802-1 is a single agreement between the client and the engineer-contractor for all preliminary design, final design, and construction services for the project. Services listed in the 20 articles that make up the body of this agreement include providing all supplies, materials, equipment, and labor required for the design and construction of the project. The engineer-contractor's design services include preparation of schematic design studies, design development documents, working drawings and specifications, and review of all shop drawings during construction.

Four exhibits and four appendices are attached to this agreement. The four exhibits provide forms for work orders, change orders, progress payments, and certificates of substantial completion. The four appendices include provisions regarding the basis for charges for engineering and design services, charges for construction services, other documents intended to be included as part of the agreement between the parties, and provisions concerning resolution of disputes. It is expected that the parties to this document will prepare their own exhibits and appendices according to the instructions in the guide sheet to this document.

Basic Relationship and Duties of the Parties

The NSPE document assumes either a Type C design/build arrangement like that shown in Figure 12.3, or a Type D arrangement illustrated in Figure 12.4. In each case, the client contracts with a single design/build firm for all design and construction services required for the project. The difference between the Type C and D arrangements served by the AIA documents (Figures 12.1 and 12.2), and the Type C and D arrangements served by the NSPE document (Figures 12.3 and 12.4), is that under the NSPE agreement, the design/build firm does not subcontract out to a separate engineer or contractor the design or construction services required for the project. The AIA, which does contemplate design/build subcontracting to third parties, publishes forms of agreement between the design/builder and third parties (A491 and B901), while the NSPE does not publish forms of agreement between the engineer-contractor as design/builder, and third parties.

Figure 12.3

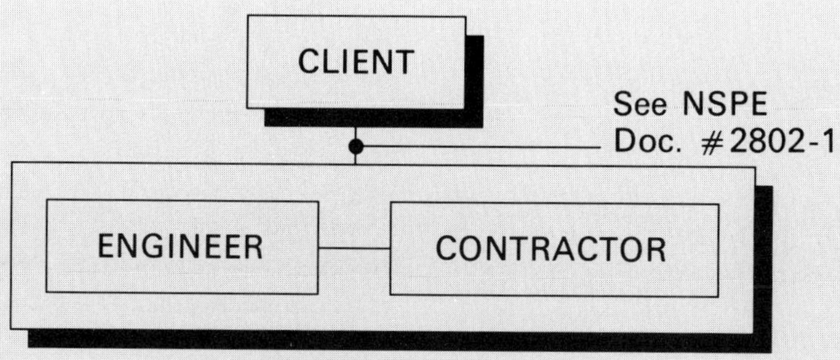

Type C Design/Build
Using NSPE Standard Form Document

Figure 12.4

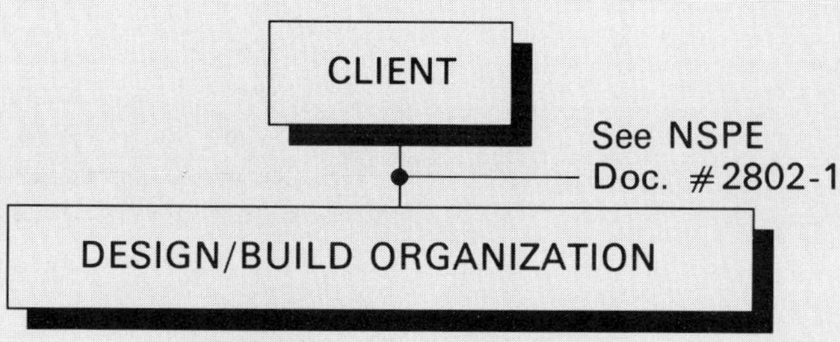

Type D Design/Build
Using NSPE Standard Form Document

Like the AIA documents, the NSPE document creates a fundamentally different set of relationships between clients, engineers, and contractors from that which traditionally exists in the industry. For example, the basic structure of the NSPE agreement assumes that the engineer-contractor is a joint venture or a single design/build firm. As such, it makes no sense, nor does the agreement provide, for the engineer-contractor or the engineer component of the engineer-contractor, to have any connection with the administration of the construction-related portions of the agreement or of the engineer-contractor's conformance with the requirements of the contract documents. While the engineer-contractor is obligated by the agreement to complete the project in accordance with the contract documents, there is no party advising the client as to whether or not this is happening, or to what extent the engineer-contractor should be paid for its services at any point during the construction phase. The engineer-contractor does not act as the client's representative or in the client's interest during the construction phase.

The absence of a fiduciary or professional relationship between the client and the engineer-contractor may, as a matter of good business, or by legal mandate, have to be disclosed to the client. However, unlike the AIA documents, which state clearly that there is no professional or fiduciary relationship between the client and the architect, there is no similar disclosure in the NSPE document informing the client of the absence of a professional or fiduciary relationship between the client and the engineering component of the design/build firm. This may be a problem in those jurisdictions in which such disclosure is required, but it can be solved easily by inclusion of appropriate contract language in the document.

Answers to questions concerning licensing requirements can be extracted from this document. Paragraph 3.2 of Document 2802-1 draws a distinction between the engineer-contractor's obligation to "provide, furnish and perform" engineering and design services, and merely to "provide and furnish" the labor and services necessary to construct the project. It seems to be the parties' intent in this document that the engineer-contractor actually perform required design services itself, not provide them through others. This language would therefore require that the engineering component of the design/build firm be properly licensed and registered, and that subcontracting design services out to others, whether or not they are properly licensed, is not what the agreement contemplates. In some jurisdictions, there may be questions as to whether the contractor component of the design/build firm must also be properly licensed in the appropriate design discipline.

In this NSPE document, the engineering and design services that the engineer-contractor is obligated to perform include schematic design studies, design development documents, and working drawings and specifications "to the extent required for the performance of the work." This contract language suggests a somewhat more subjective standard by which to assess the documentation and level of information required than the language contained in the AIA documents, which state that the documentation and information be similar to that customarily needed or required by subcontractors and approval granting authorities. Since the engineer-contractor is also performing the work, the engineer-contractor can, to a significant degree, determine the extent and type of information to be included in the drawings and specifications.

It is also interesting to note that the definition of "contract documents" in Article 2 of the NSPE agreement does not include drawings and specifications prepared by the engineer-contractor unless those are specifically enumerated as such by the parties in Appendix C of the NSPE agreement. If the parties do not state clearly in the agreement whether or not the drawings and specifications to be prepared by the engineer-contractor are included in the definition of "contract documents," then all references in the agreement to "contract documents" would exclude the drawings and specifications. This interpretation may be unintended by the parties, and may not be enforced by the courts or by arbitrators when attempting to resolve disputes.

During the construction phase of the project, Paragraph 11.1 of the NSPE document requires the engineer-contractor to perform the work in accordance with the contract documents. Indeed, in Paragraph 9.1 the engineer-contractor warrants that it shall do so. However, since the engineer-contractor can, to a significant degree, determine the content of the contract documents (assuming the definition of "contract documents" includes the drawings and specifications prepared by the engineer-contractor), then the engineer-contractor can effectively limit the extent of its obligations and limit the risks associated with its failure to perform in accordance with the requirements of the contract documents, although on most projects there are practical limits to how little need be included in the contract documents.

Special Considerations for Users of This Document

One of the practical difficulties encountered using design/build standard form documents is getting the parties to conform their actions to the terms of the agreements. This problem may be exacerbated on projects using the NSPE document since, unlike the AIA documents, the contract language of the NSPE document does not indicate in express terms the nontraditional nature of the engineer's role on the project. The parties' attention is therefore not drawn to the matter.

There are several other important issues connected with the use or adaptation of this document to a specific project which warrant some consideration during the drafting and negotiation process.

Absence of Comprehensive General Conditions

It is important to note that the set of general conditions or obligations by the engineer-contractor in this document is not nearly as detailed as those found in documents for traditionally structured projects. As a result, the client is not afforded as comprehensive a set of rights or checks with respect to the engineer-contractor as the client might otherwise enjoy. This is due, in large part, to the fact that there is no party administering the construction contract on behalf of the client who is in a position to enforce compliance with its terms during the course of construction.

Compensation

Paragraph 5.1 describes the engineer-contractor's compensation as the "contract sum of" some dollar figure. This is a lump sum fee, or a single amount for all design and construction services required by the NSPE agreement for the project, and is also intended to cover all charges for the services described in appendices A and B of the NSPE agreement. The written instructions regarding use of these appendices, however, describe a number of other forms of compensation other than a lump sum amount, such as a percentage of cost, actual payroll cost multiplied by a factor, payroll cost plus a percentage, or payroll cost plus a fixed fee. Paragraph 5.1 of the NSPE agreement must be coordinated with these appendices, therefore, so that the provisions in the agreement concerning the engineer-contractor's compensation for the project are consistent.

Insurance

According to the terms of Paragraph 13.1, the engineer-contractor is obligated to indemnify the client against certain losses occurring during performance of the work that result from the negligence of the engineer-contractor. The financial extent of the indemnification obligation is limited by the amount of insurance coverage that the engineer-contractor is obligated to carry for the project. This clause requires the client to carefully review the types and amounts of insurance coverage required of the engineer-contractor, and the risks of loss to the client on the project.

It should be noted that there is no obligation in Article 16, which lists the various types and amounts of insurance required to be carried by the engineer-contractor, to carry Professional Liability Insurance to protect against damages for its negligent acts, errors, or omissions. The project's failure to comply with codes, handicapped access requirements, or zoning matters are also not covered by the engineer-contractor's indemnification obligation in Paragraph 13.1, or the contractor's guaranty in Paragraph 9.1, nor is the engineer-contractor required by Article 16 to carry insurance to cover losses as a result of this contingency. These are risks that a client should consider when negotiating an agreement with the engineer-contractor using the NSPE standard form design/build document.

Assignment Clause

An *assignment* clause prohibits either party from assigning or transferring its contractual obligations to a third party, or to assign the entire agreement to another party. There is no clause in the NSPE agreement prohibiting assignment of the agreement by either party. The absence of an assignment clause, therefore, permits the parties to do so at their discretion.

For instance, under this NSPE document, the client could assign the agreement to another party, thus establishing a new "client" for the engineer-contractor. The engineer-contractor, in turn, could assign its obligation to provide or perform design and construction services to other design professionals and contractors. Neither of these situations is contemplated by the terms of the agreement, and any attempt by either party to take advantage of the absence of this clause may have serious consequences for the other.

Integration Clause

Furthermore, unlike the AIA standard form design/build documents, there is no integration clause in the NSPE document. The absence of an integration clause indicates that the NSPE agreement was not intended by the parties to be a complete expression of their respective rights, duties, and obligations on the project. Prior agreements, written or oral, as long as they can be proved, can later be used to help shape the agreement or to shade its interpretation.

Corporate Seal

Finally, a *corporate seal* appears above the signature line in this document. In some jurisdictions, certain legal consequences may be attached to a "sealed instrument" or a document that is "under seal." For instance, a contract under seal in Massachusetts has the effect of extending the statute of limitations. This clause should be reviewed to determine the effect, if any, that a sealed instrument may have on the agreement, and specifically on the guaranty and indemnification clauses in the agreement.

AGC Standard Form Design/Build Documents

The Associated General Contractors of America (AGC) is the largest representative organization of contractors in the United States. The AGC publishes a set of seven comprehensive standard form design/build documents that are some of the most widely used sets of documents in the industry. Some of these documents are used independently, some in conjunction with others. These documents are reproduced in their entirety in Appendix D and include:

- AGC Document No. 400, Preliminary Design-Build Agreement (1980 Edition)
- AGC Document No. 410, Standard Form of Design-Build Agreement and General Conditions Between Owner and Contractor (1982 Edition)
- AGC Document No. 415, Standard Form of Design-Build Agreement and General Conditions Between Owner and Contractor (Where the Basis of Compensation is a Lump Sum) (1986 Edition)
- AGC Document No. 420, Standard Form of Agreement Between Contractor and Architect (1985 Edition)
- AGC Document No. 430, Conditions Between Contractor and Subcontractor for Design-Build (1982 Edition)
- AGC Document No. 450, Standard Design-Build Subcontract Agreement with Subcontractor Not Providing Design (1983 Edition)
- AGC Document No. 450-1, Standard Design-Build Subcontract Agreement with Subcontractor Providing Design (1983 Edition)

Basic Structure and Organization of the Documents

AGC Document No. 400

Document No. 400 is a simple two-page agreement that describes the contractor's responsibilities for furnishing the design of the project. It provides for design services rendered in three traditional phases: schematic design, design development, and working drawings and specifications. This document contemplates development by the contractor of a guaranteed maximum price (GMP) for the design and construction of the project based on the completed design development documents. The working drawings and specifications are intended to confirm the GMP, not to act as the basis for establishing the GMP.

Document No. 400 is intended to cover only required design services. If the client elects to proceed with the project after the contractor has provided the working drawings and specifications, then it is expected that the client and the contractor will enter into a second written agreement regarding construction services. This second agreement is to be attached to Document No. 400 as an exhibit. By virtue of this arrangement, the client has the opportunity to terminate its relationship with the contractor by merely striking the language obligating it to contract with the contractor for construction services and to proceed with the project using another contractor. In this manner, Document No. 400 is similar to AIA Document A191.

Document 400, which covers only the contractor's pre-construction services, isn't really appropriate for use with the other design/build documents, since the two other agreements between the contractor and owner (documents 410 and 415) include essentially the same design services as those described in Document No. 400. Rather, Document No. 400 is intended to be used with traditionally structured standard form construction contracts, whether published by the AGC or other organizations, that deal only with construction phase services.

AGC Document Nos. 410 *and* 415

In the documents numbered 410 and 415, the client contracts with the contractor for all required design and construction services. Document No. 410 is organized into 16 articles; Document No. 415 has 13 articles. The three additional articles in Document No. 410 result from the establishment in Article 5 of a guaranteed maximum price. Article 6 in Document No. 415 describes the contractor's lump sum compensation for performing services and constructing the project. The remaining twelve articles in each document address issues such as identification of the construction team and the responsibilities of the parties, scheduling, change procedures, insurance and indemnification obligations, restrictions on assignment and choice of governing law, miscellaneous provisions (to be completed by the parties), procedures for resolving disputes by arbitration or, if necessary, termination of the agreement.

Unlike each of the three AIA documents in which the Part 1 agreements provide for design services to be performed only through preliminary design, AGC Document No. 410 states that design services be provided through completion of working drawings and specifications. In the AIA standard form design/build documents, this latter activity is performed in the Part 2 agreements.

The pre-construction services described in documents 410 and 415 are divided into three phases: schematic design studies, design development documents, and working drawings and specifications. The documents numbered 410 and 415 also describe the contractor's responsibilities regarding the construction of the project. Since the contractor has either agreed with the client in Document No. 410 on a guaranteed maximum price (GMP) for the project, or has agreed with the owner in Document No. 415 on a lump sum fee for the design and construction of the project, the contractor does not provide the client with any cost estimating or value engineering services in connection with the project. It follows that since the extent of the client's financial obligation is known and agreed to in advance in the contract, there is little reason for the client to require these services of the contractor.

Furthermore, there is nothing in the AGC owner-contractor documents (numbers 400, 410, and 415), such as exists in Subparagraphs 2.1.1 of the AIA documents, disclaiming any contractual, professional, or fiduciary relationship between the owner and the design professional retained by the contractor. The instructions clearly recommend consultation with insurance advisors, especially with respect to the implications of errors and omissions on liability insurance.

AGC Document No. 420

Document No. 420 is used in conjunction with documents 410 and 415. With minor modifications it is equally appropriate for use with other design professionals. It is organized into twelve articles that provide a description of the architect's and the contractor's responsibilities, the architect's compensation, changes in the work, contract time scheduling, ownership rights and use of the documents prepared by the architect, termination procedures, insurance for the architect, indemnification, arbitration, and other provisions regarding the extent of the agreement between the contractor and the architect and the parties' choice of governing law.

Document No. 420 states in its instruction sheet that it is for use with Document No. 410. Although it doesn't indicate so in the instruction sheet (due, most likely, to an earlier publication date), it would also seem appropriate to use Document No. 420 with Document No. 415. The instructions suggest consultation with an attorney and with insurance carriers if documents are to be modified. There is also a statement to the effect that nothing contained in the documents is intended to conflict with local, state, or federal laws or regulations.

AGC Document No. 430

Document No. 430 is the conditions of the contract between the contractor and the subcontractor which determine the subcontractor's obligations on the project. This document also establishes general administrative procedures between the contractor and the subcontractor.

There are fifteen articles in Document No. 430 that discuss typical contractor-subcontractor topics defining the commercial terms, the respective rights and obligations of the parties, the performance of the work, and various administrative matters. Like Document 420, Document No. 430 also includes a set of instructions to contractors concerning its use with other AGC design/build documents. Document No. 430 states in its instruction sheet that it is intended to be used with documents 450 and 450-1. It should also be noted that Document No. 430 states specifically that the conditions included in this document differ from those in Document No. 410. If these two documents are used together, a careful review and modification of the conditions in one or both of the standard form documents would be warranted. The instructions recommend legal consultation if the document is to be modified, as well as professional advice concerning insurance matters. These instructions also state that the provisions in the documents should comply with local, state, and federal laws and regulations.

AGC Document Nos. 450 and 450-1

The documents numbered 450 and 450-1 are forms of agreement between the contractor and each of his or her subcontractors. In Document No. 450, the subcontractor performs in his or her traditional capacity and does not provide design services. In Document 450-1, the subcontractor does provide design services. Each document contains seven articles that include provisions describing the scope of work and the subcontractor's obligations, project scheduling, changes in the subcontractor's work, miscellaneous provisions regarding contractor approval of the subcontractor's work, allocations of costs for correcting unacceptable work, subcontractor's compensation, insuring the subcontractor during the life of the project, and establishing the contract's governing law.

The only differences between these two documents is that in Document 450-1, there are a few additions to the text which recognize the subcontractor's obligation to provide design services. In Paragraph 1.3 of Article 1, two clauses are added which state that the subcontractor is to "furnish by properly licensed and qualified architects or engineers, all necessary professional architectural and engineering design services for the design of the [subcontractor's portion of the project]" and that the subcontractor is to submit in a timely manner to the contractor, design development and working drawings, shop drawings, specifications, and other data for the subcontractor's portion of the project. Article 2 includes an obligation on the subcontractor's part to provide necessary personnel to complete the design of the subcontractor's portion of the project. Finally, Paragraph 6.3 of Article 6 obligates the subcontractor to provide a certificate of insurance to the contractor in a stated amount "to protect himself and the Contractor from claims arising out of the performance of professional services caused by any errors, omissions, or negligent acts for which he is legally liable."

Basic Relationship and Duties of the Parties

AGC documents 400, 410, and 415 clearly contemplate a Type B design/build organizational structure like that depicted in Figure 12.5. In this arrangement, the client contracts with the contractor for all design and construction services required for the project. Using Document No. 420, the contractor then subcontracts separately with the architect (or with any other design professional) for all required design services. Using documents 430 and 450, the contractor also subcontracts with the various subcontractors for required construction services.

A variation of this Type B structure is illustrated in Figure 12.6. Here, the contractor subcontracts with the design professional for only a portion of the design services required for the project, and subcontracts through document nos. 430 and 450-1 with one or more subcontractors who provide design services through separate design professionals for their respective portions of the project.

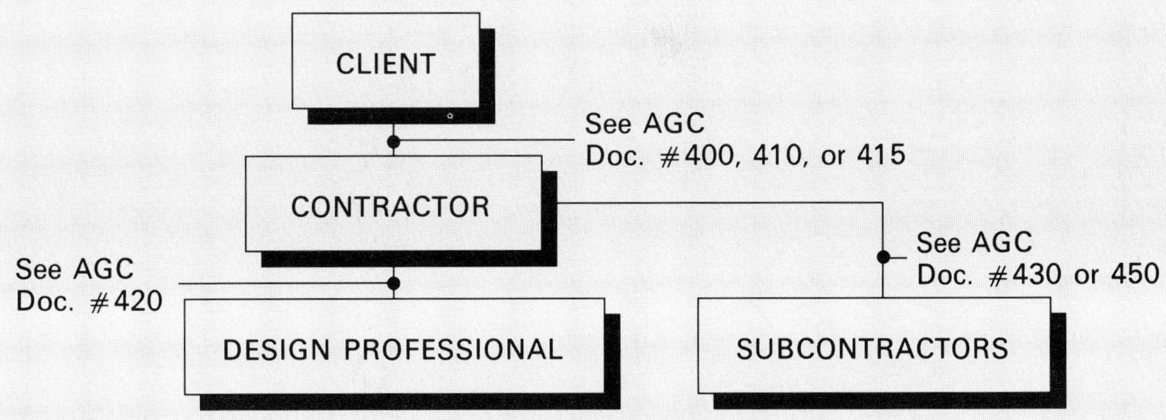

Type B Design/Build
Using AGC Standard Form Documents

Figure 12.5

A third organizational structure suggested by documents numbered 430 and 450-1 is described in Figure 12.7 in which only a portion of the project is constructed on a Type B design/build basis. The remaining portion of the project is organized in a traditional manner. Using this approach, the client retains a design professional, as he or she would on any traditionally structured project, to provide design services to the client for all but certain portions of the project. The client then contracts separately with the contractor to provide required construction services for the project, and also to provide, through subcontractors retained by the contractor, design services for certain portions of the project not included in the services provided by the client's design professional.

Regardless of whether the contractor or the client retains the design professional, in either case a subcontractor to the contractor acts as a design/build subcontractor providing design and construction services for its portion of the project. This organizational form is used fairly often in certain building types such as speculative office buildings, in which the client or the contractor may retain the services of a design professional for the architectural, structural, and selected portions of the project, while the contractor provides, through its mechanical/electrical subcontractor, and with or without assistance from the design professional, required design and construction services for this portion of the project.

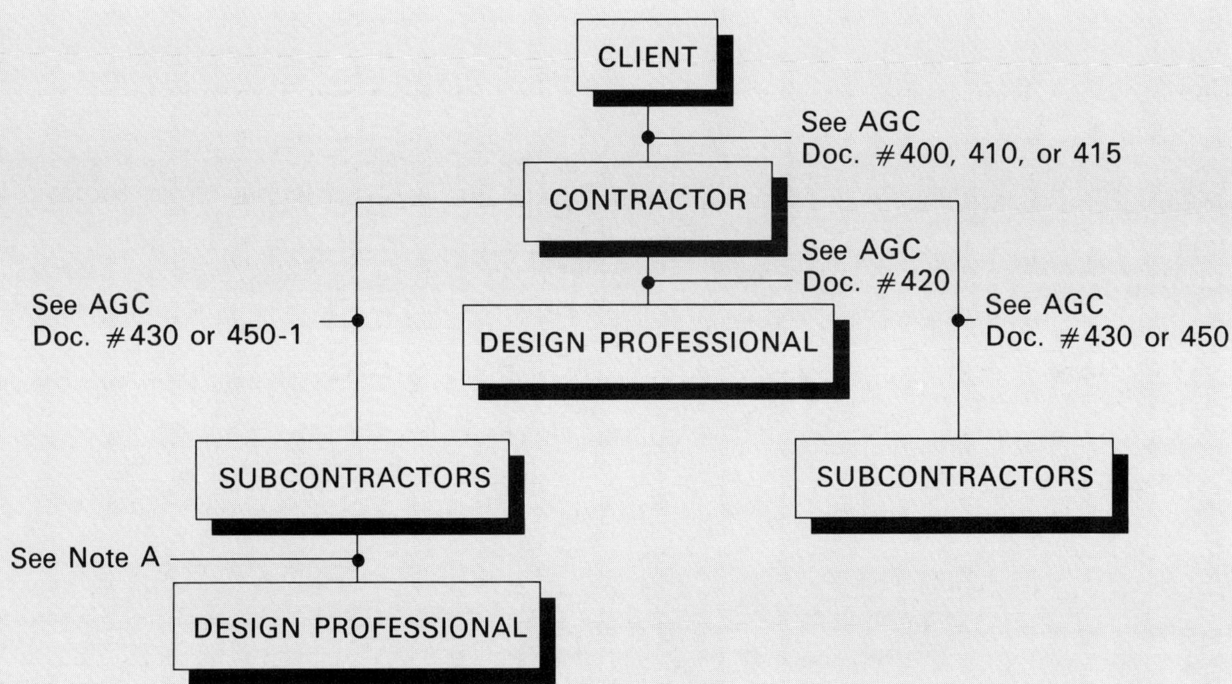

Type B Design/Build
Using AGC Standard Form Documents

Note A: The AGC does not publish a contractor-design professional agreement.

Figure 12.6

Unlike the AIA documents, the AGC owner-contractor documents (numbers 400, 410, and 415) do not contain any disclaimer regarding the absence of a professional or fiduciary relationship between the owner and the design professional, whether that design professional is retained by the contractor or by a subcontractor. While documents 410 and 415 state that design services will be "furnished" by the contractor pursuant to an agreement between the contractor and the design professional, neither of those documents, nor documents 400 or 420, is intended to create any contractual, professional, or fiduciary relationship between the client and the design professional. As such, a disclaimer to this effect may be necessary to avoid confusion later in the project.

Although knowledgeable parties will be aware of licensing, registration, and corporate practice issues in design/build, some standard form documents are more explicit than others in stating their requirements. For instance, the documents numbered 410 and 415 refer specifically to the contractor's obligation regarding design services as "furnishing" such services according to an agreement between the contractor and the design professional. Those jurisdictions that distinguish between "furnishing" and "performing" services would likely determine that the contractor was not practicing design without a license. Document No. 400, however, does not make a such a statement, although it does indicate that the various studies, designs, and other documents will be "prepared by the Architect/Engineer." But the "Architect/Engineer" could be a component of the contractor, in which case the courts may require that the contractor be licensed in design.

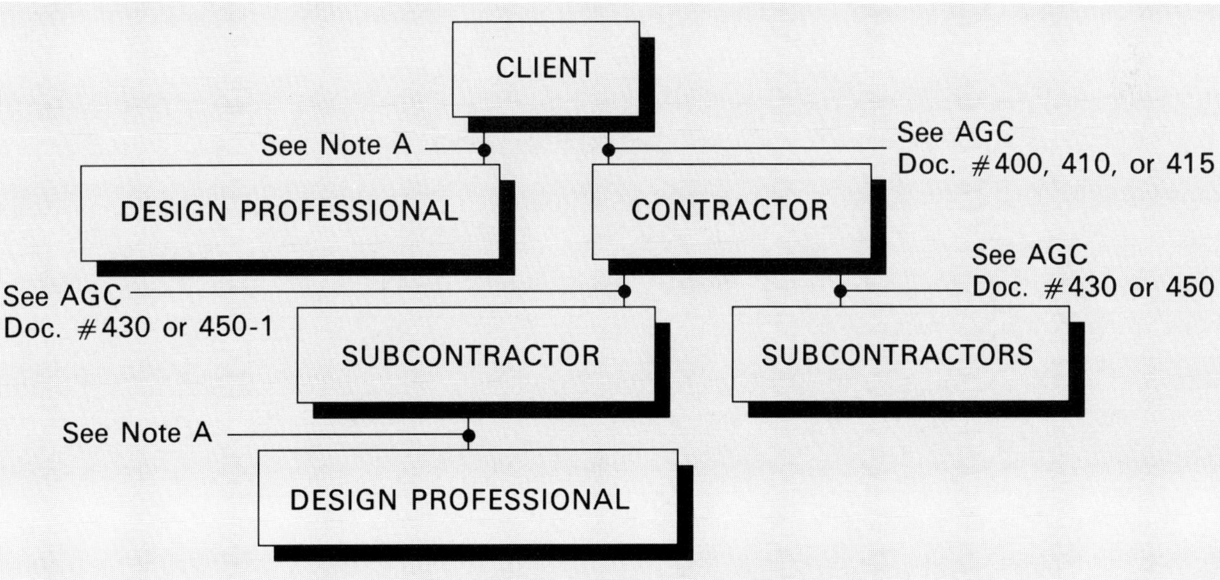

Type B Design/Build (a portion of the project)
Using AGC Standard Form Documents

Note A: The AGC does not publish a contractor-design professional agreement.

Figure 12.7

Although the three agreements between the contractor and the client (documents 400, 410, and 415) do not indicate that the design professionals retained by the contractor must be licensed, Document No. 450-1, the agreement between contractor and subcontractor where the subcontractor is to provide design services, does state that the subcontractor will provide necessary design services "by properly licensed and qualified architects or engineers." It is curious that this statement is included in a subcontract agreement and not in the principal agreement between the client and the contractor. It provides further evidence that the parties agreed that the contractor itself will not be providing design services of the sort for which a license is required, but that these services are to be subcontracted by the contractor to others who are properly licensed.

Special Considerations for Users of These Documents

It is critical for all parties using standard form design/build documents to conform their activities to the nontraditional roles established by these documents. It may be even more critical on a project using AGC documents than one using AIA documents, since the AIA documents define more explicitly the new role of the design professional on a design/build project and his or her contractual and professional limitations. Clients who ignore changes in the relationships created by these documents but, rather, view use of the design/build approach as a convenient vehicle to speed construction, reduce costs, and create a single point of responsibility, will likely have difficulty accepting the design professional's distant relationship to the client on these projects. Parties who have a clear understanding of their roles and who conform to the AGC documents will substantially reduce the incidence of disputes.

The AGC documents are a very comprehensive set of design/build documents since they include subcontractor agreements and their associated general conditions. They provide an even broader spectrum of standard form agreements for use on design/build projects than the AIA. However, as with any set of documents, they have their shortcomings, and use of AGC standard form design/build documents may have unintended or undesirable consequences for the parties.

Absence of Comprehensive General Conditions

Like the AIA and NSPE documents, there is no comprehensive set of general conditions in the AGC documents governing the contractor's obligations to the client. The general conditions that are included are quite abbreviated in nature. Clients must understand that they are not afforded as comprehensive a set of rights or checks with respect to the contractor under an AGC design/build project as they would likely have under a traditionally structured project, in which the documents recognize the traditional role of the design professional as the client's independent representative.

Establishment of Guaranteed Maximum Price in Document No. 410

The documents numbered 410 and 415 are both standard form agreements and general conditions between the owner (client) and the contractor. However, in Document No. 410, the contractor establishes a GMP for the project, while in Document No. 415, the owner and contractor agree on a lump sum amount for the contractor's compensation. These two documents are similar in most other respects.

Document No. 410 may be a bit confusing to parties in one rather significant way. In Paragraph 6.1, the contractor guarantees the client that the maximum price of the project will not exceed a stated amount, and that this amount will be called the Guaranteed Maximum Price. This paragraph is to be completed by the parties at the time of the contract's execution.

However, Subparagraph 2.1.2 states that during the second phase of the project, the contractor is to prepare design development documents. The paragraph goes on to state that these design development documents are to be "the basis to establish a Guaranteed Maximum Price for the design and construction of the Project."

How can the design development documents be used as the basis for determining the guaranteed maximum price at the beginning of the project, when the design development documents will not be prepared until some later point in time? Appropriate modification of this document at the time of its negotiation and execution will be required to clarify this incongruity.

Use of Document No. 430 with Document No. 450-1

Document No. 430, Conditions Between Contractor and Subcontractor for Design-Build, indicates in its instructions that it is intended for use with Document No. 450-1, Standard Design-Build Subcontract Agreement with Subcontractor Providing Design (as well as with Document No. 450 in which the subcontractor does not provide the design but acts in a traditional subcontractor's role on the project). Likewise, Document No. 450-1 indicates that it is to be used in conjunction with Document No. 430.

As previously indicated, Document No. 450-1 requires the subcontractor to furnish design services by properly licensed architects and engineers. This document does not require the subconsultant's architect or engineer to provide any services during construction, including contract administration responsibilities with respect to the subconsultant's subcontract, interpreting its own documents, or reviewing shop drawings of its own design work. However, the contractor's architect/engineer in Article 3 of Document No. 430 does have at least some of these responsibilities and authorities.

In Article 3 of Document No. 430, the contractor's architect/engineer has the authority to reject work that does not conform to the subcontractor's subcontract. Usually the design professional who prepared the design documents makes that judgment, rather than a third party. Notwithstanding, it may be useful for a party other than the party who is responsible for the construction of the work, to judge conformance of the work with the design requirements. To the extent that this is true, it is interesting that these documents do not let the subcontractor monitor the construction of its own design work as the contractor is permitted to do under its contract with the client.

It also appears, in Article 3 of Document No. 430, that the contractor's architect/engineer is to review shop drawings for conformance with the design concept and the information given in the subcontract. Of course, the design concept was prepared by the subcontractor's architect or engineer, not the contractor's. It seems more sensible for the party who created and developed the design concept to judge whether or not another's performance is consistent with the design concept.

On the other hand, Article 3 of Document No. 430 does make clear that the contractor's architect/engineer is to provide interpretations of the drawings and specifications only. The drawings and specifications are described elsewhere in the conditions as those documents furnished to the subcontractor by the contractor. As such, they do not include the designs of the subcontractor's architects or engineers. Therefore, the contractor's architect/engineer is not to provide interpretations of the subcontractor's design work. But since the subcontractor's agreement with the contractor does not indicate that the subcontractor's architect's or engineers are to provide such services, then who is? As a practical matter, in order to reject work of the subcontractor that does not conform to the subcontract, the contractor's architect/engineer must, of necessity, interpret the design work of the subcontractor.

While the role of the contractor's architect/engineer as described in Document No. 430 seems appropriate with respect to subcontractors not providing design services and using Document No. 450, the interplay between the contractor's architect/engineer and the subcontractor's architects and engineers on projects using Document No. 450-1, where the subcontractor is providing design services, should be closely examined by the parties on each project and a clear understanding of their respective design professionals' roles and responsibilities should be established and articulated in the appropriate contract forms.

Differences in Contract Conditions

As noted previously, the instructions to Document No. 430 indicate that the conditions contained in that document differ from those contained in documents 410 and 415. It is likely that the contractor will want to assure him or herself that the subcontractor owes the contractor the same duties and obligations that the contractor owes to the client. A careful review of the two sets of general conditions by the parties is warranted to avoid inconsistencies or unintended results.

For instance, in documents 410 and 415, the contractor agrees to indemnify the owner for claims for certain types of bodily injury and property damage resulting from the contractor's operations. While in some respects the extent of the subcontractor's indemnification obligation to the contractor in Document No. 430 is more extensive than the contractor's obligation to the client, nonetheless the subcontractor's obligation is limited to those situations in which it is wholly or partially negligent. The contractors obligation, on the other hand, is not limited to situations in which the contractor's negligence was the cause of the injury or damage.

It is possible, therefore, that the contractor could be liable to the client under its indemnification clause for matters arising out of the non-negligent work of the subcontractor which results in loss to the client, but for which the subcontractor would not be obligated to indemnify the contractor. This is not likely to be the parties' intention. A careful review of these clauses by the contractor's legal and insurance advisors may be necessary to ensure that the contract language does not place certain parties at undue risk.

Using Nonstandard Form Documents

While the AIA, NSPE, and AGC standard form design/build documents are appropriate for use on most construction projects, clearly there are cases in which substantial modifications would have to be made to the documents, on projects for which their use is not recommended.

For example, language may need to be added to the documents used on those projects in which the design/build firm is providing financing or assuming an equity interest, or providing full turnkey services. Additionally, government agencies are typically required to comply with statutory or regulatory procurement policies that require the inclusion of mandated terms and conditions or administrative procedures.

None of the documents is likely to be appropriate for very large or complex projects such as nuclear power plants or regional utility distribution systems. On such projects, the specific responsibilities and scope of services of the design/build firm are so unique that only custom-made documents can adequately deal with the issues involved. Clients on these projects, however, often have the resources to obtain experienced and qualified individuals to ensure that the custom-made documents are sufficient for use.

While nonstandard form design/build documents may be appropriate for use on some projects, parties who are unfamiliar with the documents must use caution to review these documents and understand their implications. Of course, this holds true for any unfamiliar document. The party who is thoroughly familiar with a document is at a tremendous advantage, both in terms of increased leverage and bargaining power, and in the ability to reallocate risk to other parties.

Summary

Clients, contractors, and design professionals, particularly those involved in design/build, should use written documents to define and record their contractual agreements. There are three major national organizations that publish standard form agreements for use in a variety of construction projects including design/build: the American Institute of Architects, the National Society of Professional Engineers, and the Association of General Contractors.

The AIA publishes a set of three standard form design/build documents: Owner-Design/Builder, Design/Builder-Contractor, and Design/Builder-Architect. These two-part documents are some of the most widely used documents in the industry and are intended to be used together. They assume Type C or Type D design/build arrangements in which the client contracts with the design/build firm for design and construction services which are, in turn, performed by an architect and contractor subcontracted to the design/build firm.

The NSPE publishes a standard form agreement also for use on types C or D design/build. This document is a single agreement between the client and the engineer-contractor for all design and construction services required for the project. It is expected that four exhibits and four appendices will be attached to this document outlining provisions for payment, change orders, dispute resolutions, and so forth.

The AGC publishes a set of seven standard form documents for use on a variety of Type B design/build projects. Some of these documents are used alone, some in conjunction with other documents. Each document contains a series of articles outlining the rights and responsibilities of each party on the project.

Users of these standard form design/build documents should understand that the relationships they establish are fundamentally different from those in traditionally structured projects. As such, project participants need to acknowledge, as indeed the AIA documents do, that there is no fiduciary relationship that exists between the client and the design professional in design/build, and that often users of these documents need to decipher the contract language to determine the applicability of licensing requirements in each project. Furthermore, there are other issues unique to each set of documents that may unintentionally create problems for the document's users and which need to be considered before any agreement is signed. These include the absence of general conditions, integration clauses, choice of law and dispute resolution clauses, insurance clauses, and so forth.

Regardless, design/build participants, unless they have the resources and expertise to draft their own documents, are likely to be equitably served by the standard form agreements published by these national design professional and contractor organizations. Design/build participants, or clients and construction professionals contemplating involvement in design/build, are urged to consult with a qualified professional advisor.

Appendices

Appendix

Table of Contents

CODE OF ETHICS

For Engineers

PREAMBLE

Engineering is an important and learned profession. The members of the profession recognize that their work has a direct and vital impact on the quality of life for all people. Accordingly, the services provided by engineers require honesty, impartiality, fairness and equity, and must be dedicated to the protection of the public health, safety and welfare. In the practice of their profession, engineers must perform under a standard of professional behavior which requires adherence to the highest principles of ethical conduct on behalf of the public, clients, employers and the profession.

I. FUNDAMENTAL CANONS

Engineers, in the fulfillment of their professional duties, shall:

1. Hold paramount the safety, health and welfare of the public in the performance of their professional duties.
2. Perform services only in areas of their competence.
3. Issue public statements only in an objective and truthful manner.
4. Act in professional matters for each employer or client as faithful agents or trustees.
5. Avoid deceptive acts in the solicitation of professional employment.

II. RULES OF PRACTICE

1. Engineers shall hold paramount the safety, health and welfare of the public in the performance of their professional duties.
   a. Engineers shall at all times recognize that their primary obligation is to protect the safety, health, property and welfare of the public. If their professional judgment is overruled under circumstances where the safety, health, property or welfare of the public are endangered, they shall notify their employer or client and such other authority as may be appropriate.
   b. Engineers shall approve only those engineering documents which are safe for public health, property and welfare in conformity with accepted standards.
   c. Engineers shall not reveal facts, data or information obtained in a professional capacity without the prior consent of the client or employer except as authorized or required by law or this Code.
   d. Engineers shall not permit the use of their name or firm name nor associate in business ventures with any person or firm which they have reason to believe is engaging in fraudulent or dishonest business or professional practices.
   e. Engineers having knowledge of any alleged violation of this Code shall cooperate with the proper authorities in furnishing such information or assistance as may be required.
2. Engineers shall perform services only in the areas of their competence:
   a. Engineers shall undertake assignments only when qualified by education or experience in the specific technical fields involved.
   b. Engineers shall not affix their signatures to any plans or documents dealing with subject matter in which they lack competence, nor to any plan or document not prepared under their direction and control.
   c. Engineers may accept assignments and assume responsibility for coordination of an entire project and sign and seal the engineering documents for the entire project, provided that each technical segment is signed and sealed only by the qualified engineers who prepared the segment.
3. Engineers shall issue public statements only in an objective and truthful manner.
   a. Engineers shall be objective and truthful in professional reports, statements or testimony. They shall include all relevant and pertinent information in such reports, statements or testimony.
   b. Engineers may express publicly a professional opinion on technical subjects only when that opinion is founded upon adequate knowledge of the facts and competence in the subject matter.
   c. Engineers shall issue no statements, criticisms or arguments on technical matters which are inspired or paid for by interested parties, unless they have prefaced their comments by explicitly identifying the interested parties on whose behalf they are speaking, and by revealing the existence of any interest the engineers may have in the matters.
4. Engineers shall act in professional matters for each employer or client as faithful agents or trustees.
   a. Engineers shall disclose all known or potential conflicts of interest to their employers or clients by promptly informing them of any business association, interest, or other circumstances which could influence or appear to influence their judgment or the quality of their services.
   b. Engineers shall not accept compensation, financial or otherwise, from more than one party for services on the same project, or for services pertaining to the same project, unless the circumstances are fully disclosed to, and agreed to by, all interested parties.
   c. Engineers shall not solicit or accept financial or other valuable consideration, directly or indirectly, from contractors, their agents, or other parties in connection with work for employers or clients for which they are responsible.
   d. Engineers in public service as members, advisors or employees of a governmental body or department shall not participate in decisions with respect to professional services solicited or provided by them or their organizations in private or public engineering practice.
   e. Engineers shall not solicit or accept a professional contract from a governmental body on which a principal or officer of their organization serves as a member.
5. Engineers shall avoid deceptive acts in the solicitation of professional employment.
   a. Engineers shall not falsify or permit misrepresentation of their, or their associates', academic or professional qualifications. They shall not misrepresent or exaggerate their degree of responsibility in or for the subject matter of prior assignments. Brochures or other presentations incident to the solicitation of employment shall not misrepresent pertinent facts concerning employers, employees, associates, joint venturers or past accomplishments with the intent and purpose of enhancing their qualifications and their work.
   b. Engineers shall not offer, give, solicit or receive, either directly or indirectly, any political contribution in an amount intended to influence the award of a contract by public authority, or which may be reasonably construed by the public of having the effect or intent to influence the award of a contract. They shall not offer any gift, or other valuable consideration in order to secure work. They shall not pay a commission, percentage or brokerage fee in order to secure work except to a bona fide employee or bona fide established commercial or marketing agencies retained by them.

III. PROFESSIONAL OBLIGATIONS

1. Engineers shall be guided in all their professional relations by the highest standards of integrity.
   a. Engineers shall admit and accept their own errors when proven wrong and refrain from distorting or altering the facts in an attempt to justify their decisions.
   b. Engineers shall advise their clients or employers when they believe a project will not be successful.
   c. Engineers shall not accept outside employment to the detriment of their regular work or interest. Before accepting any outside employment, they will notify their employers.
   d. Engineers shall not attempt to attract an engineer from another employer by false or misleading pretenses.
   e. Engineers shall not actively participate in strikes, picket lines, or other collective coercive action.
   f. Engineers shall avoid any act tending to promote their own interest at the expense of the dignity and integrity of the profession.
2. Engineers shall at all times strive to serve the public interest.
   a. Engineers shall seek opportunities to be of constructive service in civic affairs and work for the advancement of the safety, health and well-being of their community.
   b. Engineers shall not complete, sign, or seal plans and/or specifications that are not of a design safe to the public health and welfare and in conformity with accepted engineering standards. If the client or employer insists on such unprofessional conduct, they shall notify the proper authorities and withdraw from further service on the project.
   c. Engineers shall endeavor to extend public knowledge and appreciation of engineering and its achievements and to protect the engineering profession from misrepresentation and misunderstanding.
3. Engineers shall avoid all conduct or practice which is likely to discredit the profession or deceive the public.
   a. Engineers shall avoid the use of statements containing a material misrepresentation of fact or omitting a material fact necessary to keep statements from being misleading or intended or likely to create an unjustified expectation; statements containing prediction of future success; statements containing an opinion as to the quality of the Engineers' services; or statements intended or likely to attract clients by the use of showmanship, puffery, or self-laudation, including the use of slogans, jingles, or sensational language or format.
   b. Consistent with the foregoing, Engineers may advertise for recruitment of personnel.
   c. Consistent with the foregoing, Engineers may prepare articles for the lay or technical press, but such articles shall not imply credit to the author for work performed by others.
4. Engineers shall not disclose confidential information concerning the business affairs or technical processes of any present or former client or employer without his consent.

a. Engineers in the employ of others shall not without the consent of all interested parties enter promotional efforts or negotiations for work or make arrangements for other employment as a principal or to practice in connection with a specific project for which the Engineer has gained particular and specialized knowledge.

b. Engineers shall not, without the consent of all interested parties, participate in or represent an adversary interest in connection with a specific project or proceeding in which the Engineer has gained particular specialized knowledge on behalf of a former client or employer.

5. Engineers shall not be influenced in their professional duties by conflicting interests.

a. Engineers shall not accept financial or other considerations, including free engineering designs, from material or equipment suppliers for specifying their product.

b. Engineers shall not accept commissions or allowances, directly or indirectly, from contractors or other parties dealing with clients or employers of the Engineer in connection with work for which the Engineer is responsible.

6. Engineers shall uphold the principle of appropriate and adequate compensation for those engaged in engineering work.

a. Engineers shall not accept remuneration from either an employee or employment agency for giving employment.

b. Engineers, when employing other engineers, shall offer a salary according to professional qualifications.

7. Engineers shall not attempt to obtain employment or advancement or professional engagements by untruthfully critizing other engineers, or by other improper or questionable methods.

a. Engineers shall not request, propose, or accept a professional commission on a contingent basis under circumstances in which their professional judgment may be compromised.

b. Engineers in salaried positions shall accept part-time engineering work only to the extent consistent with policies of the employer and in accordance with ethical consideration.

c. Engineers shall not use equipment, supplies, laboratory, or office facilities of an employer to carry on outside private practice without consent.

8. Engineers shall not attempt to injure, maliciously or falsely, directly or indirectly, the professional reputation, prospects, practice or employment of other engineers, nor untruthfully criticize other engineers' work. Engineers who believe others are guilty of unethical or illegal practice shall present such information to the proper authority for action.

a. Engineers in private practice shall not review the work of another engineer for the same client, except with the knowledge of such engineer, or unless the connection of such engineer with the work has been terminated.

b. Engineers in governmental, industrial or educational employ are entitled to review and evaluate the work of other engineers when so required by their employment duties.

c. Engineers in sales or industrial employ are entitled to make engineering comparisons of represented products with products of other suppliers.

9. Engineers shall accept responsibility for their professional activities; provided, however, that Engineers may seek indemnification for professional services arising out of their practice for other than gross negligence, where the Engineer's interests cannot otherwise be protected.

a. Engineers shall conform with state registration laws in the practice of engineering.

b. Engineers shall not use association with a nonengineer, a corporation, or partnership, as a "cloak" for unethical acts, but must accept personal responsibility for all professional acts..

10. Engineers shall give credit for engineering work to those to whom credit is due, and will recognize the proprietary interests of others.

a. Engineers shall, whenever possible, name the person or persons who may be individually responsible for designs, inventions, writings, or other accomplishments.

b. Engineers using designs supplied by a client recognize that the designs remain the property of the client and may not be duplicated by the Engineer for others without express permission.

c. Engineers, before undertaking work for others in connection with which the Engineer may make improvements, plans, designs, inventions, or other records which may justify copyrights or patents, should enter into a positive agreement regarding ownership.

d. Engineers' designs, data, records, and notes referring exclusively to an employer's work are the employer's property.

11. Engineers shall cooperate in extending the effectiveness of the profession by interchanging information and experience with other engineers and students, and will endeavor to provide opportunity for the professional development and advancement of engineers under their supervision.

a. Engineers shall encourage engineering employees' efforts to improve their education.

b. Engineers shall encourage engineering employees to attend and present papers at professional and technical society meetings.

c. Engineers shall urge engineering employees to become registered at the earliest possible date.

d. Engineers shall assign a professional engineer duties of a nature to utilize full training and experience, insofar as possible, and delegate lesser functions to subprofessionals or to technicians.

e. Engineers shall provide a prospective engineering employee with complete information on working conditions and proposed status of employment, and after employment will keep employees informed of any changes.

"By order of the United States District Court for the District of Columbia, former Section 11(c) of the NSPE Code of Ethics prohibiting competitive bidding, and all policy statements, opinions, rulings or other guidelines interpreting its scope, have been rescinded as unlawfully interfering with the legal right of engineers, protected under the antitrust laws, to provide price information to prospective clients; accordingly, nothing contained in the NSPE Code of Ethics, policy statements, opinions, rulings or other guidelines prohibits the submission of price quotations or competitive bids for engineering services at any time or in any amount."

Statement by NSPE Executive Committee

In order to correct misunderstandings which have been indicated in some instances since the issuance of the Supreme Court decision and the entry of the Final Judgment, it is noted that in its decision of April 25, 1978, the Supreme Court of the United States declared: "The Sherman Act does not require competitive bidding."

It is further noted that as made clear in the Supreme Court decision:

1. Engineers and firms may individually refuse to bid for engineering services.
2. Clients are not required to seek bids for engineering services.
3. Federal, state, and local laws governing procedures to procure engineering services are not affected, and remain in full force and effect.
4. State societies and local chapters are free to actively and aggressively seek legislation for professional selection and negotiation procedures by public agencies.
5. State registration board rules of professional conduct, including rules prohibiting competitive bidding for engineering services, are not affected and remain in full force and effect. State registration boards with authority to adopt rules of professional conduct may adopt rules governing procedures to obtain engineering services.
6. As noted by the Supreme Court, "nothing in the judgment prevents NSPE and its members from attempting to influence governmental action . . ."

Note:
In regard to the question of application of the Code to corporations vis-a-vis real persons, business form or type should not negate nor influence conformance of individuals to the Code. The Code deals with professional services, which services must be performed by real persons. Real persons in turn establish and implement policies within business structures. The Code is clearly written to apply to the Engineer and it is incumbent on a member of NSPE to endeavor to live up to its provisions. This applies to all pertinent sections of the Code.

NSPE Publication No. 1102 as revised January 1987

SEAL·OF·THE·AMERICAN·INSTITVTE·OF·ARCHITECTS·MDCCCLVII

CODE OF ETHICS AND PROFESSIONAL CONDUCT

1987

Preamble

Members of The American Institute of Architects are dedicated to the highest standards of professionalism, integrity and competence. The following principles are guidelines for the conduct of members in fulfilling those obligations. They apply to all professional activities, wherever they occur. They address responsibilities to the public, which the profession serves and enriches; to the clients and users of architecture, and in the building industries, who help to shape the built environment; and to the art and science of architecture, that continuum of knowledge and creation which is the heritage and legacy of the profession.

This Code is arranged in three tiers of statements: Canons, Ethical Standards and Rules of Conduct. The Canons are broad principles of conduct. The Ethical Standards are more specific goals towards which members should aspire in professional performance and behavior. The Rules of Conduct are mandatory, the violation of which is grounds for disciplinary action by the Institute. The Rules of Conduct in some instances implement more than one Canon or Ethical Standard.

Commentary is provided for some of the Rules of Conduct. That commentary is meant to clarify or elaborate the intent of the rule. The commentary is not part of the Code. Enforcement will turn on application of the Rules of Conduct alone. But the commentary will assist those seeking to conform their conduct to the Code and those charged with its enforcement.

CANON I
GENERAL OBLIGATIONS

MEMBERS SHOULD MAINTAIN AND ADVANCE THEIR KNOWLEDGE OF THE ART AND SCIENCE OF ARCHITECTURE, RESPECT THE BODY OF ARCHITECTURAL ACCOMPLISHMENT AND CONTRIBUTE TO ITS GROWTH; LEARNED AND UNCOMPROMISED PROFESSIONAL JUDGMENT SHOULD TAKE PRECEDENCE OVER ANY OTHER MOTIVE IN THE PURSUIT OF THE ART AND SCIENCE OF ARCHITECTURE.

E.S. 1.1 Knowledge and Skill: Members should strive to improve their professional knowledge and skill.

R. 1.101 In practicing architecture, members shall demonstrate a consistent pattern of reasonable care and competence, and shall apply the technical knowledge and skill which is ordinarily applied by architects of good standing practicing in the same locality.

Commentary: By requiring a "consistent pattern" of adherence to the common law standard of competence, this rule allows for discipline of a member who more than infrequently does not achieve that standard. Isolated instances of minor lapses would not provide the basis for discipline.

R. 1.102 Members shall not undertake to provide professional services if their competence is substantially impaired by physical or mental disabilities.

E.S. 1.2 Standards of Excellence: Members should continually seek to raise the standards of aesthetic excellence, architectural education, research, training and practice.

E.S. 1.3 Public Understanding: Members should strive to improve public appreciation and understanding of architecture and the functions and responsibilities of architects.

E.S. 1.4 Allied Arts & Industries: Members should promote allied arts and contribute to the knowledge and capability of the building industries as a whole.

CANON II
OBLIGATIONS TO THE PUBLIC

MEMBERS SHOULD EMBRACE THE SPIRIT AND LETTER OF THE LAW GOVERNING THEIR PROFESSIONAL AFFAIRS AND SHOULD THOUGHTFULLY CONSIDER THE SOCIAL AND ENVIRONMENTAL IMPACT OF THEIR PROFESSIONAL ACTIVITIES.

E.S. 2.1 Conduct: Members should uphold the law in the conduct of their professional activities.

R. 2.101 Members shall not, in the conduct of their professional practice, knowingly violate the law.

Commentary: The violation of any law, local, state or federal, occurring in the conduct of a member's professional practice, is made the basis for discipline by this rule. R. 2.104 speaks to law violations by members occurring other than in the practice of architecture.

R. 2.102 Members shall neither offer nor make any payment or gift to a local, state or federal official with the intent of influencing the official's judgment in connection with an existing or prospective project in which the members are interested.

Commentary: This rule does not prohibit campaign contributions made in conformity with applicable federal and state campaign financing laws.

R. 2.103 Members serving in a public capacity shall not accept payments or gifts which are intended to influence their judgment.

R. 2.104 Members shall not engage in conduct involving fraud or wanton disregard of the rights of others.

Commentary: Conduct which brings into serious question a member's qualification to assume the fiduciary duties of an architect is the basis for discipline even if that conduct did not occur in the course of practice.

R. 2.105 If, in the course of their work on a project, the members become aware of a decision taken by their employer or client, against the members' advice, which violates any law or regulation and which will in the members' judgment, materially affect adversely the safety to the public of the finished project, the members shall:

(a) refuse to consent to the decision, and

(b) report the decision to the local building inspector or other public official charged with the enforcement of the applicable laws and regulations, unless the members are able to cause the matter to be satisfactorily resolved by other means.

Commentary: This rule extends only to violations of the building laws which threaten the public safety. Ethical Standard 2.1 calls on an architect to oppose technical violations of the law which are not threatening to safety, in which case discipline would not be imposed in the event that opposition is not successful. The obligation under this rule applies only to the safety of the finished project, an obligation coextensive with the usual undertaking of an architect.

R. 2.106 Members shall not counsel or assist a client in conduct that the architect knows, or reasonably should know, is fraudulent or illegal.

Commentary: This rule extends not only to matters which an architect knows are illegal, but also to matters which an architect of reasonable competence and prudence "should know" are illegal or fraudulent.

E.S. 2.2 Natural and Cultural Heritage: Members should respect and help conserve their natural and cultural heritage while striving to improve the environment and the quality of life within it.

E.S. 2.3 Civic Responsibility: Members should be involved in civic activities as citizens and professionals, and promote public awareness of architectural issues.

R. 2.301 Members making public statements on architectural issues shall disclose when they are being compensated for making such statements or when they have an economic interest in the issue.

E.S. 2.4 Public Interest Services: Members should render public interest professional services and encourage their employees to render such services.

E.S. 2.5 Human Rights: Members should uphold human rights in all their professional endeavors.

R. 2.501 Members shall not discriminate in their professional activities on the basis of race, religion, gender, national origin, age or nondisqualifying handicap.

Commentary: This rule applies to all professional activities of the member, including but not limited to dealings with clients, colleagues and employees. It is stated with such breadth here so as to avoid repetition under the other canons.

CANON III
OBLIGATIONS TO THE CLIENT

MEMBERS SHOULD SERVE THEIR CLIENTS COMPETENTLY AND IN A PROFESSIONAL MANNER, AND SHOULD EXERCISE UNPREJUDICED AND UNBIASED JUDGMENT ON THEIR BEHALF.

E.S. 3.1 Competence: Members should serve their clients in a timely and competent manner.

R. 3.101 In performing professional services, members shall take into account applicable laws and regulations. Members may rely on the advice of other qualified persons as to the intent and meaning of such regulations.

R. 3.102 Members shall undertake to perform professional services only when they, together with those whom they may engage as consultants, are qualified by education, training, or experience in the specific technical areas involved.

Commentary: This rule is meant to ensure that members not undertake projects which are beyond their professional capacity. Members venturing into areas which require expertise they do not possess may obtain that expertise by additional education, training or through the retention of consultants with the necessary expertise.

R. 3.103 Members shall not materially alter the scope or objectives of a project without the client's consent.

R. 3.104 When acting by agreement of the parties as the independent interpreter of building contract documents and the judge of contract performance, members shall render decisions impartially, favoring neither party to the contract.

Commentary: This rule applies when the member, though paid by the owner and owing the owner loyalty, is nonetheless required to act with impartiality in fulfilling the architect's role in the typical construction industry documents.

E.S. 3.2 Conflict of Interest: Members should disclose to clients or owners significant circumstances that could be construed as conflicts of interest and should ensure that such conflicts do not compromise those interests.

R. 3.201 Members shall not accept compensation for their services from more than one party on a project unless the circumstances are fully disclosed and agreed to by all interested parties.

R. 3.202 If members have any business association, direct or indirect financial interest, or other interest which could be substantial enough to influence their judgment in connection with their performance of professional services, the members shall fully disclose to their clients or employers the nature of the business association, financial interest, or other interest, and if the clients or employers object to such association, financial interest, or other interest, the members will either terminate such association or interest or give up the commission or employment.

Commentary: These rules are intended to embrace the full range of situations which may present a member with a conflict between his interests and those of his client or employer. In some situations a conflict is easily discerned, as when the architect owns property adjacent to property upon which he has been asked to design a structure and is faced with design options which would affect the value of his property. Other instances are not so clear, and that is more frequently the case as new systems and procedures for the construction process, such as design-build, come into the market. In every case the architect must take adequate steps to ensure that the client is aware of any substantial interest which the architect has which might run counter to the interests of the client.

E.S. 3.3 Candor and Truthfulness: Members should be candid and truthful in their professional communications.

R. 3.301 Members shall not intentionally or recklessly mislead existing or prospective clients about the results that can be achieved through the use of the members' services, nor shall the members state that they can achieve results by means that violate applicable law or this Code.

Commentary: This rule is meant to preclude dishonest, reckless or illegal representations by a member either in the course of soliciting a client or during performance. For example, it would cover the conduct of an architect who provides conceptual drawings based on an inadequate site examination or without regard for zoning laws, which lead a prospective client to believe that a design could be achieved when in fact it could not.

E.S. 3.4 Confidentiality: Members should respect the confidentiality of sensitive information obtained in the course of their professional activities.

R. 3.401 Members shall not reveal information obtained in the course of their professional activities which they have been asked to maintain in confidence, or which the reasonably prudent architect would recognize as likely, if disclosed, to affect the interests of another adversely. However, under the following exceptional circumstances members may reveal such information to the extent the members reasonably believe necessary:

(a) To stop an act which creates an appreciable risk of significant harm to the public health or safety or property of others and which the members are unable to prevent in any other manner; or

(b) To establish claims or defenses on behalf of the members; or

(c) To comply with applicable law or with this Code.

Commentary: This rule embodies generally accepted standards of client confidentiality, recognizing that under certain circumstances that confidentiality must yield to other interests. Because the law does not recognize an architect-client privilege, the rule permits an architect to reveal a confidence when necessary to comply with a subpoena or other legal process.

CANON IV OBLIGATIONS TO THE PROFESSION

MEMBERS SHOULD UPHOLD THE INTEGRITY AND DIGNITY OF THE PROFESSION.

E.S. 4.1 Honesty and Fairness: Members should pursue their professional activities with honesty and fairness.

R. 4.101 Members shall comply with the registration laws and regulations governing their professional practice.

R. 4.102 Members shall not knowingly make false statements or knowingly fail to disclose a material fact requested in connection with their application for registration or their application for AIA membership.

R. 4.103 Members shall not assist the application for registration or AIA membership of a person known by the members to be unqualified with respect to education, training, experience, or character.

R. 4.104 Members having substantial information which leads to a reasonable belief that another member has committed a violation of this Code which raises a serious question as to that member's honesty, trustworthiness or fitness as a member shall report such information to the body charged with enforcing this Code.

Commentary: Often, only an architect can recognize that the behavior of another architect poses a serious question as to that other's professional integrity. In those circumstances the duty to the professional's calling requires that the matter be brought to the attention of the proper authorities. In most jurisdictions such reporting, an implementation of professional standards, is protected from a libel or slander action if the report was made in good faith. If in doubt, a member should seek counsel before reporting on another under this rule.

R. 4.105 Members shall not sign or seal drawings, specifications, reports or other professional work for which they do not have direct professional knowledge or direct supervisory control; however, in the case of those portions of such professional work prepared by the members' registered consultants, the members may sign or seal said portions of the professional work if the members have reviewed such portions, have coordinated their preparation, or intend to be responsible for their adequacy.

Commentary: The essence of this rule is that the sign or seal of a member should not be affixed to any professional work unless the member intends to accept professional responsibility for its adequacy. The requirement that the member have professional knowledge or supervisory control or have reviewed or coordinated the consultant's work is evidence of the intent to assume professional responsibility.

R. 4.106 Members speaking in their capacity as architects shall not knowingly make false statements of material fact.

R. 4.107 Members shall accurately represent their qualifications and the scope and nature of their responsibilities in connection with work for which they are claiming credit.

Commentary: This rule is meant to prevent members from claiming credit for work which they did not do, misleading others and denying other participants in a project their proper share of credit.

E.S. 4.2 Dignity and Integrity: Members should strive, through their actions, to promote the dignity and integrity of the profession, and to ensure that their representatives and employees conform their conduct to this Code.

R. 4.201 Members shall not make misleading, deceptive or false statements or claims about their professional qualifications, experience or performance.

R. 4.202 Members shall make reasonable efforts to ensure that those over whom they have supervisory authority conform their conduct to this Code.

Commentary: What constitutes "reasonable efforts" under this rule is a common sense matter. As it makes sense to ensure that those over whom the architect exercises supervision be made generally aware of the Code, it can also make sense to bring a particular provision to the attention of a particular employee when a situation is present which might give rise to violation.

CANON V
OBLIGATIONS TO COLLEAGUES

MEMBERS SHOULD RESPECT THE RIGHTS AND ACKNOWLEDGE THE PROFESSIONAL ASPIRATIONS AND CONTRIBUTIONS OF THEIR COLLEAGUES.

E.S. 5.1 Professional Environment: Members should provide their associates and employees with a suitable working environment, compensate them fairly, and facilitate their professional development.

E.S. 5.2 Professional Recognition: Members should build their professional reputation on the merits of their own service and performance and should recognize and give credit to others for the professional work they have performed.

R. 5.201 Members shall recognize and respect the professional contributions of their employees, employers and business associates.

R. 5.202 Members leaving an employer's service shall not without the permission of the employer take designs, drawings, data, reports, notes, or other materials relating to work performed in the employer's service by the members.

R. 5.203 Members shall not unreasonably withhold permission from departing employees to take copies of designs, drawings, data, reports, notes, or other materials relating to work performed by the employees in the members' service which are not confidential.

Commentary: A member may impose reasonable conditions, such as the payment of copying costs, on the right of departing employees to take copies of work performed while in the member's service.

RULES OF ENACTMENT, APPLICATION, ENFORCEMENT AND AMENDMENT

ARTICLE I ENACTMENT

The Canons of Ethics, Ethical Standards and Rules of Conduct, referred to as the "Code of Ethics and Professional Conduct," shall be adopted by the convention of the Institute, and shall take effect at such time as the resolution of adoption sets.

ARTICLE II APPLICATION

The code of Ethics and Professional Conduct applies to the professional activities of all members, associate members and members emeritus of the AIA.

ARTICLE III ENFORCEMENT

The AIA Board of Directors shall provide in the By-Laws of the Institute procedures for the enforcement of the Code of Ethics and Professional Conduct. Such procedures shall provide that:

(1) Enforcement of the Code shall be administered through a National Judicial Council, appointed by the AIA Board of Directors.

(2) Formal charges will be filed directly with the National Judicial Council by members, components or anyone directly aggrieved by the conduct of the members.

(3) The National Judicial Council shall defer action on a charge to allow a component, which wishes, an opportunity to obtain an informal settlement.

(4) Penalties which may be imposed by the National Judicial Council are:
- (a) Admonition.
- (b) Censure.
- (c) Suspension of membership for a period of time.
- (d) Termination of membership.

(5) An appellate process be established.

(6) All proceedings will be confidential, as shall the imposition of an admonishment; however, all other penalties shall be made public.

ARTICLE IV AMENDMENT

The Code of Ethics and Professional Conduct may be amended by the convention of the Institute under the same procedures as are necessary to amend the Institute's By-Laws. The Code may also be amended by the AIA Board of Directors, upon a two-thirds vote of the entire Board.

INSTRUCTION SHEET

FOR AIA DOCUMENT A191, STANDARD FORM OF AGREEMENTS BETWEEN OWNER AND DESIGN/BUILDER—FIRST EDITION

A. GENERAL INFORMATION

1. Purpose

This Document is the first edition of AIA Document A191, Standard Form of Agreements Between Owner and Design/Builder. It is intended to govern relations between the Owner and Design/Builder under the contractual organization diagramed below.

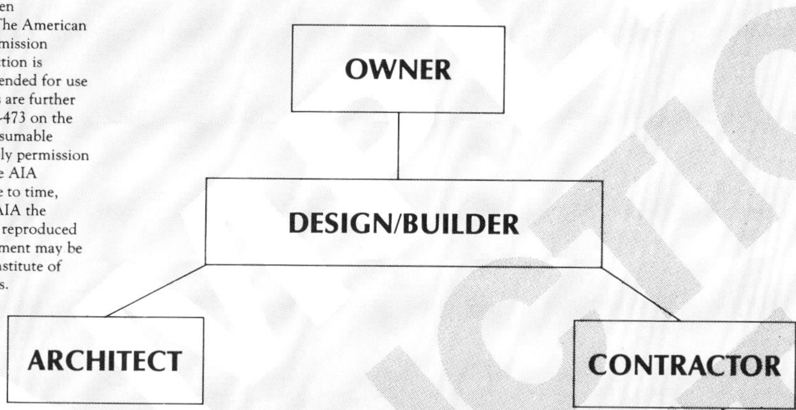

Design/build is a process in which the Owner contracts directly with one entity to provide both design and construction services. The AIA believes that if a public Owner chooses to utilize the design/build process, selection of the design/build team should be based upon objective criteria developed to evaluate the qualifications and competence of the design/build team, as with Brooks Act procurement methods.

This Document contains two Agreements which are intended to be used in sequence as the basis for the agreements between the Owner and the Design/Builder when the Owner seeks to have a single entity responsible for both the design and the construction of a project. The first Agreement, known as Part 1, covers the services of preliminary design and budgeting. The second Agreement, known as Part 2, covers the final design and construction. It is intended that the parties first enter into the Part 1 Agreement to determine the feasibility and scope of the Project, and thereafter enter into the Part 2 Agreement. Before signing Part 1 the parties should also reach substantial agreement on the terms of Part 2, except for the scope of the Project and compensation. Although it is anticipated that the parties entering into the Part 1 Agreement will also enter into the Part 2 Agreement, the parties may conclude their relationship after Part 1 is performed rather than continuing on to Part 2.

The Design/Builder's organization may take a variety of legal forms. Among others, design/build may be performed by a sole proprietorship, a partnership, a joint venture or a corporation. An architect or architectural firm may directly contract to perform design/build services or, alternatively, may form a separate corporate entity or joint venture for design/build, although these options are not explicitly stated in the Document. The AIA does not currently publish documents governing this type of joint venture.

Prior to entering into either Agreement in this Document, architects who wish to act as design/builders should contact their legal, insurance and management advisors. Several states have strong prohibitions or barriers against design/build practices under their laws regulating architectural registration, contractor licensing or incorporation of professionals. The management of money and personnel in a design/build venture is more extensive and complex than in the typical architectural practice. In addition, professional liability insurance for design/build may be difficult to obtain or limited in scope. For these reasons, it is expected that in most situations an architect will wish to establish a separate design/build firm. This firm may then subcontract the design work to the parent architectural firm through the use of AIA Document B901, listed below.

2. Related Documents

AIA Document A191 is published in conjunction with the following related documents:

A491, Standard Form of Agreements Between Design/Builder and Contractor

B901, Standard Form of Agreements Between Design/Builder and Architect

These documents are intended to govern the Design/Builder's relations with separate architects and contractors.

3. Use of Non-AIA Forms

If a non-AIA document or a mixture of AIA documents and non-AIA documents is used, particular care must be taken to achieve consistency of language and intent. If there are any significant omissions, additions or variances from the terms of the related standard AIA forms, both legal and insurance counsel should be consulted. Of particular concern is the need for consistency between the Owner-Design/Builder Agreements and any other agreements for portions of the design or construction entered into by the Design/Builder and others.

4. Letter Forms of Agreement

Letter forms of agreement are generally discouraged by the AIA, as is the performance of some or all professional services based on oral agreements or understandings. The AIA forms have been developed through more than ninety years of experience and have been tested repeatedly in courts. They are carefully coordinated with other AIA documents.

5. Use of Current Documents

Prior to using any AIA document, the user should consult the AIA or an AIA component chapter to determine the current edition of each document.

6. Reproduction

AIA Document A191 is a copyrighted document and may not be reproduced or excerpted from in whole or in part without the express written permission of the AIA prior to reproduction. This Document is intended for use as a "consumable" publication without any implied consent to duplicate except under the limited license described below.

Purchasers of the A191 Document are entitled by license to reproduce a maximum of ten copies of the completed or executed document for use only in connection with a particular Project.

B. COMPLETING THE A191 FORM

1. Modifications

As with all AIA documents, users are encouraged to consult an attorney with respect to completing or modifying the form. Legal counsel should also be sought concerning the effect of state and local law on the terms of each Agreement. In particular, legal counsel should be consulted with respect to registration laws, duties imposed by building codes, interest charges and arbitration. Generally, modifications may be accomplished by describing changes to the printed text in Article 10 of the relevant Agreement, or by attaching and referencing a separate amendment sheet. If deletions are needed, these should be accomplished by striking through with a line, or by amendment. It is not recommended that deletions be made by erasing, whiting out or taping over provisions in this Document.

2. Cover Page (Same for Part 1 and Part 2)

Date: The date of the Agreement is the date when the Agreement becomes legally effective. It may be the date that an oral agreement was reached, the date the Agreement was originally submitted to the Owner, the date authorizing action was taken or the date of actual execution. Design/build services should not be performed prior to the effective date of the Agreement.

Parties: Parties to the Agreement should be identified using the full legal names and addresses under which the Agreement will be executed, including designation of the legal status of the parties: sole proprietorship, partnership, joint venture, unincorporated association, corporation (general, closed or professional), etc.

Project: The proposed Project should be described in sufficient detail to identify (1) the official name or title of the facility, (2) the location of the site, if known, (3) the proposed building type or use, and (4) the size, capacity or scope of the Project, if known.

Architectural Services: Although the architect may not be a party to the Agreement between Owner and Design/Builder, it is customary to identify the architect in agreements of this kind.

3. Part 1 Agreement: Preliminary Design and Budgeting

a) Article 9—Basis of Compensation

Subparagraph 9.1.1

Describe the basis of computing compensation for Basic Services under this subparagraph. Although there is no standard method of computing compensation for design/build services, analogous methods may be found in the AIA publication *Compensation Guidelines for Architectural and Engineering Services* (1978 edition). Several methods may be used on a particular project. When more than one method is used, each method should reference the appropriate services listed in Article 2 and Article 10. This may be done by titling them "Method A," "Method B," etc.

Subparagraph 9.1.2
Insert the amount of initial payment as referred to in Subparagraph 5.1.1.

Subparagraph 9.1.3
Describe the manner in which subsequent monthly payments will be made to the Design/Builder.

Subparagraph 9.2.1
Describe the basis of computing additional compensation.

Subparagraph 9.3.1
List reimbursable expenses, if any.

Subparagraph 9.3.2
Insert a multiple for reimbursable expenses, if any.

Subparagraph 9.5.1
Insert rate of interest, if other than the legal rate.

Paragraph 9.7
Insert the number of months after which the compensation levels will be renegotiated.

b) Article 10—Other Conditions and Provisions

Paragraph 10.1
Insert the date for commencement of Work and the number of calendar days in which the Work is to be completed.

Paragraph 10.2
Insert Basic Services not described in Article 2.

4. Part 2 Agreement: Final Design and Construction

a) Article 13—Basis of Compensation

Subparagraph 13.1.1
Insert basis of compensation, such as stipulated sum, percentage fee or cost of the Work (defining cost), unit prices, cash allowances or contingencies, if any.

Subparagraph 13.2.1
List reimbursable expenses, if any.

Subparagraph 13.2.2
Insert a multiple for reimbursable expenses.

Subparagraph 13.3.1
Insert rate of interest, if other than the legal rate.

b) Article 14—Other Provisions

Paragraph 14.1
Insert the date of commencement and the number of days allowed for performance of the Contract.

Paragraph 14.2
Insert Basic Services not described in Article 2.

Paragraph 14.3
State the date of each month on which the Design/Builder will submit Applications for Payment.

Paragraph 14.4
List elements of proposal to clearly define the scope of Work.

C. EXECUTION OF THE AGREEMENTS

Persons executing (signing) each Agreement should indicate the capacity in which they are acting (e.g., president, secretary, partner, etc.) and the authority under which they are executing the Agreement. Evidence of authority to sign on behalf of each party should be obtained. Where appropriate, a copy of the resolution or bylaw authorizing the individual to act on behalf of the firm or entity should be attached.

THE AMERICAN INSTITUTE OF ARCHITECTS

AIA Document A191

Standard Form of Agreements Between Owner and Design/Builder

1985 EDITION

THIS DOCUMENT HAS IMPORTANT LEGAL CONSEQUENCES; CONSULTATION WITH AN ATTORNEY IS ENCOURAGED.

TABLE OF ARTICLES

THE AMERICAN INSTITUTE OF ARCHITECTS

AIA Document A191

Standard Form of Agreement Between Owner and Design/Builder

1985 EDITION

THIS DOCUMENT HAS IMPORTANT LEGAL CONSEQUENCES; CONSULTATION WITH AN ATTORNEY IS ENCOURAGED.

This Document comprises two separate Agreements: Part 1 Agreement—Preliminary Design and Budgeting and Part 2 Agreement—Final Design and Construction. Hereinafter, the Part 1 Agreement is referred to as Part 1 and the Part 2 Agreement is referred to as Part 2. Before executing Part 1, the parties should reach substantial agreement on Part 2.

PART 1 AGREEMENT—PRELIMINARY DESIGN AND BUDGETING

AGREEMENT

made as of the day of in the year of Nineteen Hundred and

BETWEEN the Owner:
(Name and address)

and the Design/Builder:
(Name and address)

For the following Project:
(Include Project name, location and detailed description of scope.)

The architectural services described in Article 2 will be provided by the following person or entity who is lawfully licensed to practice architecture:
(Name and address)

The Owner and the Design/Builder agree as set forth below.

Terms and Conditions—Part 1 Agreement

ARTICLE 1
GENERAL PROVISIONS

1.1 BASIC DEFINITIONS

1.1.1 The Project is the total design and construction for which the Design/Builder is responsible under Part 1, including all professional design services and all labor, materials and equipment used or incorporated in such design and construction.

1.1.2 The Work comprises the completed construction designed under the Project and includes labor necessary to produce such construction, and materials and equipment incorporated or to be incorporated in such construction.

1.2 EXECUTION, CORRELATION AND INTENT

1.2.1 This Part 1 shall be signed in not less than duplicate by the Owner and Design/Builder.

1.2.2 Nothing contained in the Design/Builder Contract Documents shall create a professional obligation or contractual relationship between the Owner and any third party.

1.3 OWNERSHIP AND USE OF DOCUMENTS

1.3.1 The drawings, specifications and other documents furnished by the Design/Builder are instruments of service and shall not become the property of the Owner whether or not the Project for which they are made is commenced. Drawings, specifications and other documents furnished by the Design/Builder shall not be used by the Owner on other projects, for additions to this Project or, unless the Design/Builder is in default under Part 1, for completion of this Project by others, except by written agreement relating to use, liability and compensation.

1.3.2 Submission or distribution of documents to meet official regulatory requirements or for other purposes in connection with the Project is not to be construed as publication in derogation of the Design/Builder's or the Architect's common law copyrights or other reserved rights. The Owner shall own neither the documents nor the copyrights.

ARTICLE 2
DESIGN/BUILDER

2.1 SERVICES AND RESPONSIBILITIES

2.1.1 Design services shall be performed by qualified architects, engineers and other professionals selected and paid by the Design/Builder. The professional obligations of such persons shall be undertaken and performed in the interest of the Design/Builder. Construction services shall be performed by qualified construction contractors and suppliers, selected and paid by the Design/Builder and acting in the interest of the Design/Builder. Nothing contained in Part 1 shall create any professional obligation or contractual relationship between such persons and the Owner.

2.1.2 The Design/Builder shall be responsible to the Owner for acts and omissions of the Design/Builder's employees and parties in privity of contract with the Design/Builder to perform a portion of the Work, including their agents and employees.

2.2 BASIC SERVICES

2.2.1 The Design/Builder's Basic Services are as described below and in Article 10.

2.2.2 The Design/Builder shall review the Owner's program to ascertain requirements of the Project and shall review such requirements with the Owner.

2.2.3 The Design/Builder shall provide, after consultation with the Owner, a preliminary evaluation of the program and Project budget, each in terms of the other.

2.2.4 The Design/Builder shall review with the Owner alternative approaches to design and construction of the Project.

2.2.5 The Design/Builder shall submit to the Owner a Proposal including the completed Preliminary Design Documents, a statement of the proposed contract sum, a proposed schedule for completion of the Work under Part 2 and all other information necessary to complete Part 2. Preliminary Design Documents shall consist of preliminary design drawings, outline specifications and other documents to fix and describe the size, quality and character of the entire Project, its architectural, structural, mechanical and electrical systems, and the materials and such other elements of the Project as may be appropriate. If the Proposal is accepted by the Owner, they shall then execute Part 2. Modifications to the Proposal before execution of Part 2 shall be recorded in writing as an addendum and be identified in the Contract Documents of Part 2.

2.3 ADDITIONAL SERVICES

All other services requested by the Owner and mutually agreed to in writing by the Owner and Design/Builder in Part 1, including, among others, changes in Project scope and program, shall constitute Additional Services and shall be paid for by the Owner as provided in Part 1.

ARTICLE 3
OWNER

3.1 The Owner shall provide information regarding requirements for the Project, including but not limited to the Owner's design objectives, constraints and criteria.

3.2 If the Owner provides a budget for the Project, it shall explicitly include as separate line items contingencies for changes in the design and construction, and other costs which are the responsibility of the Owner. No budget shall constitute a fixed limit of construction cost unless such limit has been agreed to in writing by the Design/Builder.

3.3 The Owner shall designate a representative authorized to act on the Owner's behalf with respect to the Project. The Owner or such authorized representative shall examine the documents submitted by the Design/Builder and shall promptly render decisions pertaining thereto to avoid delay in the orderly progress of design and construction.

3.4 The Owner shall cooperate with the Design/Builder in identifying required permits, licenses and inspections, and shall take appropriate action with reasonable promptness.

3.5 Prior to commencement of Basic Services, the Owner shall furnish a legal description and a certified land survey of the site, giving, as applicable, grades and lines of streets, alleys, pavements and adjoining property; rights-of-way, restrictions, easements, encroachments, zoning, deed restrictions, elevations and contours of the site; locations, dimensions and complete data pertaining to existing buildings, other improvements and trees; and full information concerning available services and utility lines, both public and private, above and below grade, including inverts and depths.

3.6 The Owner shall furnish services of geotechnical engineers and other consultants when such services are deemed necessary by the Design/Builder. Geotechnical engineers or other consultants shall be selected by mutual agreement. Such services shall include, as required, applicable test borings, test pits, soil bearing values, percolation tests, air and water pollution tests, and other necessary operations for determining subsoil, air and water conditions, with reports and appropriate professional recommendations.

3.7 The services, information, surveys and reports required by Paragraphs 3.5 and 3.6 shall be furnished at the Owner's expense, and the Design/Builder shall be entitled to rely upon their accuracy and completeness.

3.8 If the Owner observes or otherwise becomes aware of any fault or defect in the Work, the Owner shall give prompt written notice thereof to the Design/Builder.

3.9 The Owner shall furnish required information and services and shall render decisions with reasonable promptness to avoid delay in the orderly progress of the Design/Builder's services.

3.10 The Owner shall communicate with contractors only through the Design/Builder.

ARTICLE 4
TIME

4.1 The Design/Builder shall provide the Basic and Additional Services as expeditiously as is consistent with reasonable skill and care and shall complete the services in the time provided in Article 10.

ARTICLE 5
PAYMENTS

5.1 The initial payment provided in Article 9 shall be made upon execution of this Part 1 and credited to the Owner's account as provided in Subparagraph 9.1.2.

5.2 Subsequent payments for Part 1 Basic Services, Additional Services and Reimbursable Expenses shall be made monthly on the basis set forth in Article 9.

5.3 Within ten days of the Owner's receipt of a properly submitted Application for Payment, the Owner shall make payment to the Design/Builder.

5.4 Payments due the Design/Builder under Part 1 which are not paid when due shall bear interest from the date due at the rate specified in Paragraph 9.5, or in the absence of a specified rate, at the legal rate prevailing where the principal office of the Design/Builder is located.

ARTICLE 6
ARBITRATION

6.1 Claims, disputes and other matters in question between the parties to Part 1 arising out of or relating to Part 1 shall be decided by arbitration in accordance with the Construction Industry Arbitration Rules of the American Arbitration Association then in effect unless the parties agree otherwise. No arbitration arising out of or relating to Part 1 shall include, by consolidation or joinder or in any other manner, an additional person not a party to Part 1 except by written consent containing specific reference to Part 1 and signed by the Owner, Design/Builder and any other person sought to be joined. Consent to arbitration involving an additional person or persons shall not constitute consent to arbitration of a dispute not described therein or with a person not named therein. This provision shall be specifically enforceable in any court of competent jurisdiction.

6.2 Notice of demand for arbitration shall be filed in writing with the other party to Part 1 and with the American Arbitration Association. The demand shall be made within a reasonable time after the claim, dispute or other matter in question has arisen. In no event shall the demand for arbitration be made after the date when the applicable statute of limitations would bar institution of a legal or equitable proceeding based on such claim, dispute or other matter in question.

6.3 The award rendered by arbitrators shall be final, and judgment may be entered upon it in accordance with applicable law in any court having jurisdiction.

6.4 Unless otherwise agreed in writing, the Design/Builder shall carry on the services and maintain progress during any arbitration proceedings, and the Owner shall continue to make payments to the Design/Builder in accordance with Part 1.

6.5 This Article 6 shall survive completion or termination of Part 1.

ARTICLE 7
MISCELLANEOUS PROVISIONS

7.1 This Part 1 shall be governed by the law of the place where the principal office of the Design/Builder is located.

7.2 The table of contents and the headings of articles and paragraphs are for convenience only and shall not modify rights and obligations created by Part 1.

7.3 In case a provision of Part 1 is held to be invalid, illegal or unenforceable, the validity, legality and enforceability of the remaining provisions shall not be affected.

7.4 SUCCESSORS AND ASSIGNS

7.4.1 This Part 1 shall be binding on successors, assigns and legal representatives of and persons in privity of contract with the Owner or Design/Builder. Neither party shall assign, sublet or transfer an interest in Part 1 without written consent of the other.

7.4.2 This Paragraph 7.4 shall survive completion or termination of Part 1.

7.5 EXTENT OF AGREEMENT

7.5.1 Part 1 represents the entire agreement for Preliminary Design and Budgeting and supersedes all prior negotiations, representations or agreements. Part 1 may be amended only by written instrument signed by both Owner and Design/Builder.

7.6 In case of termination of the Architect, the Design/Builder shall provide the services of another lawfully licensed person or entity against whom the Owner makes no reasonable objection.

ARTICLE 8
TERMINATION OF THE AGREEMENT

8.1 Part 1 may be terminated by either party upon seven days' written notice should the other party fail substantially to perform in accordance with its terms through no fault of the party initiating the termination.

8.2 Part 1 may be terminated by the Owner upon at least seven days' written notice to the Design/Builder in the event that the Project is permanently abandoned.

8.3 In the event of termination not the fault of the Design/Builder, the Design/Builder shall be compensated for services performed to termination date, together with Reimbursable Expenses then due and Termination Expenses. Termination Expenses are expenses directly attributable to termination, including a reasonable amount for overhead and profit, for which the Design/Builder is not otherwise compensated under Part 1.

ARTICLE 9
BASIS OF COMPENSATION

The Owner shall compensate the Design/Builder in accordance with Article 5, Payments, and the other provisions of Part 1 as described below.

9.1 COMPENSATION FOR BASIC SERVICES

9.1.1 FOR BASIC SERVICES, compensation shall be as follows:

9.1.2 AN INITIAL PAYMENT of dollars ($) shall be made upon execution of Part 1 and credited to the Owner's account as follows:

9.1.3 SUBSEQUENT PAYMENTS shall be as follows:

9.2 COMPENSATION FOR ADDITIONAL SERVICES

9.2.1 FOR ADDITIONAL SERVICES, compensation shall be as follows:

9.3 REIMBURSABLE EXPENSES

9.3.1 Reimbursable Expenses are in addition to Compensation for Basic and Additional Services and include actual expenditures made by the Design/Builder and the Design/Builder's employees and contractors in the interest of the Project for the expenses listed as follows:

9.3.2 FOR REIMBURSABLE EXPENSES, compensation shall be a multiple of ( ) times the amounts expended.

9.4 DIRECT PERSONNEL EXPENSE is defined as the direct salaries of personnel engaged on the Project, and the portion of the cost of their mandatory and customary contributions and benefits related thereto, such as employment taxes and other statutory employee benefits, insurance, sick leave, holidays, vacations, pensions and similar contributions and benefits.

9.5 INTEREST PAYMENTS

9.5.1 The rate of interest for past due payments shall be as follows:

(Usury laws and requirements under the Federal Truth in Lending Act, similar state and local consumer credit laws and other regulations at the Owner's and Design/Builder's principal places of business, at the location of the Project and elsewhere may affect the validity of this provision. Specific legal advice should be obtained with respect to deletion, modification or other requirements, such as written disclosures or waivers.)

9.6 IF THE SCOPE of the Project is changed materially, the amount of compensation shall be equitably adjusted.

9.7 The compensation set forth herein shall be equitably adjusted if through no fault of the Design/Builder the services have not been completed within ( ) months of the date of Part 1.

ARTICLE 10
OTHER PROVISIONS

10.1 The Basic Services to be performed shall be commenced on and, subject to authorized adjustments and to delays not caused by the Design/Builder, shall be completed in ( ) calendar days.

10.2 The Basic Services beyond those described in Article 2 are:

This Part 1 entered into as of the day and year first written above.

OWNER	DESIGN/BUILDER
______________________	______________________
______________________	______________________
______________________	______________________
BY ______________________	BY ______________________

THE AMERICAN INSTITUTE OF ARCHITECTS

AIA Document A191

Standard Form of Agreement Between Owner and Design/Builder

1985 EDITION

THIS DOCUMENT HAS IMPORTANT LEGAL CONSEQUENCES; CONSULTATION WITH AN ATTORNEY IS ENCOURAGED.

This Document comprises two separate Agreements: Part 1 Agreement—Preliminary Design and Budgeting and Part 2 Agreement—Final Design and Construction. Hereinafter, the Part 1 Agreement is referred to as Part 1 and the Part 2 Agreement is referred to as Part 2.

PART 2 AGREEMENT—FINAL DESIGN AND CONSTRUCTION

AGREEMENT

made as of the day of in the year of Nineteen Hundred and

BETWEEN the Owner:
(Name and address)

and the Design/Builder:
(Name and address)

For the following Project:
(Include Project name, location and detailed description of scope.)

The architectural services described in Article 2 will be provided by the following person or entity who is lawfully licensed to practice architecture:
(Name and address)

The Owner and the Design/Builder agree as set forth below.

Terms and Conditions—Part 2 Agreement

ARTICLE 1
GENERAL PROVISIONS

1.1 BASIC DEFINITIONS

1.1.1 The Contract Documents consist of the Design/Builder's Proposal identified in Article 14, this Part 2, the Construction Documents approved by the Owner in accordance with Subparagraph 2.2.2 below and Modifications issued after execution of Part 2. A Modification is a Change Order or a written amendment to Part 2 signed by both parties. These form the Contract, and are as fully a part of the Contract as if attached to this Part 2 or repeated herein.

1.1.2 The Project is the total design and construction for which the Design/Builder is responsible under Part 2, including all professional design services and all labor, materials and equipment used or incorporated in such design and construction.

1.1.3 The Work comprises the completed construction designed under the Project and includes labor necessary to produce such construction, and materials and equipment incorporated or to be incorporated in such construction.

1.2 EXECUTION, CORRELATION AND INTENT

1.2.1 This Part 2 shall be signed in not less than duplicate by the Owner and Design/Builder.

1.2.2 It is the intent of the Owner and Design/Builder that the Contract Documents include all items necessary for proper execution and completion of the Work. The Contract Documents are complementary, and what is required by any one shall be as binding as if required by all. Work not covered in the Contract Documents will not be required unless it is consistent with and is reasonably inferable from the Contract Documents as being necessary to produce the intended results. Words and abbreviations which have well-known technical or trade meanings are used in the Contract Documents in accordance with such recognized meanings.

1.3 OWNERSHIP AND USE OF DOCUMENTS

1.3.1 The drawings, specifications and other documents furnished by the Design/Builder are instruments of service and shall not become the property of the Owner whether or not the Project for which they are made is commenced. Drawings, specifications and other documents furnished by the Design/Builder shall not be used by the Owner on other projects, for additions to this Project or, unless the Design/Builder is in default under Part 2, for completion of this Project by others, except by written agreement relating to use, liability and compensation.

1.3.2 Submission or distribution of documents to meet official regulatory requirements or for other purposes in connection with the Project is not to be construed as publication in derogation of the Design/Builder's or the Architect's common law copyrights or other reserved rights. The Owner shall own neither the documents nor the copyrights.

ARTICLE 2
DESIGN/BUILDER

2.1 SERVICES AND RESPONSIBILITIES

2.1.1 Design services shall be performed by qualified architects, engineers and other professionals selected and paid by the Design/Builder. The professional obligations of such persons shall be undertaken and performed in the interest of the Design/Builder. Construction services shall be performed by qualified construction contractors and suppliers, selected and paid by the Design/Builder and acting in the interest of the Design/Builder. Nothing contained in Part 2 shall create any professional obligation or contractual relationship between such persons and the Owner.

2.2 BASIC SERVICES

2.2.1 The Design/Builder's Basic Services are described below and in Article 14.

2.2.2 Based on the Design/Builder's Proposal, the Design/Builder shall submit Construction Documents for review and approval by the Owner. Construction Documents shall include technical drawings, schedules, diagrams and specifications, setting forth in detail the requirements for construction of the Work, and shall:

- **.1** develop the intent of the Design/Builder's Proposal in greater detail;
- **.2** provide information customarily necessary for the use of those in the building trades; and
- **.3** include documents customarily required for regulatory agency approvals.

2.2.3 The Design/Builder shall assist the Owner in filing documents required to obtain necessary approvals of governmental authorities having jurisdiction over the Project.

2.2.4 Unless otherwise provided in the Contract Documents, the Design/Builder shall provide or cause to be provided and shall pay for design services, labor, materials, equipment, tools, construction equipment and machinery, water, heat, utilities, transportation and other facilities and services necessary for proper execution and completion of the Work, whether temporary or permanent and whether or not incorporated or to be incorporated in the Work.

2.2.5 The Design/Builder shall be responsible for and shall coordinate all construction means, methods, techniques, sequences and procedures.

2.2.6 The Design/Builder shall keep the Owner informed of the progress and quality of the Work.

2.2.7 If requested in writing by the Owner, the Design/Builder, with reasonable promptness and in accordance with time limits agreed upon, shall interpret the requirements of the Contract Documents and initially shall decide, subject to demand for arbitration, claims, disputes and other matters in question relating to performance thereunder by both Owner and Design/Builder. Such interpretations and decisions shall be in writing, shall not be presumed to be correct and shall be given such weight as the arbitrator(s) or the court shall determine.

2.2.8 The Design/Builder shall correct Work which does not conform to the Construction Documents.

2.2.9 The Design/Builder warrants to the Owner that materials and equipment incorporated in the Work will be new unless otherwise specified, and that the Work will be of good quality, free from faults and defects, and in conformance with the Contract Documents. Work not conforming to these requirements shall be corrected in accordance with Article 9.

2.2.10 The Design/Builder shall pay all sales, consumer, use and similar taxes which were in effect at the time the Design/Builder's Proposal was first submitted to the Owner, and shall secure and pay for building and other permits and governmental fees, licenses and inspections necessary for the proper execution and completion of the Work which are either customarily secured after execution of Part 2 or are legally required at the time the Design/Builder's Proposal was first submitted to the Owner.

2.2.11 The Design/Builder shall give notices and comply with laws, ordinances, rules, regulations and lawful orders of public authorities relating to the Project.

2.2.12 The Design/Builder shall pay royalties and license fees. The Design/Builder shall defend suits or claims for infringement of patent rights and shall save the Owner harmless from loss on account thereof, except that the Owner shall be responsible for such loss when a particular design, process or product of a particular manufacturer is required by the Owner. However, if the Design/Builder has reason to believe the use of a required design, process or product is an infringement of a patent, the Design/Builder shall be responsible for such loss unless such information is promptly given to the Owner.

2.2.13 The Design/Builder shall be responsible to the Owner for acts and omissions of the Design/Builder's employees and parties in privity of contract with the Design/Builder to perform a portion of the Work, including their agents and employees.

2.2.14 The Design/Builder shall keep the premises free from accumulation of waste materials or rubbish caused by the Design/Builder's operations. At the completion of the Work, the Design/Builder shall remove from and about the Project the Design/Builder's tools, construction equipment, machinery, surplus materials, waste materials and rubbish.

2.2.15 The Design/Builder shall prepare Change Orders for the Owner's approval and execution in accordance with Part 2 and shall have authority to make minor changes in the design and construction consistent with the intent of Part 2 not involving an adjustment in the contract sum or an extension of the contract time. The Design/Builder shall promptly inform the Owner, in writing, of minor changes in the design and construction.

2.2.16 The Design/Builder shall notify the Owner when the Work or an agreed upon portion thereof is substantially completed by issuing a Certificate of Substantial Completion which shall establish the Date of Substantial Completion, shall state the responsibility of each party for security, maintenance, heat, utilities, damage to the Work and insurance, shall include a list of items to be completed or corrected and shall fix the time within which the Design/Builder shall complete items listed therein. Disputes between the Owner and Design/Builder regarding the Certificate of Substantial Completion shall be resolved by arbitration.

2.2.17 The Design/Builder shall maintain in good order at the site one record copy of the drawings, specifications, product data, samples, shop drawings, Change Orders and other Modifications, marked currently to record changes made during construction. These shall be delivered to the Owner upon completion of the design and construction and prior to final payment.

ARTICLE 3
OWNER

3.1 The Owner shall designate a representative authorized to act on the Owner's behalf with respect to the Project. The Owner or such authorized representative shall examine documents submitted by the Design/Builder and shall promptly render decisions pertaining thereto to avoid delay in the orderly progress of the Work.

3.2 The Owner may appoint an on-site project representative to observe the Work and to have such other responsibilities as the Owner and Design/Builder agree in writing prior to execution of Part 2.

3.3 The Owner shall cooperate with the Design/Builder in securing building and other permits, licenses and inspections, and shall pay the fees for such permits, licenses and inspections if the cost of such fees is not identified as being included in the Design/Builder's Proposal.

3.4 The Owner shall furnish services by land surveyors, geotechnical engineers and other consultants for subsoil, air and water conditions, in addition to those provided under Part 1 when such services are deemed necessary by the Design/Builder to carry out properly the design services under this Part 2.

3.5 The Owner shall furnish structural, mechanical, chemical, geotechnical and other laboratory or on-site tests, inspections and reports as required by law or the Contract Documents.

3.6 The services, information, surveys and reports required by Paragraphs 3.4 and 3.5 shall be furnished at the Owner's expense, and the Design/Builder shall be entitled to rely upon their accuracy and completeness.

3.7 If the Owner observes or otherwise becomes aware of a fault or defect in the Work or nonconformity with the Design or Construction Documents, the Owner shall give prompt written notice thereof to the Design/Builder.

3.8 The Owner shall furnish required information and services and shall promptly render decisions pertaining thereto to avoid delay in the orderly progress of the design and construction.

3.9 The Owner shall, at the request of the Design/Builder and upon execution of Part 2, provide a certified or notarized statement of funds available for the Project and their source.

3.10 The Owner shall communicate with contractors only through the Design/Builder.

ARTICLE 4
TIME

4.1 The Design/Builder shall provide services as expeditiously as is consistent with reasonable skill and care and the orderly progress of design and construction.

4.2 Time limits stated in the Contract Documents are of the essence of Part 2. The Work to be performed under Part

2 shall commence upon execution of a notice to proceed unless otherwise agreed and, subject to authorized Modifications, Substantial Completion shall be achieved as indicated in Article 14.

4.3 The Date of Substantial Completion of the Work or an agreed upon portion thereof is the date when construction or an agreed upon portion thereof is sufficiently complete so the Owner can occupy and utilize the Work or agreed upon portion thereof for its intended use.

4.4 The schedule provided in the Design/Builder's Proposal shall include a construction schedule consistent with Paragraph 4.2 above.

4.5 If the Design/Builder is delayed in the progress of the Project by acts or neglect of the Owner, Owner's employees, separate contractors employed by the Owner, changes ordered in the Work not caused by the fault of the Design/Builder, labor disputes, fire, unusual delay in transportation, adverse weather conditions not reasonably anticipatable, unavoidable casualties, or other causes beyond the Design/Builder's control, or by delay authorized by the Owner's pending arbitration or another cause which the Owner and Design/Builder agree is justifiable, the contract time shall be reasonably extended by Change Order.

ARTICLE 5
PAYMENTS

5.1 PROGRESS PAYMENTS

5.1.1 The Design/Builder shall deliver to the Owner itemized Applications for Payment in such detail as indicated in Article 14.

5.1.2 Within ten days of the Owner's receipt of a properly submitted and correct Application for Payment, the Owner shall make payment to the Design/Builder.

5.1.3 The Application for Payment shall constitute a representation by the Design/Builder to the Owner that, to the best of the Design/Builder's knowledge, information and belief, the design and construction have progressed to the point indicated; the quality of the Work covered by the application is in accordance with the Contract Documents; and the Design/Builder is entitled to payment in the amount requested.

5.1.4 The Design/Builder shall pay each contractor, upon receipt of payment from the Owner, out of the amount paid to the Design/Builder on account of such contractor's work, the amount to which said contractor is entitled in accordance with the terms of the Design/Builder's contract with such contractor. The Design/Builder shall, by appropriate agreement with each contractor, require each contractor to make payments to subcontractors in similar manner.

5.1.5 The Owner shall have no obligation to pay or to be responsible in any way for payment to a contractor of the Design/Builder except as may otherwise be required by law.

5.1.6 No progress payment or partial or entire use or occupancy of the Project by the Owner shall constitute an acceptance of Work not in accordance with the Contract Documents.

5.1.7 The Design/Builder warrants that: (1) title to Work, materials and equipment covered by an Application for Payment will pass to the Owner either by incorporation in construction or upon receipt of payment by the Design/Builder, whichever occurs first; (2) Work, materials and equipment covered by previous Applications for Payment are free and clear of liens, claims, security interests or encumbrances, hereinafter referred to as "liens"; and (3) no Work, materials or equipment covered by an Application for Payment will have been acquired by the Design/Builder, or any other person performing work at the site or furnishing materials or equipment for the Project, subject to an agreement under which an interest therein or an encumbrance thereon is retained by the seller or otherwise imposed by the Design/Builder or such other person.

5.1.8 If the Contract provides for retainage, then at the date of Substantial Completion or occupancy of the Work or any agreed upon portion thereof by the Owner, whichever occurs first, the Design/Builder may apply for and the Owner, if the Design/Builder has satisfied the requirements of Paragraph 5.2.1 and any other requirements of the Contract relating to retainage, shall pay the Design/Builder the amount retained, if any, for the Work or for the portion completed or occupied, less the reasonable value of incorrect or incomplete Work. Final payment of such withheld sum shall be made upon correction or completion of such Work.

5.2 FINAL PAYMENT

5.2.1 Neither final payment nor amounts retained, if any, shall become due until the Design/Builder submits to the Owner (1) an affidavit that payrolls, bills for materials and equipment, and other indebtedness connected with the Project for which the Owner or Owner's property might be liable have been paid or otherwise satisfied, (2) consent of surety, if any, to final payment, (3) a certificate that insurance required by the Contract Documents is in force following completion of the Work, and (4) if required by the Owner, other data establishing payment or satisfaction of obligations, such as receipts, releases and waivers of liens arising out of Part 2, to the extent and in such form as may be designated by the Owner. If a contractor refuses to furnish a release or waiver required by the Owner, the Design/Builder may furnish a bond satisfactory to the Owner to indemnify the Owner against such lien. If such lien remains unsatisfied after payments are made, the Design/Builder shall reimburse the Owner for moneys the latter may be compelled to pay in discharging such lien, including all costs and reasonable attorneys' fees.

5.2.2 Final payment constituting the entire unpaid balance due shall be paid by the Owner to the Design/Builder upon the Owner's receipt of the Design/Builder's final Application for Payment when the Work has been completed and the Contract fully performed except for those responsibilities of the Design/Builder which survive final payment.

5.2.3 The making of final payment shall constitute a waiver of all claims by the Owner except those arising from:

- **.1** unsettled liens;
- **.2** faulty or defective Work appearing after Substantial Completion;
- **.3** failure of the Work to comply with requirements of the Contract Documents; or
- **.4** terms of special warranties required by the Contract Documents.

5.2.4 Acceptance of final payment shall constitute a waiver of all claims by the Design/Builder except those previously made in writing and identified by the Design/Builder as unsettled at the time of final Application for Payment.

5.3 INTEREST PAYMENTS

5.3.1 Payments due the Design/Builder under Part 2 which are not paid when due shall bear interest from the date due at the rate specified in Article 13, or in the absence of a specified rate, at the legal rate prevailing where the principal improvements are to be located.

ARTICLE 6
PROTECTION OF PERSONS AND PROPERTY

6.1 The Design/Builder shall be responsible for initiating, maintaining and providing supervision of safety precautions and programs in connection with the Work.

6.2 The Design/Builder shall take reasonable precautions for safety of, and shall provide reasonable protection to prevent damage, injury or loss to: (1) employees on the Work and other persons who may be affected thereby; (2) the Work and materials and equipment to be incorporated therein; and (3) other property at or adjacent to the site.

6.3 The Design/Builder shall give notices and comply with applicable laws, ordinances, rules, regulations and orders of public authorities bearing on the safety of persons and property and their protection from damage, injury or loss.

6.4 The Design/Builder shall be liable for damage or loss (other than damage or loss to property insured under the property insurance provided or required by the Contract Documents to be provided by the Owner) to property at the site caused in whole or in part by the Design/Builder, a contractor of the Design/Builder or anyone directly or indirectly employed by either of them, or by anyone for whose acts they may be liable, except damage or loss attributable to the acts or omissions of the Owner, the Owner's separate contractors or anyone directly or indirectly employed by them or by anyone for whose acts they may be liable and not attributable to the fault or negligence of the Design/Builder.

ARTICLE 7
INSURANCE AND BONDS

7.1 DESIGN/BUILDER'S LIABILITY INSURANCE

7.1.1 The Design/Builder shall purchase and maintain in a company or companies authorized to do business in the state in which the Work is located such insurance as will protect the Design/Builder from claims set forth below which may arise out of or result from operations under the Contract by the Design/Builder or by a contractor of the Design/Builder, or by anyone directly or indirectly employed by any of them, or by anyone for whose acts they may be liable:

.1 claims under workers' or workmen's compensation, disability benefit and other similar employee benefit laws which are applicable to the Work to be performed;

.2 claims for damages because of bodily injury, occupational sickness or disease, or death of the Design/Builder's employees under any applicable employer's liability law;

.3 claims for damages because of bodily injury, sickness or disease, or death of persons other than the Design/Builder's employees;

.4 claims for damages covered by usual personal injury liability coverage which are sustained (1) by a person as a result of an offense directly or indirectly related to employment of such person by the Design/Builder or (2) by another person;

.5 claims for damages, other than to the Work at the site, because of injury to or destruction of tangible property, including loss of use; and

.6 claims for damages for bodily injury or death of a person or property damage arising out of ownership, maintenance or use of a motor vehicle.

7.1.2 The insurance required by the above Subparagraph 7.1.1 shall be written for not less than limits of liability specified in the Contract Documents or required by law, whichever are greater.

7.1.3 The Design/Builder's liability insurance shall include contractual liability insurance applicable to the Design/Builder's obligations under Paragraph 11.7.

7.1.4 Certificates of Insurance, and copies of policies if requested, acceptable to the Owner shall be delivered to the Owner prior to commencement of design and construction. These Certificates as well as insurance policies required by this Paragraph shall contain a provision that coverage will not be cancelled or allowed to expire until at least thirty days' prior written notice has been given to the Owner. If any of the foregoing insurance coverages are required to remain in force after final payment, an additional certificate evidencing continuation of such coverage shall be submitted along with the application for final payment.

7.2 OWNER'S LIABILITY INSURANCE

7.2.1 The Owner shall be responsible for purchasing and maintaining, in a company or companies authorized to do business in the state in which the principal improvements are to be located, Owner's liability insurance to protect the Owner against claims which may arise from operations under this Project.

7.3 PROPERTY INSURANCE

7.3.1 Unless otherwise provided under this Part 2, the Owner shall purchase and maintain, in a company or companies authorized to do business in the state in which the principal improvements are to be located, property insurance upon the Work at the site to the full insurable value thereof. Property insurance shall include interests of the Owner, the Design/Builder, and their respective contractors and subcontractors in the Work. It shall insure against perils of fire and extended coverage and shall include all risk insurance for physical loss or damage including, without duplication of coverage, theft, vandalism and malicious mischief. If the Owner does not intend to purchase such insurance for the full insurable value of the entire Work, the Owner shall inform the Design/Builder in writing prior to commencement of the Work. The Design/Builder may then effect insurance for the Work at the site which will protect the interests of the Design/Builder and the Design/Builder's contractors and subcontractors, and by appropriate Change Order the cost thereof shall be charged to the Owner. If the Design/Builder is damaged by failure of the Owner to purchase or maintain such insurance without notice to the Design/Builder, then the Owner shall bear all reasonable costs properly attributable thereto. If not covered under the all risk insurance or not otherwise provided in the Contract Documents, the Design/Builder shall effect and maintain similar property insurance on portions of the Work stored off-site or in transit when such portions of the Work are to be included in an Application for Payment.

7.3.2 Unless otherwise provided under this Part 2, the Owner shall purchase and maintain such boiler and machinery insurance as may be required by the Contract Documents or by law and which shall specifically cover such insured objects during installation and until final acceptance by the Owner. This insurance shall cover interests of the Owner, the Design/Builder, and the Design/Builder's contractors and subcontractors in the Work.

7.3.3 A loss insured under Owner's property insurance is to be adjusted with the Owner and made payable to the Owner as trustee for the insureds, as their interests may appear, subject to requirements of any applicable mortgagee clause and of Subparagraph 7.3.8. The Design/Builder shall pay contractors their shares of insurance proceeds received by the Design/Builder, and by appropriate agreement, written where legally required for validity, shall require contractors to make payments to their subcontractors in similar manner.

7.3.4 Before an exposure to loss may occur, the Owner shall file with the Design/Builder a copy of each policy required by this Paragraph 7.3. Each policy shall contain only those endorsements specifically related to this Project. Each policy shall contain a provision that the policy will not be cancelled or allowed to expire until at least thirty days' prior written notice has been given the Design/Builder.

7.3.5 If the Design/Builder requests in writing that insurance for risks other than those described herein or for other special hazards be included in the property insurance policy, the Owner shall, if possible, obtain such insurance, and the cost thereof shall be charged to the Design/Builder by appropriate Change Order.

7.3.6 The Owner and Design/Builder waive all rights against each other and the contractors, subcontractors, agents and employees, each of the other, for damages caused by fire or other perils to the extent covered by property insurance obtained pursuant to this Paragraph 7.3 or other property insurance applicable to the Work, except such rights as they may have to proceeds of such insurance held by the Owner as trustee. The Owner or Design/Builder, as appropriate, shall require from contractors and subcontractors by appropriate agreements, written where legally required for validity, similar waivers each in favor of other parties enumerated in this Paragraph 7.3. The policies shall be endorsed to include such waivers of subrogation.

7.3.7 If required in writing by a party in interest, the Owner as trustee shall provide, upon occurrence of an insured loss, a bond for proper performance of the Owner's duties. The cost of required bonds shall be charged against proceeds received as trustee. The Owner shall deposit proceeds so received in a separate account and shall distribute them in accordance with such agreement as the parties in interest may reach, or in accordance with an arbitration award in which case the procedure shall be as provided in Article 10. If after such loss no other special agreement is made, replacement of damaged Work shall be covered by appropriate Change Order.

7.3.8 The Owner, as trustee, shall have power to adjust and settle a loss with insurers unless one of the parties in interest shall object, in writing, within ten days after occurrence of loss, to the Owner's exercise of this power. If such objection be made, the Owner as trustee shall make settlement with the insurers in accordance with the decision of arbitration as provided in Article 10. If distribution of insurance proceeds by arbitration is required, the arbitrators will direct such distribution.

7.3.9 If the Owner finds it necessary to occupy or use a portion or portions of the Work before Substantial Completion, such occupancy or use shall not commence prior to a time agreed to by the Owner and Design/Builder and to which the insurance company or companies providing property insurance have consented by endorsement to the policy or policies. The property insurance shall not lapse or be cancelled on account of such partial occupancy or use. Consent of the Design/Builder and of the insurance company or companies to such occupancy or use shall not be unreasonably withheld.

7.4 LOSS OF USE INSURANCE

7.4.1 The Owner, at the Owner's option, may purchase and maintain such insurance as will insure the Owner against loss of use of the Owner's property due to fire or other hazards, however caused. The Owner waives all rights of action against the Design/Builder, and its contractors and their agents and employees, for loss of use of the Owner's property, including consequential losses due to fire or other hazards, however caused, to the extent covered by insurance under this Paragraph 7.4.

7.5 PERFORMANCE BOND AND PAYMENT BOND

7.5.1 The Owner shall have the right to require the Design/Builder to furnish bonds covering the faithful performance of the Contract and the payment of all obligations arising thereunder if and as required in the Contract Documents or in Article 14.

ARTICLE 8
CHANGES IN THE WORK

8.1 CHANGE ORDERS

8.1.1 A Change Order is a written order signed by the Owner and Design/Builder, and issued after execution of Part 2, authorizing a change in the Work or adjustment in the contract sum or contract time. The contract sum and contract time may be changed only by Change Order.

8.1.2 The Owner, without invalidating Part 2, may order changes in the Work within the general scope of Part 2 consisting of additions, deletions or other revisions, and the contract sum and contract time shall be adjusted accordingly. Such changes in the Work shall be authorized by Change Order, and shall be performed under applicable conditions of the Contract Documents.

8.1.3 If the Owner requests the Design/Builder to submit a proposal for a change in the Work and then elects not to proceed with the change, a Change Order shall be issued to reimburse the Design/Builder for any costs incurred for Design Services or proposed revisions to the Contract Documents.

8.1.4 Cost or credit to the Owner resulting from a change in the Work shall be determined in one or more of the following ways:

- **.1** by mutual acceptance of a lump sum properly itemized and supported by sufficient substantiating data to permit evaluation;
- **.2** by unit prices stated in the Contract Documents or subsequently agreed upon;

.3 by cost to be determined in a manner agreed upon by the parties and a mutually acceptable fixed or percentage fee; or

.4 by the method provided below.

8.1.5 If none of the methods set forth in Clauses 8.1.4.1, 8.1.4.2 or 8.1.4.3 is agreed upon, the Design/Builder, provided a written order signed by the Owner is received, shall promptly proceed with the Work involved. The cost of such Work shall then be determined on the basis of reasonable expenditures and savings of those performing the Work attributable to the change, including the expenditures for design services and revisions to the Contract Documents. In case of an increase in the contract sum, the cost shall include a reasonable allowance for overhead and profit. In case of the methods set forth in Clauses 8.1.4.3 and 8.1.4.4, the Design/Builder shall keep and present an itemized accounting together with appropriate supporting data for inclusion in a Change Order. Unless otherwise provided in the Contract Documents, cost shall be limited to the following: cost of materials, including sales tax and cost of delivery; cost of labor, including social security, old age and unemployment insurance, and fringe benefits required by agreement or custom; workers' or workmen's compensation insurance; bond premiums; rental value of equipment and machinery; additional costs of supervision and field office personnel directly attributable to the change; and fees paid to architects, engineers and other professionals. Pending final determination of cost to the Owner, payments on account shall be made on the Application for Payment. The amount of credit to be allowed by the Design/Builder to the Owner for deletion or change which results in a net decrease in the contract sum will be actual net cost. When both additions and credits covering related Work or substitutions are involved in a change, the allowance for overhead and profit shall be figured on the basis of the net increase, if any, with respect to that change.

8.1.6 If unit prices are stated in the Contract Documents or subsequently agreed upon, and if quantities originally contemplated are so changed in a proposed Change Order that application of agreed unit prices to quantities proposed will cause substantial inequity to the Owner or Design/Builder, applicable unit prices shall be equitably adjusted.

8.2 CONCEALED CONDITIONS

8.2.1 If concealed or unknown conditions of an unusual nature that affect the performance of the Work and vary from those indicated by the Contract Documents are encountered below ground or in an existing structure other than the Work, which conditions are not ordinarily found to exist or which differ materially from those generally recognized as inherent in work of the character provided for in this Part 2, notice by the observing party shall be given promptly to the other party and, if possible, before conditions are disturbed and in no event later than twenty-one days after first observance of the conditions. The contract sum shall be equitably adjusted for such concealed or unknown conditions by Change Order upon claim by either party made within twenty-one days after the claimant becomes aware of the conditions.

8.3 REGULATORY CHANGES

8.3.1 The Design/Builder shall be compensated for changes in the Work necessitated by the enactment or revision of codes, laws or regulations subsequent to the submission of the Design/Builder's Proposal under Part 1.

ARTICLE 9
CORRECTION OF WORK

9.1 The Design/Builder shall promptly correct Work rejected by the Owner or known by the Design/Builder to be defective or failing to conform to the Construction Documents, whether observed before or after Substantial Completion and whether or not fabricated, installed or completed, and shall correct Work under this Part 2 found to be defective or nonconforming within a period of one year from the date of Substantial Completion of the Work or designated portion thereof, or within such longer period provided by any applicable special warranty in the Contract Documents.

9.2 Nothing contained in this Article 9 shall be construed to establish a period of limitation with respect to other obligations of the Design/Builder under this Part 2. Paragraph 9.1 relates only to the specific obligation of the Design/Builder to correct the Work, and has no relationship to the time within which the obligation to comply with the Contract Documents may be sought to be enforced, nor to the time within which proceedings may be commenced to establish the Design/Builder's liability with respect to the Design/Builder's obligations other than correction of the Work.

9.3 If the Design/Builder fails to correct defective Work as required or persistently fails to carry out Work in accordance with the Contract Documents, the Owner, by written order signed personally or by an agent specifically so empowered by the Owner in writing, may order the Design/Builder to stop the Work, or any portion thereof, until the cause for such order has been eliminated; however, the Owner's right to stop the Work shall not give rise to a duty on the part of the Owner to exercise the right for benefit of the Design/Builder or other persons or entities.

9.4 If the Design/Builder defaults or neglects to carry out the Work in accordance with the Contract Documents and fails within seven days after receipt of written notice from the Owner to commence and continue correction of such default or neglect with diligence and promptness, the Owner may give a second written notice to the Design/Builder and, seven days following receipt by the Design/Builder of that second written notice and without prejudice to other remedies the Owner may have, correct such deficiencies. In such case an appropriate Change Order shall be issued deducting from payments then or thereafter due the Design/Builder costs of correcting such deficiencies. If the payments then or thereafter due the Design/Builder are not sufficient to cover the amount of the deduction, the Design/Builder shall pay the difference to the Owner. Such action by the Owner shall be subject to arbitration.

ARTICLE 10
ARBITRATION

10.1 Claims, disputes and other matters in question between the parties to this Part 2 arising out of or relating to Part 2 shall be decided by arbitration in accordance with the Construction Industry Arbitration Rules of the American Arbitration Association then in effect unless the parties agree otherwise. No arbitration arising out of or relating to this Part 2 shall include, by consolidation or joinder or in any other manner, an additional person not a party to Part 2 except by written consent containing specific reference to Part 2 and signed by the Owner, Design/Builder and any other person sought to be joined. Consent to arbitration involving an additional person or persons shall not constitute consent to arbitration of a dispute not described or with a person not named therein. This provision shall be specifically enforceable in any court of competent jurisdiction.

10.2 Notice of demand for arbitration shall be filed in writing with the other party to this Part 2 and with the American Arbitration Association. The demand shall be made within a reasonable time after the claim, dispute or other matter in question has arisen. In no event shall the demand for arbitration be made after the date when the applicable statute of limitations would bar institution of a legal or equitable proceeding based on such claim, dispute or other matter in question.

10.3 The award rendered by arbitrators shall be final, and judgment may be entered upon it in accordance with applicable law in any court having jurisdiction.

10.4 Unless otherwise agreed in writing, the Design/Builder shall carry on the Work and maintain its progress during any arbitration proceedings, and the Owner shall continue to make payments to the Design/Builder in accordance with the Contract Documents.

10.5 This Article 10 shall survive completion or termination of Part 2.

ARTICLE 11
MISCELLANEOUS PROVISIONS

11.1 This Part 2 shall be governed by the law of the place where the Work is located.

11.2 The table of contents and the headings of articles and paragraphs are for convenience only and shall not modify rights and obligations created by this Part 2.

11.3 In case a provision of Part 2 is held to be invalid, illegal or unenforceable, the validity, legality and enforceability of the remaining provisions shall not be affected.

11.4 SUBCONTRACTS

11.4.1 The Design/Builder, as soon as practicable after execution of Part 2, shall furnish to the Owner in writing the names of the persons or entities the Design/Builder will engage as contractors for the Project.

11.4.2 Nothing contained in the Design/Builder Contract Documents shall create a professional obligation or contractual relationship between the Owner and any third party.

11.5 WORK BY OWNER OR OWNER'S CONTRACTORS

11.5.1 The Owner reserves the right to perform work related to, but not part of, the Project and to award separate contracts in connection with other work at the site. If the Design/Builder claims that delay or additional cost is involved because of such action by the Owner, the Design/Builder shall make such claims as provided in Subparagraph 11.6.

11.5.2 The Design/Builder shall afford the Owner's separate contractors reasonable opportunity for introduction and storage of their materials and equipment for execution of their work. The Design/Builder shall incorporate and coordinate the Design/Builder's Work with work of the Owner's separate contractors as required by the Contract Documents.

11.5.3 Costs caused by defective or ill-timed work shall be borne by the party responsible.

11.6 CLAIMS FOR DAMAGES

11.6.1 Should either party to Part 2 suffer injury or damage to person or property because of an act or omission of the other party, the other party's employees or agents, or another for whose acts the other party is legally liable, claim shall be made in writing to the other party within a reasonable time after such injury or damage is or should have been first observed.

11.7 INDEMNIFICATION

11.7.1 To the fullest extent permitted by law, the Design/Builder shall indemnify and hold harmless the Owner and the Owner's consultants and separate contractors, any of their subcontractors, sub-subcontractors, agents and employees from and against claims, damages, losses and expenses, including but not limited to attorneys' fees, arising out of or resulting from performance of the Work. These indemnification obligations shall be limited to claims, damages, losses or expenses (1) that are attributable to bodily injury, sickness, disease or death, or to injury to or destruction of tangible property (other than the Work itself) including loss of use resulting therefrom, and (2) to the extent such claims, damages, losses or expenses are caused in whole or in part by negligent acts or omissions of the Design/Builder, the Design/Builder's contractors, anyone directly or indirectly employed by either or anyone for whose acts either may be liable, regardless of whether or not they are caused in part by a party indemnified hereunder. Such obligation shall not be construed to negate, abridge or otherwise reduce other rights or obligations of indemnity which would otherwise exist as to a party or person described in this Paragraph 11.7.

11.7.2 In claims against the Owner or its consultants and its contractors, any of their subcontractors, sub-subcontractors, agents or employees by an employee of the Design/Builder, its contractors, anyone directly or indirectly employed by them or anyone for whose acts they may be liable, the indemnification obligation under this Paragraph 11.7 shall not be limited by a limitation on amount or type of damages, compensation or benefits payable by or for the Design/Builder, or a Design/Builder's contractor, under workers' or workmen's compensation acts, disability benefit acts or other employee benefit acts.

11.8 SUCCESSORS AND ASSIGNS

11.8.1 This Part 2 shall be binding on successors, assigns, and legal representatives of and persons in privity of contract with the Owner or Design/Builder. Neither party shall assign, sublet or transfer an interest in Part 2 without the written consent of the other.

11.8.2 This Paragraph 11.8 shall survive completion or termination of Part 2.

11.9 In case of termination of the Architect, the Design/Builder shall provide the services of another lawfully licensed person or entity against whom the Owner makes no reasonable objection.

11.10 EXTENT OF AGREEMENT

11.10.1 Part 2 represents the entire agreement between the Owner and Design/Builder and supersedes Part 1 and prior negotiations, representations or agreements. Part 2 may be amended only by written instrument signed by both Owner and Design/Builder.

ARTICLE 12
TERMINATION OF THE AGREEMENT

12.1 TERMINATION BY THE OWNER

12.1.1 This Part 2 may be terminated by the Owner upon fourteen days' written notice to the Design/Builder in the event that the Project is abandoned. If such termination occurs, the Owner shall pay the Design/Builder for Work completed and for proven loss sustained upon materials, equipment, tools, and construction equipment and machinery, including reasonable profit and applicable damages.

12.1.2 If the Design/Builder defaults or persistently fails or neglects to carry out the Work in accordance with the Contract Documents or fails to perform the provisions of Part 2, the Owner may give written notice that the Owner intends to terminate Part 2. If the Design/Builder fails to correct the defaults, failure or neglect within seven days after being given notice, the Owner may then give a second written notice and, after an additional seven days, the Owner may without prejudice to any other remedy make good such deficiencies and may deduct the cost thereof from the payment due the Design/Builder or, at the Owner's option, may terminate the employment of the Design/Builder and take possession of the site and of all materials, equipment, tools and construction equipment and machinery thereon owned by the Design/Builder and finish the Work by whatever method the Owner may deem expedient. If the unpaid balance of the contract sum exceeds the expense of finishing the Work, the excess shall be paid to the Design/Builder, but if the expense exceeds the unpaid balance, the Design/Builder shall pay the difference to the Owner.

12.2 TERMINATION BY THE DESIGN/BUILDER

12.2.1 If the Owner fails to make payment when due, the Design/Builder may give written notice of the Design/Builder's intention to terminate Part 2. If the Design/Builder fails to receive payment within seven days after receipt of such notice by the Owner, the Design/Builder may give a second written notice and, seven days after receipt of such second written notice by the Owner, may terminate Part 2 and recover from the Owner payment for Work executed and for proven losses sustained upon materials, equipment, tools, and construction equipment and machinery, including reasonable profit and applicable damages.

ARTICLE 13
BASIS OF COMPENSATION

The Owner shall compensate the Design/Builder in accordance with Article 5, Payments, and the other provisions of this Part 2 as described below.

13.1 COMPENSATION

13.1.1 FOR BASIC SERVICES, as described in Paragraphs 2.2.2 through 2.2.17, and for any other services included in Article 14 as part of Basic Services, Basic Compensation shall be as follows:

13.2 REIMBURSABLE EXPENSES

13.2.1 Reimbursable Expenses are in addition to the compensation for Basic and Additional Services and include actual expenditures made by the Design/Builder in the interest of the Project for the expenses listed as follows:

13.2.2 FOR REIMBURSABLE EXPENSES, compensation shall be a multiple of ( ) times the amounts expended.

13.3 INTEREST PAYMENTS

13.3.1 The rate of interest for past due payments shall be as follows:

(Usury laws and requirements under the Federal Truth in Lending Act, similar state and local consumer credit laws and other regulations at the Owner's and Design/Builder's principal places of business, at the location of the Project and elsewhere may affect the validity of this provision. Specific legal advice should be obtained with respect to deletion, modification or other requirements, such as written disclosures or waivers.)

ARTICLE 14
OTHER PROVISIONS

14.1 The Basic Services to be performed shall be commenced on and, subject to authorized adjustments and to delays not caused by the Design/Builder, Substantial Completion shall be achieved in ( ) calendar days.

14.2 The Basic Services beyond those described in Article 2 are:

14.3 The Design/Builder shall submit an Application for Payment on the of each month.

14.4 The Design/Builder's Proposal includes:
(List below: this Part 2, Supplementary and other Conditions, the drawings, the specifications, and Modifications, showing page or sheet numbers in all cases and dates where applicable to define the scope of Work.)

This Part 2 entered into as of the day and year first written above.

OWNER	DESIGN/BUILDER
______________________	______________________
______________________	______________________
______________________	______________________
BY ______________________	BY ______________________

INSTRUCTION SHEET

FOR AIA DOCUMENT A491, STANDARD FORM OF AGREEMENTS BETWEEN DESIGN/BUILDER AND CONTRACTOR—FIRST EDITION

A. GENERAL INFORMATION

1. Purpose

This Document is the first edition of AIA Document A491, Standard Form of Agreements Between Design/Builder and Contractor. It is intended to govern relations between the Design/Builder and Contractor under the contractual organization diagramed below.

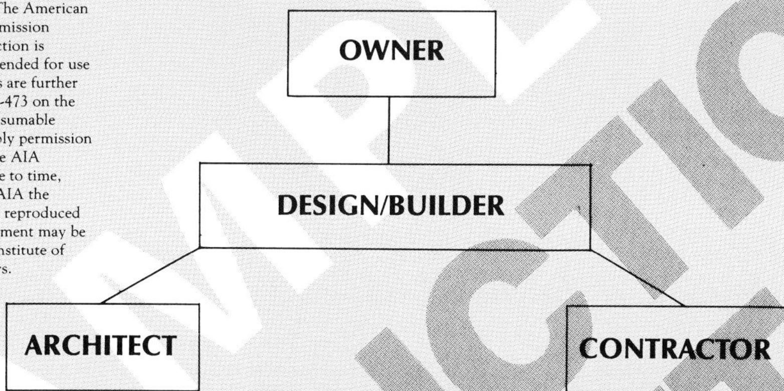

Design/build is a process in which the Owner contracts directly with one entity to provide both design and construction services. The AIA believes that if a public Owner chooses to utilize the design/build process, selection of the design/build team should be based upon objective criteria developed to evaluate the qualifications and competence of the design/build team, as with Brooks Act procurement methods.

This Document contains two Agreements which are intended to be used in sequence as the basis for the agreements between the Design/Builder and the Contractor when the Owner seeks to have a single entity responsible for both the design and the construction of a project. The first Agreement, known as Part 1, covers management consulting services to be provided by the Contractor during the preliminary design and budgeting phase of the Project. The second Agreement, known as Part 2, covers construction. It is intended that the parties first enter into the Part 1 Agreement to provide cost estimating, scheduling and value engineering for the Project, and thereafter enter into the Part 2 Agreement. Before signing Part 1 the parties should also reach substantial agreement on the terms of Part 2, except for the scope of the Project and compensation. Although it is anticipated that the parties entering into the Part 1 Agreement will also enter into the Part 2 Agreement, the parties may conclude their relationship after Part 1 is performed rather than continuing on to Part 2.

2. Related Documents

AIA Document A491 is published in conjunction with the following related documents:

A191, Standard Form of Agreements Between Owner and Design/Builder
B901, Standard Form of Agreements Between Design/Builder and Architect

3. Use of Non-AIA Forms

If a non-AIA document or a mixture of AIA documents and non-AIA documents is used, particular care must be taken to achieve consistency of language and intent. If there are any significant omissions, additions or variances from the terms of the related standard AIA forms, both legal and insurance counsel should be consulted.

4. Letter Forms of Agreement

Letter forms of agreement are generally discouraged by the AIA, as is the performance of some or all services based on oral agreements or understandings. The AIA forms have been developed through more than ninety years of experience and have been tested repeatedly in courts. They are carefully coordinated with other AIA documents.

5. Use of Current Documents

Prior to using any AIA document, the user should consult the AIA or an AIA component chapter to determine the current edition of each document.

6. Reproduction

AIA Document A491 is a copyrighted document and may not be reproduced or excerpted from in whole or in part without the express written permission of the AIA prior to reproduction. This Document is intended for use as a "consumable" publication without any implied consent to duplicate except under the limited license described below.

Purchasers of the A491 Document are entitled by license to reproduce a maximum of ten copies of the completed or executed document for use only in connection with a particular Project.

B. COMPLETING THE A491 FORM

1. Modifications

As with all AIA documents, users are encouraged to consult an attorney with respect to completing or modifying the form. Legal counsel should also be sought concerning the effect of state and local law on the terms of each Agreement. In particular, legal counsel should be consulted with respect to interest charges, arbitration and duties imposed by building codes. Generally, modifications may be accomplished by describing changes to the printed text in Article 10 of Part 1 or Article 14 of Part 2, or by attaching and referencing a separate amendment sheet. If deletions are needed, these should be accomplished by striking through with a line, or by amendment. It is not recommended that deletions be made by erasing, whiting out or taping over provisions in this Document.

2. Cover Page (Same for Part 1 and Part 2)

Date: The date of the Agreement is the date when the Agreement becomes legally effective. It may be the date that an oral agreement was reached, the date the Agreement was originally submitted to the Design/Builder, the date authorizing action was taken or the date of actual execution. Services should not be performed prior to the effective date of the Agreement.

Parties: Parties to this Agreement should be identified using the full legal names and addresses under which the Agreement will be executed, including designation of the legal status of the parties: sole proprietorship, partnership, joint venture, unincorporated association, corporation (general, closed or professional), etc.

Project: The proposed Project should be described in sufficient detail to identify (1) the official name or title of the facility, (2) the location of the site, if known, (3) the proposed building type or use, and (4) the size, capacity or scope of the Project, if known.

Owner: Although the Owner is not a party to the Agreement Between Design/Builder and Contractor, it is customary to identify the Owner in agreements of this kind.

3. Part 1 Agreement: Pre-Construction

a) Article 9—Basis of Compensation

Subparagraph 9.1.1
Describe the basis of computing compensation for Basic Services under this subparagraph. Several methods may be used on a particular project. When more than one method is used, each method should reference the appropriate services listed in Article 2 and Article 10. This may be done by titling them "Method A," "Method B," etc.

Subparagraph 9.1.2
Insert the amount of initial payment as referred to in Paragraph 5.1.

Subparagraph 9.1.3
Describe the manner in which subsequent progress payments will be made to the Contractor.

Subparagraph 9.2.1
Describe the basis of computing additional compensation.

Subparagraph 9.3.1
List reimbursable expenses, if any.

Subparagraph 9.3.2
Insert a multiple for reimbursable expenses, if any.

Subparagraph 9.5.1
Insert rate of interest, if other than the legal rate.

Paragraph 9.7
Insert the number of months after which the compensation levels will be renegotiated.

b) Article 10—Other Conditions and Provisions

Paragraph 10.1
Insert the date for commencement of Work and the number of calendar days in which the Work is to be completed.

Paragraph 10.2
Insert Basic Services not described in Article 2.

4. **Part 2 Agreement: Construction**

a) **Article 13—Basis of Compensation**

Paragraph 13.2
Insert basis of compensation, such as stipulated sum, percentage fee or cost of the Work (defining cost), unit prices, cash allowances or contingencies, if any. Insert Contract Sum.

Paragraph 13.3
State the date of each month on which the Contractor will submit Applications for Payment.

Paragraph 13.4
Insert rate of interest, if other than the legal rate.

b) **Article 14—Other Provisions**

Paragraph 14.1
Describe the Contractor's scope of Work.

Paragraph 14.2
Insert the date of commencement and the number of days allowed for performance of the Contract.

Paragraph 14.3
List the Contract Documents.

Paragraph 14.4
Insert the Contractor's insurance coverage, such as amounts and limits on property insurance, workers' or workmen's compensation, or liability insurance.

Paragraph 14.6
Insert temporary facilities and services to be provided by the Design/Builder.

C. EXECUTION OF THE AGREEMENTS

Persons executing (signing) each Agreement should indicate the capacity in which they are acting (e.g., president, secretary, partner, etc.) and the authority under which they are executing the Agreement. Evidence of authority to sign on behalf of each party should be obtained. Where appropriate, a copy of the resolution or bylaw authorizing the individual to act on behalf of the firm or entity should be attached.

THE AMERICAN INSTITUTE OF ARCHITECTS

AIA Document A491

Standard Form of Agreements Between Design/Builder and Contractor

1985 EDITION

THIS DOCUMENT HAS IMPORTANT LEGAL CONSEQUENCES; CONSULTATION WITH AN ATTORNEY IS ENCOURAGED.

TABLE OF ARTICLES

PART 1 AGREEMENT—PRE-CONSTRUCTION

PART 2 AGREEMENT—CONSTRUCTION

A491-1985
COVER PAGE

THE AMERICAN INSTITUTE OF ARCHITECTS

AIA Document A491

Standard Form of Agreement Between Design/Builder and Contractor

1985 EDITION

THIS DOCUMENT HAS IMPORTANT LEGAL CONSEQUENCES; CONSULTATION WITH AN ATTORNEY IS ENCOURAGED.

This Document comprises two separate Agreements: Part 1 Agreement—Pre-Construction and Part 2 Agreement—Construction. Before executing Part 1, the parties should reach substantial agreement on Part 2. Hereinafter the Part 1 Agreement is referred to as Part 1 and the Part 2 Agreement is referred to as Part 2. This Document is intended for use with AIA Document A191, Owner-Design/Builder Agreement.

PART 1 AGREEMENT—PRE-CONSTRUCTION

AGREEMENT

made as of the day of in the year of Nineteen Hundred and

BETWEEN the Design/Builder:
(Name and address)

and the Contractor:
(Name and address)

For the following Project:
(Include Project name, location and detailed description of scope.)

The Owner is:
(Name and address)

The Design/Builder and the Contractor agree as set forth below.

Terms and Conditions—Part 1 Agreement

ARTICLE 1
GENERAL PROVISIONS

1.1 BASIC DEFINITIONS

1.1.1 The Project is the total design and construction for which the Design/Builder is responsible under a separate agreement with the Owner, including all professional design services and all labor, materials and equipment used or incorporated in such design and construction.

1.1.2 The Work comprises the completed construction designed under the Project and to be performed by the Contractor under Part 2. The Work includes labor necessary to produce such construction, and materials and equipment incorporated or to be incorporated in such construction.

1.2 EXECUTION, CORRELATION AND INTENT

1.2.1 This Part 1 shall be signed in not less than duplicate by the Design/Builder and Contractor.

1.3 OWNERSHIP AND USE OF DOCUMENTS

1.3.1 The drawings, specifications and other documents furnished by the Design/Builder are instruments of service and shall not become the property of the Contractor whether or not the Project for which they are made is commenced. Drawings, specifications and other documents furnished by the Design/Builder shall not be used by the Contractor on other projects, for additions to this Project or for completion of this Project by others except by written agreement relating to use, liability and compensation.

1.3.2 Submission or distribution of documents to meet official regulatory requirements or for other purposes in connection with the Project is not to be construed as publication in derogation of the Architect's common law copyrights or other reserved rights. The Contractor shall own neither the documents nor the copyrights.

ARTICLE 2
CONTRACTOR

2.1 BASIC SERVICES

2.1.1 The Contractor's Basic Services are described below and in Article 10.

2.1.2 The Contractor shall, after consultation with the Design/Builder, prepare a preliminary evaluation of the program and budget provided by the Design/Builder for the Work.

2.1.3 The Contractor shall review with the Design/Builder alternative approaches to design and construction of the Project.

2.1.4 The Contractor shall provide estimates of Construction Cost, by line items, showing the quantity assumptions for labor, materials and equipment.

2.1.5 The Contractor shall provide value engineering services to the extent required in Article 10.

2.1.6 The Contractor shall provide scheduling services for pre-construction and construction activities to the extent required in Article 10.

2.2 ADDITIONAL SERVICES

2.2.1 All other services requested by the Design/Builder and mutually agreed to in writing by the Design/Builder and Contractor in Part 1, including, among others, changes in Project scope and program, shall constitute Additional Services and shall be paid for by the Design/Builder as provided in Part 1.

ARTICLE 3
DESIGN/BUILDER

3.1 The Design/Builder shall provide information regarding requirements for the Project, including but not limited to the Owner's design objectives, constraints and criteria.

3.2 The Design/Builder shall designate a representative authorized to act on the Design/Builder's behalf with respect to the Project. The Design/Builder or such authorized representative shall examine the documents submitted by the Contractor and shall promptly render decisions pertaining thereto to avoid delay in the orderly progress of the Contractor's Services.

3.3 The Design/Builder agrees to obtain the services of qualified architects, engineers, other professionals, other construction contractors and suppliers, as necessary for the proper execution of the Project, using professionals whose professional obligations are undertaken and performed in the interest of the Design/Builder.

3.4 Prior to commencement of Basic Services, the Design/Builder shall furnish a legal description and a certified land survey of the site, giving, as applicable, grades and lines of streets, alleys, pavements and adjoining property; rights-of-way, restrictions, easements, encroachments, zoning, deed restrictions, elevations and contours of the site; locations, dimensions and complete data pertaining to existing buildings, other improvements and trees; and full information concerning available services and utility lines, both public and private and above and below grade, including inverts and depths.

3.5 The Design/Builder shall provide the Contractor with Preliminary Design Documents consisting of preliminary design drawings, outline specifications and other documents to fix and describe the size, quality and character of the entire Project, its architectural, structural, mechanical and electrical systems, and the materials and such other elements of the Project as may be appropriate.

3.6 The Design/Builder shall furnish services of geotechnical engineers and other consultants when such services are deemed necessary by the Design/Builder. Such services shall include, as required, applicable test borings, test pits, soil bearing values, percolation tests, air and water pollution tests, and other necessary operations for determining subsoil, air and water conditions, with reports and appropriate professional recommendations.

3.7 The services, information, surveys and reports required by Paragraphs 3.3 through 3.6 shall be the responsibility of the Design/Builder, and the Contractor shall be entitled to rely upon their accuracy and completeness.

3.8 The Design/Builder shall furnish required information and services and shall render decisions with reasonable promptness to avoid delay in the orderly progress of the Contractor's services.

ARTICLE 4
TIME

4.1 The Contractor shall provide the Basic and Additional Services as expeditiously as is consistent with reasonable skill and care, and shall complete the services in the time provided in Article 10.

ARTICLE 5
PAYMENTS

5.1 The initial payment provided in Article 9 shall be made upon execution of Part 1 and shall be the minimum payment under Part 1.

5.2 Subsequent payments for Basic Services, Additional Services and Reimbursable Expenses shall be made monthly on the basis set forth in Article 9.

5.3 Within twenty days of the Design/Builder's receipt of a properly submitted Application for Payment, the Design/Builder shall make payment to the Contractor.

5.4 Payments due the Contractor under Part 1 which are not paid when due shall bear interest from the date due at the rate specified in Paragraph 9.7, or in the absence of a specified rate, at the legal rate prevailing where the principal office of the Contractor is located.

ARTICLE 6
ARBITRATION

6.1 Claims, disputes and other matters in question between the parties to Part 1 arising out of or relating to Part 1 shall be decided by arbitration in accordance with the Construction Industry Arbitration Rules of the American Arbitration Association then in effect unless the parties agree otherwise. No arbitration arising out of or relating to Part 1 shall include, by consolidation or joinder or in any other manner, an additional person not a party to Part 1 except by written consent containing specific reference to Part 1 and signed by the Design/Builder, Contractor and any other person sought to be joined. Consent to arbitration involving an additional person or persons shall not constitute consent to arbitration of a dispute not described therein or with a person not named therein. This provision shall be specifically enforceable in any court of competent jurisdiction.

6.2 Notice of demand for arbitration shall be filed in writing with the other party to Part 1 and with the American Arbitration Association. The demand shall be made within a reasonable time after the claim, dispute or other matter in question has arisen. In no event shall the demand for arbitration be made after the date when the applicable statute of limitations would bar institution of a legal or equitable proceeding based on such claim, dispute or other matter in question.

6.3 The award rendered by arbitrators shall be final, and judgment may be entered upon it in accordance with applicable law in any court having jurisdiction.

6.4 Unless otherwise agreed in writing, the Contractor shall carry on the services and maintain progress during any arbitration proceedings, and the Design/Builder shall continue to make payments to the Contractor in accordance with Part 1.

6.5 This Article 6 shall survive completion or termination of Part 1.

ARTICLE 7
MISCELLANEOUS PROVISIONS

7.1 This Part 1 shall be governed by the law of the place where the principal office of the Design/Builder is located.

7.2 The table of contents and the headings of articles and paragraphs are for convenience only and shall not modify rights and obligations created by Part 1.

7.3 In case a provision of Part 1 is held invalid, illegal or unenforceable, the validity, legality and enforceability of the remaining provisions shall not be affected.

7.4 SUCCESSORS AND ASSIGNS

7.4.1 This Part 1 shall be binding on successors, assigns and legal representatives of and persons in privity of contract with the Design/Builder or Contractor. Neither party shall assign or transfer an interest in Part 1 without written consent of the other.

7.4.2 This Paragraph 7.4 shall survive completion or termination of Part 1.

7.5 EXTENT OF AGREEMENT

7.5.1 Part 1 represents the entire agreement and supersedes all prior negotiations, representations or agreements. Part 1 may be amended only by written instrument signed by both Design/Builder and Contractor.

ARTICLE 8
TERMINATION OF THE AGREEMENT

8.1 This Part 1 may be terminated by either party upon seven days' written notice should the other party fail substantially to perform in accordance with its terms through no fault of the party initiating the termination.

8.2 Part 1 may be terminated by the Design/Builder upon at least seven days' written notice to the Contractor in the event that the Project is permanently abandoned.

8.3 In the event of termination not the fault of the Contractor, the Contractor shall be compensated for services performed to termination date, together with Reimbursable Expenses then due and Termination Expenses. Termination Expenses are expenses directly attributable to termination, including a reasonable amount for overhead and profit, for which the Contractor is not otherwise compensated under Part 1.

ARTICLE 9
BASIS OF COMPENSATION

The Design/Builder shall compensate the Contractor in accordance with Article 5, Payments, and the other provisions of Part 1 as described below.

9.1 COMPENSATION FOR BASIC SERVICES

9.1.1 FOR BASIC SERVICES, compensation shall be as follows:

9.1.2 AN INITIAL PAYMENT of dollars ($) shall be made upon execution of Part 1 and credited to the Contractor's account as follows:

9.1.3 SUBSEQUENT PAYMENTS shall be as follows:

9.2 COMPENSATION FOR ADDITIONAL SERVICES

9.2.1 FOR ADDITIONAL SERVICES, compensation shall be as follows:

9.3 REIMBURSABLE EXPENSES

9.3.1 Reimbursable Expenses are in addition to Compensation for Basic and Additional Services and include actual expenditures made by the Contractor and the Contractor's employees and subcontractors in the interest of the Project for the expenses listed as follows:

9.3.2 FOR REIMBURSABLE EXPENSES, compensation shall be a multiple of ( ) times the amounts expended.

9.4 DIRECT PERSONNEL EXPENSE is defined as the direct salaries of personnel engaged on the Project and the portion of the cost of their mandatory and customary contributions and benefits related thereto, such as employment taxes and other statutory employee benefits, insurance, sick leave, holidays, vacations, pensions and similar contributions and benefits.

9.5 INTEREST PAYMENTS

9.5.1 The rate of interest for past due payments shall be as follows:

(Usury laws and requirements under the Federal Truth in Lending Act, similar state and local consumer credit laws and other regulations at the Design/Builder's and Contractor's principal places of business, at the location of the Project and elsewhere may affect the validity of this provision. Specific legal advice should be obtained with respect to deletion, modification or other requirements, such as written disclosures or waivers.)

9.6 IF THE SCOPE of the Project or of the Contractor's services is changed materially, the amount of compensation shall be equitably adjusted.

9.7 The compensation set forth herein shall be equitably adjusted if through no fault of the Contractor the services have not been completed within ( ) months of the date of Part 1.

ARTICLE 10
OTHER PROVISIONS

10.1 The Basic Services to be performed shall be commenced on and, subject to authorized adjustments and to delays not caused by the Contractor, shall be completed in ( ) calendar days.

10.2 The Basic Services beyond those described in Article 2 are:

This Part 1 entered into as of the day and year first written above.

DESIGN/BUILDER	CONTRACTOR
BY	BY

THE AMERICAN INSTITUTE OF ARCHITECTS

AIA Document A491

Standard Form of Agreement Between Design/Builder and Contractor

1985 EDITION

THIS DOCUMENT HAS IMPORTANT LEGAL CONSEQUENCES; CONSULTATION WITH AN ATTORNEY IS ENCOURAGED.

This Document comprises two separate Agreements: Part 1 Agreement—Pre-Construction and Part 2 Agreement—Construction. Hereinafter, the Part 1 Agreement is referred to as Part 1 and the Part 2 Agreement is referred to as Part 2. This Document is intended for use with AIA Document A191, Owner-Design/Builder Agreement.

PART 2 AGREEMENT—CONSTRUCTION

AGREEMENT

made as of the day of in the year of Nineteen Hundred and

BETWEEN the Design/Builder:
(Name and address)

and the Contractor:
(Name and address)

For the following Project:
(Include Project name, location and detailed description of scope.)

The Owner is:
(Name and address)

The Design/Builder and the Contractor agree as set forth below.

Terms and Conditions—Part 2 Agreement

ARTICLE 1
GENERAL PROVISIONS

1.1 BASIC DEFINITIONS

1.1.1 The Contract Documents for this Contract consist of this Part 2, the drawings, specifications and other documents identified in Article 14, the Construction Documents issued after execution of Part 2 and agreed upon by the parties to this Contract, and Modifications. A Modification is a written amendment to Part 2 signed by both parties, or a Change Order. These form the Contract, and are as fully a part of the Contract as if attached to this Part 2 or repeated herein.

1.1.2 The Project is the total design and construction for which the Design/Builder is responsible under a separate agreement with the Owner, including all professional services and all labor, materials and equipment used or incorporated in such design and construction.

1.1.3 The Work comprises the completed construction designed under the Project and required by the Contract Documents. The Work includes labor necessary to produce such construction, and materials and equipment incorporated or to be incorporated in such construction.

1.2 EXECUTION, CORRELATION AND INTENT

1.2.1 This Part 2 shall be signed in not less than duplicate by the Design/Builder and Contractor.

1.2.2 It is the intent of the Design/Builder and Contractor that the Contract Documents include items necessary for proper execution and completion of the Work and that they shall be binding upon the Design/Builder and Contractor. Work not covered in the Contract Documents will not be required unless it is consistent with and is reasonably inferable from the Contract Documents as being necessary to complete the Work. Words and abbreviations which have well-known technical or trade meanings are used in the Contract Documents in accordance with such recognized meanings.

1.3 OWNERSHIP AND USE OF DOCUMENTS

1.3.1 The drawings, specifications and other documents furnished by the Design/Builder are instruments of service and shall not become the property of the Contractor whether or not the Project for which they are made is commenced. Drawings, specifications and other documents furnished by the Design/Builder shall not be used by the Contractor on other projects, for additions to this Project or for completion of this Project by others except by written agreement relating to use, liability and compensation.

1.3.2 Submission or distribution of documents to meet official regulatory requirements or for other purposes in connection with the Project is not to be construed as publication in derogation of the Architect's common law copyrights or other reserved rights. The Contractor shall own neither the documents nor the copyrights.

ARTICLE 2
CONTRACTOR

2.1 SERVICES AND RESPONSIBILITIES

2.1.1 The Contractor agrees to obtain the services of qualified Subcontractors and suppliers as necessary to perform the Work in the interest of the Design/Builder.

2.2 INDEPENDENT CONTRACTOR STATUS

2.2.1 In the performance of this Contract, the Contractor shall operate as an independent contractor and not as an agent of the Design/Builder or Owner.

2.3 SUPERVISION AND CONSTRUCTION PROCEDURES

2.3.1 The Contractor shall supervise and direct the Work, using the Contractor's best skill and attention. The Contractor shall be solely responsible for all construction means, methods, techniques, sequences and procedures and for coordinating all portions of the Work under the Contract. The Contractor shall be responsible to the Design/Builder for acts and omissions of the Contractor's employees, Subcontractors and their agents and employees, and other persons performing the Work.

2.3.2 The Contractor, as soon as practicable after execution of Part 2, shall furnish to the Design/Builder in writing the names of the persons or entities proposed for each of the principal portions of the Work. Contracts between the Contractor and each Subcontractor shall (1) require each such Subcontractor, to the extent of the Work to be performed by the Subcontractor, to conform to the Contract Documents and to assume in favor of the Contractor the obligations and responsibilities which the Contractor, by these Documents, assumes in favor of the Design/Builder; and (2) provide each Subcontractor with the rights and remedies provided to the Contractor against the Design/Builder by these Documents.

ARTICLE 3
DESIGN/BUILDER

3.1 RESPONSIBILITIES

3.1.1 The Design/Builder shall provide Construction Documents for use by the Contractor. Construction Documents shall include technical drawings, schedules, diagrams and specifications setting forth in detail the requirements for construction of the Work, and shall:

- **.1** develop the intent of the Design/Builder's proposal in greater detail;
- **.2** provide information customarily necessary for the use of those in the building trades; and
- **.3** include documents customarily required for regulatory agency approvals.

3.2 SERVICES PROVIDED BY THE DESIGN/BUILDER

3.2.1 The Design/Builder shall cooperate with the Contractor in scheduling and performing the Design/Builder's work to avoid conflicts or interference in the Work. As soon as practicable after execution of this Part 2, the Design/Builder shall provide the Contractor a copy of the estimated progress schedule of the Project which the Design/Builder has prepared and submitted for the Owner's information, together with such additional scheduling details as will enable the Contractor to plan and perform the Work properly. The Contractor shall be notified promptly of subsequent changes in the progress schedule and additional scheduling details.

3.3 COMMUNICATIONS

3.3.1 The Design/Builder shall promptly notify the Contractor of Modifications to the Project which affect Part 2 and which were issued or entered into subsequent to the execution of Part 2.

3.3.2 The Design/Builder shall not give instructions or orders directly to employees or workers of the Contractor except to persons designated as authorized representatives of the Contractor.

ARTICLE 4
TIME

4.1 The Contractor shall provide labor, materials, equipment and services as expeditiously as is consistent with reasonable skill and care and the orderly progress of the Work.

4.2 Time limits stated in this Part 2 are of the essence. The Work to be performed under Part 2 shall commence upon execution unless otherwise agreed and, subject to authorized Modifications, Substantial Completion shall be achieved as indicated in Article 14.

4.3 The date of Substantial Completion of the Contractor's Work or a designated portion thereof is the date when construction or a designated portion thereof is sufficiently complete so the Owner can occupy and utilize the Work or designated portion thereof for its intended use.

4.4 The Contractor, immediately after being awarded the Contract, shall prepare and submit for the Design/Builder's information a progress schedule for the Contractor's portion of the Work. The progress schedule shall be related to the entire Project to the extent required by the Contract Documents, and shall provide for expeditious and practicable execution of the Work.

4.5 If the Contractor is delayed in the progress of the Work by acts or neglect of the Owner or Design/Builder, separate contractors employed by the Owner, changes ordered in the Work not caused by the fault of the Contractor, labor disputes, fire, unusual delay in transportation, adverse weather conditions not reasonably anticipatable, unavoidable casualties, or other causes beyond the Contractor's control, or another cause which the Design/Builder agrees is justifiable, the Contract Time shall be reasonably extended by Change Order.

ARTICLE 5
PAYMENTS

5.1 Unless otherwise provided in the Contract Documents, the Design/Builder shall pay the Contractor each progress payment and the final payment under this Contract within ten working days after receipt of payment from the Owner, except as provided in Article 13. The amount of each progress payment to the Contractor shall be based on the percentage of completion allowed to the Design/Builder and shall reflect the percentage actually retained, if any, from payments to the Design/Builder plus, to the extent permitted by the Contract Documents, the amount allowed for materials and equipment suitably stored by the Contractor, less the aggregate of previous payments to the Contractor.

5.2 The Design/Builder may decline to make payment or partial payment because of: (1) defective Work of the Contractor not remedied; (2) third party claims or liens filed or reasonable evidence indicating probable filing of such claims or liens; (3) failure of the Contractor to make payments to Subcontractors, suppliers or workers; (4) reasonable doubt that the Contractor's Work can be completed for the unpaid balance of the Contract Sum; (5) damage to the Design/Builder or another contractor; (6) reasonable evidence that the Contractor's Work will not be completed within the Contract Time; or (7) persistent failure to carry out the Work in accordance with the Contract Documents.

5.3 PROGRESS PAYMENTS

5.3.1 The Contractor shall deliver to the Design/Builder itemized Applications for Payment in such detail as indicated in Article 13.

5.3.2 Within twenty days of the Design/Builder's receipt of a properly submitted Application for Payment, the Design/Builder shall make payment to the Contractor.

5.3.3 The Application for Payment shall constitute a representation by the Contractor to the Design/Builder that the construction has progressed to the point indicated; the quality of the Work covered by the application is in accordance with the Contract Documents; and the Contractor is entitled to payment in the amount requested.

5.3.4 Upon receipt of payment from the Design/Builder, the Contractor shall pay each Subcontractor, out of the amount paid to the Contractor on account of such Subcontractor's work, the amount to which said Subcontractor is entitled. The Contractor shall, by appropriate agreement with each Subcontractor, require each Subcontractor to make payments to its sub-subcontractors in a similar manner.

5.3.5 The Owner and the Design/Builder shall have no obligation to pay or to be responsible in any way for the payment of moneys to a Subcontractor except as may otherwise be required by law.

5.3.6 No progress payment or partial or entire use or occupancy of the Project by the Owner shall constitute an acceptance of Work not in accordance with the Contract Documents.

5.3.7 The Contractor warrants that: (1) title to Work, materials and equipment covered by an Application for Payment will pass to the Design/Builder either by incorporation in construction or upon receipt of payment by the Contractor, whichever occurs first; (2) Work, materials and equipment covered by previous Applications for Payment are free and clear of liens, claims, security interests or encumbrances, hereinafter referred to as "liens"; and (3) no Work, materials or equipment covered by an Application for Payment will have been acquired by the Contractor, or any other person performing Work at the site or furnishing materials or equipment for the Project, subject to an agreement under which an interest therein or an encumbrance thereon is retained by the seller or otherwise imposed by the Contractor or such other person.

5.3.8 If the Contract provides for retainage, then at the date of Substantial Completion of the Contractor's Work or occupancy of the Contractor's Work or any designated portion thereof by the Owner, whichever occurs first, the Contractor may apply for and the Design/Builder, if the Contractor has satisfied the requirements of Paragraph 5.2.1 and any other requirements of the Contract relating to retainage, shall pay the Contractor amounts retained, if any, for the Work or for the designated portion completed or occupied, less the reasonable value of incorrect or incomplete Work. Final payment of such withheld sum shall be made upon correction or completion of such Work.

5.4 FINAL PAYMENT

5.4.1 Neither final payment nor amounts retained, if any, shall become due until the Contractor submits to the Design/Builder (1) an affidavit that payrolls, bills for materials and equipment, and other indebtedness connected with the Work for which the Design/Builder or Owner's property might be liable have been paid or otherwise satisfied, (2) consent of surety, if any, to final payment, (3) a certificate that insurance required by the Contract Documents is in force following completion of the Work, and (4) if required by the Design/Builder, other data establishing payment or satisfaction of obligations, such as receipts, releases and waivers of liens arising out of Part 2, to the extent and in such form as may be designated by the Design/Builder. If a Subcontractor refuses to furnish a release or waiver required by the Design/Builder, the Contractor may furnish a bond satisfactory to the Design/Builder to indemnify the Design/Builder against such lien. If such lien remains unsatisfied after payments are made, the Contractor shall reimburse the Design/Builder for moneys the latter may be compelled to pay in discharging such lien, including all costs and reasonable attorneys' fees.

5.4.2 Final payment constituting the entire unpaid balance due shall be paid by the Design/Builder to the Contractor upon the Design/Builder's receipt of the Contractor's final Application for Payment when the Work has been completed and the Contract fully performed.

5.4.3 The making of final payment shall constitute a waiver of all claims by the Design/Builder except those arising from:

- **.1** unsettled liens;
- **.2** faulty or defective Work appearing after Substantial Completion;
- **.3** failure of the Work to comply with requirements of the Contract Documents; or
- **.4** terms of special warranties required by the Contract Documents.

5.4.4 Acceptance of final payment shall constitute a waiver of all claims by the Contractor except those previously made in writing and identified by the Contractor as unsettled at the time of final Application for Payment.

5.5 INTEREST PAYMENTS

5.5.1 Payments due the Contractor and unpaid under Part 2 which are not paid when due shall bear interest from the date due at the rate specified in Article 13, or in the absence of a specified rate, at the legal rate prevailing where the principal improvements are to be located.

ARTICLE 6
PROTECTION OF PERSONS AND PROPERTY

6.1 The Contractor shall be responsible for initiating, maintaining and providing supervision of safety precautions and programs in connection with the Work.

6.2 The Contractor shall take reasonable precautions for safety of, and shall provide reasonable protection to prevent damage, injury or loss to: (1) employees on the Work and other persons who may be affected thereby; (2) the Work and materials and equipment to be incorporated therein; and (3) other property at or adjacent to the site.

6.3 The Contractor shall give notices and comply with applicable laws, ordinances, rules, regulations and orders of public authorities bearing on the safety of persons and property and their protection from damage, injury or loss.

6.4 The Contractor shall be liable for damage or loss (other than damage or loss to property insured under the property insurance provided or required by the Contract Documents) to property at the site caused in whole or in part by the Contractor, a Subcontractor of the Contractor or anyone directly or indirectly employed by either of them, or by anyone for whose acts they may be liable, except damage or loss attributable to the acts or omissions of the Design/Builder, the Design/Builder's or Owner's separate contractors, or anyone directly or indirectly employed by them or by anyone for whose acts they may be liable, and not attributable to the fault or negligence of the Contractor.

ARTICLE 7
INSURANCE AND BONDS

7.1 CONTRACTOR'S LIABILITY INSURANCE

7.1.1 The Contractor shall purchase and maintain in a company or companies authorized to do business in the state in which the Work is located such insurance as will protect the Contractor from claims set forth below which may arise out of or result from operations under the Contract, and for which the Contractor may be legally liable, whether or not such operations be by the Contractor or by a Subcontractor or by anyone directly or indirectly employed by either of them, or by anyone for whose acts they may be liable:

- **.1** claims under workers' or workmen's compensation, disability benefit and other similar employee benefit laws which are applicable to the Work to be performed;
- **.2** claims for damages because of bodily injury, occupational sickness or disease, or death of the Contractor's employees under any applicable employer's liability law;
- **.3** claims for damages because of bodily injury, sickness or disease, or death of persons other than the Contractor's employees;
- **.4** claims for damages covered by usual personal injury liability coverage which are sustained (1) by a person as a result of an offense directly or indirectly related to employment of such person by the Contractor or (2) by another person;
- **.5** claims for damages, other than to the Work at the site, because of injury to or destruction of tangible property, including loss of use; and
- **.6** claims for damages for bodily injury or death of a person or property damage arising out of ownership, maintenance or use of a motor vehicle.

7.1.2 The insurance required by the above subparagraph shall be written for not less than limits of liability specified in Article 14 or required by law, whichever are greater.

7.1.3 The Contractor's liability insurance shall include contractual liability insurance applicable to the Contractor's obligations under Paragraph 11.7.

7.1.4 Certificates of Insurance, and copies of policies if requested, acceptable to the Design/Builder shall be delivered to the Design/Builder prior to commencement of construction. These Certificates as well as insurance policies required by this paragraph shall contain a provision that coverage will not be cancelled or allowed to expire until at least thirty days' prior written notice has been given to the Design/Builder. If any of the foregoing insurance coverages are required to remain in force after final payment, an additional certificate evidencing continuation of such coverage shall be submitted along with the application for final payment.

7.2 DESIGN/BUILDER'S LIABILITY INSURANCE

7.2.1 The Design/Builder shall be responsible for purchasing and maintaining, in a company or companies authorized to do business in the state in which the principal improvements are to be located, liability insurance to protect the Design/Builder against claims which may arise from operations in connection with this Project.

7.3 PROPERTY INSURANCE

7.3.1 Unless otherwise provided, the Design/Builder shall provide, or cause to be provided, and maintain, in a company or companies authorized to do business in the state in which the principal improvements are to be located, property insurance upon the Work at the site to the full insurable value thereof. Property insurance shall include interests of the Owner, Design/Builder, Contractor and Subcontractors in the Work. It shall insure against perils of fire and extended coverage and shall include all risk insurance for physical loss or damage, including, without duplication of coverage, theft, vandalism and malicious mischief. If the Design/Builder does not intend to provide or cause to be provided such insurance for the full insurable value of the entire Work, the Design/Builder shall inform the Contractor in writing prior to commencement of the Work. The Contractor may then effect insurance which will protect the interests of the Contractor and Subcontractors in the Work, and by appropriate Change Order the cost thereof shall be charged to the Design/Builder. If the Contractor is damaged by failure of the Design/Builder to provide or maintain such insurance without notice to the Contractor, then the Design/Builder shall bear all reasonable costs properly attributable thereto. If not covered under the all risk insurance or not otherwise provided in the Contract Documents, the Contractor shall effect and maintain similar property insurance on portions of the Work stored off-site or in transit when such portions of the Work are to be included in an Application for Payment.

7.3.2 The Design/Builder shall provide or cause to be provided and maintain such boiler and machinery insurance as may be required by the Contract Documents or by law which shall specifically cover such insured objects during installation and until final acceptance by the Owner. This insurance shall cover interests of the Owner, Design/Builder, Contractor and Subcontractors in the Work.

7.3.3 A loss insured under the Design/Builder's property insurance is to be adjusted with the Owner and made payable to the Owner as trustee for the insureds, as their interests may appear, subject to requirements of any applicable mortgagee clause. The Contractor shall pay Subcontractors their shares of insurance proceeds received by the Contractor, and by appropriate agreement, written where legally required for validity, shall require Subcontractors to make payment to their sub-subcontractors in similar manner.

7.3.4 Before an exposure to loss may occur, the Design/Builder shall file with the Contractor a copy of each policy required by this Paragraph 7.3. Each policy shall contain only those endorsements specifically related to this Project.

7.3.5 If the Contractor requests in writing that insurance for risks other than those described herein or for other special hazards be included in the property insurance policy, the Design/Builder shall, if possible, obtain such insurance, and the cost thereof shall be charged to the Contractor by appropriate Change Order.

7.3.6 The Design/Builder and the Contractor waive all rights against (1) each other and other contractors, subcontractors, sub-subcontractors, the Architect, consultants, agents and employees, each of the other, and (2) the Owner and separate contractors, if any, and their subcontractors and sub-subcontractors for damages caused by fire and other perils to the extent covered by any property insurance applicable to the Work, except such rights as they may have to the proceeds of such insurance held by the Owner as trustee. The Design/Builder or the Contractor, as appropriate, shall require of the Owner, the Architect, other contractors and subcontractors by appropriate agreements, written where legally required for validity, similar waivers each in favor of other parties enumerated in this Paragraph 7.3.

7.3.7 If required in writing by a party in interest, the Owner as trustee shall provide, upon occurrence of an insured loss, a bond for proper performance of the Owner's duties. The cost of required bonds shall be charged against proceeds received as Trustee. The Owner shall deposit in a separate account proceeds so received, and the Owner shall distribute them in accordance with such agreement as the parties in interest may reach, or in accordance with an arbitration award in which case the procedure shall be as provided in Article 10. If after such loss no other special agreement is made, replacement of damaged work shall be covered by appropriate Change Order.

7.3.8 The Owner, as trustee, shall have power to adjust and settle a loss with insurers unless one of the parties in interest shall object, in writing, within ten days after occurrence of loss, to the Owner's exercise of this power. If such objection be made, the Owner as trustee shall, in that case, make settlement with the insurers in accordance with the decision of arbitration as provided in Article 10. If distribution of insurance proceeds by arbitration is required, the arbitrators will direct such distribution.

7.4 PERFORMANCE BOND AND PAYMENT BOND

7.4.1 The Design/Builder shall have the right to require the Contractor to furnish bonds covering the faithful performance of the Contract and the payment of all obligations arising thereunder if and as required in the Bidding Documents, in the Contract Documents or in Article 14 of this Part 2.

ARTICLE 8
CHANGES IN THE WORK

8.1 CHANGE ORDERS

8.1.1 A Change Order is a written order signed by the Design/Builder, and issued after execution of Part 2, authorizing a change in the Work or adjustment in the Contract Sum or Contract Time. The Contract Sum and Contract Time may be changed only by Change Order.

8.1.2 The Design/Builder, without invalidating Part 2, may order changes in the Work within the general scope of Part 2 consisting of additions, deletions or other revisions, and the Contract Sum and Contract Time shall be adjusted accordingly. Such changes in the Work shall be authorized by Change Order, and shall be performed under applicable conditions of the Contract Documents.

8.1.3 Cost or credit to the Design/Builder resulting from a change in the Work shall be determined in one or more of the following ways:

- **.1** by mutual acceptance of a lump sum properly itemized and supported by sufficient substantiating data to permit evaluation;
- **.2** by unit prices stated in the Contract Documents or subsequently agreed upon;
- **.3** by cost to be determined in a manner agreed upon by the parties and a mutually acceptable fixed or percentage fee; or
- **.4** by the method provided below.

8.1.4 If none of the methods set forth in Clauses 8.1.3.1, 8.1.3.2 or 8.1.3.3 is agreed upon, the Contractor, provided a written order signed by the Design/Builder is received, shall promptly proceed with the Work involved. The cost of such Work shall then be determined on the basis of reasonable expenditures and savings of those performing the Work attributable to the change, including, in case of an increase in the Contract Sum, a reasonable allowance for overhead and profit. In such case, the Contractor shall keep and present an itemized accounting together with appropriate supporting data for inclusion in a Change Order. Unless otherwise provided in the Contract Documents, cost shall be limited to the following: cost of materials, including sales tax and cost of delivery; cost of labor, including social security, old age and unemployment insurance, and fringe benefits required by agreement or custom; workers' or workmen's compensation insurance; bond premiums; rental value of equipment and machinery; and additional costs of supervision and field office personnel directly attributable to the change. Pending final determination of cost to the Design/Builder, payments on account shall be made on the Application for Payment. When both additions and credits covering related Work or substitutions are involved in a change, the allowance for overhead and profit shall be figured on the basis of the net increase, if any, with respect to that change.

8.1.5 If unit prices are stated in the Contract Documents or subsequently agreed upon, and if quantities originally contemplated are so changed in a proposed Change Order that application of agreed unit prices to quantities proposed will cause substantial inequity to the Design/Builder or Contractor, applicable unit prices shall be equitably adjusted.

8.2 CONCEALED CONDITIONS

8.2.1 If concealed or unknown conditions of an unusual nature that affect the performance of the Work and vary from those indicated by the Contract Documents are encountered below ground or in an existing structure other than the Work, which conditions are not ordinarily found to exist or which differ materially from those generally recognized as inherent in work of the character provided for in this Part 2, notice by the observing party shall be given promptly to the other party, if possible before conditions are disturbed and in no event later than twenty-one days after first observance of the conditions. The Contract Sum shall be equitably adjusted for such concealed or unknown conditions by Change Order upon claim by either party made within twenty-one days after claimant becomes aware of the conditions.

8.3 REGULATORY CHANGES

8.3.1 The Contractor shall be compensated for changes in the Work necessitated by the enactment or revision of codes, laws or regulations subsequent to the execution of Part 2.

ARTICLE 9
CORRECTION OF WORK

9.1 The Contractor shall promptly correct Work rejected by the Design/Builder or known by the Contractor to be defective or failing to conform to the Construction Documents, whether observed before or after Substantial Completion and whether or not fabricated, installed or completed, and shall correct Work under this Contract found to be defective or nonconforming within a period of one year from the date of Substantial Completion of the Work or designated portion thereof, or within such longer period provided by any applicable special warranty in the Contract Documents.

9.2 Nothing contained in this Article 9 shall be construed to establish a period of limitation with respect to other obligations of the Contractor under this Agreement. Paragraph 9.1 relates only to the specific obligation of the Contractor to correct the Work, and has no relationship to the time within which the obligation to comply with the Contract Documents may be sought to be enforced, nor to the time within which proceedings may be commenced to establish the Contractor's liability with respect to the Contractor's obligations other than correction of the Work.

9.3 If the Contractor fails to correct defective Work as required or persistently fails to carry out Work in accordance with the Contract Documents, the Design/Builder may issue a written order to the Contractor to stop the Work, or any portion thereof, until the cause for such order has been eliminated; however, the Design/Builder's right to stop the Work shall not give rise to a duty on the part of the Design/Builder to exercise the right for benefit of the Contractor or other persons or entities.

9.4 If the Contractor defaults or neglects to carry out the Work in accordance with the Contract Documents and fails within seven days after receipt of written notice from the Design/Builder to commence and continue correction of such default or neglect with diligence and promptness, the Design/Builder may give a second written notice to the Contractor and, seven days following receipt by the Contractor of that second written notice and without prejudice to other remedies the Design/Builder may have, correct such deficiencies. In such case an appropriate Change

Order shall be issued deducting from payments then or thereafter due the Contractor costs of correcting such deficiencies. If the payments then or thereafter due the Contractor are not sufficient to cover the amount of the deduction, the Contractor shall pay the difference to the Design/Builder. Such action by the Design/Builder shall be subject to arbitration.

ARTICLE 10
ARBITRATION

10.1 Claims, disputes and other matters in question between the parties to Part 2 arising out of or relating to Part 2 shall be decided by arbitration in accordance with the Construction Industry Arbitration Rules of the American Arbitration Association then in effect unless the parties agree otherwise. No arbitration arising out of or relating to Part 2 shall include, by consolidation or joinder or in any other manner, an additional person not a party to Part 2 except by written consent containing specific reference to Part 2 and signed by the Design/Builder, Contractor and any other person sought to be joined. Consent to arbitration involving an additional person or persons shall not constitute consent to arbitration of a dispute not described therein or with a person not named therein. This provision shall be specifically enforceable in any court of competent jurisdiction.

10.2 Notice of demand for arbitration shall be filed in writing with the other party to Part 2 and with the American Arbitration Association. The demand shall be made within a reasonable time after the claim, dispute or other matter in question has arisen. In no event shall the demand for arbitration be made after the date when the applicable statute of limitations would bar institution of a legal or equitable proceeding based on such claim, dispute or other matter in question.

10.3 The award rendered by arbitrators shall be final, and judgment may be entered upon it in accordance with applicable law in any court having jurisdiction.

10.4 Unless otherwise agreed in writing, the Contractor shall maintain its progress during any arbitration proceeding, and the Design/Builder shall continue to make payments to the Contractor in accordance with the Contract Documents.

10.5 This Article 10 shall survive completion or termination of Part 2.

ARTICLE 11
MISCELLANEOUS PROVISIONS

11.1 This Part 2 shall be governed by the law of the place where the Work is located.

11.2 The table of contents and the headings of articles and paragraphs are for convenience only and shall not modify rights and obligations created by this Part 2.

11.3 In case a provision of Part 2 is held to be invalid, illegal or unenforceable, the validity, legality and enforceability of the remaining provisions shall not be affected.

11.4 SUBCONTRACTS

11.4.1 A Subcontractor is a person or entity having a direct contract with the Contractor.

11.4.2 Nothing contained in the Contract Documents shall create a contractual relationship between the Owner and the Contractor or Subcontractors of the Contractor.

11.5 WORK BY DESIGN/BUILDER AND OWNER OR SEPARATE CONTRACTORS

11.5.1 The Design/Builder and Owner reserve the right to perform work related to the Project and to award separate contracts in connection with other portions of the Project or other work at the site. If the Contractor claims that delay or additional cost is involved because of such action by the Owner or Design/Builder, the Contractor shall make such claims as provided in Subparagraph 11.6.

11.5.2 The Contractor shall afford the Owner's and Design/Builder's separate contractors reasonable opportunity for introduction and storage of their materials and equipment for execution of their work, and shall incorporate and coordinate the Contractor's Work with work of the Owner's and Design/Builder's separate contractors as required by the Construction Documents.

11.5.3 Costs caused by defective or ill-timed Work shall be borne by the party responsible.

11.6 CLAIMS FOR DAMAGES

11.6.1 Should either party to Part 2 suffer injury or damage to person or property because of an act or omission of the other party, the other party's employees or agents, or another for whose acts the other party is legally liable, claim shall be made in writing to the other party within a reasonable time after such injury or damage is or should have been first observed.

11.7 INDEMNIFICATION

11.7.1 To the fullest extent permitted by law, the Design/Builder and the Contractor shall indemnify and hold harmless each other, their respective consultants, contractors, subcontractors, sub-subcontractors, agents and employees from and against claims, damages, losses and expenses, including but not limited to attorneys' fees, arising out of or resulting from performance of the Work or of professional services for this Project. The indemnification obligations under this Subparagraph 11.7.1 shall not be limited with respect to amount or type of damages, compensation or benefits required to be paid under workers' or workmen's compensation acts, disability benefit acts or other employee benefit acts. These indemnification obligations shall be limited to claims, damages, losses or expenses (1) that are attributable to bodily injury, sickness, disease or death, or to injury to or destruction of tangible property (other than the Work itself) including loss of use resulting therefrom, and (2) to the extent such claims, damages, losses or expenses are caused in whole or part by negligent acts or omissions of the Design/Builder, the Contractor or anyone directly or indirectly employed by either, or anyone for whose acts either may be liable, regardless of whether or not they are caused in part by a party indemnified hereunder. Such obligation shall not be construed to negate, abridge or otherwise reduce other rights or obligations of indemnity which would otherwise exist as to a party or person described in this Paragraph 11.7.

11.7.2 These indemnification obligations shall be further limited to the extent of responsibility for the claims, damages, losses and expenses on a comparative basis of fault and responsibility between the Design/Builder and the Contractor, and between others obligated to indemnify or to be indemnified hereunder. "Comparative basis of fault and responsibility" shall be determined on the basis of existing facts independently of any statutory or judicial definition which might otherwise be deemed to be applicable.

11.8 SUCCESSORS AND ASSIGNS

11.8.1 This Part 2 shall be binding on successors, assigns and legal representatives of and persons in privity of contract with the Design/Builder or Contractor. Neither party shall assign, sublet or transfer an interest in Part 2 without the written consent of the other.

11.8.2 This Paragraph 11.8 shall survive completion or termination of Part 2.

11.9 EXTENT OF AGREEMENT

11.9.1 Part 2 represents the entire agreement between the Design/Builder and Contractor and supersedes Part 1 and prior negotiations, representations or agreements. Part 2 may be amended only by written instrument signed by both the Design/Builder and Contractor.

ARTICLE 12
TERMINATION OF THE AGREEMENT

12.1 TERMINATION BY THE DESIGN/BUILDER

12.1.1 This Part 2 may be terminated by the Design/Builder upon at least seven days' written notice to the Contractor in the event that the Project is abandoned. If such termination occurs, the Design/Builder shall pay the Contractor for Work completed and for proven loss sustained upon materials, equipment, tools, and construction equipment and machinery, including reasonable profit and applicable damages.

12.1.2 If the Contractor defaults or persistently fails or neglects to carry out the Work in accordance with the Contract Documents or fails to perform the provisions of the Agreement, the Design/Builder may give written notice that the Design/Builder intends to terminate the Agreement. If the Contractor fails to correct the Contractor's defaults or fails to perform within seven days after being given notice, the Design/Builder may, after seven additional days' written notice to the Contractor and without prejudice to any other remedy the Design/Builder may have, make good such deficiencies and may deduct the cost thereof from the payment due the Contractor or, at the Design/Builder's option, may terminate the employment of the Contractor and take possession of the site and of all materials, equipment, tools and construction equipment and machinery thereon owned by the Contractor and finish the Work by whatever method the Design/Builder may deem expedient. If the unpaid balance of the Contract Sum exceeds the expense of finishing the Work, the excess shall be paid to the Contractor, but if the expense exceeds the unpaid balance, the Contractor shall pay the difference to the Design/Builder.

12.2 TERMINATION BY THE CONTRACTOR

12.2.1 If the Design/Builder fails to make payment when due, the Contractor may give written notice of the Contractor's intention to terminate Part 2. If the Contractor fails to receive payment within seven days after receipt of such notice by the Design/Builder, the Contractor may give a second written notice and, seven days after receipt of such second written notice by the Design/Builder, may terminate Part 2 and recover from the Design/Builder payment for Work executed and for proven losses sustained upon materials, equipment, tools, and construction equipment and machinery, including reasonable profit and applicable damages.

ARTICLE 13
BASIS OF COMPENSATION

13.1 The Design/Builder shall compensate the Contractor in accordance with Article 5, Payments, and other provisions of this Part 2 as described below.

13.2 The basis of compensation, including retainage provisions, if any, shall be:

The Contract Sum is ( ).

13.3 The Contractor shall submit an Application for Payment on the of each month.

13.4 The interest rate to be applied in Article 5, Paragraph 5.4, shall be:

(Usury laws and requirements under the Federal Truth in Lending Act, similar state and local consumer credit laws and other regulations at the Design/Builder's and Contractor's principal places of business, at the location of the Project and elsewhere may affect the validity of this provision. Specific legal advice should be obtained with respect to deletion, modification or other requirements, such as written disclosures or waivers.)

ARTICLE 14
OTHER PROVISIONS

14.1 The Contractor's scope of Work is:
(List below the Conditions of the Contract [General, Supplementary and other Conditions], the drawings, the specifications, and any addenda and accepted alternates, showing page or sheet numbers in all cases and dates where applicable. Define the scope of Work.)

14.2 The scope of Work to be performed shall be commenced on and, subject to authorized adjustments, Substantial Completion shall be achieved in ( ) calendar days, which shall be the Contract Time.

14.3 The Contract Documents include:
(List specific documents and indicate dates.)

14.4 The Contractor's insurance coverage shall be:

14.5 The Contractor shall provide a performance bond and payment bond in the full amount of the Contract Sum.

14.6 The Design/Builder shall provide the following temporary facilities and services:

This Part 2 entered into as of the day and year first written above.

DESIGN/BUILDER	CONTRACTOR
______________________	______________________
______________________	______________________
______________________	______________________
BY ____________________	BY ____________________

INSTRUCTION SHEET

FOR AIA DOCUMENT B901, STANDARD FORM OF AGREEMENTS BETWEEN DESIGN/BUILDER AND ARCHITECT—FIRST EDITION

A. GENERAL INFORMATION

1. Purpose

This Document is the first edition of AIA Document B901, Standard Form of Agreements Between Design/Builder and Architect. It is intended to govern relations between the Design/Builder and Architect under the contractual organization diagramed below.

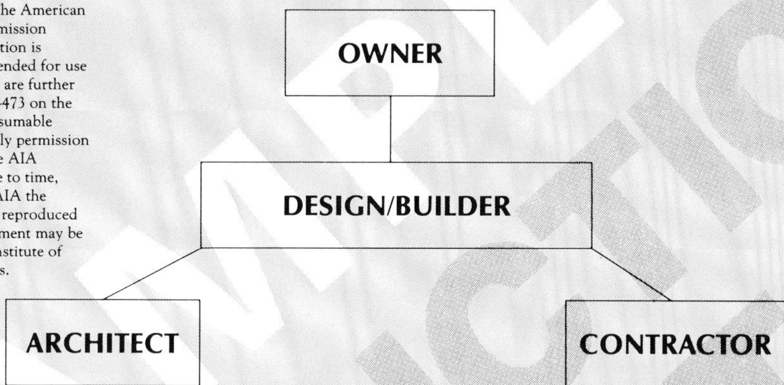

Design/build is a process in which the Owner contracts directly with one entity to provide both design and construction services. The AIA believes that if a public Owner chooses to utilize the design/build process, selection of the design/build team should be based upon objective criteria developed to evaluate the qualifications and competence of the design/build team, as with Brooks Act procurement methods.

This Document contains two Agreements which are intended to be used in sequence as the basis for the agreements between the Design/Builder and the Architect. The first Agreement, known as Part 1, covers the services of preliminary design. The second Agreement, known as Part 2, covers the services of final design. The segmentation of services between Part 1 and Part 2 is meant to parallel the typical sequence of services found in Owner-Design/Builder agreements. Although it is anticipated that the parties entering into the Part 1 Agreement will also enter into the Part 2 Agreement, the parties may conclude their relationship after Part 1 is performed rather than continuing on to Part 2.

The Design/Builder may take a variety of legal forms, and it is possible that this party may be a separate corporate entity or joint venture formed by the Architect which subcontracts the design work to the Architect's separate firm. Prior to proceeding in this fashion or entering into either Agreement in this Document with any other entity, architects are advised to contact their legal, insurance and management advisors. Several states have strong prohibitions or barriers against design/build practices under their laws regulating architectural registration, contractor licensing or incorporation of professionals.

2. Related Documents

AIA Document B901 is published in conjunction with the following related documents:

A191, Standard Form of Agreements Between Owner and Design/Builder
A491, Standard Form of Agreements Between Design/Builder and Contractor

These documents are intended to govern relations between the Owner and the Design/Builder and between the Design/Builder and a separate contractor.

3. Use of Non-AIA Forms

If a non-AIA document or a mixture of AIA documents and non-AIA documents is used in conjunction with this Document, particular care must be taken to achieve consistency of language and intent. If there are any significant omissions, additions or variances from the terms of the related standard AIA forms, both legal and insurance counsel should be consulted. Of particular concern is the need for consistency among these Agreements, Owner-Design/Builder Agreements and any other agreements for portions of the design or construction entered into by the Architect and others.

4. Letter Forms of Agreement

Letter forms of agreement are generally discouraged by the AIA, as is the performance of some or all professional services based on oral agreements or understandings. The AIA forms have been developed through more than ninety years of experience and have been tested repeatedly in courts. They are carefully coordinated with other AIA documents.

5. Use of Current Documents

Prior to using any AIA document, the user should consult the AIA or an AIA component chapter to determine the current edition of each document.

6. Reproduction

AIA Document B901 is a copyrighted document and may not be reproduced or excerpted from in whole or in part without the express written permission of the AIA prior to reproduction. This Document is intended for use as a "consumable" publication without any implied consent to duplicate except under the limited license described below.

Purchasers of the B901 Document are entitled by license to reproduce a maximum of ten copies of the completed or executed document for use only in connection with a particular Project.

B. COMPLETING THE B901 FORM

1. Modifications

As with all AIA documents, users are encouraged to consult an attorney with respect to completing or modifying the form. Legal counsel should also be sought concerning the effect of state and local law on the terms of each Agreement. In particular, legal counsel should be consulted with respect to registration laws, duties imposed by building codes, interest charges and arbitration. Generally, modifications may be accomplished by describing changes to the printed text in Article 10 of the relevant Agreement, or by attaching and referencing a separate amendment sheet. If deletions are needed, these should be accomplished by striking through with a line, or by amendment. It is not recommended that deletions be made by erasing, whiting out or taping over provisions in the Document.

2. Cover Page (Same for Part 1 and Part 2)

Date: The date of the Agreement is the date when the Agreement becomes legally effective. It may be the date that an oral agreement was reached, the date the Agreement was originally submitted to the Design/Builder, the date authorizing action was taken or the date of actual execution. Professional services should not be performed prior to the effective date of the Agreement.

Parties: Parties to the Agreement should be identified using the full legal names and addresses under which the Agreement will be executed, including designation of the legal status of the parties: sole proprietorship, partnership, joint venture, unincorporated association, corporation (general, closed or professional), etc.

Project: The proposed Project should be described in sufficient detail to identify (1) the official name or title of the facility, (2) the location of the site, if known, (3) the proposed building type or use, and (4) the size, capacity or scope of the Project, if known.

Owner: Although the Owner is not a party to the Agreement between Design/Builder and Architect, it is customary to identify the Owner in agreements of this kind.

3. Part 1 Agreement: Preliminary Design

a) Article 9—Basis of Compensation

Subparagraph 9.1.1
Describe the basis of computing compensation for Basic Services under this subparagraph. Methods for computing compensation may be found in the AIA publication *Compensation Guidelines for Architectural and Engineering Services* (1978 edition). Several methods may be used on a particular project. When more than one method is used, each method should reference the appropriate services listed in Article 2 and Article 10. This may be done by titling them "Method A," "Method B," etc.

Subparagraph 9.1.2
Insert the amount of initial payment as referred to in Subparagraph 5.1.1.

Subparagraph 9.1.3
Describe the manner in which subsequent periodic payments will be made to the Architect, as referred to in Paragraph 5.2.

Subparagraph 9.2.1
Describe the basis of computing additional compensation.

Subparagraph 9.3.1
Insert a multiple for reimbursable expenses, if any.

Subparagraph 9.5.1
Insert rate of interest, if other than the legal rate.

Paragraph 9.7
Insert the number of months after which the compensation levels will be renegotiated.

b) **Article 10—Other Provisions**

Paragraph 10.1
Insert the date for commencement of Work and the number of calendar days in which the Work is to be completed.

Paragraph 10.2
Insert Basic Services not described in Article 2.

4. **Part 2 Agreement: Final Design**

a) **Article 9—Basis of Compensation**

Subparagraph 9.1.1
Describe the basis of computing compensation for Basic Services under this subparagraph. Methods for computing compensation may be found in the AIA publication *Compensation Guidelines for Architectural and Engineering Services* (1978 edition). Several methods may be used on a particular project. When more than one method is used, each method should reference the appropriate services listed in Article 2 and Article 10. This may be done by titling them "Method A," "Method B," etc.

Subparagraph 9.1.2
Insert amount of initial payment.

Subparagraph 9.1.3
Describe the manner in which subsequent periodic payments will be made to the Architect, as referred to in Paragraph 5.2.

Subparagraph 9.2.1
Describe compensation for additional services.

Subparagraph 9.3.1
Insert a multiple for reimbursable expenses, if any.

Subparagraph 9.5.1
Insert rate of interest, if other than the legal rate.

Paragraph 9.7
Insert the number of months after which the compensation levels will be renegotiated.

b) **Article 10—Other Provisions**

Paragraph 10.1
Insert the date of commencement and the number of days allowed for performance of Basic Services.

Paragraph 10.2
Insert Basic Services not described in Article 2.

C. EXECUTION OF THE AGREEMENTS

Persons executing (signing) each Agreement should indicate the capacity in which they are acting (e.g., president, secretary, partner, etc.) and the authority under which they are executing the Agreement. Evidence of authority to sign on behalf of each party should be obtained. Where appropriate, a copy of the resolution or bylaw authorizing the individual to act on behalf of the firm or entity should be attached.

THE AMERICAN INSTITUTE OF ARCHITECTS

AIA Document B901

Standard Form of Agreements Between Design/Builder and Architect

1985 EDITION

THIS DOCUMENT HAS IMPORTANT LEGAL CONSEQUENCES; CONSULTATION WITH AN ATTORNEY IS ENCOURAGED.

TABLE OF ARTICLES

PART 1 AGREEMENT—PRELIMINARY DESIGN

PART 2 AGREEMENT—FINAL DESIGN

THE AMERICAN INSTITUTE OF ARCHITECTS

AIA Document B901

Standard Form of Agreement Between Design/Builder and Architect

1985 EDITION

THIS DOCUMENT HAS IMPORTANT LEGAL CONSEQUENCES; CONSULTATION WITH AN ATTORNEY IS ENCOURAGED.

This Document comprises two separate Agreements: Part 1 Agreement—Preliminary Design and Part 2 Agreement—Final Design. Hereinafter, the Part 1 Agreement is referred to as Part 1 and the Part 2 Agreement is referred to as Part 2. Before executing Part 1, the parties should reach substantial agreement on Part 2. This Document is intended for use with AIA Document A191, Owner-Design/Builder Agreement.

PART 1 AGREEMENT—PRELIMINARY DESIGN

AGREEMENT

made as of the day of in the year of Nineteen Hundred and

BETWEEN the Design/Builder:
(Name and address)

and the Architect:
(Name and address)

For the following Project:
(Include Project name, location and detailed description of scope.)

The Owner is:
(Name and address)

The Design/Builder and the Architect agree as set forth below.

Terms and Conditions—Part 1 Agreement

ARTICLE 1
GENERAL PROVISIONS

1.1 BASIC DEFINITIONS

1.1.1 The Project is the total design and construction for which the Design/Builder is responsible under a separate agreement with the Owner, including all professional design services and all labor, materials and equipment used or incorporated in such design and construction.

1.1.2 The Work comprises the completed construction designed by the Architect under the Project and includes labor necessary to produce such construction, and materials and equipment incorporated or to be incorporated in such construction.

1.2 EXECUTION, CORRELATION AND INTENT

1.2.1 This Part 1 shall be signed in not less than duplicate by the Design/Builder and the Architect.

1.2.2 Nothing contained in the Design/Builder Contract Documents shall create a professional obligation or contractual relationship between the Design/Builder and any third party.

1.3 OWNERSHIP AND USE OF DOCUMENTS

1.3.1 The drawings, specifications and other documents furnished by the Architect are instruments of service and shall not become the property of the Design/Builder whether or not the Project for which they are made is commenced. If Part 2 is not executed, the Design/Builder shall not use the documents prepared by the Architect without the written permission of the Architect. Drawings, specifications and other documents furnished by the Architect shall not be used by the Design/Builder on other projects, for additions to this Project or, unless the Architect is in default under Part 1, for completion of this Project by others, except by written agreement relating to use, liability and compensation.

1.3.2 Submission or distribution of documents to meet official regulatory requirements or for other purposes in connection with the Project is not to be construed as publication in derogation of the Architect's common law copyrights or other reserved rights. The Design/Builder shall own neither the documents nor the copyrights.

ARTICLE 2
ARCHITECT

2.1 BASIC SERVICES

2.1.1 The Architect's Basic Services are as described below and in Article 10 and include normal structural, mechanical and electrical engineering services. The professional obligations of the Architect are undertaken and performed in the interest of the Design/Builder. Nothing contained in Part 1 shall create any professional obligation or contractual relationship between the Architect and the Owner. All communications between the Architect and the Owner shall pass through the Design/Builder unless otherwise directed by the Design/Builder.

2.1.2 The Architect shall review the program furnished by the Design/Builder to ascertain requirements of the Project and shall review such requirements with the Design/Builder.

2.1.3 The Architect shall provide, after consultation with the Design/Builder, a preliminary evaluation of the program and Project budget, each in terms of the other.

2.1.4 The Architect shall review with the Design/Builder alternative approaches to design and construction of the Project.

2.1.5 The Architect shall provide Preliminary Design Documents consisting of preliminary design drawings, outline specifications and other documents to fix and describe the size, quality and character of the Work, including its architectural, structural, mechanical and electrical systems, and the materials and such other elements of the Project as may be appropriate.

2.2 ADDITIONAL SERVICES

2.2.1 The following services are not included in Basic Services unless so identified in Article 10. They shall be provided if authorized or confirmed in writing by the Design/Builder, and they shall be paid for by the Design/Builder as provided in this Agreement, in addition to compensation for Basic Services.

2.2.2 Providing analyses and programming for the requirements of the Project.

2.2.3 Providing financial feasibility or other special studies.

2.2.4 Providing planning surveys, site evaluations, environmental studies or comparative studies of prospective sites, and preparing special surveys, studies and submissions required for approvals of governmental authorities or others having jurisdiction over the Project.

2.2.5 Providing services relative to future facilities, systems and equipment which are not intended to be constructed in Part 2.

2.2.6 Providing services to investigate existing conditions or facilities or to make measured drawings thereof, or to verify the accuracy of drawings or other information furnished by the Design/Builder.

2.2.7 Preparing documents more detailed than the preliminary design documents to permit early ordering of materials or start of construction prior to execution of Part 2.

2.2.8 Providing coordination for Work performed or to be performed by persons other than those engaged and coordinated by a single general contractor.

2.2.9 Providing services in connection with the work of consultants other than those retained by the Architect.

2.2.10 Providing detailed estimates of construction cost, analyses of owning and operating costs, or detailed quantity surveys or inventories of materials, equipment and labor.

2.2.11 Providing interior design and other similar services required for or in connection with the selection, procurement or installation of furniture, furnishings and related equipment.

2.2.12 Providing services for planning tenant or rental spaces.

2.2.13 Providing landscape design services in conjunction with the selection and installation of plant material.

2.2.14 Making revisions in drawings, specifications or other documents when such revisions are inconsistent with written approvals or instructions previously given, are required by the enactment or revision of codes, laws or regulations subsequent to the preparation of such documents or are due to other causes not solely within the control of the Architect.

2.2.15 Making investigations, surveys, valuations, inventories or detailed appraisals and valuations of existing facilities and services required in connection with construction performed by the Design/Builder.

2.2.16 Preparing to serve or serving as a witness in connection with any public hearing, arbitration proceeding or legal proceeding.

2.2.17 Providing services of consultants for other than the normal architectural, structural, mechanical and electrical engineering services for the Project.

2.2.18 Providing any other services not otherwise included in this Agreement or not customarily furnished in accordance with generally accepted architectural practice.

ARTICLE 3
DESIGN/BUILDER

3.1 The Design/Builder shall provide information regarding requirements for the Project including but not limited to design objectives, constraints and criteria.

3.2 If the Design/Builder provides a budget for the Project, it shall explicitly include as separate line items contingencies for changes in the design and construction, and other costs which are the responsibility of the Design/Builder. No budget shall constitute a fixed limit of construction cost unless such limit has been agreed to in writing by the Architect.

3.3 The Design/Builder shall designate a representative authorized to act on the Design/Builder's behalf with respect to the Project. The Design/Builder or such authorized representative shall examine the documents submitted by the Architect and shall promptly render decisions pertaining thereto to avoid delay in the orderly progress of the Architect's services.

3.4 Prior to commencement of Basic Services, the Design/Builder shall furnish a legal description and a certified land survey of the site, giving, as applicable, grades and lines of streets, alleys, pavements and adjoining property; rights-of-way, restrictions, easements, encroachments, zoning, deed restrictions, elevations and contours of the site; locations, dimensions and complete data pertaining to existing buildings, other improvements and trees; and full information concerning available services and utility lines, both public and private and above and below grade, including inverts and depths.

3.5 The Design/Builder shall furnish services of geotechnical engineers and other consultants when such services are deemed necessary by the Architect. Such services shall include, as required, applicable test borings, test pits, soil bearing values, percolation tests, air and water pollution tests, and other necessary operations for determining subsoil, air and water conditions, with reports and appropriate professional recommendations.

3.6 The Design/Builder shall furnish all cost estimating services required for the Project.

3.7 The services, information, surveys and reports required by Paragraphs 3.4 through 3.6 shall be furnished by the Design/Builder without expense to the Architect, and the Architect shall be entitled to rely upon their accuracy and completeness.

3.8 The Design/Builder shall furnish required information and services and shall promptly render decisions to avoid delay in the orderly progress of the Architect's services.

ARTICLE 4
TIME

4.1 The Architect shall perform the Basic and Additional Services as expeditiously as is consistent with professional skill and care and shall complete services in the time provided in Article 10.

ARTICLE 5
PAYMENTS

5.1 The initial payment provided in Article 9 shall be made upon execution of this Part 1 and shall be the minimum payment under Part 1.

5.2 Subsequent payments for Basic Services, Additional Services and Reimbursable Expenses shall be made monthly on the basis set forth in Article 9.

5.3 Payments due the Architect under Part 1 which are not paid when due shall bear interest from the date due at the rate specified in Paragraph 9.5, or in the absence of a specified rate, at the legal rate prevailing where the principal office of the Architect is located.

5.4 REIMBURSABLE EXPENSES

5.4.1 Reimbursable Expenses are in addition to the Compensation for Basic and Additional Services and include actual expenditures made by the Architect and the Architect's employees and consultants in the interest of the Project for the expenses listed in the following subparagraphs.

5.4.2 Expense of transportation in connection with the Project; living expenses in connection with out-of-town travel; long-distance communications; and fees paid for securing approval of authorities having jurisdiction over the Project.

5.4.3 Expense of reproductions, postage and handling of drawings, specifications and other documents, excluding reproductions for the office use of the Architect and the Architect's consultants.

5.4.4 Expense of data processing, computer time and photographic production techniques when used in connection with Additional Services.

5.4.5 If authorized in advance by the Design/Builder, expense of overtime work requiring higher than regular rates.

5.4.6 Expense of renderings, models and mock-ups requested by the Design/Builder.

5.4.7 Expense of any additional insurance coverage or limits, including professional liability insurance, requested by the Design/Builder in excess of that normally carried by the Architect and the Architect's consultants.

ARTICLE 6
ARBITRATION

6.1 Claims, disputes and other matters in question between the parties to this Part 1 arising out of or relating to Part 1 shall be decided by arbitration in accordance with the Construction Industry Arbitration Rules of the American Arbitration Association then in effect unless the parties agree otherwise. No arbitration arising out of or relating to Part 1 shall include, by consolidation or joinder or in any other manner, an additional person not a party to Part 1 except by written consent containing specific reference to Part 1 and signed by the Architect, Design/Builder and any other person sought to be joined. Consent to arbitration involving an additional person or persons shall not constitute consent to arbitration of a dispute not described therein or with a person not named therein. This provision shall be specifically enforceable in any court of competent jurisdiction.

6.2 Notice of demand for arbitration shall be filed in writing with the other party to Part 1 and with the American Arbitration Association. The demand shall be made within a reasonable time after the claim, dispute or other matter in question has arisen. In no event shall the demand for arbitration be made after the date when the applicable statute of limitations would bar institution of a legal or equitable proceeding based on such claim, dispute or other matter in question.

6.3 The award rendered by arbitrators shall be final, and judgment may be entered upon it in accordance with applicable law in any court having jurisdiction.

6.4 Unless otherwise agreed in writing, the Architect shall carry on the services and maintain progress during any arbitration proceedings, and the Design/Builder shall continue to make payments to the Architect in accordance with Part 1.

6.5 This Article 6 shall survive completion or termination of Part 1.

ARTICLE 7
MISCELLANEOUS PROVISIONS

7.1 This Part 1 shall be governed by the law of the place where the principal office of the Architect is located.

7.2 The table of contents and the headings of articles and paragraphs are for convenience only and shall not modify rights and obligations created by Part 1.

7.3 In case a provision of Part 1 is held to be invalid, illegal or unenforceable, the validity, legality and enforceability of the remaining provisions shall not be affected.

7.4 SUCCESSORS AND ASSIGNS

7.4.1 This Part 1 shall be binding on successors, assigns, and legal representatives of and persons in privity of contract with the Design/Builder or Architect. Neither party shall assign or transfer an interest in Part 1 without written consent of the other. The Design/Builder shall not transfer to any other person or entity the instruments of service prepared under Part 1 without written consent of the Architect.

7.4.2 This Paragraph 7.4 shall survive completion or termination of Part 1.

7.5 EXTENT OF AGREEMENT

7.5.1 Part 1 represents the entire agreement for Preliminary Design and supersedes all prior negotiations, representations or agreements. Part 1 may be amended only by written instrument signed by both Design/Builder and Architect.

ARTICLE 8
TERMINATION OF THE AGREEMENT

8.1 Part 1 may be terminated by either party upon seven days' written notice should the other party fail substantially to perform in accordance with its terms through no fault of the party initiating the termination.

8.2 Part 1 may be terminated by the Design/Builder upon at least seven days' written notice to the Architect in the event that the Project is permanently abandoned.

8.3 In the event of termination the Architect shall be compensated for services properly performed to termination date. If the termination is not due to the fault of the Architect, the Architect shall also be paid Termination Expenses. Termination Expenses are expenses directly attributable to termination, including a reasonable amount for overhead and profit, for which the Architect is not otherwise compensated under Part 1.

ARTICLE 9
BASIS OF COMPENSATION

The Design/Builder shall compensate the Architect in accordance with Article 5, Payments, and the other provisions of Part 1 as described below.

9.1 COMPENSATION FOR BASIC SERVICES

9.1.1 FOR BASIC SERVICES, compensation shall be as follows:

9.1.2 AN INITIAL PAYMENT of dollars ($) shall be made upon execution of Part 1 and credited to the Design/Builder's account as follows:

9.1.3 SUBSEQUENT PAYMENTS shall be as follows:

9.2 COMPENSATION FOR ADDITIONAL SERVICES

9.2.1 FOR ADDITIONAL SERVICES, compensation shall be as follows:

9.3 REIMBURSABLE EXPENSES

9.3.1 FOR REIMBURSABLE EXPENSES, compensation shall be a multiple of ( ) times the amounts expended.

9.4 IF A MULTIPLE OF DIRECT PERSONNEL EXPENSE is the basis of compensation, Direct Personnel Expense is defined as the direct salaries of all the Architect's personnel engaged on the Project, and the portion of the cost of their mandatory and customary contributions and benefits related thereto, such as employment taxes and other statutory employee benefits, insurance, sick leave, holidays, vacations, pensions and similar contributions and benefits.

9.5 INTEREST PAYMENTS

9.5.1 The rate of interest for past due payments shall be as follows:

(Usury laws and requirements under the Federal Truth in Lending Act, similar state and local consumer credit laws and other regulations at the Design/Builder's and Architect's principal places of business, at the location of the Project and elsewhere may affect the validity of this provision. Specific legal advice should be obtained with respect to deletion, modification or other requirements, such as written disclosures or waivers.)

9.6 IF THE SCOPE of the Project or of the Architect's services is changed materially, the compensation shall be equitably adjusted.

9.7 The compensation set forth herein shall be equitably adjusted if through no fault of the Architect the services have not been completed within ( ) months of the date of Part 1.

ARTICLE 10
OTHER PROVISIONS

10.1 The Basic Services to be performed shall be commenced on and, subject to authorized adjustments and to delays not caused by the Architect, including those resulting from the required performance of Additional Services, shall be completed in ( ) calendar days.

10.2 The Basic Services beyond those described in Article 2 are:

This Part 1 entered into as of the day and year first written above.

DESIGN/BUILDER	ARCHITECT
______________________	______________________
______________________	______________________
______________________	______________________
BY ______________________	BY ______________________

THE AMERICAN INSTITUTE OF ARCHITECTS

AIA Document B901

Standard Form of Agreement Between Design/Builder and Architect

1985 EDITION

THIS DOCUMENT HAS IMPORTANT LEGAL CONSEQUENCES; CONSULTATION WITH AN ATTORNEY IS ENCOURAGED.

This Document comprises two separate Agreements: Part 1 Agreement—Preliminary Design and Part 2 Agreement—Final Design. Hereinafter, the Part 1 Agreement is referred to as Part 1 and the Part 2 Agreement is referred to as Part 2. This Document is intended for use with AIA Document A191, Owner-Design/Builder Agreement.

PART 2 AGREEMENT—FINAL DESIGN

AGREEMENT

made as of the day of in the year of Nineteen Hundred and

BETWEEN the Design/Builder:
(Name and address)

and the Architect:
(Name and address)

For the following Project:
(Include Project name, location and detailed description of scope.)

The Owner is:
(Name and address)

The Design/Builder and Architect agree as set forth below.

Terms and Conditions—Part 2 Agreement

ARTICLE 1
GENERAL PROVISIONS

1.1 BASIC DEFINITIONS

1.1.1 The Project is the total design and construction for which the Design/Builder is responsible under a separate agreement with the Owner, including all professional design services and all labor, materials and equipment used or incorporated in such design and construction.

1.1.2 The Work comprises the completed construction designed by the Architect under the Project and includes labor necessary to produce such construction, and materials and equipment incorporated or to be incorporated in such construction.

1.1.3 The Contractor is the person or entity undertaking the construction of the Work for the Design/Builder and identified as such in the Agreement Between Design/Builder and Contractor.

1.2 EXECUTION, CORRELATION AND INTENT

1.2.1 This Part 2 shall be signed in not less than duplicate by the Design/Builder and the Architect.

1.3 OWNERSHIP AND USE OF DOCUMENTS

1.3.1 The drawings, specifications and other documents furnished by the Architect are instruments of service and shall not become the property of the Design/Builder whether or not the Work for which they are made is commenced. Drawings, specifications and other documents furnished by the Architect shall not be used by the Design/Builder on other projects, for additions to this Project or, unless the Architect is in default under this Part 2, for completion of this Project by others, except by written agreement relating to use, liability and compensation.

1.3.2 Submission or distribution of documents to meet official regulatory requirements or for other purposes in connection with the Project is not to be construed as publication in derogation of the Architect's common law copyrights or other reserved rights. The Design/Builder shall own neither the documents nor the copyrights.

ARTICLE 2
ARCHITECT

2.1 BASIC SERVICES

2.1.1 The Architect's Basic Services are as described below and in Article 10, and include normal structural, mechanical and electrical engineering services. The professional obligations of the Architect are undertaken and performed in the interest of the Design/Builder. Nothing contained in Part 2 shall create any professional obligation or contractual relationship between the Architect and the Owner, the Contractor or any party other than the Design/Builder. All communications between the Architect and the Owner or Contractor shall pass through the Design/Builder unless otherwise directed by the Design/Builder.

2.1.2 Based upon the Preliminary Design Documents contained in the Design/Builder's Proposal, the Architect shall provide Construction Documents for review and approval by the Design/Builder. The Construction Documents shall consist of drawings and specifications setting forth in detail the requirements for construction of the Work.

2.1.3 The Architect shall assist the Design/Builder in filing documents required to obtain necessary approvals of governmental authorities having jurisdiction over the Project; however, this shall not be construed as requiring the Architect to provide any services not otherwise described in this paragraph or Article 10.

2.1.4 Unless otherwise indicated in Article 10, the Architect shall, during the construction of the Work, provide the services described in Subparagraphs 2.1.5 through 2.1.15.

2.1.5 Instructions to the Contractor shall be forwarded through the Design/Builder. The Architect shall have authority to act on behalf of the Design/Builder only to the extent provided in Part 2.

2.1.6 The Architect shall visit the site at intervals appropriate to the stage of construction or as otherwise agreed by the Architect in writing to become generally familiar with the progress and quality of the Work and to determine in general if the Work is proceeding in accordance with the Construction Documents. However, the Architect shall not be required to make exhaustive or continuous on-site inspections to check the quality or quantity of the Work. On the basis of such on-site observations as an architect, the Architect shall keep the Design/Builder informed of the progress and quality of the Work, and shall endeavor to guard the Design/Builder against defects and deficiencies in the Work of the Contractor.

2.1.7 The Architect shall not have control or charge of and shall not be responsible for construction means, methods, techniques, sequences or procedures, or for safety precautions and programs in connection with the Work, for the acts or omissions of the Contractor, the Contractor's subcontractors or any other persons performing any of the Work, or for the failure of any of them to carry out the Work in accordance with the Construction Documents.

2.1.8 The Architect shall at all times have access to the Work wherever it is in preparation or progress.

2.1.9 The Architect shall provide written or graphic interpretations of the Construction Documents necessary for the proper execution or progress of the Work with reasonable promptness on written request of the Design/Builder, and shall, upon written request of the Design/Builder, provide written opinions, within a reasonable time, on all matters relating to the execution of the Work or the interpretation of the Construction Documents.

2.1.10 Whenever, in the Architect's reasonable opinion, it is necessary or advisable for the implementation of the intent of the Construction Documents, the Design/Builder shall provide special inspection or testing of the Work by qualified laboratories or experts, whether or not such Work be then fabricated, installed or completed.

2.1.11 The Architect shall review and approve or take other appropriate action upon Contractor's submittals such as shop drawings, product data and samples forwarded to the Architect by the Design/Builder, but only for conformance with the design concept of the Work and with the information given in the Construction Documents. The Design/Builder shall require the Contractor to review and approve such submittals and apply the Contractor's approval stamp prior to submittal. The Architect's approval of a specific item shall not indicate approval of an assembly of which the item is a component.

2.1.12 The extent of the duties, responsibilities and limitations of authority of the Architect as a Design/Builder's representative during construction shall not be modified or extended without written consent of the Design/Builder, the Contractor and the Architect.

2.1.13 If the Design/Builder and Architect agree that more extensive representation at the site than is described above in Subparagraphs 2.1.4 through 2.1.12 shall be provided or is legally required, the Architect shall provide one or more Project Representatives to assist the Architect in carrying out such responsibilities at the site.

2.1.14 Such Project Representatives shall be selected, employed and directed by the Architect, and the Architect shall be compensated therefor as mutually agreed between the Design/Builder and the Architect as set forth in an exhibit appended to Part 2, which shall describe the duties, responsibilities and limitations of authority of such Project Representatives.

2.1.15 Through the observations by such Project Representatives, the Architect shall endeavor to provide further protection for the Design/Builder against defects and deficiencies in the Work, but the furnishing of such project representation shall not modify the rights, responsibilities or obligations of the Architect as described above in this article.

2.2 ADDITIONAL SERVICES

2.2.1 The following services are not included in Basic Services unless so identified in Article 10. They shall be provided if authorized or confirmed in writing by the Design/Builder, and they shall be paid for by the Design/Builder as provided in this Part 2, in addition to the compensation for Basic Services.

2.2.2 Providing analyses and programming for the requirements of the Project.

2.2.3 Providing financial feasibility or other special studies.

2.2.4 Providing planning surveys, site evaluations, environmental studies or comparative studies of prospective sites, and preparing special surveys, studies and submissions required for approvals of governmental authorities or others having jurisdiction over the Project.

2.2.5 Providing services relative to future facilities, systems and equipment which are not intended to be constructed in Part 2.

2.2.6 Providing services to investigate existing conditions or facilities or to make measured drawings thereof, or to verify the accuracy of drawings or other information furnished by the Design/Builder.

2.2.7 Preparing documents for alternate, separate or sequential bids or purchasing.

2.2.8 Providing coordination for Work performed or to be performed by persons other than those engaged and coordinated by the Contractor.

2.2.9 Providing services in connection with the work of consultants other than those retained by the Architect.

2.2.10 Providing detailed estimates of construction cost, analyses of owning and operating costs, or detailed quantity surveys or inventories of materials, equipment and labor.

2.2.11 Providing interior design and other similar services required for or in connection with the selection, procurement or installation of furniture, furnishings and related equipment.

2.2.12 Providing services for planning tenant or rental spaces.

2.2.13 Providing landscape design services in connection with the selection and installation of plant material.

2.2.14 Making revisions in drawings, specifications or other documents when such revisions are inconsistent with written approvals or instructions previously given, are required by the enactment or revision of codes, laws or regulations subsequent to the preparation of such documents or are due to other causes not solely within the control of the Architect.

2.2.15 Preparing drawings, specifications and supporting data; evaluating the Contractor's proposals, claims and submittals; and providing other services in connection with Change Orders to the extent the adjustment in the Basic Compensation resulting from the adjusted Contract Sum is not commensurate with the services required of the Architect, provided such change orders are made necessary by causes not solely within the control of the Architect and whether or not the Work in such proposed change order is executed.

2.2.16 Making investigations, surveys, valuations, inventories or detailed appraisals and valuations of existing facilities and services required in connection with construction performed by the Design/Builder.

2.2.17 Providing consultation concerning replacement of any Work damaged by fire or other cause during construction, and furnishing services as may be required in connection with the replacement of such Work.

2.2.18 Providing services made necessary by the default of the Contractor or by major defects or deficiencies in the Work of the Contractor or by failure of performance of either the Design/Builder or Contractor under the Contract for Construction.

2.2.19 Preparing a set of reproducible record prints of drawings showing significant changes in the Work made during construction based on marked-up prints, drawings and other data furnished by the Design/Builder to the Architect.

2.2.20 Providing extensive assistance in the utilization of any equipment or system, such as initial start-up or testing, adjusting and balancing, preparation of operation and maintenance manuals, training personnel for operation and maintenance, and consultation during operation.

2.2.21 Providing services after issuance to the Design/Builder of the Contractor's final Certificate for Payment more than sixty days after the date of substantial completion of the Work.

2.2.22 Preparing to serve or serving as a witness in connection with any public hearing, arbitration proceeding or legal proceeding.

2.2.23 Providing services of consultants for other than the normal architectural, structural, mechanical and electrical engineering services for the Project.

2.2.24 Providing administration of the Contract between the Design/Builder and the Contractor by acting as the representative of the Design/Builder; undertaking direct correspondence or negotiations with the Contractor on behalf of the Design/Builder; assisting with the bidding of the Work and selection of the Contractor; evaluating claims made by the Contractor; evaluating Applications for Payment submitted by the Contractor and issuing Certificates for Payment for amounts due by the Design/Builder to the Contractor; making site visits and evaluating lists of uncompleted work prepared by the Contractor in connection with the issuance of a Certificate of Substantial Completion, or preparing such lists; making site visits and reviewing or forwarding to the Design/Builder for review material submitted in connection with the Contractor's Application for Final Payment, and issuing a Certificate for Final Payment; and similar administrative services. The extent of the Architect's authority and responsibility in connection with such services as are requested by the Design/Builder shall be as mutually agreed by the Architect and the Design/Builder and shall be recorded in writing and appended to this Part 2. The issuance of a Certificate for Payment shall constitute a representation by the Architect to the Design/Builder, based on the Architect's observations at the site as provided in Subparagraph 2.1.6 and on the data comprising the Contractor's Application for Payment, that the Work has progressed to the point indicated; that, to the best of the Architect's knowledge, information and belief, the quality of the Work is in accordance with the Construction Documents (subject to an evaluation of the Work for conformance with the Construction Documents upon Substantial Completion, to the results of any subsequent tests required by or performed under the Construction Documents, to minor deviations from the Construction Documents correctable prior to completion and to any specific qualifications stated in the Certificate for Payment); and that the Contractor is entitled to payment in the amount certified. However, the issuance of a Certificate for Payment shall not be a representation that the Architect has made any examination to ascertain how and for what purpose the Contractor has used the moneys paid on account of the Contract Sum.

2.2.25 Providing any other services not otherwise included in this Agreement or not customarily furnished in accordance with generally accepted architectural practice.

ARTICLE 3
DESIGN/BUILDER

3.1 The Design/Builder shall designate a representative authorized to act on the Design/Builder's behalf with respect to the Project. The Design/Builder or such authorized representative shall examine documents submitted by the Architect and shall promptly render decisions pertaining thereto to avoid delay in the orderly progress of the services.

3.2 The Design/Builder shall furnish further services by land surveyors, geotechnical engineers and other consultants for subsoil, air and water conditions, in addition to those provided under Part 1, when such services are deemed necessary by the Architect to carry out properly the Architect's services under Part 2.

3.3 The Design/Builder shall furnish structural, mechanical, chemical, geotechnical and other laboratory or on-site tests, inspections and reports as required by law or the Construction Documents.

3.4 The Design/Builder shall furnish all cost estimating services required for the Project.

3.5 The services, information, surveys and reports required by Paragraphs 3.2 through 3.4 shall be furnished by the Design/Builder without expense to the Architect, and the Architect shall be entitled to rely upon their accuracy and completeness.

3.6 The Design/Builder shall furnish required information and services and shall promptly render decisions to avoid delay in the orderly progress of the Architect's services.

3.7 If the Design/Builder observes or otherwise becomes aware of a fault or defect in the Work or nonconformity with the Preliminary Design or Construction Documents, the Design/Builder shall give prompt written notice thereof to the Architect.

ARTICLE 4
TIME

4.1 The Architect shall perform Basic and Additional Services as expeditiously as is consistent with professional skill and care, and shall complete services in the time provided in Article 10.

ARTICLE 5
PAYMENTS

5.1 The initial payment described in Article 9 shall be made upon execution of Part 2, and shall be the minimum payment under Part 2.

5.2 Subsequent payments for Basic Services, Additional Services and Reimbursable Expenses shall be made monthly on the basis set forth in Article 9.

5.3 REIMBURSABLE EXPENSES

5.3.1 Reimbursable Expenses are in addition to the Compensation for Basic and Additional Services and include actual expenditures made by the Architect and the Architect's employees and consultants in the interest of the Project for the expenses listed in the following Subparagraphs 5.3.2 through 5.3.7.

5.3.2 Expense of transportation in connection with the Project; living expenses in connection with out-of-town travel; long-distance communications; and fees paid for securing approval of authorities having jurisdiction over the Project.

5.3.3 Expense of reproductions, postage and handling of drawings, specifications and other documents, excluding reproductions for the office use of the Architect and the Architect's consultants.

5.3.4 Expense of data processing, computer time and photographic production techniques when used in connection with Additional Services.

5.3.5 If authorized in advance by the Design/Builder, expense of overtime work requiring higher than regular rates.

5.3.6 Expense of renderings, models and mock-ups requested by the Design/Builder.

5.3.7 Expense of any additional insurance coverage or limits, including professional liability insurance, requested by the Design/Builder in excess of that normally carried by the Architect and the Architect's consultants.

5.4 INTEREST PAYMENTS

5.4.1 Payments due the Architect under Part 2 which are not paid when due shall bear interest from the date due at the rate specified in Article 9, or in the absence of a specified rate, at the legal rate prevailing where the principal improvements are to be located.

ARTICLE 6
ARBITRATION

6.1 Claims, disputes and other matters in question between the parties to Part 2 arising out of or relating to Part 2 shall be decided by arbitration in accordance with the Construction Industry Arbitration Rules of the American Arbitration Association then in effect unless the parties agree otherwise. No arbitration arising out of or relating to Part 2 shall include, by consolidation or joinder or in any other manner, any additional person not a party to Part 2 except by written consent containing specific reference to Part 2 and signed by the Architect, Design/Builder and any other person sought to be joined. Consent to arbitration involving an additional person or persons shall not constitute consent to arbitration of a dispute not described therein or with a person not named therein. This provision shall be specifically enforceable in any court of competent jurisdiction.

6.2 Notice of demand for arbitration shall be filed in writing with the other party to Part 2 and with the American Arbitration Association. The demand shall be made within a reasonable time after the claim, dispute or other matter in question has arisen. In no event shall the demand for arbitration be made after the date when the applicable statute of limitations would bar institution of a legal or equitable proceeding based on such claim, dispute or other matter in question.

6.3 The award rendered by arbitrators shall be final, and judgment may be entered upon it in accordance with applicable law in any court having jurisdiction.

6.4 Unless otherwise agreed in writing, the Architect shall carry on the services and maintain progress during any arbitration proceedings, and the Design/Builder shall continue to make payments to the Architect in accordance with Part 2.

6.5 This Article 6 shall survive completion or termination of Part 2.

ARTICLE 7
MISCELLANEOUS PROVISIONS

7.1 This Part 2 shall be governed by the law of the place where the principal office of the Architect is located.

7.2 The table of contents and the headings of articles and paragraphs are for convenience only and shall not modify rights and obligations created by Part 2.

7.3 In case a provision of Part 2 is held to be invalid, illegal or unenforceable, the validity, legality and enforceability of the remaining provisions shall not be affected.

7.4 SUCCESSORS AND ASSIGNS

7.4.1 This Part 2 shall be binding on successors, assigns, and legal representatives of and persons in privity of contract with the Design/Builder or the Architect. Neither party shall assign, sublet or transfer an interest in Part 2 without the written consent of the other. The Design/Builder shall not transfer to any other person or entity the instruments of service prepared under Part 2 without written consent of the Architect.

7.4.2 This Paragraph 7.4 shall survive completion or termination of Part 2.

7.5 EXTENT OF AGREEMENT

7.5.1 Part 2 represents the entire agreement between the Design/Builder and Architect and supersedes Part 1 and prior negotiations, representations or agreements. Part 2 may be amended only by written instrument signed by both Design/Builder and Architect.

7.6 The Design/Builder and the Architect waive all rights against (1) each other and the contractors, subcontractors, sub-subcontractors, consultants, agents and employees, each of the other, and (2) the Owner and separate contractors, if any, and their subcontractors and sub-subcontractors for damages caused by fire and other perils to the extent covered by any property insurance applicable to the Work, except such rights as they may have to the proceeds of such insurance. The Design/Builder or the Architect, as appropriate, shall require of the Owner, contractor, subcontractors, sub-subcontractors and consultants by appropriate agreements, written where legally required for validity, similar waivers each in favor of all other parties enumerated in this paragraph.

7.7 INDEMNIFICATION

7.7.1 To the fullest extent permitted by law, the Design/Builder and the Architect shall indemnify each other and hold each other harmless, and also the respective contractors, subcontractors, sub-subcontractors, consultants, agents and employees, each of the other, from and against claims, damages, losses and expenses, including but not limited to attorneys' fees, arising out of or resulting from performance of the Work or of professional services under Part 2. The indemnification obligations under this Subparagraph 7.7.1 shall not be limited with respect to amount or type of damages, compensation or benefits required to be paid by or for the Architect or Design/Builder or a subcontractor under workers' or workmen's compensation acts, disability benefit acts or other employee benefit acts. Such obligation shall not be construed to negate, abridge or otherwise reduce other rights or obligations of indemnity which would otherwise exist as to a party or person described in this Paragraph 7.7.

7.7.2 The indemnification obligations hereunder shall be limited to claims, damages, losses and expenses that are (1) attributable to bodily injury, sickness, disease or death, or to injury to or destruction of tangible property (other than the Work itself), including loss of use resulting therefrom, and (2) caused in whole or in part by negligent acts or omissions of the Architect or the Design/Builder, anyone directly or indirectly employed by either, or anyone for whose acts either may be liable.

7.7.3 The indemnification obligations hereunder shall be further limited to the extent of responsibility for the claims, damages, losses and expenses on a comparative basis of fault and responsibility between the Architect and the Design/Builder, and between others obligated to indemnify or to be indemnified hereunder. "Comparative basis of fault and responsibility" shall be determined on the basis of existing facts independently of any statutory or judicial definition which might otherwise be deemed to be applicable.

ARTICLE 8
TERMINATION OF THE AGREEMENT

8.1 Part 2 may be terminated by either party upon seven days' written notice should the other party fail substantially to perform in accordance with its terms through no fault of the party initiating the termination.

8.2 Part 2 may be terminated by the Design/Builder upon seven days' written notice to the Architect in the event that the Project is permanently abandoned.

8.3 If the Design/Builder fails to make payment when due, the Architect may give written notice of the Architect's intention to terminate Part 2. If the Architect fails to receive payment within seven days after giving such notice, the Architect may, without prejudice to any other remedy the Architect may have, give a second written notice and terminate Part 2.

8.4 In the event of termination, the Architect shall be compensated for all services properly performed to the termination date. If the termination is not due to the fault of the Architect, the Architect shall also be paid Termination Expenses. Termination Expenses are expenses directly attributable to termination, including a reasonable amount for overhead and profit, for which the Architect is not otherwise compensated under Part 2.

ARTICLE 9
BASIS OF COMPENSATION

The Design/Builder shall compensate the Architect in accordance with Article 5, Payments, and the other provisions of Part 2 as described below.

9.1 COMPENSATION FOR BASIC SERVICES

9.1.1 FOR BASIC SERVICES, compensation shall be as follows:

9.1.2 AN INITIAL PAYMENT of dollars ($) shall be made upon execution of this Agreement and credited to the Design/Builder's account as follows:

9.1.3 SUBSEQUENT PAYMENTS shall be as follows:

9.2 COMPENSATION FOR ADDITIONAL SERVICES

9.2.1 FOR ADDITIONAL SERVICES, compensation shall be as follows:

9.3 REIMBURSABLE EXPENSES

9.3.1 FOR REIMBURSABLE EXPENSES, compensation shall be a multiple of ( ) times the amounts expended.

9.4 IF A MULTIPLE OF DIRECT PERSONNEL EXPENSE is the basis of compensation, Direct Personnel Expense is defined as the direct salaries of all the Architect's personnel engaged on the Project, and the portion of the cost of their mandatory and customary contributions and benefits related thereto, such as employment taxes and other statutory employee benefits, insurance, sick leave, holidays, vacations, pensions and similar contributions and benefits.

9.5 INTEREST PAYMENTS

9.5.1 The rate of interest for past due payments shall be as follows:

(Usury laws and requirements under the Federal Truth in Lending Act, similar state and local consumer credit laws and other regulations at the Design/Builder's and Architect's principal places of business, at the location of the Project and elsewhere may affect the validity of this provision. Specific legal advice should be obtained with respect to deletion, modification or other requirements, such as written disclosures or waivers.)

9.6 IF THE SCOPE of the Project or of the Architect's services is changed materially, the amounts of compensation shall be equitably adjusted.

9.7 IF THE SERVICES covered by this Agreement have not been completed within ( ) months of the date hereof, through no fault of the Architect, the compensation, rates and multiples set forth herein shall be equitably adjusted.

ARTICLE 10
OTHER PROVISIONS

10.1 The Basic Services to be performed shall be commenced on and, subject to authorized adjustments and to delays not caused by the Architect, including those resulting from the required performance of Additional Services, shall be completed in ( ) calendar days.

10.2 The Basic Services beyond those described in Article 2 are:

This Part 2 entered into as of the day and year first written above.

DESIGN/BUILDER	ARCHITECT
____________________	____________________
____________________	____________________
____________________	____________________
BY ____________________	BY ____________________

This document has important legal consequences; consultation with an attorney is encouraged with respect to its completion or modification.

STANDARD FORM OF AGREEMENT Between Owner and Engineer-Contractor for Design and Construction Services

Issued by
PROFESSIONAL ENGINEERS IN CONSTRUCTION
A practice division of the

NATIONAL SOCIETY OF PROFESSIONAL ENGINEERS

2029 K STREET, N.W., WASHINGTON, D.C. 20006

NSPE 2802-1 CP 5C 1/77/REPRINT 1M 11/83

Guide Sheet for Completing Standard Form of Agreement Between Owner and Engineer-Contractor for Design and Construction Services

APPENDICES AND EXHIBITS—There are four appendices and four exhibits referenced in the body of the Standard Form of Agreement. In preparing the final contract document for signature, sample copies, in the form normally used by the Engineer-Contractor, should be attached. As referenced in the Standard Form of Agreement, these attachments are as follows:

EXHIBIT A—Work Order. Attach as "Exhibit A" the form to be used by the owner in authorizing additions, deletions or modifications in the work. *See Section 1.8, Article 1.*

EXHIBIT B—Change Order. Attach as "Exhibit B" the form to be used by the owner in authorizing an adjustment in the contract sum or time for completion. *See Section 1.9, Article 1.*

EXHIBIT C—Progress Payment. Attach as "Exhibit C" the form to be used by the Engineer-Contractor as invoice for work completed during the preceding month. *See Article 6.*

EXHIBIT D—Certificate of Substantial Completion. Attach as "Exhibit D" the form to be used by the Engineer-Contractor as a certificate of substantial completion. *See Article 7.*

APPENDIX A—Charge for Engineering and Design Services. Attach as "Appendix A" a statement of the basis for charge for engineering and design services. Such charges may be on the basis of a lump sum, a percentage, actual payroll cost multiplied by a factor, payroll cost plus a percentage, or payroll cost plus a fixed fee. *See Article 2 and Article 5.*

APPENDIX B—Charge for Construction. Attach as "Appendix B" a statement of the basis for charge for construction. Such charges may be on the basis of a lump sum, guaranteed maximum price, cost plus a fixed fee, cost plus a percentage, or a unit price. *See Article 2 and Article 5.*

APPENDIX C—Additional Contract Documents. Attach as "Appendix C" any other documents pertinent to the Agreement.

APPENDIX D—Resolution of Disputes. Attached to the Standard Form as Appendix D-1 and Appendix D-2 are subsidiary documents providing for resolution of disputes by either arbitration or legal proceedings. The appropriate document should be appended to the final Agreement as "Appendix D." *See Article 20.*

Index of Articles

STANDARD FORM OF AGREEMENT BETWEEN OWNER AND ENGINEER-CONTRACTOR FOR DESIGN AND CONSTRUCTION SERVICES

THIS AGREEMENT made as of the day of 197 , by and between

(hereinafter called "Owner"),

and

(hereinafter called "Engineer-Contractor").

WITNESSETH:

That in consideration of the mutual covenants and agreements herein contained, the parties hereto do hereby covenant and agree as follows:

ARTICLE 1: DEFINITIONS

1.1 OWNER: "Owner" shall mean the above-named organization designated as "Owner," its successors and assigns.

1.2 OWNER'S REPRESENTATIVE: "Owner's Representative" shall mean ______________________ or such other person as may be designated by the Owner on written notice to Engineer-Contractor, to act as its representative.

1.3 ENGINEER-CONTRACTOR: "Engineer-Contractor" shall mean the above-named organization designated as "Engineer-Contractor," its successors and assigns.

1.4 ENGINEER-CONTRACTOR'S REPRESENTATIVE: "Engineer-Contractor's Representative" shall mean ______________________ or such other person as may be designated by Engineer-Contractor on written notice to Owner to act as its representative.

1.5 JOB SITE (CONSTRUCTION AREA): "Job site" shall mean only the specific area known and designated as Lot ________, Block __________ on the Tax Assessment Map of the ________________ of ________________, County of ______________________, State of ______________.

1.6 WORK: "Work" shall cover all labor, materials and services necessary to produce the engineering and design services and the construction required by the contract documents.

1.7 DATE OF SUBSTANTIAL COMPLETION: "Date of substantial completion" of the work or a designated portion thereof is the date when: (i) the construction is sufficiently completed in accordance with the contract documents so that Owner may occupy the work or designated portion thereof for the use for which it is intended, or (ii) Owner obtains a temporary certificate or a permanent certificate of occupancy for the work.

1.8 WORK ORDER: A "Work order" is a written order to the Engineer-Contractor in form similar to Exhibit A annexed hereto, signed by the Owner's Representative, issued after the execution of the contract, authorizing the Engineer-Contractor to make additions, deletions or modifications in the work to be performed by Engineer-Contractor.

1.9 CHANGE ORDER: A "Change order" is a written order to the Engineer-Contractor in form similar to Exhibit B annexed hereto, prepared by Engineer-Contractor, signed by the Owner's Representative, issued after the execution of the contract, authorizing an adjustment (if any) in the contract sum to be paid to Engineer-Contractor or an adjustment in the time for the completion of the work countersigned by Engineer-Contractor's Representative.

ARTICLE 2: CONTRACT DOCUMENTS

2.1 The contract documents shall consist of all of the following:

2.1.1 This contract, together with Appendix A and Appendix B annexed hereto, and any amendments or modifications thereto, including any signed work order or signed change order.

2.1.2 All other documents described in Appendix C annexed hereto and made a part hereof.

2.2 In the event of conflict between this contract and the provisions of the other contract documents, this contract shall control. In the event of any conflict between the provisions of the contract documents, other than this contract, the latest approved document shall control.

2.3 All contract documents hereinafter submitted by Engineer-Contractor for the approval of Owner in connection with the performance of the work shall be deemed approved unless Owner makes written objection thereto within eight (8) working days after receipt thereof.

ARTICLE 3: SCOPE OF THE WORK

3.1 The totality of the obligations imposed upon Engineer-Contractor as set forth in 3.2 and 3.3 shall constitute the scope of the work covered by and to be performed under this contract.

1

3.2 The Engineer-Contractor shall provide, furnish and perform all necessary engineering and design services and provide and furnish all necessary supplies, materials and equipment and all necessary labor and services required for the design and construction of the

(INCLUDE DESCRIPTION OF PROJECT)

in accordance with the contract documents.

3.3 The engineering and design services to be performed by Engineer-Contractor under this contract shall cover all of the following to the extent required for the performance of the work:

3.3.1 Preparation of schematic design studies consisting of drawings and other documents illustrating the scope and relationship of the various components of the work.

3.3.2 Preparation of design development documents consisting of drawings and other documents which shall fix and describe the size and the character of the work.

3.3.3 Preparation of working drawings and specifications setting forth in detail the requirements for the performance of the work.

3.3.4 Review of all shop drawings, samples and other submissions for conformance with the design concept of the work and for compliance with the drawings and specifications.

3.4 The Engineer-Contractor shall not be liable to Owner or otherwise responsible for damage or injury to the work or for additional costs or delays in the performance of the work arising out of or caused by concealed, latent or unforeseen surface or sub-surface conditions: (i) differing from those indicated in the contract documents, or (ii) not specifically disclosed to Engineer-Contractor in writing prior to the commencement of the work.

3.5 The Engineer-Contractor shall not be liable to Owner or otherwise responsible for damage or injury to the work or for additional costs or delays in the performance of the work arising out of or caused by reason of the Engineer-Contractor relying upon or acting upon incorrect or inaccurate written information furnished the Engineer-Contractor by Owner or its agents and representatives.

ARTICLE 4: TIME OF COMMENCEMENT AND COMPLETION

The work to be performed under this contract shall be commenced as of the ________ day next following the execution of this contract and shall be completed within such time schedule as shall be mutually agreed to by the Owner and Engineer-Contractor.

ARTICLE 5: CONTRACT SUM

5.1 The Owner shall pay the Engineer-Contractor for the performance of the work, subject to additions and deductions by change order as provided in Article 12, in current funds, the contract sum of __________dollars. The said contract sum shall cover the entire charge for engineering and design services as set forth in Appendix A hereof and the entire charge for construction as set forth in Appendix B hereof.

ARTICLE 6: PROGRESS PAYMENTS

6.1 On or before the 10th day of the first full month following the commencement of the work and continuing thereafter on or before the 10th day of each succeeding month, Engineer-Contractor shall submit to Owner an invoice for payment in the form similar to Exhibit C annexed hereto and made a part hereof, covering all work performed during the preceding month, including all work performed pursuant to change orders. The invoice for payment shall contain a pro rata share of the Engineer-Contractor's overhead and fee and shall also contain a mobilization charge in the amount of __________dollars which shall be part of the contract sum.

6.2 The invoice for payment shall show:

6.2.1 Charge for all engineering work performed during the preceding month.

6.2.2 Charge for all construction work performed during the preceding month, including the value of construction material, the payment of which Engineer-Contractor is liable for, whether or not such construction material is delivered to the job site.

6.3 Within twenty (20) days after submission of the invoice for payment, Owner shall make a progress payment to Engineer-Contractor in an amount equal to the aggregate sum of the following:

6.3.1 100% of the aggregate amount of the charge for engineering shown on the invoice for payment.

6.3.2 95% of the aggregate amount of the charge for construction shown on the invoice for payment.

6.4 Interest at the rate of one and one-half (1½%) per cent per month shall be paid on the unpaid balance of any invoice for payment, exclusive of retainage withheld in accordance with 6.5 not paid by Owner within twenty (20) days from the date of receipt thereof. Such interest shall be in addition to the contract sum to be paid Engineer-Contractor pursuant to this agreement.

6.5 The Owner shall hold a retainage of five (5%) per cent of the charge for construction as shown on each monthly invoice for payment submitted, until such time as Engineer-Contractor has completed 50% of the work to be performed. Thereafter, no additional retainage shall be held by Owner.

6.5.1 All retainage held by Owner shall bear interest at the prime rate of interest charged by __________ as of the last day of each month, calculated from the date of withholding of the retainage and all such interest shall belong exclusively to Engineer-Contractor.

6.6 Each invoice for payment shall contain Engineer-Contractor's certification that the work described in the invoice has been completed in accordance with the contract documents, that all due items are paid for, for which previous certificates were issued and payments received, and that the amount of the payment shown on the invoice is now due Engineer-Contractor.

ARTICLE 7: PAYMENT TO ENGINEER-CONTRACTOR FOLLOWING SUBSTANTIAL COMPLETION

7.1 When the Engineer-Contractor determines that the work or a designated portion thereof is substantially complete, the Engineer-Contractor shall prepare and submit to Owner a certificate of substantial completion in form similar to Exhibit D annexed hereto, which certificate shall fix the date of substantial completion. The Engineer-Contractor shall attach to the certificate a list of items to be completed or corrected by Engineer-Contractor before final payment. If at such time as Engineer-Contractor submits the certificate of substantial completion, Engineer-Contractor shall have obtained a certificate of occupancy for the work, then the date of substantial completion as set forth in the certificate of substantial completion shall be binding on Owner. If the certificate of substantial completion is not accompanied by a certificate of occupancy, the Owner shall have seven (7)

2

days after receipt of the certificate of substantial completion to make written objection thereto. Any objection on the part of Owner shall be in such specific detail as to adequately apprise Engineer-Contractor of the basis for the objection. In the event Owner does not make objection within the prescribed time, the work shall be deemed to be substantially complete as of the date specified in the certificate of substantial completion.

7.2 Upon the date of substantial completion of the work, Owner shall release all retainage to Engineer-Contractor together with accrued interest thereon, less a sum equal to twice the estimate of the cost required to complete any corrective and incomplete work and any punch list items, as mutually agreed to by Owner and Engineer-Contractor. The final cost of the work will be reconciled within thirty (30) days following the final completion of the work.

ARTICLE 8: FINAL PAYMENT

8.1 The Owner shall make final payment within forty-five (45) days after completion of the work, provided the contract be then fully performed, subject however, to the provisions of 8.2 of this contract.

8.2 At the completion of the work and before final acceptance and approval is given by Owner, Engineer-Contractor shall furnish to Owner a complete release of liens, if any, signed by the Engineer-Contractor and all subcontractors and materialmen connected with the project. If any subcontractor or materialmen connected with the project refuses to furnish such release of liens, Engineer-Contractor may furnish Owner with a bond duly issued by a bonding company authorized to do business in the State in which the work is to be performed in form satisfactory to Owner indemnifying Owner against any such lien, which bond shall remain in full force and effect until the lien is discharged of record or otherwise satisfied.

8.3 At such time as the Owner shall make final payment to Engineer-Contractor under 8.1 hereof, Owner and Engineer-Contractor shall exchange releases by the terms of which each party shall release the other from any and all liability, loss and damages arising out of or resulting from the performance of the work by Engineer-Contractor hereunder, excluding however any guaranty which shall be given by Engineer-Contractor under Article 9 hereof.

ARTICLE 9: ENGINEER-CONTRACTOR'S GUARANTY

9.1 Engineer-Contractor, subject to the provisions of 9.2 and 9.3 hereof, guarantees that the work shall be performed in a skillful and workmanlike manner, free from defects in workmanship and in conformance with the contract documents. This guaranty is expressly in lieu of all other guaranties and warranties, express or implied, including any warranties of merchantability and fitness. Engineer-Contractor's liability for its guaranty hereunder shall be limited to remedying, at its own expense, any defect in the workmanship proximately resulting from the failure of Engineer-Contractor to perform the work in a skillful and workmanlike manner, provided however: (i) that such defect shall manifest itself on or before the expiration of the first year next following the date of substantial completion, and (ii) that Owner shall give notice in writing to Engineer-Contractor of such defect on or before the expiration of the first year next following the date of substantial completion. In lieu of remedying such defect in the work, Engineer-Contractor, with the concurrence of Owner, may pay Owner the cost of repair thereof.

9.2 Engineer-Contractor does not guarantee nor warrant, either expressly or impliedly, the materials in or workmanship of supplies, materials, equipment or machinery manufactured by third parties and furnished and installed by Engineer-Contractor in the performance of the work, but Engineer-Contractor shall endeavor to obtain from all vendors and suppliers and assign to Owner the customary warranties and guaranties of such vendors and suppliers with respect thereto and Engineer-Contractor shall, at the sole cost and expense of Owner, render reasonable assistance to Owner when requested in order to enable Owner to enforce such warranties and guaranties by the third party manufacturers or suppliers.

9.3 Engineer-Contractor does not guarantee nor warrant the quality or suitability of any process to be used by Owner in the completed facility or any product to be manufactured by Owner in the completed facility.

ARTICLE 10: RESPONSIBILITIES OF OWNER

The Owner, at its sole cost and expense, shall:

10.1 Cooperate with the Engineer-Contractor in all respects.

10.2 Designate in writing a person to act as Owner's Representative with respect to the work to be performed under this agreement and such person shall have complete authority to transmit instructions to the Engineer-Contractor through Engineer-Contractor's Representative, receive information and interpret and define Owner's policies and decisions with respect to all aspects of the work covered by this agreement.

10.3 Provide full information with respect to the scope of the work to be performed by Engineer-Contractor.

10.4 Give prompt written notice to Engineer-Contractor whenever the Owner observes or otherwise becomes aware of any defect in the work covered by this agreement.

10.5 Guarantee access to and make all provisions for the Engineer-Contractor to enter upon public and private lands as required for the Engineer-Contractor to perform its work under this agreement.

10.6 Make available a convenient and adequate source of water and electricity and furnish telephone service and all other utilities required for the performance of the work.

10.7 Furnish all property and topographic surveys describing the physical characteristics and legal limits of the job site and necessary utility locations at the job site required for the performance of the work.

10.8 Furnish necessary borings and soils engineering required for the performance of the work.

10.9 Provide at the job site for the benefit and use of Engineer-Contractor in the performance of the work, sufficient trailer space, parking space and storage space for materials and construction equipment.

10.10 Make application to all federal, state and municipal jurisdictional agencies and obtain all governmental approvals, permits, licenses and variances required for the performance of the work.

10.11 Not cause any other construction to be undertaken in the immediate area of the job site where the work is to be performed by Engineer-Contractor under this agreement without the consent of Engineer-Contractor.

10.12 In addition to the contract sum, pay all sales and use taxes imposed upon Engineer-Contractor in the performance of the work.

ARTICLE 11: RESPONSIBILITIES OF ENGINEER-CONTRACTOR

The Engineer-Contractor shall:

11.1 Cause the work to be performed in accordance with the contract documents, using its best skill and attention.

11.2 Provide and pay for all labor, materials, equipment, tools, construction equipment and machinery, transportation and other facilities and services necessary for the execution and completion of the work.

3

11.3 At all times during the performance of the work, keep the premises free from accumulation of waste materials or rubbish caused by its operations. At the completion of the work, Engineer-Contractor shall remove all its waste materials and rubbish from and about the job site as well as its tools, construction equipment, machinery and surplus materials and shall leave the job site "broom clean" or its equivalent.

11.4 Assist Owner in making application to all federal, state and municipal jurisdictional agencies for the purpose of obtaining all governmental approvals, permits, licenses and variances required for the performance of the work, provided nevertheless, that Owner shall be responsible for the actual obtainment of all such approvals, permits, licenses and variances.

ARTICLE 12: CHANGES IN THE WORK

12.1 The Owner, without invalidating the contract, may order changes in the work consisting of additions, deletions or modifications and the contract sum and the time for the completion of the work shall be adjusted accordingly. All such changes in the work shall be authorized by a work order and thereafter confirmed by a change order in the manner hereinafter provided for.

12.2 The Engineer-Contractor shall not be required to proceed with any additions, deletions or modifications to the work unless in pursuance to a signed work order. Should the work to be performed by Engineer-Contractor under any work order result in an increase in the cost of the work, the Owner shall be obligated to pay Engineer-Contractor the total cost of the additional work which shall include the aggregate sum of the following:

- **12.2.1** Subcontracts and purchase orders .... at cost
- **12.2.2** Field craft labor .... at cost (__ × bare salary)
- **12.2.3** Field and office construction services ....at cost (__ × bare salary)
- **12.2.4** Corporate overhead .... __of the aggregate sum of 12.2.1, 12.2.2 and 12.2.3.
- **12.2.5** Engineer-Contractor's Fee .... __of the aggregate sum of 12.2.1, 12.2.2, 12.2.3 and 12.2.4
- **12.2.6** Design and engineering .... __ × bare salary

12.3 The cost or net credit to the Owner resulting from a change in the work as above provided shall be confirmed by a change order. Thereupon, the time for the completion of the work shall be adjusted accordingly. The contract sum shall be adjusted upwards or downwards by the amount of any additional cost to Owner or credited to Owner resulting from any change in the work caused by change order. The refusal by Owner to execute a change order shall not relieve Owner of its obligation to pay Engineer-Contractor the full cost of any additional work performed by Engineer-Contractor pursuant to a work order.

ARTICLE 13: INDEMNIFICATION BY ENGINEER-CONTRACTOR

13.1 Engineer-Contractor, within the limits of its insurance coverage as provided in Article 16 hereof, shall indemnify and save harmless Owner from and against any loss, liability or damages which may be sustained by Owner by reason of injury or death to persons or damage to tangible property occurring during the performance of the work and resulting from the negligence of Engineer-Contractor, its subcontractors, agents or employees.

13.2 The Engineer-Contractor shall indemnify and save harmless Owner from all costs, fees, damages and expenses arising out of or resulting from any charge or encumbrance in the nature of a laborer's, mechanic's or materialman's lien asserted by a party or parties other than Engineer-Contractor in connection with the performance of the work.

ARTICLE 14: INDEMNIFICATION BY OWNER

Owner shall indemnify and save harmless Engineer-Contractor from and against any and all loss, liability and damages (including reasonable attorneys' fees) arising out of any claim, suit or legal proceeding to recover damages for wrongful death, bodily injury, illness or disease or injury to, or destruction of, tangible property alleged to be caused either directly or indirectly by any substance, condition, element or material or any combination of the foregoing: (i) produced by Owner or emitted or released by Owner either intentionally or unintentionally, from the facilities herein agreed to be designed and/or constructed by Engineer-Contractor for the benefit of Owner, or (ii) used by Engineer-Contractor or incorporated by Engineer-Contractor into the work herein agreed to be performed by Engineer-Contractor for the benefit of Owner if specifically required by Owner or if necessary for the planned use of the work.

ARTICLE 15: PATENT INDEMNIFICATION

15.1 The Owner shall not cause Engineer-Contractor to use any design, process or equipment which would infringe upon any patent right held by any third party.

15.2 Owner shall indemnify and save Engineer-Contractor harmless from and against all liability, damages and expenses arising out of any suit or action brought against Engineer-Contractor for use of any design, process or equipment required by the Owner, based upon a claim that any design, process or equipment incorporated in the work infringes upon any invention, design, process or device which is the subject of a patent.

ARTICLE 16: ENGINEER-CONTRACTOR'S LIABILITY INSURANCE

16.1 The Engineer-Contractor shall purchase and maintain all of the insurance described in 16.1.1 through 16.1.3 hereof, for not less than the limits of liability therein specified so as to protect Engineer-Contractor from claims under workmen's compensation acts and other employee benefits acts, from claims for damages because of bodily injury, including death, and from claims for damage to property which may arise out of or result from the Engineer-Contractor's operations under this contract, whether such operations be by Engineer-Contractor or by any subcontractor or anyone directly or indirectly employed by any of them.

16.1.1. Workmen's compensation, including occupational disease in accordance with the statutory requirements set forth by the state in which the work is to be performed and employer's liability insurance covering all Engineer-Contractor's employees engaged in the performance of this contract in the minimum sum of $250,000.00.

16.1.2 Comprehensive general liability insurance, including Engineer-Contractor's protective liability and contractual liability insurance covering death or bodily injury with minimum limits of $250,000.00 per person and $1,000,000.00 for any one accident and property damage coverage with minimum limits of $250,000.00 for any one accident and $500,000.00 in the aggregate. The contractual liability insurance shall insure the hold harmless and indemnification agreement contained in 13.1 of this contract.

16.1.3 Comprehensive automobile liability insurance covering Engineer-Contractor for claims arising from owned, hired and non-owned vehicles covering death or bodily injury with minimum limits of $100,000.00 per person and $300,000.00 for any one accident and property damage coverage with minimum limits of $50,000.00 for any one accident.

16.2 Certificates of insurance covering all of the insurance required to be maintained by Engineer-Contractor shall be filed with the Owner.

ARTICLE 17: OWNER'S INSURANCE

17.1 Owner, at its own expense, shall obtain and maintain until completion of the work, builder's all risk insurance which shall insure against the perils of fire, flooding, extended coverage, theft, vandalism and malicious mischief, containing a limit of not less than the full amount of the contract sum, which insurance may, at Owner's election, contain a deductible excluding the first $500.00 of any loss. This insurance shall include the interest of the Owner, Engineer-Contractor and subcontractors. The loss, if any, under such insurance is to be made adjustable with and payable to Owner, Engineer-Contractor and subcontractors, as their interests may appear. The policy for such insurance shall be issued by an insurance carrier authorized to do business in the state in which the work is to be performed and shall not be cancelled or substantially modified without at least thirty (30) days' advance written notice to the Engineer-Contractor.

17.2 The Owner shall include Engineer-Contractor as an additional insured under the following described policies of insurance now held by Owner.

17.2.1 Comprehensive general liability insurance.

17.2.2 Comprehensive automobile liability insurance.

17.2.3 Certificates of insurance, naming Engineer-Contractor as an additional insured under the above described policies, shall be filed with Engineer-Contractor.

17.3 The Owner shall be liable for damage or destruction to or for the loss or theft of any supplies, materials or equipment in transit to the job site required for the performance of the work, which shall be ordered by Owner or by Engineer-Contractor in the name of Owner.

ARTICLE 18: TERMINATION OF THE AGREEMENT BY OWNER

18.1 The Owner may, upon ten (10) days' written notice and upon the occurrence of any event of default by Engineer-Contractor as provided in 18.2, terminate this agreement. Upon receipt of such notice of termination, Engineer-Contractor shall also take all steps necessary for its orderly and safe disengagement from and protection of the work.

18.2 The Engineer-Contractor shall be in default under this agreement upon the occurrence of any of the following mentioned events:

18.2.1 Insolvency or bankruptcy of Engineer-Contractor or the making of any assignment for the benefit of creditors, or the filing of any petition for bankruptcy or reorganization by Engineer-Contractor.

18.2.2 The willful breach of any material provision of this agreement by Engineer-Contractor and the failure by Engineer-Contractor to take prompt action to remedy same within ten (10) days of the receipt of written notice from Owner.

18.3 In the event of Engineer-Contractor's default, Owner shall have the right to terminate the employment of Engineer-Contractor and to take possession of the work and of all materials, tools and appliances thereon with the right to their continued use, without obligation, until such time as the work is completed, and to finish the work by any reasonable method Owner may deem expedient.

18.4 Should Owner terminate the contract, Owner shall pay Engineer-Contractor a sum equal to the value of the total work completed to date of termination, including: (i) all engineering and design services, and (ii) all construction work, and Owner shall also pay Engineer-Contractor a pro rata portion of Engineer-Contractor's fee and overhead. In addition thereto, Owner shall pay Engineer-Contractor a cancellation charge sufficient to cover all costs and expenses incurred by Engineer-Contractor for the orderly and safe disengagement from and protection of the work. Owner shall also reimburse Engineer-Contractor for all cancellation charges and/or disengaging charges for which Engineer-Contractor may be liable to its own subcontractors and materialmen.

ARTICLE 19: TERMINATION OF THE AGREEMENT BY ENGINEER-CONTRACTOR

19.1 The Engineer-Contractor may, upon the occurrence of any event of default by Owner as provided in 19.3 and upon ten (10) days written notice to Owner, terminate this agreement without prejudice to any legal remedies or rights it may possess, and recover from Owner payment for the entire unpaid balance of the aggregate sum due Engineer-Contractor for the performance of the work completed as of the date of termination, including the cost of all supplies, materials, equipment and design services, the cost of which Engineer-Contractor shall be legally obligated to satisfy.

19.2 In addition to such sums as are due Engineer-Contractor under the provisions of Article 5, Owner shall also pay Engineer-Contractor:

19.2.1 A termination charge equal to ______ percent of the contract sum plus a cancellation charge equal to ______ percent of the contract sum, which cancellation charge shall cover all costs and expenses incurred by Engineer-Contractor for the orderly and safe disengagement from and protection of the work.

19.2.2 Such retainage as shall be held by Owner as of the effective date of the notice of termination.

19.2.3 All cancellation charges which Engineer-Contractor shall become obligated to pay any subcontractor or materialman of Engineer-Contractor.

19.2.4 The amount of such damages as Engineer-Contractor shall become obligated to pay any subcontractor, or materialman of Engineer-Contractor or any third party by reason of the termination of the agreement by Engineer-Contractor.

19.3 The Owner shall be in default of this agreement upon the occurrence of any of the following mentioned events:

19.3.1 Insolvency or bankruptcy of Owner or the making of any assignment for the benefit of creditors or the filing of any petition for bankruptcy or reorganization by Owner.

19.3.2 The willful breach of any provision of this agreement by Owner and the failure by Owner to remedy same within ten (10) days of the receipt of written notice thereof from Engineer-Contractor.

19.3.3 The willful failure without cause to make payment on any application for payment within thirty (30) days from submission thereof. Should Owner in good faith dispute a portion of any application for payment, it shall still be required to make timely payment of the undisputed portion of such application for payment and its failure to do so shall constitute an act of default.

19.4 In lieu of terminating the contract as above provided, upon the happening of any of the events above mentioned, Engineer-Contractor may stop the performance of the work or the progress of the work until such time as the default is remedied without prejudice to any other legal remedy or right it may possess. The election by Engineer-Contractor to stop the work as herein provided shall not be deemed a waiver of Engineer-Contractor's right to terminate the agreement.

19.5 All monies due Engineer-Contractor upon termination of this agreement shall bear interest at the prime rate of interest charged by ______________________________ as of the last day of each month, calculated from the date of termination and all such interest shall belong exclusively to Engineer-Contractor.

ARTICLE 20: DISPUTES

All claims, disputes or other matters in controversy arising out of or relating to this agreement shall be determined in the manner provided for in Appendix D—annexed hereto and made a part hereof.

ARTICLE 21: FORCE MAJEURE

Engineer-Contractor shall not be responsible for any delay in the performance or progress of the work or liable for any costs or damages sustained by Owner resulting from such delay caused by any act or neglect of the Owner or Owner's Representative, or by any employee of Owner, or by any third person acting as the agent, servant or employee of the Owner, or by changes ordered in the work, or by labor disputes, including but not limited to strikes, slowdowns, job actions, picketing and secondary boycotts or by fire or other casualty loss, or by unusual delay in transportation or by acts of God or as a result of compliance with any order or request of any federal, state or municipal governmental authority or any person purporting to act therefor, or by acts of declared or undeclared war or by public disorder, riot, or civil commotion, or by any other cause beyond the control and without the fault or negligence of Engineer-Contractor. In the event of any such delay, Engineer-Contractor shall proceed with due diligence to alleviate such delay and continue the performance of all obligations hereunder. The time during which Engineer-Contractor is delayed in the performance of the work, as herein provided, shall be added to the time for completion of the work as set forth in Article 4. All additional costs or damages resulting from any delay in the performance or progress of the work caused by any act or neglect of the Owner, its agents or representatives shall be borne entirely by the Owner.

ARTICLE 22: MISCELLANEOUS PROVISIONS

22.1 Any notices required or permitted under this contract shall be deemed to be fully given if placed in a pre-paid addressed envelope and sent certified mail, if to the Owner, addressed: ______________________________

____

if to the Engineer-Contractor, addressed: ______________

____

or to such other addresses as the parties shall specify in writing to each other.

22.2 It is agreed between the parties hereto that the interpretation and enforcement of this agreement shall be in conformity with the laws of the state of ______________

22.3 In the event one or more, but not all of the provisions of this agreement are declared unlawful and/or unenforceable by a court of competent jurisdiction, such determination shall not affect the legality or enforceability of the remainder of the terms hereof.

22.4 This agreement may be executed in several counterparts, each of which so executed shall be deemed to be an original, and such counterparts shall, together, constitute and be one and the same agreement.

22.5 This agreement shall inure to the benefit of and be binding upon the parties hereto, their successors or assigns.

22.6 The Owner and Engineer-Contractor, by and through their respective signatories to this agreement, each represent to the other that they are authorized to enter into the within agreement.

ARTICLE 23: OFFER OF EMPLOYMENT

Owner and Engineer-Contractor mutually agree that each will not offer employment to, nor accept for employment, the employees of the other party for a period of six (6) months after final payment and after the completion of such other assignments as may follow arising out of this contract.

ARTICLE 24: FILING OF CONTRACT

24.1 The Owner and Engineer-Contractor covenant each with the other that a copy of this contract duly executed by the parties hereto and in form suitable for filing under the laws of the state in which the work is to be performed shall be filed by Engineer-Contractor in accordance with such laws.

24.2 Upon receipt of final payment from the Owner, Engineer-Contractor shall furnish Owner with a discharge of building contract in form suitable for filing under the laws of the state in which the work is to be performed.

24.3 In the event the laws of the state in which the work is to be performed do not provide for the filing of a copy of this contract, but do provide for the filing of another document in lieu thereof, the effect of which is to preclude the assertion of any mechanics' lien claim by any subcontractor or materialman, then the parties hereto, in cooperation with each other, shall diligently proceed to execute such other document and cause a copy of same to be filed in accordance with local law.

IN WITNESS WHEREOF, the parties hereto have caused these presents to be signed by their proper corporate officers and have affixed their corporate seals hereto the day and year first above written.

ATTEST:

By ______________ President

______________ Secretary OWNER

By ______________ President

______________ Secretary ENGINEER-CONTRACTOR

APPENDIX D-1
RESOLUTION OF DISPUTES BY ARBITRATION

1. All claims, disputes or other matters in controversy arising out of or relating to this agreement shall be determined by three (3) arbitrators, one appointed by the Owner, one appointed by the Engineer-Contractor and the third by the arbitrators so appointed.

2. Notice of demand for arbitration by either party to this agreement shall be served in writing upon the other party to this agreement and shall be made within sixty (60) days after the dispute has arisen.

3. Within thirty (30) days after either party shall have given notice of demand for arbitration, Owner and Engineer-Contractor shall each appoint his respective arbitrator and give actual notice thereof to the other party. If either party shall fail to appoint an arbitrator within the aforesaid initial thirty (30) day period and give actual notice thereof to the other party, then said defaulting party shall be deemed to have irrevocably waived its right to appoint an arbitrator and the arbitrator appointed by the party not in default shall, within thirty (30) days next following the expiration of the initial thirty (30) day period, appoint the second arbitrator and such appointment shall be binding upon the party in default. Within twenty (20) days after the appointment of the two (2) arbitrators, as above provided, the said two (2) arbitrators shall appoint a third arbitrator. In the event the two (2) arbitrators cannot select a third arbitrator within the prescribed twenty (20) day period, then either party may petition the American Arbitration Association to appoint the third arbitrator, subject to his acceptance of the procedure for arbitration as herein set forth. Neither party shall have the right to appoint an arbitrator unless the person to be appointed shall agree to serve as an arbitrator subject to the terms and conditions of this article.

4. The arbitrators, upon their appointment, and after having been duly sworn to do their duties with impartiality and fidelity, shall proceed with all reasonable dispatch to hear and determine the matter in dispute and they shall conduct all arbitration proceedings in the state in which the work is to be performed. In the event the taking of testimony in the arbitration hearing shall not be concluded within sixty (60) days after the third arbitrator shall have been selected, the arbitrators shall then expedite the hearing of the matter in dispute and take testimony on a continuous weekly basis for at least thirty-two (32) hours a week until such time as the taking of all testimony is completed and both sides have rested.

5. The Owner and Engineer-Contractor shall each pay the cost and fees of the arbitrator they select or who is selected on their behalf and one-half of the cost and fees of the third arbitrator.

6. Whenever possible and to the extent not inconsistent with the provisions of this article, the arbitration proceedings shall be conducted in accordance with the Construction Industry Arbitration Rules promulgated by the American Arbitration Association. However, the failure to comply strictly with such Rules shall not be deemed a breach of this agreement.

7. Any decision or award rendered by at least a majority of the arbitrators shall be final and judgment may be entered upon it in accordance with the laws of the state in which the arbitration proceedings shall be conducted.

8. It shall be a condition precedent to the institution of any legal proceedings by either party against the other that a decision or award shall first have been rendered by the arbitrators.

APPENDIX D-1A
RESOLUTION OF DISPUTES BY ARBITRATION

1. All claims, disputes and other matters in question arising out of, or relating to, this agreement or the breach thereof, shall be decided by arbitration in accordance with the Construction Industry Arbitration Rules of the American Arbitration Association then obtaining unless the parties mutually agree otherwise. This agreement to arbitrate shall be specifically enforceable under the prevailing arbitration law.

2. Notice of the demand for arbitration shall be filed in writing with the other party or parties to this agreement and with the American Arbitration Association. The demand shall be made within a reasonable time after the claim, dispute or other matter in question has arisen. In no event shall the arbitration be made after the date when institution of legal or equitable proceedings based on such claim, dispute or other matter in question would be barred by the applicable statute of limitations.

3. The arbitrators shall conduct all arbitration proceedings in the state in which the work is to be performed. The award rendered by the arbitrators shall be final and judgment may be entered upon it in accordance with applicable law in any court having jurisdiction thereof.

4. It shall be a condition precedent to the institution of any legal proceedings by either party against the other that a decision or award shall first have been rendered by the arbitrators.

APPENDIX D-2
RESOLUTION OF DISPUTES BY LEGAL PROCEEDINGS

All claims, disputes or other matters in controversy arising out of or relating to this agreement shall be determined in the local courts of the state in which the work is to be performed.

THE ASSOCIATED GENERAL CONTRACTORS

PRELIMINARY DESIGN-BUILD AGREEMENT

This **AGREEMENT** made this ______________ day of ______________________________

19________ between ____

hereinafter called the **OWNER,** and ____

____, hereinafter called the **CONTRACTOR.**

The Owner and Contractor agree as set forth below:

1. The Owner engages the Contractor to cause certain preliminary design work and construction estimates to be made to determine the cost of designing and constructing

hereinafter called the "Project," for the Owner.

2. The Contractor shall be responsible for furnishing the Design of the Project. The Owner and Contractor shall develop a design phase schedule. PHASE 1: Based upon the Owner's Project requirements, schematic Design Studies will be prepared by the Architect/Engineer. These Schematics are for the purpose of assisting the Owner in determining the feasibility of the Project. PHASE 2: Upon approval of Schematic Designs and authorization from the Owner to proceed, the Architect/Engineer shall prepare Design Development Documents to fix the size and character of the Project as to structural, mechanical and electrical systems, materials and other appropriate essential items in the Project. These Development Documents are the basis to establish a Guaranteed Maximum Price for the design and construction of the Project. PHASE 3: From approved Design Development Documents the Architect/Engineer will prepare working Drawings and Specifications setting forth in detail the requirements for the construction of the Project, and based upon codes, laws or regulations which have been enacted at the time of their preparation. These Working Drawings and Specifications will confirm the Guaranteed Maximum Price and, if the Owner elects to proceed with the Project, the Owner and Contractor will enter into a further agreement in the form attached hereto and marked Exhibit A. Construction of the Project shall be in accordance with these Drawings and Specifications as approved by the Owner. The Drawings and Specifications shall remain the property of the Contractor and are not to be used by the Owner on other projects without the written consent of the Contractor.

3. For performing or causing the performance of these services, the Owner agrees to pay the contractor as follows:

a) SCHEMATIC DESIGN STUDIES — PHASE 1. Compensation for this Phase will be in the amount of ____________________. This compensation is to be paid

b) DESIGN DEVELOPMENT DOCUMENTS — PHASE 2. Compensation for this Phase will be in the amount of ____________. This compensation is to be paid

c) WORKING DRAWINGS AND SPECIFICATIONS — PHASE 3. Compensation for this Phase will be in the amount of ________

__________________________. This compensation is to be paid

4. The Architect/Engineer will be

5. If the Owner elects not to proceed after any Phase, the Owner has no further obligations to the Contractor other than the payment of his compensation as set out in Paragraph 3. If the Owner desires to proceed through construction, the compensation in Article 3 above will be credited toward the Fee in the final contract for construction. (Final Fee will be reduced by compensation already paid.)

6. If the Owner provides full information regarding his requirements for the Project and makes the necessary decisions for the design and construction estimates to proceed in an orderly manner, it is anticipated that the design will be sufficiently complete for the development of a Guaranteed Maximum Price by

CONTRACTOR

____

ATTEST:

____

By ______________________________

Date ______________________________

OWNER

____

ATTEST:

____

By ______________________________

Date ______________________________

AGC DOCUMENT NO. 400 • PRELIMINARY DESIGN BUILD AGREEMENT • APRIL 1980

THE ASSOCIATED GENERAL CONTRACTORS

STANDARD FORM OF DESIGN-BUILD AGREEMENT AND GENERAL CONDITIONS BETWEEN OWNER AND CONTRACTOR

This Document has important legal and insurance consequences; consultation with an attorney and insurance consultants and carriers is encouraged with respect to its completion or modification.

AGREEMENT

Made this day of in the year of Nineteen Hundred and

BETWEEN the Owner, and

the Contractor.

For services in connection with the following described Project: (Include complete Project location and scope)

The Owner and the Contractor agree as set forth below:

Certain provisions of this document have been derived, with modifications, from the following documents published by The American Institute of Architects: AIA Document A111 Owner-Contractor Agreement, © 1976; AIA Document A201 General Conditions, © 1976 by The American Institute of Architects. Usage made of AIA language, with the permission of AIA, does not imply AIA endorsement or approval of this document. Further reproduction of copyrighted AIA materials without separate written permission from AIA is prohibited.

INDEX

ARTICLE 1

The Construction Team and Extent of Agreement

THE CONTRACTOR accepts the relationship of trust and confidence established between him and the Owner by this Agreement. He agrees to furnish the architectural, engineering and construction services set forth herein and agrees to furnish efficient business administration and superintendence, and to use his best efforts to complete the Project in the best and soundest way and in the most expeditious and economical manner consistent with the interests of the Owner.

1.1 *The Construction Team:* The Contractor, the Owner, and the Architect/Engineer called the "Construction Team" shall work from the beginning of design through construction completion. The services of
, as the Architect/Engineer, will be furnished by the Contractor pursuant to an agreement between the Contractor and the Architect/Engineer.

1.2 *Extent of Agreement:* This Agreement represents the entire agreement between the Owner and the Contractor and supersedes all prior negotiations, representations or agreements. When the Drawings and Specifications are complete, they shall be identified by amendment to this Agreement. This Agreement shall not be superseded by any provisions of the documents for construction and may be amended only by written instrument signed by both Owner and Contractor.

1.3 *Definitions:* The Project is the total construction to be designed and constructed of which the Work is a part. The Work comprises the completed construction required by the Drawings and Specifications. The term day shall mean calendar day unless otherwise specifically designated.

ARTICLE 2

Contractor's Responsibilities

2.1 Contractor's Services

2.1.1 The Contractor shall be responsible for furnishing the Design and for the construction of the Project. The Owner and Contractor shall develop a design and construction phase schedule and the Owner shall be responsible for prompt decisions and approvals so as to maintain the approved schedule.

2.1.2 The Owner and Contractor shall develop a design phase schedule. *PHASE 1:* Based upon the Owner's Project requirements, schematic Design Studies will be prepared by the Architect/Engineer. These Schematics are for the purpose of assisting the Owner in determining the feasibility of the Project. *PHASE 2:* Upon approval of Schematic Designs and authorization from the Owner to proceed, the Architect/Engineer shall prepare Design Development Documents to fix the size and character of the Project as to structural, mechanical and electrical systems, materials and other appropriate essential items in the Project. These Development Documents are the basis to establish a Guaranteed Maximum Price for the design and construction of the Project. *PHASE 3:* From approved Design Development Documents the Architect/Engineer will prepare working Drawings and Specifications setting forth in detail the requirements for the construction of the Project, and based upon codes, laws or regulations which have been enacted at the time of their preparation. These Working Drawings and Specifications will be used to confirm the Guaranteed Maximum Price. Construction of the Project shall be in accordance with these Drawings and Specifications as approved by the Owner. The Drawings and Specifications shall remain the property of the Contractor and are not to be used by the Owner on other projects without the written consent of the Contractor. If the working Drawings and Specifications have not been completed and a Guaranteed Maximum Price has been established prior to the completion of the working Drawings and Specifications, the Contractor, the Architect/Engineer and the Owner will work closely together to monitor the design in accordance with prior approvals so as to ensure that the Project can be constructed within the Guaranteed Maximum Price. As these working Drawings and Specifications are being completed, the Contractor will keep the Owner advised of the effects of any Owner requested changes on the Contract Time Schedule and/or the Guaranteed Maximum Price.

2.1.3 The Contractor will assist the Owner in securing permits necessary for the construction of the Project.

2.2 Responsibilities With Respect to Construction

2.2.1 The Contractor will provide all construction supervision, inspection, labor, materials, tools, construction equipment and subcontracted items necessary for the execution and completion of the Project.

2.2.2 The Contractor will pay all sales, use, gross receipts and similar taxes related to the Work provided by the Contractor which have been legally enacted at the time of execution of this Agreement and for which the Contractor is liable.

2.2.3 The Contractor will prepare and submit for the Owner's approval an estimated progress schedule for the Project. This schedule shall indicate the dates for the starting and completion of the various stages of the design and construction. It shall be revised as required by the conditions of the Work and those conditions and events which are beyond the Contractor's control.

2.2.4 The Contractor shall at all times keep the premises free from the accumulation of waste materials or rubbish caused by his operations. At the completion of the Work, he shall remove all of his waste material and rubbish from and around the Project as well as all his tools, construction equipment, machinery and surplus materials.

2.2.5 The Contractor will give all notices and comply with all laws and ordinances legally enacted at the date of execution of the Agreement, which govern the proper execution of the Work.

2.2.6 The Contractor shall take necessary precautions for the safety of his employees on the Work, and shall comply with all applicable provisions of federal, state and municipal safety laws to prevent accidents or injury to persons on, about or adjacent to the Project site. He shall erect and properly maintain, at all times, as required by the conditions and progress of Work, necessary safeguards for the protection of workmen and the public. It is understood and agreed, however, that the Contractor shall have no responsibility for the elimination or abatement of safety hazards created or otherwise resulting from Work at the job site carried on by other persons or firms directly employed by the Owner as separate contractors or by the Owner's tenants, and the Owner agrees to cause any such separate contractors and tenants to abide by and fully adhere to all applicable provisions of federal, state and municipal safety laws and regulations and to comply with all reasonable requests and directions of the Contractor for the elimination or abatement of any such safety hazards at the job site.

2.2.7 The Contractor shall keep such full and detailed accounts as may be necessary for proper financial management under this Agreement. The system shall be satisfactory to the Owner, who shall be afforded access to all the Contractor's records, books, correspondence, instructions, drawings, receipts, vouchers, memoranda and similar data relating to this Agreement. The Contractor shall preserve all such records for a period of three years after the final payment or longer where required by law.

2.3 Royalties and Patents

2.3.1 The Contractor shall pay all royalties and license fees for materials, methods and systems incorporated in the work. He shall defend all suits or claims for infringement of any patent rights and shall save the Owner harmless from loss on account thereof except when a particular design, process or product is specified by the Owner. In such case the Contractor shall be responsible for such loss only if he has reason to believe that the design, process or product so specified is an infringement of a patent, and fails to give such information promptly to the Owner.

2.4 Warranties and Completion

2.4.1 The Contractor warrants to the Owner that all materials and equipment furnished under this Agreement will be new, unless otherwise specified, and that all Work will be of good quality, free from improper workmanship and defective materials and in conformance with the Drawings and Specifications. The Contractor agrees to correct all Work performed by him under this Agreement which proves to be defective in material and workmanship within a period of one year from the Date of Substantial Completion as defined in Paragraph 5.2, or for such longer periods of time as may be set forth with respect to specific warranties contained in the Specifications.

2.4.2 The Contractor will secure required certificates of inspection, testing or approval and deliver them to the Owner.

2.4.3 The Contractor will collect all written warranties and equipment manuals and deliver them to the Owner.

2.4.4 The Contractor with the assistance of the Owner's maintenance personnel, will direct the checkout of utilities and operations of systems and equipment for readiness, and will assist in their initial start-up and testing.

2.5 Additional Services

2.5.1 The Contractor will provide the following additional services upon the request of the Owner. A written agreement between the Owner and Contractor shall define the extent of such additional services and the amount and manner in which the Contractor will be compensated for such additional services.

2.5.2 Services related to investigation, appraisals or evaluations of existing conditions, facilities or equipment, or verification of the accuracy of existing drawings or other Owner-furnished information.

2.5.3 Services related to Owner-furnished equipment, furniture and furnishings which are not a part of this Agreement.

2.5.4 Services for tenant or rental spaces not a part of this Agreement.

2.5.5 Obtaining and training maintenance personnel or negotiating maintenance service contracts.

ARTICLE 3

Owner's Responsibilities

3.1 The Owner shall provide full information regarding his requirements for the Project.

3.2 The Owner shall designate a representative who shall be fully acquainted with the Project, and has authority to approve changes in the scope of the Project, render decisions promptly, and furnish information expeditiously and in time to meet the dates set forth in Subparagraph 2.2.3.

3.3 The Owner shall furnish for the site of the Project all necessary surveys describing the physical characteristics, soils reports and subsurface investigations, legal limitations, utility locations, and a legal description.

3.4 The Owner shall secure and pay for necessary approvals, easements, assessments and charges required for the construction, use, or occupancy of permanent structures or for permanent changes in existing facilities.

3.5 The Owner shall furnish such legal services as may be necessary for providing the items set forth in Paragraph 3.4, and such auditing services as he may require.

3.6 If the Owner becomes aware of any fault or defect in the Project or non-conformance with the Drawings or Specifications, he shall give prompt written notice thereof to the Contractor.

3.7 The Owner shall provide the insurance for the Project as provided in Paragraph 12.4.

3.8 The Owner shall bear the costs of any bonds that may be required.

3.9 The services and information required by the above paragraphs shall be furnished with reasonable promptness at the Owner's expense and the Contractor shall be entitled to rely upon the accuracy and the completeness thereof.

3.10 The Owner shall furnish reasonable evidence satisfactory to the Contractor, prior to commencing Work and at such future times as may be required, that sufficient funds are available and committed for the entire Cost of the Project. Unless such reasonable evidence is furnished, the Contractor is not required to commence or continue any Work, or may, if such evidence is not presented within a reasonable time, stop Work upon 15 days notice to the Owner. The failure of the Contractor to insist upon the providing of this evidence at any one time shall not be a waiver of the Owner's obligation to make payments pursuant to this Agreement nor shall it be a waiver of the Contractor's right to request or insist that such evidence be provided at a later date.

3.11 The Owner shall have no contractual obligation to the Contractor's Subcontractors and shall communicate with such Subcontractors only through the Contractor.

ARTICLE 4

Subcontracts

4.1 All portions of the Work that the Contractor does not perform with his own forces shall be performed under subcontracts.

4.2 A Subcontractor is a person or entity who has a direct contract with the Contractor to perform any Work in connection with the Project. The term Subcontractor does not include any separate contractor employed by the Owner or the separate contractors' subcontractors.

4.3 No contractual relationship shall exist between the Owner and any Subcontractor. The Contractor shall be responsible for the management of the Subcontractors in the performance of their Work.

ARTICLE 5

Contract Time Schedule

5.1 The Work to be performed under this Agreement shall be commenced on or about and shall be substantially completed on or about

5.2 The Date of Substantial Completion of the Project or a designated portion thereof is the date when construction is sufficiently complete in accordance with the Drawings and Specifications so the Owner can occupy or utilize the Project or designated portion thereof for the use for which it is intended. Warranties called for by this Agreement or by the Drawings and Specifications shall commence on the Date of Substantial Completion of the Project or designated portion thereof. This date shall be established by a Certificate of Substantial Completion signed by the Owner and Contractor and shall state their respective responsibilities for security, maintenance, heat, utilities, damage to the Work and insurance. This Certificate shall also list the items to be completed or corrected and fix the time for their completion and correction.

5.3 If the Contractor is delayed at any time in the progress of the Project by any act or neglect of the Owner or by any separate contractor employed by the Owner, or by changes order in the Project, or by labor disputes, fire, unusual delay in transportation, adverse weather conditions not reasonably anticipatable, unavoidable casualties, or any causes beyond the Contractor's control, or a delay authorized by the Owner pending arbitration, then the Date for Substantial Completion shall be extended by Change Order for the period of time caused by such delay.

Guaranteed Maximum Price

6.1 The Contractor guarantees that the maximum price to the Owner for the Cost of the Project as set forth in Article 8, and the Contractor's Fee as set forth in Article 7, will not exceed
Dollars ($), which sum shall be called the Guaranteed Maximum Price.

6.2 The Guaranteed Maximum Price is based upon laws, codes, and regulations in existence at the date of its establishment and upon criteria, Drawings, and Specifications as set forth below:

6.3 The Guaranteed Maximum Price will be modified for delays caused by the Owner and for Changes in the Project, all pursuant to Article 9.

6.4 Allowances included in the Guaranteed Maximum Price are as set forth below:

6.5 Whenever the cost is more than or less than the Allowance, the Guaranteed Maximum Price shall be adjusted by Change Order.

ARTICLE 7

Contractor's Fee

7.1 In consideration of the performance of the Agreement, the Owner agrees to pay to the Contractor in current funds as compensation for his services a Fee as follows:

7.2 Adjustment in Fee shall be made as follows:

7.2.1 For Changes in the Project as provided in Article 9, the Contractor's Fee shall be adjusted as follows:

7.2.2 For delays in the Project not the responsibility of the Contractor, there will be an equitable adjustment in the fee to compensate the Contractor for his increased expenses.

7.2.3 In the event the Cost of the Project plus the Contractor's Fee shall be less than the Guaranteed Maximum Price as adjusted by Change Orders, the resulting savings will be shared by the Owner and the Contractor as follows:

7.2.4 The Contractor shall be paid an additional fee in the same proportion as set forth in 7.2.1 if the Contractor is placed in charge of managing the replacement of insured or uninsured loss.

7.3 The Contractor shall be paid monthly that part of his Fee proportionate to the percentage of Work completed, the balance, if any, to be paid at the time of final payment.

7.4 Including in the Contractor's Fee are the following:

7.4.1 Salaries or other compensation of the Contractor's employees at the principal office and branch offices, except employees listed in Subparagraph 8.2.3.

7.4.2 General operating expenses of the Contractor's principal and branch offices other than the field office.

7.4.3 Any part of the Contractor's capital expenses, including interest on the Contractor's capital employed for the Project.

7.4.4 Overhead or general expenses of any kind, except as may be expressly included in Article 8.

7.4.5 Costs in excess of the Guaranteed Maximum Price.

ARTICLE 8

Cost of the Project

8.1 The term Cost of the Project shall mean costs necessarily incurred in the design and construction of the Project and shall include the items set forth below in this Article. The Owner agrees to pay the Contractor for the Cost of the Project as defined in this Article. Such payment shall be in addition to the Contractor's Fee stipulated in Article 7.

8.2. Cost Items

8.2.1 All architectural, engineering and consulting fees and expenses incurred in designing and constructing the Project.

8.2.2 Wages paid for labor in the direct employ of the Contractor in the performance of the Work under applicable collective bargaining agreements, or under a salary or wage schedule agreed upon by the Owner and the Contractor, and including such welfare or other benefits, if any, as may be payable with respect thereto.

8.2.3 Salaries of Contractor's employees when stationed at the field office, in whatever capacity employed, employees engaged on the road expediting the production or transportation of material and equipment and employees from the main or branch office performing the functions listed below:

8.2.4 Cost of all employee benefits and taxes for such items as unemployment compensation and social security, insofar as such cost is based on wages, salaries, or other remuneration paid to employees of the Contractor and included in the Cost of the Project under Subparagraphs 8.2.1, 8.2.2 and 8.2.3.

8.2.5 Reasonable transportation, traveling and hotel and moving expenses of the Contractor or of his officers or employees incurred in discharge of duties connected with the Project.

8.2.6 Cost of all materials, supplies and equipment incorporated in the Project, including costs of transportation and storage thereof.

8.2.7 Payments made by the Contractor to Subcontractors for Work performed pursuant to contract under this Agreement.

8.2.8 Cost, including transportation and maintenance, of all materials, supplies, equipment, temporary facilities and hand tools not owned by the workmen, which are employed or consumed in the performance of the Work, and cost less salvage value on such items used, but not consumed, which remain the property of the Contractor.

8.2.9 Rental charges of all necessary machinery and equipment, exclusive of hand tools, used at the site of the Work, whether rented from the Contractor or others, including installations, repairs and replacements, dismantling, removal, costs of lubrication, transportation and delivery costs thereof, at rental charges consistent with those prevailing in the area.

8.2.10 Cost of the premiums for all insurance which the Contractor is required to procure by this Agreement or is deemed necessary by the Contractor.

8.2.11 Sales, use, gross receipts or similar taxes related to the Project, imposed by any governmental authority, and for which the Contractor is liable.

8.2.12 Permit fees, licenses, tests, royalties, damages for infringement of patents and costs of defending suits therefor for which the Contractor is responsible under Subparagraph 2.3.1 and deposits lost for causes other than the Contractor's negligence.

8.2.13 Losses, expenses or damages to the extent not compensated by insurance or otherwise (including settlement made with the written approval of the Owner), and the cost of corrective work.

8.2.14 Minor expenses such as telegrams, long-distance telephone calls, telephone service at the site, expressage, and similar petty cash items in connection with the Project.

8.2.15 Cost of removal of all debris.

8.2.16 Costs incurred due to an emergency affecting the safety of persons and property.

8.2.17 Cost of data processing services required in the performance of the services outlined in Article 2.

8.2.18 Legal costs reasonably and properly resulting from prosecution of the Project for the Owner.

8.2.19 All costs directly incurred in the performance of the Project and not included in the Contractor's Fee as set forth in Paragraph 7.4.

ARTICLE 9

Changes in the Project

9.1 The Owner, without invalidating this Agreement, may order Changes in the Project within the general scope of this Agreement consisting of additions, deletions or other revisions, the Guaranteed Maximum Price, if established, the Contractor's Fee, and the Contract Time Schedule being adjusted accordingly. All such Changes in the Project shall be authorized by Change Order.

9.1.1 A Change Order is a written order to the Contractor signed by the Owner or his authorized agent and issued after the execution of this Agreement, authorizing a Change in the Project and/or an adjustment in the Guaranteed Maximum Price, the Contractor's Fee or the Contract Time Schedule. Each adjustment in the Guaranteed Maximum Price resulting from a Change Order shall clearly separate the amount attributable to the Cost of the Project and the Contractor's Fee.

9.1.2 The increase or decrease in the Guaranteed Maximum Price resulting from a Change in the Project shall be determined in one or more of the following ways:

9.1.2.1 by mutual acceptance of a lump sum properly itemized and supported by sufficient substantiating data to permit evaluation; or

9.1.2.2 by unit prices stated in this Agreement or subsequently agreed upon; or

9.1.2.3 by cost to be determined as defined in Article 8 and a mutual acceptable fixed or percentage fee; or

9.1.2.4 by the method provided in Subparagraph 9.1.3.

9.1.3 If none of the methods set forth in Clauses 9.1.2.1 through 9.1.2.3 is agreed upon, the Contractor, provided he receives a written order signed by the Owner, shall promptly proceed with the Work involved. The cost of such Work shall then be determined on the basis of the reasonable expenditures and savings of those performing the Work attributed to the change, including, in the case of an increase in the Guaranteed Maximum Price, a reasonable increase in the Contractor's Fee. In such case, and also under Clauses 9.1.2.3 and 9.1.2.4 above, the Contractor shall keep and present, in such form as the Owner may prescribe, an itemized accounting together with appropriate supporting data of the increase in the Cost of the Project as outlined in Article 8. The amount of decrease in the Guaranteed Maximum Price to be allowed by the Contractor to the Owner for any deletion or change which results in a net decrease in cost will be the amount of the actual net decrease. When both additions and credits are involved in any one change, the increase in Fee shall be figured on the basis of net increase, if any.

9.1.4 If unit prices are stated in this Agreement or subsequently agreed upon, and if the quantities originally contemplated are so changed in a proposed Change Order or as a result of several Change Orders that application of the agreed unit prices to the quantities of Work proposed will cause substantial inequity to the Owner or the Contractor, the applicable unit prices and the Guaranteed Maximum Price shall be equitably adjusted.

9.1.5 Should concealed conditions encountered in the performance of the Work below the surface of the ground or should concealed or unknown conditions in an existing structure be at variance with the conditions indicated by the Drawings, Specifications, or Owner-furnished information or should unknown physical conditions below the surface of the ground or should concealed or unknown conditions in an existing structure of an unusual nature, differing materially from those ordinarily encountered and generally recognized as inherent in work of the character provided for in this Agreement, be encountered, the Guaranteed Maximum Price and the Contract Time Schedule shall be equitably adjusted by Change Order upon claim by either party made within a reasonable time after the first observance of the conditions.

9.2 Claims for Additional Cost or Time

9.2.1 If the Contractor wishes to make a claim for an increase in the Guaranteed Maximum Price, or increase in his Fee or an extension in the Contract Time Schedule, he shall give the Owner written notice thereof within a reasonable time after the occurrence of the event giving rise to such claim. This notice shall be given by the Contractor before proceeding to execute the Work, except in an emergency endangering life or property in which case the Contractor shall act, at his discretion, to prevent threatened damage, injury or loss. Claims arising from delay shall be made within a reasonable time after the delay. Increases based upon design and estimating costs with respect to possible changes requested by the Owner, shall be made within a reasonable time after the decision is made not to proceed with the change. No such claim shall be valid unless so made. If the Owner and the Contractor cannot agree on the amount of the adjustment in the Guaranteed Maximum Price, the Contractor's Fee or Contract Time Schedule, it shall be determined pursuant to the provisions of Article 16. Any change in the Guaranteed Maximum Price, the Contractor's Fee or Contract Time Schedule resulting from such claim shall be authorized by Change Order.

9.3 Minor Changes in the Project

9.3.1 The Owner will have authority to order minor Changes in the Work not involving an adjustment in the Guaranteed Maximum Price or an extension of the Contract Time Schedule and not inconsistent with the intent of the Drawings and Specifications. Such Changes may be effected by written order and shall be binding on the Owner and the Contractor.

9.4 Emergencies

9.4.1 In any emergency affecting the safety of persons or property, the Contractor shall act, at his discretion, to prevent threatened damage, injury or loss. Any increase in the Guaranteed Maximum Price or extension of time claimed by the Contractor on account of emergency work shall be determined as provided in this Article.

ARTICLE 10

Discounts

All discounts for prompt payment shall accrue to the Owner to the extent the Cost of the Project is paid directly by the Owner or from a fund made available by the Owner to the Contractor for such payments. To the extent the Cost of the Project is paid with funds of the Contractor, all cash discounts shall accrue to the Contractor. All trade discounts, rebates and refunds, and all returns from sale of surplus materials and equipment, shall be credited to the Cost of the Project.

ARTICLE 11

Payments to the Contractor

11.1 Payments shall be made by the Owner to the Contractor according to the following procedure:

11.1.1 On or before the _______________ day of each month after Work has commenced, the Contractor shall submit to the Owner an Application for Payment in such detail as may be required by the Owner based on the Work completed and materials stored on the site and/or at locations approved by the Owner along with a proportionate amount of the Contractor's Fee for the period ending on the _______________ day of the month.

11.1.2 Within ten (10) days after his receipt of each monthly Application for Payment, the Owner shall pay directly to the Contractor the appropriate amounts for which Application for Payment is made therein. This payment request shall deduct the aggregate of amounts previously paid by the Owner.

11.1.3 If the Owner should fail to pay the Contractor at the time the payment of any amount becomes due, then the Contractor may, at any time thereafter, upon serving written notice that he will stop Work within five (5) days after receipt of the notice by the Owner, and after such five (5) day period, stop the Project until payment of the amount owing has been received. Written notice shall be deemed to have been duly served if sent by certified mail to the last business address known to him who gives the notice.

11.1.4 Payments due but unpaid shall bear interest at the rate the Owner is paying on his construction loan or at the legal rate, whichever is higher.

11.2 The Contractor warrants and guarantees that title to all Work, materials and equipment covered by an Application for Payment whether incorporated in the Project or not, will pass to the Owner upon receipt of such payment by the Contractor free and clear of all liens, claims, security interests or encumbrances hereinafter referred to as Liens.

11.3 No Progress Payment nor any partial or entire use or occupancy of the Project by the Owner shall constitute an acceptance of any Work not in accordance with the Drawings and Specifications.

11.4 Final payment constituting the unpaid balance of the Cost of the Project and the Contractor's Fee shall be due and payable when the Project is delivered to the Owner, ready for beneficial occupancy, or when the Owner occupies the Project, whichever event first occurs, provided that the Project be then substantially completed and this Agreement substantially performed. If there should remain minor items to be completed, the Contractor and the Owner shall list such items and the Contractor shall deliver, in writing, his guarantee to complete said items within a reasonable time thereafter. The Owner may retain a sum equal to 150% of the estimated cost of completing any unfinished items, provided that said unfinished items are listed separately and the estimated cost of completing any unfinished items is likewise listed separately. Thereafter, the Owner shall pay to the Contractor, monthly, the amount retained for incomplete items as each of said items is completed.

11.5 Before issuance of Final Payment, the Owner may request satisfactory evidence that all payrolls, materials bills and other indebtedness connected with the Project have been paid or otherwise satisfied.

11.6 The making of Final Payment shall constitute a waiver of all claims by the Owner except those rising from:

11.6.1. Unsettled Liens.

11.6.2 Improper workmanship or defective materials appearing within one year after the Date of Substantial Completion.

11.6.3 Failure of the Work to comply with the Drawings and Specifications.

11.6.4 Terms of any special guarantees required by the Drawings and Specifications.

11.7 The acceptance of Final Payment shall constitute a waiver of all claims by the Contractor except those previously made in writing and unsettled.

ARTICLE 12

Insurance, Indemnity and Waiver of Subrogation

12.1 Indemnity

12.1.1 The Contractor agrees to indemnify and hold the Owner harmless from all claims for bodily injury and property damage (other than the Work itself and other property insured under Paragraph 12.4) that may arise from the Contractor's operations under this Agreement.

12.1.2 The Owner shall cause any other contractor who may have a contract with the Owner to perform work in the areas where Work will be performed under this Agreement, to agree to indemnify the Owner and the Contractor and hold them harmless from all claims for bodily injury and property damage (other than property insured under Paragraph 12.4) that may arise from that contractor's operations. Such provisions shall be in a form satisfactory to the Contractor.

12.2 Contractor's Liability Insurance

12.2.1 The Contractor shall purchase and maintain such insurance as will protect him from the claims set forth below which may arise out of or result from the Contractor's operations under this Agreement whether such operations be by himself or by any Subcontractor or by anyone directly or indirectly employed by any of them, or by anyone for whose acts any of them may be liable:

12.2.1.1 Claims under workers' compensation, disability benefit and other similar employee benefit acts which are applicable to the Work to be performed.

12.2.1.2 Claims for damages because of bodily injury, occupational sickness or disease, or death of his employees under any applicable employer's liability law.

12.2.1.3 Claims for damages because of bodily injury, or death of any person other than his employees.

12.2.1.4 Claims for damages insured by usual personal injury liability coverage which are sustained (1) by any person as a result of an offense directly or indirectly related to the employment of such person by the Contractor or (2) by any other person.

12.2.1.5 Claims for damages, other than to the Work itself, because of injury to or destruction of tangible property, including loss of use therefrom.

12.2.1.6 Claims for damages because of bodily injury or death of any person or property damage arising out of the ownership, maintenance or use of any motor vehicle.

12.2.2 The Comprehensive General Liability Insurance shall include premises-operations (including explosion, collapse and underground coverage) elevators, independent contractors, completed operations, and blanket contractual liability on all written contracts, all including broad form property damage coverage.

12.2.3 The Contractor's Comprehensive General and Automobile Liability Insurance, as required by Subparagraphs 12.2.1 and 12.2.2 shall be written for not less than limits of liability as follows:

a. Comprehensive General Liability
   1. Bodily Injury — -$________ Each Occurrence (Completed Operations)
      $________ Aggregate
   2. Property Damage — -$________ Each Occurrence
      $________ Aggregate

b. Comprehensive Automobile Liability
   1. Bodily Injury — -$________ Each Person
      $________ Each Occurrence
   2. Property Damage — -$________ Each Occurrence

12.2.4 Comprehensive General Liability Insurance may be arranged under a single policy for the full limits required or by a combination of underlying policies with the balance provided by an Excess or Umbrella Liability policy.

12.2.5 The foregoing policies shall contain a provision that coverages afforded under the policies will not be cancelled or not renewed until at least sixty (60) days' prior written notice has been given to the Owner. Certificates of Insurance showing such coverages to be in force shall be filed with the Owner prior to commencement of the Work.

12.3 Owner's Liability Insurance

12.3.1 The Owner shall be responsible for purchasing and maintaining his own liability insurance and, at his option, may purchase and maintain such insurance as will protect him against claims which may arise from operations under this Agreement.

12.4 Insurance to Protect Project

12.4.1 The Owner shall purchase and maintain property insurance in a form acceptable to the Contractor upon the entire Project for the full cost of replacement as the time of any loss. This insurance shall include as named insureds the Owner, the Contractor, Subcontractors and Subsubcontractors and shall insure against loss from the perils of Fire, Extended Coverage, and shall include "All Risk" insurance for physical loss or damage including, without duplication of coverage, at least theft, vandalism, malicious mischief, transit, collapse, flood, earthquake, testing, and damage resulting from defective design, workmanship or material. The Owner will increase limits of coverage, if necessary, to reflect estimated replacement cost. The Owner will be responsible for any co-insurance penalties or deductibles. If the Project covers an addition to or is adjacent to an existing building, the Contractor, Subcontractors and Subsubcontractors shall be named as additional insureds under the Owner's Property Insurance covering such building and its contents.

12.4.1.1 If the Owner finds it necessary to occupy or use a portion or portions of the Project prior to Substantial Completion thereof, such occupancy shall not commence prior to a time mutually agreed to by the Owner and the Contractor and to which the insurance company or companies providing the property insurance have consented by endorsement to the policy or policies. This insurance shall not be cancelled or lapsed on account of such partial occupancy. Consent of the Contractor and of the insurance company or companies to such occupancy or use shall not be unreasonably withheld.

12.4.2 The Owner shall purchase and maintain such boiler and machinery insurance as may be required or necessary. This insurance shall include the interests of the Owner, the Contractor, Subcontractors and Subsubcontractors in the Work.

12.4.3 The Owner shall purchase and maintain such insurance as will protect the Owner and the Contractor against loss of use of Owner's property due to those perils insured pursuant to Subparagraph 12.4.1. Such policy will provide coverage for expediting expenses of materials, continuing overhead of the Owner and the Contractor, necessary labor expense including overtime, loss of income by the Owner and other determined exposures. Exposures of the Owner and the Contractor shall be determined by mutual agreement and separate limits of coverage fixed for each item.

12.4.4 The Owner shall file a copy of all policies with the Contractor before an exposure to loss may occur. Copies of any subsequent endorsements will be furnished to the Contractor. The Contractor will be given sixty (60) days notice of cancellation, non-renewal, or any endorsements restricting or reducing coverage. If the Owner does not intend to purchase such insurance, he shall inform the Contractor in writing prior to the commencement of the Work. The Contractor may then effect insurance which will protect the interest of himself, the Subcontractors and their Subsubcontractors in the Project, the cost of which shall be a Cost of the Project pursuant to Article 8, and the Guaranteed Maximum Price shall be increased by Change Order. If the Contractor is damaged by failure of the Owner to purchase or maintain such insurance or to so notify the Contractor, the Owner shall bear all reasonable costs properly attributable thereto.

12.5 Property Insurance Loss Adjustment

12.5.1 Any insured loss shall be adjusted with the Owner and the Contractor and made payable to the Owner and Contractor as trustees for the insureds, as their interests may appear, subject to any applicable mortgagee clause.

12.5.2 Upon the occurrence of an insured loss, monies received will be deposited in a separate account and the trustees shall make distribution in accordance with the agreement of the parties in interest, or in the absence of such agreement, in accordance with an arbitration award pursuant to Article 16. If the trustees are unable to agree between themselves on the settlement of the loss, such dispute shall also be submitted to arbitration pursuant to Article 16.

12.6 Waiver of Subrogation

12.6.1 The Owner and Contractor waive all rights against each other, the Architect/Engineer, Subcontractors and Subsubcontractors for damages caused by perils covered by insurance provided under Paragraph 12.4, except such rights as they may have to the proceeds of such insurance held by the Owner and Contractor as trustees. The Contractor shall require similar waivers from all Subcontractors and Subsubcontractors.

12.6.2 The Owner and Contractor waive all rights against each other and the Architect/Engineer, Subcontractors and Subsubcontractors for loss or damage to any equipment used in connection with the Project which loss is covered by any property insurance. The Contractor shall require similar waivers from all Subcontractors and Subsubcontractors.

12.6.3 The Owner waives subrogation against the Contractor, Architect/Engineer, Subcontractors, and Subsubcontractors on all property and consequential loss policies carried by the Owner on adjacent properties and under property and consequential loss policies purchased for the Project after its completion.

12.6.4 If the policies of insurance referred to in this Paragraph require an endorsement to provide for continued coverage where there is a wavier of subrogation, the owners of such policies will cause them to be so endorsed.

ARTICLE 13

Termination of the Agreement And Owner's Right to Perform Contractor's Obligations

13.1 Termination by the Contractor

13.1.1 If the Project is stopped for a period of thirty (30) days under an order of any court or other public authority having jurisdiction, or as a result of an act of government, such as a declaration of a national emergency making materials unavailable, through no act or fault of the Contractor or if the Project should be stopped for a period of thirty (30) days by the Contractor for the Owner's failure to make payment thereon, then the Contractor may, upon seven days' written notice to the Owner, terminate this Agreement and recover from the Owner payment for all Work executed, the Contractor's Fee earned to date, and for any proven loss sustained upon any materials, equipment, tools, construction equipment and machinery, including reasonable profit and damages.

13.2 Owner's Right to Perform Contractor's Obligations and Termination by the Owner for Cause

13.2.1 If the Contractor fails to perform any of his obligations under this Agreement, including any obligation he assumes to perform Work with his own forces, the Owner may, after seven days' written notice, during which period the Contractor fails to perform such obligation, make good such deficiencies. The Guaranteed Maximum Price, if any, shall be reduced by the cost to the Owner of making good such deficiencies.

13.2.2 If the Contractor is adjudged a bankrupt, or if he makes a general assignment for the benefit of his creditors, or if a receiver is appointed on account of his insolvency, or if he persistently or repeatedly refuses or fails, except in cases for which extension of time is provided, to supply enough properly skilled workmen or proper materials, or if he fails to make proper payment to Subcontractors or for materials or labor, or persistently disregards laws, ordinances, rules, regulations or orders of any public authority having jurisdiction, or otherwise is guilty of a substantial violation of a provision of this Agreement, then the Owner may, without prejudice to any right or remedy and after giving the Contractor and his surety, if any, seven (7) days' written notice, during which period the Contractor fails to cure the violation, terminate the employment of the Contractor and take possession of the site and of all materials, equipment, tools, construction equipment and machinery thereon owned by the Contractor and may finish the Work by whatever reasonable method he may deem expedient. In such case, the Contractor shall not be entitled to receive any further payment until the Work is finished nor shall he be relieved from his obligations assumed under Article 6.

13.3 Termination by Owner Without Cause

13.3.1 If the Owner terminates the Agreement other than pursuant to Article 13.2.2, he shall reimburse the Contractor for any unpaid Cost of the Project due him under Article 8, plus the unpaid balance of the Contractor's Fee. If the Contractor's Fee is based upon a percentage of the Cost of the Project, the Fee shall be calculated upon the adjusted Guaranteed Maximum Cost, if any, otherwise to a reasonable estimated Cost of the Project when completed. The Owner shall also pay to the Contractor fair compensation, either by purchase or rental at the election of the Owner, for any equipment retained. In case of such termination of this Agreement the Owner shall further assume and become liable for obligations, commitments and unsettled claims that the Contractor has previously undertaken or incurred in good faith in connection with said Work. The Contractor shall, as a condition of receiving the payments referred to in this Article 13, execute and deliver such papers and take all such steps, including the legal assignment of his contractual rights, as the Owner may require for the purpose of fully vesting in the Owner the rights and benefits of the Contractor under such obligations or commitments.

ARTICLE 14

Assignment and Governing Law

14.1 Neither the Owner nor the Contractor shall assign his interest in this Agreement without the written consent of the other except as to the assignment of proceeds.

14.2 This Agreement shall be governed by the law in effect at the location of this Project.

ARTICLE 15

Miscellaneous Provisions

ARTICLE 16

Arbitration

16.1 All claims, disputes and other matters in question arising out of, or relating to, this Agreement or the breach thereof, except with respect to the Architect/Engineer's decision on matters relating to artistic effect, and except for claims which have been waived by the making or acceptance of Final Payment shall be decided by arbitration in accordance with the Construction Industry Arbitration Rules of the American Arbitration Association then obtaining unless the parties mutually agree otherwise. This agreement to arbitrate shall be specifically enforceable under the prevailing arbitration law.

16.2 Notice of the demand for arbitration shall be filed in writing with the other party to this Agreement and with the American Arbitration Association. The demand for arbitration shall be made within a reasonable time after the claim, dispute or other matter in question has arisen, and in no event shall it be made when institution of legal or equitable proceedings based on such claim, dispute or other matter in question would be barred by the applicable statute of limitations.

16.3 The award rendered by the arbitrators shall be final and judgment may be entered upon it in accordance with applicable law in any court having jurisdiction thereof.

16.4 Unless otherwise agreed in writing, the Contractor shall carry on the Work and maintain the Contract Time Schedule during any arbitration proceedings and the Owner shall continue to make payments in accordance with this Agreement.

16.5 All claims which are related to or dependent upon each other shall be heard by the same arbitrator or arbitrators, even though the parties are not the same, unless a specific contract prohibits such consolidation.

16.6 These provisions relating to mandatory arbitration shall not be applicable to a claim asserted in an action in a state or federal court by a person who is under no obligation to arbitrate such claim with either of the parties to this Agreement insofar as the parties to this Agreement may desire to assert any rights of indemnity or contribution with respect to the subject matter of such action.

This Agreement entered into as of the day and year first written above.

ATTEST: OWNER:

ATTEST: CONTRACTOR:

THE ASSOCIATED GENERAL CONTRACTORS

STANDARD FORM OF DESIGN-BUILD AGREEMENT AND GENERAL CONDITIONS BETWEEN OWNER AND CONTRACTOR

(WHERE THE BASIS OF COMPENSATION IS A LUMP SUM)

This Document has important legal and insurance consequences; consultation with an attorney and insurance consultants and carriers is encouraged with respect to its completion or modification.

AGREEMENT

Made this day of in the year of Nineteen Hundred

and **BETWEEN** the Owner, and

the Contractor.

For services in connection with the following described Project: (Include complete Project location and scope)

The Owner and the Contractor agree as set forth below:

AGC DOCUMENT NO. 415 • STANDARD FORM OF DESIGN-BUILD AGREEMENT AND GENERAL CONDITIONS BETWEEN OWNER AND CONTRACTOR (LUMP SUM) • FEBRUARY 1986

INDEX

ARTICLE 1

The Construction Team and Extent of Agreement

1.1 *THE CONSTRUCTION TEAM:* The Contractor, the Owner, and the Architect/Engineer called the "Construction Team" shall work from the beginning of design through construction completion. The services of ______________________ as the Architect/Engineer will be furnished by the Contractor pursuant to an agreement between the Contractor and the Architect/Engineer.

1.2 *EXTENT OF AGREEMENT:* This Agreement represents the entire agreement between the Owner and the Contractor and supersedes all prior negotiations, representations or agreements. When the Drawings and Specifications are complete, they shall be identified by amendment to this Agreement. This Agreement shall not be superseded by any provisions of the documents for construction and may be amended only by written instrument signed by both Owner and Contractor.

1.3 *DEFINITIONS:* The Project is the total construction to be designed and constructed of which the Work is a part. The Work comprises the completed construction required by the Drawings and Specifications. The term day shall mean calendar day unless otherwise specifically designated.

ARTICLE 2

Contractor's Responsibilities

2.1 Contractor's Services

2.1.1 The Contractor shall be responsible for furnishing the Design and for the Construction of the Project. The Contractor shall develop a design and construction phase schedule and the Owner shall be responsible for prompt decisions and approvals so as to maintain the approved schedule. Any design, engineering, architectural, or other professional service required to be performed under this Agreement shall be performed by duly licensed personnel.

2.1.2 The Contractor shall prepare and the Owner approve a design phase schedule as follows: PHASE 1: Based upon the Owner's Project requirements, schematic Design Studies will be prepared by the Architect/Engineer. These Schematics are for the purpose of assisting the Owner in determining the feasibility of the project. PHASE 2: Upon approval of Schematic Designs and authorization from the Owner to proceed, the Architect/Engineer shall prepare Design Development documents to fix the size and character of the Project as to structural, mechanical and electrical systems, materials and other appropriate essential items in the Project. These Development Documents are the basis for the design and construction of the Project. PHASE 3: From approved Design Development Documents the Architect/Engineer will prepare working Drawings and Specifications setting forth in detail the requirements for the construction of the Project, and based upon codes, laws or regulations which have been enacted at the time of their preparation.

2.1.3 The Contractor, the Architect/Engineer and the Owner will work closely together to monitor the design in accordance with prior approvals so as to ensure that the Project can be constructed within the Lump Sum as defined in Article 6. As these working Drawings and Specifications are being completed, the Contractor will keep the Owner advised of the effects of any Owner requested changes on the Contract Time Schedule and/or the Lump Sum. *Construction of the Project shall be in accordance with these Drawings and Specifications as approved by the Owner. The Drawings and Specifications shall remain the property of the Contractor and are not to be used by the Owner on this or other projects without the written consent of the Contractor.*

2.1.4 After the completion of any Phase as set forth in Article 2.1.2, if the Project is no longer feasible from the standpoint of the Owner, the Owner may terminate this Agreement and pay the Contractor pursuant to Article 10.3.1.

2.1.5 The Contractor will assist the Owner in securing permits necessary for the construction of the Project.

2.2 Responsibilities With Respect to Construction

2.2.1 The Contractor will provide all construction supervision, inspection, labor, materials, tools, construction equipment and subcontracted items necessary for the execution and completion of the Project.

2.2.2 The Contractor will pay all sales, use, gross receipts and similar taxes related to the Work provided by the Contractor which have been legally enacted at the time of execution of this Agreement and for which the Contractor is liable.

2.2.3 The Contractor will prepare and submit for the Owner's approval an estimated progress schedule for the Project. This schedule shall indicate the dates for the starting and completion of the various stages of the design and construction. It shall be revised as required by the conditions of the Work and those conditions and events which are beyond the Contractor's control.

2.2.4 The Contractor shall at all times keep the premises free from the accumulation of waste materials or rubbish caused by his operations. At the completion of the Work, he shall remove all of his waste material and rubbish from and around the Project as well as all his tools, construction equipment, machinery and surplus materials.

2.2.5 The Contractor will give all notices and comply with all laws and ordinances legally enacted at the date of execution of the Agreement, which govern the proper execution of the Work.

2.2.6 The Contractor shall take necessary precautions for the safety of his employees on the Work, and shall comply with all applicable provisions of federal, state and municipal safety laws to prevent accidents or injury to persons on, about or adjacent to the Project site. He shall erect and properly maintain, at all times, as required by the conditions and progress of Work, necessary safeguards for the protection of workmen and the public. It is understood and agreed, however, that the Contractor shall have no responsibility for the elimination or abatement of safety hazards created or otherwise resulting from Work at the job site carried on by other persons or firms directly employed by the Owner as separate contractors or by the Owner's tenants, and the Owner agrees to cause any such separate contractors and tenants to abide by and fully adhere to all applicable provisions of federal, state and municipal safety laws and regulations and to comply with all reasonable requests and directions of the Contractor for the elimination or abatement of any such safety hazards at the job site.

2.2.7 The Contractor shall keep such full and detailed accounts as may be necessary for proper financial management under this Agreement. The system shall be satisfactory to the Owner, who shall be afforded access to all the Contractor's records, books, correspondence, instructions, drawings, receipts, vouchers, memoranda and similar data relating to this Agreement. The Contractor shall preserve all such records for a period of three years after the final payment or longer where required by law.

2.3 Royalties and Patents

2.3.1 The Contractor shall pay all royalties and license fees for materials, methods and systems incorporated in the work. He shall defend all suits or claims for infringement of any patent rights and shall save the Owner harmless from loss on account thereof except when a particular design, process or product is specified by the Owner. In such case the Contractor shall be responsible for such loss only if he has reason to believe that the design, process or product so specified is an infringement of a patent, and fails to give such information promptly to the Owner.

2.4 Warranties and Completion

2.4.1 The Contractor warrants to the Owner that all materials and equipment furnished under this Agreement will be new, unless otherwise specified, and that all Work will be of good quality, free from improper workmanship and defective materials and in conformance with the Drawings and Specifications. The Contractor agrees to correct all Work performed by him under this Agreement which proves to be defective in material and workmanship within a period of one year from the Date of Substantial Completion as defined in Paragraph 5.2, or for such longer periods of time as may be set forth with respect to specific warranties contained in the Specifications. This warranty is expressly in lieu of all other rights and remedies at law or in equity.

2.4.2 The Contractor will secure required certificates of inspection, testing or approval and deliver them to the Owner.

2.4.3 The Contractor will collect all written warranties and equipment manuals and deliver them to the Owner.

2.4.4 The Contractor, with the assistance of the Owner's maintenance personnel, will direct the checkout of utilities and operations of systems and equipment for readiness, and will assist in their initial start-up and testing.

2.5 Additional Services

2.5.1 The Contractor will provide the following additional services upon the request of the Owner. A written agreement between the Owner and Contractor shall define the extent of such additional services and the amount and manner in which the Contractor will be compensated for such additional services.

2.5.2 Services related to investigation, appraisals or evaluations of existing conditions, facilities or equipment, or verification of the accuracy of existing drawings or other Owner-furnished information.

2.5.3 Services related to Owner-furnished equipment, furniture and furnishings which are not a part of this Agreement.

2.5.4 Services for tenant or rental spaces not a part of this Agreement.

2.5.5 Obtaining and training maintenance personnel or negotiating maintenance service contracts.

ARTICLE 3

Owner's Responsibilities

3.1 The Owner shall provide full information regarding his requirements for the Project.

3.2 The Owner shall designate a representative who shall be fully acquainted with the Project, and has authority to approve changes in the scope of the Project, render decisions promptly, and furnish information expeditiously and in time to meet the dates set forth in Subparagraph 2.2.3.

3.3 The Owner shall furnish for the site of the Project all necessary surveys describing the physical characteristics, soils reports and subsurface investigations, legal limitations, utility locations, and a legal description.

3.4 The Owner shall secure and pay for all necessary approvals, easements, assessments and charges required for the construction, use, or occupancy of permanent structures or for permanent changes in existing facilities.

3.5 The Owner shall furnish such legal services as may be necessary for providing the items set forth in Paragraph 3.4, and such auditing services as he may require.

3.6 If the Owner becomes aware of any fault or defect in the Project or non-conformance with the Drawings or Specifications, he shall give prompt written notice thereof to the Contractor.

3.7 The Owner shall provide the insurance for the Project as provided in Paragraph 9.4.

3.8 The Owner shall bear the costs of any bonds that may be required.

3.9 The services and information required by the above paragraphs shall be furnished with reasonable promptness at the Owner's expense and the Contractor shall be entitled to rely upon the accuracy and the completeness thereof.

3.10 The Owner shall furnish reasonable evidence satisfactory to the Contractor, prior to commencing Work and at such future times as may be required, that sufficient funds are available and committed for the entire Cost of the Project. Unless such reasonable evidence is furnished, the Contractor is not required to commence or continue any Work, or may, if such evidence is not presented within a reasonable time, stop Work upon 15 days notice to the Owner. The failure of the Contractor to insist upon the providing of this evidence at any one time shall not be a waiver of the Owner's obligation to make payments pursuant to this Agreement, nor shall it be a waiver of the Contractor's right to request or insist that such evidence be provided at a later date.

3.11 The Owner shall have no contractual obligation to the Contractor's Subcontractors and shall communicate with such Subcontractors only through the Contractor.

ARTICLE 4

Subcontracts

4.1 All portions of the Work that the Contractor does not perform with his own forces shall be performed under subcontracts.

4.2 A Subcontractor is a person or entity who has a direct contract with the Contractor to perform any Work in connection with the Project. The term Subcontractor does not include any separate contractor employed by the Owner or the separate contractors' subcontractors.

4.3 No contractual relationship shall exist between the Owner and any Subcontractor. The Contractor shall be responsible for the management of the Subcontractors in the performance of their Work.

ARTICLE 5

Contract Time Schedule

5.1 The Work to be performed under this Agreement shall be commenced on or about and shall be substantially completed on or about

5.2 The Date of Substantial Completion of the Project or a designated portion thereof is the date when construction is sufficiently complete in accordance with the Drawings and Specifications so the Owner can occupy or utilize the Project or designated portion thereof for the use for which it is intended. Warranties called for by this Agreement or by the Drawings and Specifications shall commence on the Date of Substantial Completion of the Project or designated portion thereof. This date shall be established by a Certificate of Substantial Completion signed by the Owner and Contractor and shall state their respective responsibilities for security, maintenance, heat, utilities, damage to the Work and insurance. This Certificate shall also list the items to be completed or corrected and fix the time for their completion and correction.

5.3 If the Contractor is delayed at any time in the progress of the Project by any act or neglect of the Owner or by any separate contractor employed by the Owner, or by changes ordered in the Project, or by labor disputes, fire, unusual delay in transportation, adverse weather conditions not reasonably anticipated, unavoidable casualties, or any causes beyond the Contractor's control, or a delay authorized by the Owner pending arbitration, then the Date for Substantial Completion shall be extended by Change Order for the period caused by such delay.

ARTICLE 6

Lump Sum Price

6.1 The Lump Sum price for the Project is ($).

6.2 The Lump Sum is based upon laws, codes, and regulations in existence at the date of its establishment and upon criteria, Drawings, and Specifications as set forth in this agreement.

6.3 The Lump Sum will be modified for delays caused by the Owner and for Changes in the Project, all pursuant to Article 7.

6.4 Allowances

6.4.1 Allowances included in the Lump Sum are as set forth below:

6.4.2 Whenever the cost is more than or less than the Allowance, the Lump Sum shall be adjusted by Change Order as provided in Article 7.

ARTICLE 7

Changes in the Project

7.1 The Owner, without invalidating this Agreement, may order Changes in the Project within the general scope of this Agreement consisting of additions, deletions or other revisions. The Lump Sum, and the Contract Time Schedule shall be adjusted accordingly. All such Changes in the Project shall be authorized by Change Order.

7.1.1 A Change Order is a written order to the Contractor signed by the Owner or his authorized agent and issued after the execution of this Agreement, authorizing a Change in the Project and/or an adjustment in the Lump Sum or the Contract Time Schedule.

7.1.2 The increase or decrease in the Lump Sum resulting from a Change in the Project shall be determined in one or more of the following ways:

7.1.2.1 by mutual acceptance of a lump sum properly itemized and supported by sufficient substantiating data to permit evaluation; or

7.1.2.2 by unit prices stated in this Agreement or subsequently agreed upon; or

7.1.2.3 If none of the methods set forth in articles 7.1.2.1 and 7.1.2.2 is agreed upon, the Contractor shall promptly proceed with the Work required by the Change in the Project provided the Contractor receives a written order to proceed signed by the Owner. The increase in the Lump Sum shall then be determined on the basis of the reasonable costs of such Work and savings of those performing the Work attributed to the Change in the Project including a reasonable increase in the Contractor's overhead and profit. The amount of decrease in the Lum Sum to be allowed by Contractor to the Owner for any deletion or Change in the Project with results in a net decrease in cost will be the amount of the actual net decrease only. When both increases and decreases in costs of the Work are involved in any one Change in the Project, the increase in overhead and profit shall be figured on the basis of the net increase in costs, if any. Under this article and articles 7.1.2.1 and 7.1.2.2, the Contractor shall keep and present, in such form as the Owner may prescribe, an itemized accounting together with appropriate supporting data of the effect on the Lump Sum. The increase or decrease in the Lump Sum under this article and articles 7.1.2.1 and 7.1.2.2 shall be authorized by Change Order signed by the Owner or its authorized agent.

7.1.3 If unit prices are stated in this agreement or subsequently agreed upon, and if the quantities originally contemplated are so changed in a proposed Change Order or as a result of several Change Orders that application of the agreed unit prices to the quantities of Work proposed will cause substantial inequity to the Owner or the Contractor, the applicable unit prices and the Lump Sum shall be equitably adjusted.

7.1.4 Should concealed conditions encountered in the performance of the Work below the surface of the ground or should concealed or unknown conditions in an existing structure be at variance with the conditions indicated by the Drawings, Specifications, or Owner-furnished information or should unknown physical conditions below the surface of the ground or should concealed or unknown conditions in an existing structure of an unusual nature, differing materially from those ordinarily encountered and generally recognized as inherent in work of the character provided for in this Agreement, be encountered, the Lump Sum and the Contract Time Schedule shall be equitably adjusted by Change Order upon claim by either party made within a reasonable time after the first observance of the conditions.

7.2 Claims for Additional Cost or Time

7.2.1 If the Contractor wishes to make a claim for an increase in the Lump Sum or an extension in the Contract Time Schedule, he shall give the Owner written notice thereof within a reasonable time after the occurrence of the event giving rise to such claim. This notice shall be given by the Contractor before proceeding to execute the Work, except in an emergency endangering life or property in which case the Contractor shall act, at his discretion, to prevent threatened damage, injury or loss. Claims arising from delay shall be made within a reasonable time after the delay. Increases based upon design and estimating costs with respect to possible changes requested by the Owner, shall be made within a reasonable time after the decision is made not to proceed with the change. No such claim shall be valid unless so made. If the Owner and the Contractor cannot agree on the amount of the adjustment in the Lump Sum, and the Contract Time Schedule, it shall be determined pursuant to the provisions of Article 13. Any change in the Lump Sum or Contract Time Schedule resulting from such claim shall be authorized by Change Order.

7.3 Minor Changes in the Project

7.3.1 The Owner will have authority to order minor Changes in the Work not involving an adjustment in the Lump Sum or an extension of the Contract Time Schedule and not inconsistent with the intent of the Drawings and Specifications. Such Changes may be effected by written order and shall be binding on the Owner and the Contractor.

7.4 Emergencies

7.4.1 In any emergency affecting the safety of persons or property, the Contractor shall act, at his discretion, to prevent threatened damage, injury or loss. Any increase in the Lump Sum or extension of time claimed by the Contractor on account of emergency work shall be determined as provided in this Article.

ARTICLE 8

Payments to the Contractor

8.1 Payments shall be made by the Owner to the Contractor according to the following procedure:

8.1.1 On or before the ______ day of each month after Work has commenced, the Contractor shall submit to the Owner an Application for Payment in such detail as may be required by the Owner based on the Work completed and materials stored on the site and/or at locations approved by the Owner for the period ending on the ______ day of the month.

8.1.2 Within ten (10) days after his receipt of each monthly Application for Payment, the Owner shall pay directly to the Contractor the appropriate amounts for which Application for Payment is made therein. This payment request shall deduct the aggregate of amounts previously paid by the Owner.

8.1.3 If the Owner should fail to pay the Contractor at the time the payment of any amount becomes due, then the Contractor may, at any time thereafter, upon serving written notice that he will stop Work within seven (7) days after receipt of the notice by the Owner, and after such seven (7) day period, stop the Project until payment of the amount owing has been received. Written notice shall be deemed to have been duly served if sent by certified mail to the last known business address of the Owner.

8.1.4 Payments due but unpaid shall bear interest at the rate of two percentage points above the prime interest rate prevailing from time to time at the location of the Project.

8.2 The Contractor warrants and guarantees that title to all Work, materials and equipment covered by an Application for Payment whether incorporated in the Project or not, will pass to the Owner upon receipt of such payment by the Contractor free and clear of all liens, claims, security interests or encumbrances hereinafter referred to as Liens.

8.3 No Progress Payment nor any partial or entire use or occupancy of the Project by the Owner shall constitute an acceptance of any Work not in accordance with the Drawings and Specifications.

8.4 Final payment constituting the unpaid balance of the Project shall be due and payable when the Project is delivered to the Owner, ready for beneficial occupancy, or when the Owner occupies the Project, whichever event first occurs, provided that the Project be then substantially completed and this Agreement substantially performed. If there should remain minor items to be completed, the Contractor and the Owner shall list such items and the Contractor shall deliver, in writing, his guarantee to complete said items within a reasonable time thereafter. The Owner may retain a sum equal to 150 percent of the estimated cost of completing any unfinished items, provided that said unfinished items are listed separately and the estimated cost of completing any unfinished items is likewise listed separately. Thereafter, the Owner shall pay to the Contractor, monthly, the amount retained for incomplete items as each of said items is completed.

8.5 Before issuance of Final Payment, the Owner may request satisfactory evidence that all payrolls, materials bills and other indebtness connected with the Project have been paid or otherwise satisfied.

8.6 The making of Final Payment shall constitute a waiver of all claims by the Owner except those rising from: unsettled liens; improper workmanship or defective materials appearing within one year after the Date of Substantial Completion; and terms of any special guarantees required by the Drawings and Specifications.

8.7 The acceptance of Final Payment shall constitute a waiver of all claims by the Contractor except those previously made in writing and unsettled.

ARTICLE 9

Insurance, Indemnity and Waiver of Subrogation

9.1 Indemnity

9.1.1 The Contractor agrees to indemnify and hold the Owner harmless from all claims for bodily injury and property damage (other than the Work itself and other property insured under Paragraph 9.4) that may arise from the Contractor's operations under this Agreement.

9.1.2 The Owner shall cause any other contractor who may have a contract with the Owner to perform work in the areas where Work will be performed under this Agreement, to agree to indemnify the Owner and the Contractor and hold them harmless from all claims for bodily injury and property damage (other than property insured under Paragraph 9.4) that may arise from that contractor's operations. Such provisions shall be in a form satisfactory to the Contractor.

9.2 Contractor's Liability Insurance

9.2.1 The Contractor shall purchase and maintain such insurance as will protect him from the claims set forth below which may arise out of or result from the Contractor's operations under this Agreement whether such operations be by himself or by any Subcontractor or by anyone directly or indirectly employed by any of them, or by anyone for whose acts any of them may be liable:

9.2.1.1 Claims under workers' compensation, disability benefit and other similar employee benefit acts which are applicable to the Work to be performed;

9.2.1.2 Claims for damages because of bodily injury, occupational sickness or disease, or death of his employees under any applicable employer's liability law;

9.2.1.3 Claims for damages because of bodily injury, or death of any person other than his employees;

9.2.1.4 Claims for damages insured by usual personal injury liability coverage which are sustained (1) by any person as a result of an offense directly or indirectly related to the employment of such person by the Contractor or (2) by any other person;

9.2.1.5 Claims for damages, other than to the Work itself, because of injury to or destruction of tangible property, including loss of use therefrom;

9.2.1.6 Claims for damages because of bodily injury or death of any person or property damage arising out of the ownership, maintenance or use of any motor vehicle.

9.2.2 The Comprehensive General Liability Insurance shall include premises-operations (including explosion, collapse and underground coverage) elevators, independent contractors, completed operations, and blanket contractual liability on all written contracts, all including broad form property damage coverage.

9.2.3 The Contractor's Comprehensive General and Automobile Liability Insurance, as required by Subparagraphs 9.2.1 and 9.2.2 shall be written for not less than limits of liability as follows:

a. Comprehensive General Liability
   1. Bodily Injury — $ ________ Each Occurrence (Completed Operations)
      $ ________ Aggregate
   2. Property Damage — $ ________ Each Occurrence
      $ ________ Aggregate

b. Comprehensive Automobile Liability
   1. Bodily Injury — $ ________ Each Person
      $ ________ Each Occurrence
   2. Property Damage — $ ________ Each Occurrence

9.2.4 Comprehensive General Liability Insurance may be arranged under a single policy for the full limits required or by a combination of underlying policies with the balance provided by an Excess or Umbrella Liability policy.

9.2.5 The foregoing policies shall contain a provision that coverages afforded under the policies will not be cancelled or not renewed until at least sixty (60) days' prior written notice has been given to the Owner. Certificates of Insurance showing such coverages to be in force shall be filed with the Owner prior to commencement of the Work.

9.3 Owner's Liability Insurance

9.3.1 The Owner shall be responsible for purchasing and maintaining his own liability insurance and, at his option, may purchase and maintain such insurance as will protect him against claims which may arise from operations under this Agreement.

9.4 Insurance to Protect Project

9.4.1 The Owner shall purchase and maintain property insurance in a form acceptable to the Contractor upon the entire Project for the full cost of replacement at the time of any loss. This insurance shall include as named insureds the Owner, the Contractor, Subcontractors and Subsubcontractors and shall insure against loss from the perils of Fire, Extended Coverage, and shall include "All Risk" insurance for physical loss or damage including, without duplication of coverage, at least theft, vandalism, malicious mischief, transit, collapse, flood, earthquake, testing, and damage resulting from defective design, workmanship or material. The Owner will increase limits of coverage, if necessary, to reflect estimated replacement cost. The Owner will be responsible for any co-insurance penalties or deductibles. If the Project covers an addition to or is adjacent to an existing building, the Contractor, Subcontractors and Subsubcontractors shall be named as additional insureds under the Owner's Property Insurance covering such building and its contents.

9.4.1.1 If the Owner finds it necessary to occupy or use a portion or portions of the Project prior to Substantial Completion thereof, such occupany shall not commence prior to a time mutually agreed to by the Owner and the Contractor and to which the insurance company or companies providing the property insurance have consented by endorsement to the policy or policies. This insurance shall not be cancelled or lapsed on account of such partial occupancy. Consent of the Contractor and of the insurance company or companies to such occupancy or use shall not be unreasonably withheld.

9.4.2 The Owner shall purchase and maintain such boiler and machinery insurance as may be required or necessary. This insurance shall include the interests of the Owner, the Contractor, Subcontractors and Subsubcontractors in the Work.

9.4.3 The Owner shall purchase and maintain such insurance as will protect the Owner and the Contractor against loss of use of Owner's property due to those perils insured pursuant to Subparagraph 9.4.1. Such policy will provide coverage for expenses of expediting materials, continuing overhead of the Owner and the Contractor, necessary labor expense including overtime, loss of income by the Owner and other determined exposures. Exposures of the Owner and the Contractor shall be determined by mutual agreement and separate limits of coverage fixed for each item.

9.4.4 The Owner shall file a copy of all policies with the Contractor before an exposure to loss may occur. Copies of any subsequent endorsements will be furnished to the Contractor. The Contractor will be given sixty (60) days notice of cancellation, non-renewal, or any endorsements restricting or reducing coverage. If the Owner does not intend to purchase such insurance, he shall inform the Contractor in writing prior to the commencement of the Work. The Contractor may then effect insurance which will protect the interests of himself, the Subcontractors and their Subsubcontractors in the Project, the cost of which shall be added to the Lump Sum by Change Order. If the Contractor is damaged by failure of the Owner to purchase or maintain such insurance or to so notify the Contractor, the Owner shall bear all reasonable costs properly attributable thereto.

9.5 Property Insurance Loss Adjustment

9.5.1 Any insured loss shall be adjusted with the Owner and the Contractor and made payable to the Owner and Contractor as trustees for the insureds, as their interests may appear, subject to any applicable mortgagee clause.

9.5.2 Upon the occurrence of an insured loss, monies received will be deposited in a separate account and the trustees shall make distribution in accordance with the agreement of the parties in interest, or in the absence of such agreement, in accordance with an arbitration award pursuant to Article 13. If the trustees are unable to agree between themselves on the settlement of the loss, such dispute shall also be submitted to arbitration pursuant to Article 13.

9.6 Waiver of Subrogation

9.6.1 The Owner and Contractor waive all rights against each other, the Architect/Engineer, Subcontractors and Subsubcontractors for damages caused by perils covered by insurance provided under Paragraph 9.4, except such rights as they may have to the proceeds of such insurance held by the Owner and Contractor as trustees. The Contractor shall require similar waivers from all Subcontractors and Subsubcontractors.

9.6.2 The Owner and Contractor waive all rights against each other and the Architect/Engineer, Subcontractors and Subsubcontractors for loss or damage to any equipment used in connection with the Project which loss is covered by any property insurance. The Contractor shall require similar waivers from all Subcontractors and Subsubcontractors.

9.6.3 The Owner waives subrogation against the Contractor, Architect/Engineer, Subcontractors, and Subsubcontractors on all property and consequential loss policies carried by the Owner on adjacent properties and under property and consequential loss policies purchased for the Project after its completion.

9.6.4 If the policies of insurance referred to in this Paragraph require an endorsement to provide for continued coverage where there is a waiver of subrogation, the owners of such policies will cause them to be so endorsed.

ARTICLE 10

TERMINATION OF THE AGREEMENT AND OWNER'S RIGHT TO PERFORM CONTRACTOR'S OBLIGATIONS

10.1 Termination by the Contractor

10.1.1 If the Project is stopped for a period of thirty (30) days under an order of any court or other public authority having jurisdiction, or as a result of an act of government, such as a declaration of a national emergency making materials unavailable, through no act or fault of the Contractor or if the Project should be stopped for a period of thirty (30) days by the Contractor for the Owner's failure to make payment thereon, then the Contractor may, upon seven days' written notice to the Owner, terminate this Agreement and recover from the Owner payment for all Work executed, the Lump Sum earned to date, and for any proven loss sustained upon any materials, equipment, tools, construction equipment and machinery, including reasonable profit and damages.

10.2 Owner's Right to Perform Contractor's Obligations and Termination by the Owner for Cause

10.2.1 If the Contractor fails to perform any of his obligations under this Agreement, including any obligation he assumes to perform Work with his own forces, the Owner may, after seven days' written notice, during which period the Contractor fails to perform such obligation, make good such deficiencies. The Lump Sum, if any, shall be reduced by the cost to the Owner of making good such deficiencies.

10.2.2 If the Contractor is adjudged a bankrupt, or if he makes a general assignment for the benefit of his creditors, or if a receiver is appointed on account of his insolvency, or if he persistently or repeatedly refuses or fails, except in cases for which extension of time is provided, to supply enough properly skilled workmen or proper materials, or if he fails to make proper payment to Subcontractors or for materials or labor, or persistently disregards laws, ordinances, rules, regulations or orders of any public authority having jurisdiction, or otherwise is guilty of a substantial violation of a provision of this Agreement, then the Owner may, without prejudice to any right or remedy and after giving the Contractor and his surety, if any, seven (7) days' written notice, during which period the Contractor fails to cure the violation, terminate the employment of the Contractor and take possession of the site and of all materials, equipment, tools, construction equipment and machinery thereon owned by the Contractor and may finish the Work by whatever reasonable method he may deem expedient. In such case, the Contractor shall not be entitled to receive any further payment until the Work is finished nor shall he be relieved from his obligations assumed under Article 6.

10.3 Termination by Owner Without Cause

10.3.1 If the Owner terminates the Agreement other than pursuant to 10.2.2, he shall pay the Contractor the total of: (a.) Costs incurred by the Contractor in performing the Project, including initial costs and preparatory expenses; (b.) Costs incurred in settling and paying termination claims under terminated subcontracts; (c.) Accounting, legal, clerical and other expenses incurred as a result of the termination; (d.) Storage, transportation, demobilization and other costs incurred for the preservation, protection or disposition of material and equipment on the Project; (e.) Any other necessary and reasonable costs incurred by the Contractor as a result of the Owner's termination of this Agreement; (f.) Overhead at ten percent (10%) of the total amount of (a.) thorugh (e.) above; profit at ten percent (10%) of the total amount of (a) through (f) above, as adjusted pursuant to Articles 6 and 7. In calculating the amount due the Contractor under this clause, a deduction shall be made for all payments to the Contractor under this Agreement.

ARTICLE 11

Assignment and Governing Law

11.1 Neither the Owner nor the Contractor shall assign his interest in this Agreement without the written consent of the other except as to the assignment of proceeds.

11.2 This Agreement shall be governed by the law in effect at the location of this Project.

ARTICLE 12

Miscellaneous Provisions

ARTICLE 13

Arbitration

13.1 *AGREEMENT TO ARBITRATE:* All claims, disputes and matters in question arising out of, or relating to this Agreement or the breach thereof, except for claims which have been waived by the making or acceptance of final payment, and the claims described in Article 13.7, shall be decided by arbitration in accordance with the Construction Industry Arbitration Rules of the American Arbitration Association then in effect unless the parties mutually agree otherwise. This agreement to arbitrate shall be specifically enforceable under the prevailing arbitration law.

13.2 *NOTICE OF DEMAND:* Notice of the demand for arbitration shall be filed in writing with the other party to this Agreement and with the American Arbitration Association. The demand for arbitration shall be made within a reasonable time after written notice of the claim, dispute or other matter in question has been given, and in no event shall it be made after the date of final acceptance of the Work by the Owner or when institution of legal or equitable proceedings based on such claim, dispute or other matter in question would be barred by the applicable statute of limitations, whichever shall first occur. The location of the arbitration proceedings shall be the city of the Contractor's headquarters or ____________________

____

____

13.3 *AWARD:* The award rendered by the arbitrator(s) shall be final and judgment may be entered upon it in accordance with applicable law in any court having jurisdiction.

13.4 *WORK CONTINUATION AND PAYMENT:* Unless otherwise agreed in writing, the Contractor shall carry on the Work and maintain the Schedule of Work pending arbitration, and, if so, the Owner shall continue to make payments in accordance with this Agreement.

13.5 *NO LIMITATION OF RIGHTS OR REMEDIES:* Nothing in this Article shall limit any rights or remedies not expressly waived by the Contractor which the Contractor may have under lien laws or payment bonds.

13.6 *SAME ARBITRATORS:* To the maximum extent permitted by law, all claims which are related to or dependent upon each other, shall be heard by the same arbitrator or arbitrators even through the parties are not the same.

13.7 *EXCEPTIONS:* This agreement to arbitrate shall not apply to any claim of contribution or indemnity asserted by one party to this Agreement against the other party and arising out of any action brought in a state or federal court or in arbitration by a person who is under no obligation to arbitrate the subject matter of such action with either of the parties hereto. In any dispute arising over the application of this Article 13.7, the question of arbitrability shall be decided by the appropriate court and not by arbitration.

Attest: ____________________ Owner: ____________________

Attest: ____________________ Contractor: ____________________

THE ASSOCIATED GENERAL CONTRACTORS

STANDARD FORM OF AGREEMENT BETWEEN CONTRACTOR AND ARCHITECT

INSTRUCTIONS TO CONTRACTOR

1. These documents are intended to be used with AGC Document No. 410, Standard Form of Design-Build Agreement and General Conditions Between Owner and Contractor, January, 1982. Nothing contained herein is intended to conflict with local, state or federal laws or regulations. However, in all cases your attorney should be consulted to advise you on their use and any modifications. Care should be taken to assure that all modifications are correlated so the provisions of all documents are consistent.

2. Article 1 covers both the basic service and supplemental services to be performed by the architect. Any of these services which the Contractor does not desire to be performed by the Architect should be eliminated from this Agreement. The Contractor should verify that either he or the Architect includes sufficient funds for the services to be provided to the Owner based on the assumption that the Contractor is providing the Owner with a firm figure, be it lump sum or guaranteed maximum cost, for the Contractor's work and responsibilities.

3. It is recommended that all insurance matters such as the implications of errors and omissions liability, completed operations, and waiver of subrogation be reviewed with your insurance consultant and carrier.

AGC Document No. 420 • CONTRACTOR-ARCHITECT AGREEMENT • January 1985

THE ASSOCIATED GENERAL CONTRACTORS

STANDARD FORM OF AGREEMENT BETWEEN CONTRACTOR AND ARCHITECT

(See AGC Document No. 400 for Preliminary Design-Build Contract; AGC Document No. 410 for Design-Build Agreement; and General Conditions)

This Document has important legal consequences; consultation with an attorney is encouraged with respect to its completion or modification.

AGREEMENT

Made as of the day of in the year Nineteen Hundred and

BETWEEN

hereinafter referred to as the "Contractor," and
hereinafter referred to as the "Architect."

The Contractor has entered into a Contract with
hereinafter referred to as the "Owner"
for the design and construction of (include description, location and anticipated construction sequencing)

hereinafter referred to as the "Project."

The Contractor and the Architect shall cooperate in carrying out the Project in a relationship of trust and agree as set forth below:

THE ASSOCIATED GENERAL CONTRACTORS

STANDARD FORM OF AGREEMENT BETWEEN CONTRACTOR AND ARCHITECT

TABLE OF CONTENTS

ARTICLE 1

ARCHITECT'S SERVICES AND RESPONSIBILITIES

1.1 BASIC SERVICES

The Architect's Basic Services consist of the four phases described in this Paragraph 1.1 and include normal architectural, structural, mechanical and electrical engineering services. These services and those included in Paragraph 1.2 shall be provided in accordance with the Contractor's overall coordination and direction of the Project, including all necessary financial constraints.

Schematic Design Phase

1.1.1 The Architect shall review the program and Project budget furnished by the Contractor to ascertain the requirements of the Project and shall review the understanding of such requirements with the Contractor and the Owner.

1.1.2 The Architect shall review with the Contractor alternative approaches to design and construction of the Project.

1.1.3 Based on the mutually agreed upon program and Project budget requirements, the Architect shall prepare, for approval by the Contractor and the Owner, Schematic Design Documents consisting of drawings and other documents illustrating the scale and relationship of Project components.

Design Development Phase

1.1.4 Based on the approved Schematic Design Documents and any adjustments authorized by the Contractor in the program or Project budget, the Architect shall review with and prepare for approval of the Contractor and the Owner, Design Development Documents consisting of drawings and other documents to fix and describe the size and character of the entire Project as to architectural, structural, mechanical and electrical systems, materials and such other elements as may be appropriate.

Construction Documents Phase

1.1.5.1 Following the Contractor's and the Owner's approval of the Design Development Documents, the Architect shall review with and prepare for approval of the Contractor and the Owner, Construction Documents consisting of Drawings and Specifications for the construction of the Project.

1.1.5.2 The Architect shall assist the Contractor in the preparation of the necessary bidding information, bidding forms, and the General Conditions (AGC Document No. 410) and any other conditions of the contract.

Construction Phase

1.1.6.1 The Architect shall at all times have access to the Work wherever it is in preparation and progress.

1.1.6.2 The Architect shall be the interpreter of the requirements of the Drawings and Specifications. The Architect shall, within a reasonable time, render such interpretations and clarifications as are necessary for the proper execution or progress of the Work.

1.1.6.3 All interpretations of the Architect shall be consistent with the intent of and reasonably inferable from the Drawings and Specifications, and when requested, shall be in written or graphic form.

1.1.6.4 The Architect's decisions in matters relating to artistic effect shall be final if consistent with the intent of the Drawings and Specifications.

1.1.6.5 Whenever the Architect considers it necessary or advisable for the implementation of the intent of the Drawings and Specifications, he shall recommend to the Contractor special inspection or testing of the Work in accordance with the General Conditions whether or not such Work be then fabricated, installed or completed. However, neither the Architect's obligation to recommend action under this Subparagraph nor any decision made by him in good faith, either to make or not to make such recommendation, shall give rise to any duty or responsibility of the Architect to the Owner, any Subcontractor, any Sub-subcontractor, any of their agents or employees, or any other person not a party to this Agreement.

1.1.6.6 The Architect shall review and approve or take other appropriate action upon Contractor's submittals such as Shop Drawings, Product Data and Samples, but only for conformance with the design concept of the Work and with the information given in the Drawings and Specifications. Such action shall be taken with reasonable promptness so as to cause no delay. The Architect's approval of a specific item shall not indicate approval of an assembly of which the item is a component.

1.1.6.7 The Architect with the Contractor shall conduct inspections to determine the dates of Substantial Completion and Final Completion.

1.1.6.8 The Architect shall only communicate with the Owner and the Subcontractors through the Contractor.

1.1.6.9 The Architect shall not have control or charge of and shall not be responsible for construction means, methods, techniques, sequences, or procedures, or for safety precautions or programs in connection with the Work, for the acts or omissions of the Contractor, Subcontractors, or any other person performing any of the Work, or for the failure of any of them to carry out the Work in accordance with the Contract Documents.

1.2 SUPPLEMENTAL SERVICES (Optional: Those which are not applicable should be struck. Those which are accepted should remain.)

1.2.1 The Architect shall investigate existing conditions or facilities, make measured drawings thereof and verify the accuracy of drawings or other information furnished by the Contractor.

1.2.2 The Architect shall prepare a set of reproducible record drawings showing significant changes in the Work made during the construction process, based on marked-up prints, drawings and other data furnished by the Contractor to the Architect.

1.2.3 The Architect shall provide services of the following consultants in addition to those required by Paragraph 1.1 to accomplish Basic Services as follows:

1.2.4 The Architect shall visit the site to perform on site observations and to recommend to the Contractor rejection of Work which does not conform to the Drawings and Specifications, and shall provide the required personnel for such observations, for attendance at job meetings and for other consultation, including all travel expenses as follows:

1.2.5 The Architect shall provide assistance in the utilization of equipment and systems, such as initial start-up or testing, adjusting or balancing, as follows:

1.2.6 The Architect, exercising his professional judgment, shall indentify the architectural, structural, mechanical, chemical and other laboratory tests, inspections and reports, to be required, as follows:

1.2.7 The Architect shall pay fees required by governmental authorities having jurisdiction in order to produce the Drawings and Specifications described in the Schematic Design, Design Development, and Construction Document Phases of Basic Services, as follows:

1.2.8 The Architect shall provide the following number of copies of sets of Drawings and Specifications:

Schematic Design Documents: ________sets
Design Development Documents: ________sets
Construction Documents: ________sets
Bulletins: ________sets

1.2.9 The Architect shall provide interior design and other similar services required for or in connection with the selection, procurement or installation of furniture, furnishings and related equipment, as follows:

1.2.10 The Architect shall provide services for planning tenant or rental spaces, as follows:

1.2.11 The Architect shall provide further supplemental services, as follows: (Include any of the services to be provided by the Architect, such as data processing, photographic production techniques, renderings, models and mock-ups, etc.)

ARTICLE 2

CONTRACTOR'S RESPONSIBILITIES

2.1 The Contractor shall obtain from the Owner full information regarding his requirements for the Project.

2.2 The Contractor shall obtain from the Owner for the site of the Project all necessary surveys describing the physical characteristics, topography, soils reports, and sub-surface investigation, legal limitations, utility locations and a legal description.

2.3 The information required by Paragraph 2.1 and 2.2 shall be furnished with reasonable promptness and the Architect shall be entitled to rely upon the accuracy and the completeness thereof.

2.4 The Contractor shall prepare all budgets, cost estimates and schedules for the Project. The Contractor shall consult with the Architect before establishing the time necessary for the Architect to perform his services and discharge his responsibilities.

2.5 The Contractor shall carefully study and compare the Contract Documents and shall at once report to the Architect any error, inconsistency or omission he may discover.

ARTICLE 3

ARCHITECT'S COMPENSATION AND PAYMENTS

3.1 COMPENSATION

3.1.1 The Contractor shall compensate the Architect for the Basic and Supplemental Services as described in Article 1, including all overhead and expenses including travel expense, on the following basis:

3.1.2 The Contractor shall compensate the Architect for any additional services on the following basis:

3.1.3 If the Contractor makes a claim for an increase in his contract price with the Owner due to delays in the Project and if these delays have resulted in an increase in the Architect's costs, the Architect shall present his delay claim to the Contractor for his approval and for inclusion in the Contractor's claim to the Owner.

PAYMENTS

3.2 The Architect shall submit periodic Applications for Payment, and payment for services shall be made promptly in proportion to services performed. Compensation which is based on a lump sum amount or on a percentage of construction completion, shall not, at the completion of each Phase, exceed the following percentages of the total compensation:

Schematic Design Phase:	_______%
Design Development Phase:	_______%
Construction Documents Phase:	_______%
Construction Phase:	_______%
Total	_______%

3.3 The Contractor may decline to approve an Application for Payment if, in his opinion, the Application is not adequately supported. If the Architect and Contractor cannot agree on a revised amount, the Contractor shall make payment for the amount he deems appropriate.

3.4 If the Contractor should fail to pay the Architect at the time the payment of any amount becomes due, then the Architect may, at any time thereafter, upon serving written notice that he will stop work within five (5) days after receipt of the notice by the Contractor, and after such five (5) day period, stop work until payment of the amount owing has been received. Written notice shall be deemed to have been duly served if sent by certified mail to the last business address known to him who gives the notice.

3.5 The acceptance of final payment shall constitute a waiver of all claims by the Architect for compensation for services performed.

ARTICLE 4

CHANGES IN THE WORK

4.1 If the Owner or Contractor requests Changes in the Work in accordance with Contractor's Agreement with the Owner, the Architect shall furnish the Contractor with a firm figure to include in the particular Change Order to cover his compensation with respect to the Change.

4.2 If the Owner does not proceed with a Change in the Work upon receiving its estimated cost, the Architect shall be paid for his services in the absence of a prior contrary Agreement.

ARTICLE 5

CONTRACT TIME SCHEDULE

5.1 The Work to be performed under the Contractor's agreement with the Owner shall be commenced on or about and shall be substantially completed on or about

5.2 The Architect shall perform his services and discharge his responsibilities within the time schedule established pursuant to Paragraph 2.4. If he is delayed at any time by any act or neglect of the Contractor or the Owner, or by Change Orders in the Project, or any causes beyond the Architect's control, or a delay authorized by the Contractor pending arbitration, then the time allotted within the schedule for performing his services and discharging his responsibilities shall be extended for the period of such delay.

ARTICLE 6

OWNERSHIP AND USE OF DOCUMENTS

6.1 Drawings and Specifications as instruments of service are and shall remain the property of the Architect whether the Project for which they are prepared is executed or not. The Contractor shall be permitted to retain copies, including reproducible copies, of Drawings and Specifications for information and reference in connection with the Owner's use and occupancy of the Project. The Drawings and Specifications shall not be used on other projects, for additions to this Project, or for completion of this Project by others provided the Architect is not in default under this Agreement, except by agreement in writing and with appropriate compensation to the Architect.

6.2 Submission or distribution to meet official regulatory requirements or for other purposes in connection with the Project is not to be construed as publication in derogation of the Architect's rights.

ARTICLE 7

TERMINATION OF AGREEMENT

7.1 This Agreement may be terminated by either party upon seven (7) days' written notice should the other party fail substantially to perform in accordance with its terms through no fault of the party initiating the termination.

7.2 This Agreement may be terminated by the Contractor upon at least seven (7) days' written notice to the Architect in the event that the Project is permanently abandoned.

7.3 In the event of termination not the fault of the Architect, the Architect shall be compensated for all services performed to the termination date.

ARTICLE 8

INSURANCE

8.1 The Architect shall purchase and maintain such insurance as will protect him from the claims set forth below which may arise out of or result from the Architect's operations under this Agreement whether such operations be by himself or by any of his consultants or by anyone directly or indirectly employed by any of them, or by anyone for whose acts any of them may be liable:

8.1.1 Claims under workers' compensation, disability benefit and other similar employee benefit acts which are applicable to the work to be performed.

8.1.2 Claims for damages because of bodily injury, occupational sickness or disease, or death of his employees and under any applicable employer's liability law with customary limits.

8.1.3 Claims for damages because of bodily injury, or death of any person other than his employees.

8.1.4 Claims for damages insured by usual personal injury liability coverage which are sustained (1) by any person as a result of an offense directly or indirectly related to the employment of such person by the Architect or (2) by any other person.

8.1.5 Claims for damages, other than to the Work itself, because of injury to or destruction of tangible property, including loss of use therefrom.

8.1.6 Claims for damages because of bodily injury or death of any person or property damage arising out of the ownership, maintenance or use of any motor vehicle.

8.2 The Architect's Comprehensive General and Automobile Liability Insurance, as required by Paragraph 8.1 shall be written for not less than limits of liability as follows:

a.	Comprehensive General Liability	
	1. Personal Injury	$_________ Aggregate
	2. Bodily Injury	$_________ Each Occurrence
		$_________ Aggregate
	3. Property Damage	$_________ Each Occurrence
		$_________ Aggregate
b.	Comprehensive Automobile Liability	
	1. Bodily Injury	$_________ Each Person
		$_________ Each Occurrence
	2. Property Damage	$_________ Each Occurrence

8.3 Comprehensive General Liability Insurance may be arranged under a single policy for the full limits required or by a combination of underlying policies with the balance provided by an Excess or Umbrella Liability policy.

8.4 The foregoing policies shall contain a provision that coverages afforded under the policies will not be cancelled or not renewed until at least sixty (60) days' prior written notice has been given to the Contractor. Certificates of Insurance showing such coverages to be in force shall be filed with the Contractor prior to commencement of the Architect's Services.

8.5 The Architect shall furnish the Contractor an appropriate certificate, including any endorsements directly relating to this Project, indentifying the Architect's Professional Liability Insurance Coverage and stipulating amounts of coverage and deductible. Such certificate shall indicate that coverage thereunder will not be cancelled or not renewed until at least thirty (30) days' prior written notice has been given to the Contractor. If the Contractor, on review of the policy stipultations including monetary limits, requires the Architect to modify the current terms or limits, the Architect's compensation will be increased by the premium difference caused by the change and similarly increased on every policy anniversary therafter until completion of the Project or on reversion to the original terms should this occur prior to Final Completion.

8.6 With respect to any equipment or other property used by the Contractor or Architect in connection with the Work, the Contractor and Architect mutually waive their rights of recovery against each other and all Subcontractors and Owners for loss or damage caused or resulting from any peril insured under Equipment or Property policies. With respect to any equipment or property used in connection with the Work by any Subcontractor, the Contractor will require similar waivers to the Architect. If the policies of insurance referred to in this paragraph require an endorsement to provide for continued coverage where there is a waiver of subrogation, the owners of such policies will cause them to be so endorsed.

ARTICLE 9

INDEMNITY

9.1 The Architect shall indemnify the Contractor from all claims and losses arising from negligent acts, errors or omissions of the Architect in the performance of professional services under this agreement, to the extent that the Architect is responsible for such losses on a comparative basis of fault and responsibility between the Architect and the Contractor. The Architect shall have the option to assume the defense of any such claim, without prejudice to any other rights the Architect may have. The failure of the Architect to assume such defense shall not constitute a waiver of any other rights he may have.

9.2 The Contractor shall indemnify the Architect from all claims and losses arising from negligent acts, errors or omissions of the Contractor in the performance of services under this agreement or under the Contractor's agreement with the Owner to the extent that the Contractor is responsible for such losses on a comparative basis of fault and responsibility between the Contractor and the Architect.

9.3 Such indemnification by either party shall become due and owing only upon a final determination of legal liability between the parties under this Article 9.

9.4 The Contractor and Architect waive all rights to indemnification from each other and their agents and employees for claims or losses arising from negligent acts, errors or omissions arising under this agreement for any such claims or losses covered by insurance obtained by the Contractor or Architect, or which covers the project or equipment used on the project. The aforesaid waiver shall not be applicable to subrogation under 9.1 above by the Contractor's Professional Liability Insuror, if any, in the case of design claims, the defense of which was tendered to the Architect within a reasonable time after it arose. It shall also not be applicable to subrogation by the Architect's Professional Liability Insuror, if any, to claims against the Contractor under 9.2 above.

ARTICLE 10

ARBITRATION

10.1 All claims, disputes and other matters in question between the Contractor and the Architect arising out of or relating to either's obligations to the other under this Agreement, shall be decided by arbitration in accordance with the Construction Industry Arbitration Rules of the American Arbitration Association then obtaining except for those specifically excluded in this Article. This agreement to arbitrate is expressly intended to exclude any obligation to arbitrate matters arising under this Project with any person other than the parties to this Agreement and only the Contractor may initiate an arbitration proceeding against the Architect and only the Architect may initiate an arbitration proceeding against the Contractor pursuant to the terms of this Article. This Article is also expressly intended to preclude consolidation of any arbitration proceeding under this Article with any other arbitration proceeding.

10.2 Notice to the demand for arbitration shall be served upon the other party to this Agreement and filed in writing with the American Arbitration Association. The demand for arbitration shall be made within a reasonable time after the claim accrues, or the dispute or other matter in question arises, but in no event shall it be made after the date when institution of legal or equitable proceedings based upon such claim, dispute or other matter in question would be barred by the applicable statute of limitations.

10.3 The award rendered by the arbitrators shall be final and judgment may be entered thereon in accordance with the applicable law in any court having jurisdiction thereof.

10.4 Each party shall proceed with his obligations under this Agreement pending any arbitration proceedings, unless otherwise agreed in writing.

10.5 If a claim is asserted against the Contractor by the Owner, a Subcontractor or other person not a party to this Agreement which is predicated upon alleged errors or omissions in Drawings, Specifications, or other design responsibilities of the Architect, the Contractor shall promptly give notice of such design claim to the Architect and the Architect shall cooperate fully with the Contractor in the defense of such design claim. The Architect shall, if he so elects, have the right to control the defense of such design claim.

10.6 Paragraph 10.5 shall also be applicable in the event a contract claim is made in a court of law or equity and no party to that proceeding seeks to specifically enforce or assert as a defense any existing obligation to arbitrate.

10.7 This Article shall not be applicable to an action for bodily injury or property damage brought by a third party who is under no obligation to arbitrate such claim with either the Contractor or Architect, insofar as either the Contractor or Architect may desire to assert any rights of indemnity or contribution against the other with respect to the subject matter of such action.

ARTICLE 11

EXTENT OF AGREEMENT BETWEEN CONTRACTOR AND ARCHITECT

This Agreement represents the entire agreement between the Contractor and the Architect and supersedes all prior negotiations, representations or agreements.

This Agreement shall not be superseded by any provisions of the documents for construction and may be amended only by written instrument signed by both Contractor and Architect.

ARTICLE 12

GOVERNING LAW

12.1 This Agreement shall be governed by the law in effect at ______________________

This Agreement entered into as of the day and year first above written.

CONTRACTOR	ARCHITECT
By: ______________________	By: ______________________
Title: ______________________	Title: ______________________

THE ASSOCIATED GENERAL CONTRACTORS

CONDITIONS BETWEEN CONTRACTOR AND SUBCONTRACTOR FOR DESIGN-BUILD

INSTRUCTIONS FOR CONTRACTOR

1. This document is intended to be used with AGC Document No. 450, Standard Design-Build Subcontract Agreement With Subcontractor Not Providing Design, or AGC Document No. 450-1, Standard Design-Build Subcontract Agreement With Subcontractor Providing Design, as the Conditions Between the Contractor and Subcontractor. These conditions govern the obligations of the Subcontractors and in addition establish the general procedures for the administration of construction. These Conditions Between Contractor and Subcontractor differ from those in AGC Form No. 410, Standard Form of Design-Build Agreement and General Conditions Between Owner and Contractor.

2. In all cases your attorney should be consulted to advise you on their use and any modifications.

3. Nothing contained herein is intended to conflict with local, state or federal laws or regulations.

4. It is recommended all insurance matters be reviewed with your insurance consultant and carrier such as implications of errors and omission liability, completed operations, and waiver of subrogation.

5. Each article should be reviewed by the Contractor as to the applicability to a given project and contractual conditions.

6. Special conditions and terms for the project or the subcontracts should cover the following:

   – subcontractor retainages
   – payment schedules
   – insurance limits
   – builder's risk deductible, if any.

7. If the Owner does not provide Builder's Risk Insurance, Paragraph 12.2 will need to be modified.

THE ASSOCIATED GENERAL CONTRACTORS

CONDITIONS BETWEEN CONTRACTOR AND SUBCONTRACTOR FOR DESIGN-BUILD

TABLE OF CONTENTS

ARTICLES **PAGE**

ARTICLE 1

CONTRACT DOCUMENTS

1.1 DEFINITIONS

1.1.1 THE CONTRACT DOCUMENTS

The Subcontract Documents(hereinafter referred to as the Subcontract) consist of the Contract between the Contractor and the Subcontractor, the Subcontract Conditions (including any Supplementary Conditions), the Drawings (and Criteria if the drawings are not complete), the Specifications, all Addenda issued prior to execution of the Contract, and all Modifications issued after the execution of the contract. A Modification is (1) a written amendment to the Contract signed by both parties, (2) a written interpretation issued by the Architect/Engineer pursuant to Subparagraph 3.2.2; or (3) a written order for a minor change in the Work issued on the Owner's behalf pursuant to Subparagraph 13.4. In addition, the Subcontractor assumes toward the Contractor all the obligations and responsibilities which the Contractor assumes toward the Owner under the Agreement between the Owner and the Contractor. A copy of the pertinent parts of the Agreement will be made available on request. The Contract Documents do not include Bidding or Proposal Documents such as the Advertisement or Invitation To Bid, Requests for Proposals, sample forms, Subcontractors Bid or Proposal, or portions of Addenda relative to any of these, or any other documents other than those set forth in this subparagraph unless specifically set forth in the Agreement with the Subcontractor.

1.1.2 THE SUBCONTRACT

The Subcontract forms the contract with the Subcontractor. This contract represents the entire and integrated agreement and supersedes all prior negotiations, representations, or agreements, either written or oral. The Contract may be amended or modified only by a Modification as defined in Subparagraph 1.1.1.

1.1.3 THE WORK

The Work comprises the completed construction and any design required by the Subcontractor's Contract and includes all labor necessary to produce such construction required of the Contractor or a particular Subcontractor, and all materials and equipment incorporated or to be incorporated in such construction.

1.1.4 THE PROJECT

The Project is the total design and construction to be performed under the Agreement between the Owner and Contractor of which the Work is a part.

1.2 EXECUTION, CORRELATION AND INTENT

1.2.1 By executing the Subcontract, each Subcontractor represents that he has visited the site, familiarized himself with the local conditions under which the Work is to be performed and correlated his observations with the requirements of the Subcontract.

1.2.2 The intent of the Subcontract is to include all items necessary for the proper execution and completion of the Work. The documents constituting the Subcontract are complementary, and what is required by any one shall be as binding as if required by all. Work not covered in the Subcontract will not be required unless it is consistent therewith and is reasonably inferable therefrom as being necessary to produce the intended results. Words and abbreviations in the Subcontract which have well-known technical or trade meanings are used in accordance with such recognized meanings.

1.2.3 The organization of the Specifications into divisions, sections and articles, and the arrangements of Drawings shall not control the Contractor in dividing the Work among Subcontractors or in establishing the extent of Work to be performed by any trade.

1.3 OWNERSHIP AND USE OF DOCUMENTS

1.3.1 Unless otherwise provided in the Subcontract, the Subcontractor will be furnished, free of charge, all copies of Drawings and Specifications reasonably necessary for the execution of the Work.

1.3.2 All Drawings, Specifications and copies thereof furnished by the Contractor are and shall remain his property. They are to be used only with respect to this Project and are not to be used on any other project. With the exception of one contract set for each party, such documents are to be returned or suitably accounted for to the Contractor on request at the completion of the Work. Submission or distribution to meet official regulatory requirements or for other purposes in connection with the Project is not to be construed as publication in derogation of the Contractor's common law copyright or other reserved rights.

ARTICLE 2

OWNER

2.1 DEFINITION

2.1.1 The Owner is the person or entity identified as such in the Subcontract and is referred to as if singular in number and masculine in gender. The term Owner means the Owner or his authorized representative.

2.2 INFORMATION AND SERVICES REQUIRED OF THE OWNER

2.2.1 The Owner will furnish all surveys describing the physical characteristics, legal limitations and utility locations for the site of the Project, and a legal description of the site.

2.2.2 Except as provided in Subparagraph 5.7.1 the Owner will secure and pay for necessary approvals, easements, assessments and charges required for the construction, use, or occupancy of permanent structures or permanent changes in existing facilities.

2.2.3 Information or services under the Owner's control will be furnished by the Owner with reasonable promptness to avoid delay in the orderly progress of the Work.

2.2.4 The Owner shall forward all instructions to the Subcontractors through the Contractor.

ARTICLE 3

ARCHITECT/ENGINEER

3.1 DEFINITION

3.1.1 The Architect/Engineer is the person lawfully licensed to practice architecture or engineering or an entity lawfully practicing architecture or engineering and identified as such in the Agreement between the Owner and Contractor and is referred to as if singular in number and masculine in gender. The term Architect/Engineer means the Architect/Engineer or his authorized representative.

3.1.2 Nothing contained in the Contract Documents shall create any contractual relationship between the Architect/Engineer and any Subcontractor.

3.2 ARCHITECT/ENGINEER'S DUTIES DURING CONSTRUCTION

3.2.1 The Architect/Engineer shall at all times have access to the Work wherever it is in preparation and progress. When directed by the Contractor, the Subcontractor shall provide facilities for such access so the Architect/Engineer may perform his functions under these conditions.

3.2.2 The Architect/Engineer will be the interpreter of the requirements of the Drawings and Specifications. The Architect/Engineer will, within a reasonable time, render such interpretations as are necessary for the proper execution of the progress of the Work.

3.2.3 All interpretations of the Architect/Engineer shall be consistent with the intent of and reasonably inferable from the Subcontract and will be in writing or in the form of drawings. All requests for interpretations shall be directed through the Contractor. Neither the Architect/Engineer nor the Contractor will be liable to the Subcontractor for the result of any interpretation or decision rendered in good faith in such capacity.

3.2.4 The Architect/Engineer's decisions in matters relating to artistic effect will be final if consistent with the intent of the Subcontract.

3.2.5 The Architect/Engineer will have authority to reject Work which does not conform to the Subcontract. Whenever, in his opinion, he considers it necessary or advisable for the implementation of the intent of the Subcontract, he will have authority to require special inspection or testing of the Work in accordance with Subparagraph 8.7.2 whether or not such Work be then fabricated, installed or completed. However, neither the Architect/Engineer's authority to act under this Subparagraph 3.2.5, nor any decision made by him in good faith either to exercise or not to exercise such authority, shall give rise to any duty or responsibility of the Architect/Engineer to the Subcontractor, any Sub-Subcontractor, any of their agents or employees, or any other person performing any of the Work.

3.2.6 The Architect/Engineer will review and approve or take other appropriate action upon Subcontractor's submittals such as Shop Drawings, Product Data and Samples, but only for conformance with the design concept of the Work and with the information in the Subcontract. Such action shall be taken with reasonable promptness so as to cause no delay. The Architect/Engineer's approval of a specific item shall not indicate approval of an assembly of which the item is a component.

3.2.7 The Architect/Engineer along with the Contractor will conduct inspections to determine the dates of Substantial Completion and final completion.

3.2.8 The Architect/Engineer will communicate with the subcontractors through the Contractor.

ARTICLE 4

CONTRACTOR

4.1 DEFINITION

4.1.1 The Contractor is the person or entity which has entered into an agreement with the Owner to design and construct the Project and is referred to throughout the Subcontract as if singular in number and masculine in gender. The Contractor is authorized to enter into agreements with subcontractors to perform the Work necessary to complete the Project and to perform some of the construction with his own forces. The term Contractor means the Contractor acting through his authorized representative.

4.2 ADMINISTRATION OF THE CONTRACT

4.2.1 The Contractor will provide the general administration of the Project as herein described.

4.2.2 The Contractor shall have the responsibility to supervise and coordinate the Work of all Subcontractors.

4.2.3 The Contractor shall prepare and update all Construction Schedules and shall direct the Work with respect to such schedules.

4.2.4 The Contractor shall have authority to reject Work which does not conform to the Subcontract and to require any Special Inspection and Testing in accordance with Subparagraph 8.7.2.

4.2.5 The Contractor will prepare and issue Change Orders to the Subcontractors in accordance with Article 13.

4.2.6 The Contractor along with the Architect/Engineer will conduct inspections to determine the dates of Substantial Completion and final completion, and will receive and review written warranties and related documents required by the Subcontract and assembled by the Subcontractor.

4.3 CONTRACTOR'S RIGHT TO STOP THE WORK

4.3.1 If the Subcontractor fails to correct defective Work as required by Paragraph 14.2 or persistently fails to carry out the Work in accordance with the Contract Documents, the Contractor may order the Subcontractor to stop the Work, or any portion thereof, until the cause for such order has been eliminated.

4.3.2 If the Subcontractor defaults or neglects to carry out the Work in accordance with the Subcontract and fails within seven days after receipt of written notice from the Contractor to commence and continue correction of such default or neglect with diligence and promptness, the Contractor may, by written notice, and without prejudice to any other remedy he or the Owner may have, make good such deficiencies, or exercise any of the options he has in 15.2.1. In such case an appropriate Change Order shall be issued deducting from the payments then or thereafter due the Subcontractor the cost of correcting such deficiencies, including compensation for the Architect/Engineer's and Contractor's additional services made necessary by such default, neglect or failure.

ARTICLE 5

SUBCONTRACTORS

5.1 DEFINITION

5.1.1 A Subcontractor is the person or entity identified as such in the Agreement between the Contractor and a Subcontractor and is referred to throughout the Subcontract as if singular in number and masculine in gender. The term Subcontractor means the Subcontractor or his authorized representative.

5.2 REVIEW OF CONTRACT DOCUMENTS

5.2.1 The Subcontractor shall carefully study and compare the documents within the Subcontract and shall at once report to the Contractor any error, inconsistency or omission he may discover. The Subcontractor shall not be liable to the Owner, the Contractor or the Architect/Engineer for any damage resulting from any such errors, inconsistencies or omissions.

5.3 SUPERVISION AND CONSTRUCTION PROCEDURES

5.3.1 The Subcontractor shall supervise and direct the Work, using his best skill and attention. He shall be solely responsible for all construction means, methods, techniques, sequences and procedures and for coordinating all portions of the Work under the Subcontract subject to the overall coordination of the Contractor.

5.3.2 The Subcontractor shall be responsible to the Contractor for the acts and omissions of his employees and all his Sub-subcontractors and their agents and employees and other persons performing any of the Work under a contract with the Subcontractor.

5.3.3 The Subcontractor shall not be relieved from his obligations to perform the work in accordance with the Subcontract by inspections, tests or approvals required or performed by persons other than the Subcontractor.

5.4 LABOR AND MATERIALS

5.4.1 Unless otherwise specifically provided in the Subcontract, the Subcontractor shall provide and pay for all labor, materials, equipment, tools, construction equipment and machinery, transportation, and other facilities and services necessary for the proper execution and completion of the Work.

5.4.2 The Subcontractor shall at all times enforce strict discipline and good order among his employees and shall not employ on the Work any unfit person or anyone not skilled in the task assigned to him.

5.5. WARRANTY

5.5.1 The Subcontractor warrants to the Owner and the Contractor that all materials and equipment furnished under this Contract will be new unless otherwise specified, and that all Work will be of good quality, free from faults and defects and in conformance with the Subcontract. All Work not so conforming to these requirements, including substitutions not properly approved and authorized, may be considered defective. If required by the Contractor, the Subcontractor shall furnish satisfactory evidence as to the kind and quality of materials and equipment. This warranty is not limited by the provisions of Paragraph 14.2. Warranties required by the Contract Documents shall commence on the Date of Substantial Completion of the Project as established by the Certificate of Substantial Completion between the Contractor and the Owner.

5.6 TAXES

5.6.1 The Subcontractor shall pay all sales, consumer, use and other similar taxes for the Work or portions thereof provided by the Subcontractor which are legally enacted at the time bids or proposals are received, whether or not yet effective, for which he is legally liable.

5.7 PERMITS, FEES AND NOTICES

5.7.1 Unless otherwise provided in the Subcontract, the Subcontractor shall secure and pay for all permits, governmental fees, licenses and inspections necessary for the proper execution and completion of the Work, which are customarily secured after execution of the contract and which are legally required at the time bids or proposals are received.

5.7.2 The Subcontractor shall give all notices and comply with all laws, ordinances, rules, regulations and orders of any public authority bearing on the performance of the Work.

5.7.3 Unless otherwise provided in the Subcontract, it is not the responsibility of the Subcontractor to make certain that the Subcontract is in accordance with applicable laws, statutes, building codes and regulations except to the extent he has contracted to provide part of the design. If the Subcontractor observes that any of the Subcontract Documents are at variance therewith in any respect, he shall promptly notify the Contractor in writing, and any necessary changes shall be by appropriate Modification.

5.7.4 If the Subcontractor performs any Work knowing it to be contrary to such laws, ordinances, rules and regulations, and without such notice to the Contractor, he shall assume full responsibility therefor and shall bear all costs attributable thereto.

5.8 ALLOWANCES

5.8.1 The Contract Sum as defined in Paragraph 10.1.1 includes all allowances. Items covered by these allowances shall be supplied for such amounts and by such persons as the Contractor may direct.

5.8.2 Unless otherwise provided in the Subcontract:

.1 These allowances shall cover the cost to the Subcontractor, less any applicable trade discount, of the materials and equipment required by the allowance delivered at the site, and all applicable taxes;

.2 The Subcontractor's costs for unloading and handling on the site, labor, installation costs, overhead, profit and other expenses contemplated for the original allowance shall be included in the Contract Sum and not in the allowance;

.3 Whenever the cost is more than or less than the allowance, the Contract Sum shall be adjusted accordingly by Change Order, the amount of which will recognize changes, if any, in handling costs on the site, labor, installation costs, overhead, profit and other expenses.

5.9 SUPERINTENDENT

5.9.1 The Subcontractor shall employ a competent superintendent and necessary assistants who shall be in attendance at the Project site during the progress of the Work. The superintendent shall be satisfactory to the Contractor, and shall not be changed except with the consent of the Contractor, unless the superintendent proves to be unsatisfactory to the Subcontractor or ceases to be in his employ. The superintendent shall represent the Subcontractor and all communications given to the superintendent shall be as binding as if given to the Subcontractor. Important communications shall be confirmed in writing. Other communications shall be so confirmed on written request in each case.

5.10 PROGRESS SCHEDULE

5.10.1 The Subcontractor, immediately after being awarded the Contract, shall prepare and submit for the Contractor's information an estimated progress schedule for the Work. The progress schedule shall be related to the entire Project and shall provide for expeditious and practicable execution of the Work. This schedule shall indicate the dates for the starting and completion of the various stages of construction, shall be revised as required by the conditions of the Work, and shall be subject to the Contractor's approval.

5.11 DRAWINGS AND SPECIFICATIONS AT THE SITE

5.11.1 The Subcontractor shall maintain at the site for the Contractor one copy of all Drawings, Specifications, Addenda, Change Orders and other Modifications, in good order and marked currently to record all changes made during construction. These Drawings, marked to record all changes during construction, and approved Shop Drawings, Product Data and Samples shall be delivered to the Contractor for the Owner upon completion of the Work.

5.12 SHOP DRAWINGS, PRODUCT DATA AND SAMPLES

5.12.1 Shop Drawings are drawings, diagrams, schedules and other data especially prepared for the Work by the Subcontractor or any Subsubcontractor, manufacturer, supplier or distributor to illustrate some portion of the Work.

5.12.2 Product Data are illustrations, standard schedules, performance charts, instructions, brochures, diagrams and other information furnished by the Subcontractor to illustrate a material, product or system for some portion of the Work.

5.12.3 Samples are physical examples which illustrate materials, equipment or workmanship and establish standards by which the Work will be judged.

5.12.4 The Subcontractor shall review, approve and submit through the Contractor with reasonable promptness and in such sequence as to cause no delay in the Work or in the work of any separate contractor, all Shop Drawings, Product Data and Samples required by the Subcontract.

5.12.5 By approving and submitting Shop Drawings, Product Data and Samples, the Subcontractor represents that he has determined and verified all materials, field measurements, and field construction criteria related thereto, or will do so, and that he has checked and coordinated the information contained within such submittals with the requirements of the Work under the Subcontract.

5.12.6 The Contractor, if he finds such submittals to be in order, will forward them to the Architect/Engineer. If the Contractor finds them not to be complete or in proper form, he may return them to the Subcontractor for correction or completion.

5.12.7 The Subcontractor shall not be relieved of responsibility for any deviation from the requirements of the Subcontract by the Architect/Engineer's approval of Shop Drawings, Product Data or Samples under Subparagraph 3.2.6 unless the Sub contractor has specifically informed the Architect/Engineer and Contractor in writing of such deviation at the time of submission and the Architect/Engineer has given written approval to the specific deviation. The Subcontractor shall not be relieved from responsibility for errors or omissions in the Shop Drawings, Product Data or Samples by the Architect/Engineer's approval thereof.

5.12.8 The Subcontractor shall direct specific attention, in writing or on resubmitted Shop Drawings, Product Data or Samples, to revisions other than those requested by the Architect/Engineer or Contractor on previous submittals.

5.12.9 No portion of the Work requiring submission of a Shop Drawing, Product Data or Sample shall be commenced until the submittal has been approved by the Architect/Engineer. All such portions of the Work shall be in accordance with approved submittals.

5.13 USE OF SITE

5.13.1 The Subcontractor shall confine operations at the site to areas designated by the Contractor, permitted by law, ordinances, permits and the Subcontract and shall not unreasonably encumber the site with any materials or equipment.

5.14 CUTTING AND PATCHING OF WORK

5.14.1 The Subcontractor shall be responsible for all cutting, fitting or patching that may be required to complete the Work or to make its several parts fit together properly. He shall provide protection of existing Work as required.

5.14.2 The Subcontractor shall not damage or endanger any portion of the Work or the work of the Contractor or any separate contractors or subcontractors by cutting, patching or otherwise altering any work, or by excavation. The Subcontractor shall not cut or otherwise alter the work of the Contractor or any separate contractor except with the written consent of the Contractor and of such separate contractor. The Subcontractor shall not unreasonably withhold from the Contractor or any separate contractor his consent to cutting or otherwise altering the Work.

5.15 CLEANING UP

5.15.1 The Subcontractor at all times shall keep the premises free from accumulation of waste materials or rubbish caused by his operations. At the completion of the Work he shall remove all his waste materials and rubbish from and about the Project as well as all his tools, construction equipment, machinery and surplus materials.

5.15.2 If the Subcontractor fails to clean up within 24 hours after receipt of notice of noncompliance from the Contractor, the Contractor may do so and the cost thereof shall be charged to the Subcontractor.

5.16 COMMUNICATIONS

5.16.1 The Subcontractor shall forward all communications to the Owner and Architect/Engineer through the Contractor.

5.17 ROYALTIES AND PATENTS

5.17.1 The Subcontractor shall pay all royalties and license fees for materials, methods and systems incorporated in the Work. He shall defend all suits or claims for infringement of any patent rights and shall save the Owner and Contractor harmless from loss on account thereof, except that the Owner shall be responsible for all such loss when a particular design, process or the product of a particular manufacturer or manufacturers is specified by the Owner. If the Subcontractor has reason to believe that the design, process or product specified is an infringement of a patent, he shall be responsible for such loss unless he promptly gives such information to the Contractor.

5.18 INDEMNIFICATION

5.18.1 To the fullest extent permitted by law, the Subcontractor shall indemnify and hold harmless the Owner, the Contractor and the Architect/Engineer and their agents and employees from and against all claims, damages, losses, and expenses including but not limited to, attorneys' fees, arising out of or resulting from the performance of the Work, provided that any such claim, damage, loss or expense (1) is attributable to bodily injury, sickness, disease or death, or to injury to or destruction of tangible property (other than the Work itself) including the loss of use resulting therefrom, and (2) is caused in whole or in part by any negligent act or omission of the Subcontractor, any Sub-subcontractor, anyone directly or indirectly employed by any of them or anyone for whose acts any of them may be liable, regardless of whether or not it is caused in part by a party indemnified hereunder. Such obligations shall not be construed to negate, abridge or otherwise reduce any other right or obligation of indemnity which would otherwise exist as to any party or person described in this Paragraph 5.18.

5.18.2 In any and all claims against the Owner, the Contractor or the Architect/Engineer or any of their agents or employees by any employee of the Subcontractor, any Sub-subcontractor, anyone directly or indirectly employed by any of them or anyone for whose acts any of them may be liable, the indemnification obligation under this Paragraph 5.18 shall not be limited in any way by any limitation on the amount or type of damages, compensation or benefits payable by or for the Subcontractor or any Sub-subcontractor under workers' or workmen's compensation acts, disability benefit acts or other employee benefit acts.

5.18.3 The obligations of the Subcontractor under this Paragraph 5.18 shall not extend to the liability of the Architect/Engineer, his agents or employees arising out of (1) the preparation or approval of maps, drawings, opinions, reports, surveys, designs or specifications, or (2) the giving of or the failure to give directions or instruction by the Architect/Engineer, his agents or employees provided such giving or failure to give is the primary cause of the injury or damage.

ARTICLE 6

SUB-SUBCONTRACTORS

6.1 DEFINITION

6.1.1 A Sub-subcontractor is a person or entity who has a direct contract with the Subcontractor to perform any of the Work at the site. The term Sub-subcontractor is referred to throughout the Subcontract as if singular in number and masculine in gender and means a Sub-subcontractor or his authorized representative.

6.2 AWARDS OF SUB-SUBCONTRACTS AND OTHER CONTRACTS FOR PORTIONS OF THE WORK

6.2.1 Unless otherwise required by the Subcontract or in the Bidding or Proposal Documents, the Subcontractor shall furnish to the Contractor in writing, for acceptance by the Contractor in writing, the names of the persons or entities (including those who are to furnish materials or equipment fabricated to a special design) proposed for each of the principal portions of the Work. The Contractor will promptly reply to the Subcontractor in writing if the Contractor, after due investigation, has reasonable objection to any such proposed person or entity. Failure of the Contractor to reply promptly shall constitute notice of no reasonable objection.

6.2.2 The Subcontractor shall not contract with any such proposed person or entity to whom the Contractor has made reasonable objection under the provisions of Subparagraph 6.2.1. The Subcontractor shall not be required to contract with anyone to whom he has a reasonable objection.

6.2.3 If the Contractor refuses to accept any person or entity on a list submitted by the Subcontractor in response to the requirements of these conditions, the Subcontractor shall submit an acceptable substitute; however, no increase in the Contract Sum shall be allowed for any such substitution.

6.2.4 The Subcontractor shall make no substitution for any Sub-subcontractor, person or entity previously selected if the Contractor makes reasonable objection to such substitution.

6.3 SUB-SUBCONTRACTUAL RELATIONS

6.3.1 By an appropriate agreement, written where legally required for validity, the Subcontractor shall require each Sub-subcontractor, to the extent of the work to be performed by the Sub-subcontractor, to be bound to the Subcontractor by the terms of the Subcontract and to assume toward the Subcontractor all the obligations and responsibilities which the Subcontractor, by the Subcontract, assumes toward the Owner, the Contractor, or the Architect/Engineer. Said agreement shall preserve and protect the rights of the Owner, the Contractor and the Architect/Engineer under the Subcontract with respect to the Work to be performed by the Sub-subcontractor so that the subcontracting thereof will not prejudice such rights, and shall allow to the Sub-subcontractor, unless specifically provided otherwise in the Subcontractor—Sub-subcontractor agreement, the benefit of all rights, remedies and redress against the Subcontractor that the Subcontractor, by these Documents, has against the Contractor. Where appropriate, the Subcontractor shall require each Sub-subcontractor to enter into similar agreements with his Sub-subcontractors. The Subcontractor shall make available to each proposed Sub-subcontractor, prior to the execution of the Sub-subcontract, copies of the Subcontract to which the Sub-subcontractor will be bound by this Paragraph 6.3, and shall identify to the Sub-subcontractor any terms and conditions of the proposed Sub-subcontract which may be at variance with the appropriate parts of the Subcontract. Each Sub-subcontractor shall similarly make copies of parts of the Subcontract available to his Sub-subcontractors.

ARTICLE 7

SEPARATE SUBCONTRACTS

7.1 MUTUAL RESPONSIBILITY OF SUBCONTRACTORS

7.1.1 The Subcontractor shall afford the Contractor and other subcontractors reasonable opportunity for the introduction and storage of their materials and equipment and the execution of their work, and shall connect and coordinate his Work with others under the general direction of the Contractor.

7.1.2 If any part of the Subcontractor's Work depends, for proper execution or results, upon the Work of the Contractor or any separate subcontractor, the Subcontractor shall, prior to proceeding with the Work, promptly report to the Contractor any apparent discrepancies or defects in such Work that render it unsuitable for such proper execution and results. Failure of the Subcontractor so to report shall constitute an acceptance of the other subcontractor's or the Contractor's Work as fit and proper to receive his Work, except as to defects which may subsequently become apparent in such work by others.

7.1.3 Any costs caused by defective or ill-timed work shall be borne by the party responsible therefor.

7.1.4 Should the Subcontractor wrongfully cause damage to the Work or property of the Owner or to other work on the site, the Subcontractor shall promptly remedy such damage as provided in Subparagraph 11.2.5.

7.1.5 Should the Subcontractor wrongfully cause damage to the work or property of any separate subcontractor or other contractor, the Subcontractor shall, upon due notice, promptly attempt to settle with the other contractor by agreement, or otherwise resolve the dispute. If such separate contractor sues the Owner or the Contractor or initiates an arbitration proceeding against the Owner or Contractor on account of any damage alleged to have been caused by the Subcontractor, the Owner or Contractor shall notify the Subcontractor who shall defend such proceedings at the Subcontractor's expense, and if any judgment or award against the Owner or Contractor arises therefrom, the Subcontractor shall pay or satisfy it and shall reimburse the Owner or Contractor for all attorneys' fees and court or arbitration costs which the Owner or Contractor has incurred.

7.2 CONTRACTOR'S RIGHT TO CLEAN UP

7.2.1 If a dispute arises between the separate subcontractors as to their responsibility for cleaning up as required by Paragraph 5.15, the Contractor may clean up and charge the cost thereof to the subcontractors responsible therefor as the Contractor shall determine to be just.

ARTICLE 8

MISCELLANEOUS PROVISIONS

8.1 GOVERNING LAW

8.1.1 The Subcontract shall be governed by the law of the place where the Project is located.

8.2 SUCCESSORS AND ASSIGNS

8.2.1 The Contractor and the Subcontractor each binds himself, his partners, successors, assigns and legal representatives to the other party hereto and to the partners, successors, assigns and legal representatives of such other party in respect to all covenants, agreements and obligations contained in the Subcontract . Neither party to the Contract shall assign the Contract or sublet it as a whole without the written consent of the other.

8.3 WRITTEN NOTICE

8.3.1 Written notice shall be deemed to have been duly served if delivered in person to the individual or member of the firm or entity or to an officer of the corporation for whom it was intended, or if delivered at or sent by registered or certified mail to the last business address known to him who gives the notice.

8.4 CLAIMS FOR DAMAGES

8.4.1 Should either party to the Subcontract suffer injury or damage to person or property because of any act or omission of the other party of his employees, agents or others for whose acts he is legally liable, claim shall be made in writing to such other party within a reasonable time after the first observance of such injury or damage.

8.5 PERFORMANCE BOND AND LABOR AND MATERIAL PAYMENT BOND

8.5.1 The Contractor shall have the right to require the Subcontractor to furnish bonds in a form and with a corporate surety acceptable to the Contractor covering the faithful performance of the Subcontract and the payment of all obligations arising thereunder if and as required in the Subcontract.

8.6 RIGHTS AND REMEDIES

8.6.1 The duties and obligations imposed by the Subcontract shall be in addition to and not a limitation of any duties, obligations and rights otherwise imposed by law. However, the remedies provided in the Subcontract shall be the sole remedies available with respect to monetary claims either party may have against the other. Moreover, when the Subcontractor makes a claim against the Contractor for additional time or money and the Contractor presents that claim to or asserts that claim against the Owner, the Subcontractor shall be bound by the determination of the Owner, an award of arbitration, or a judgment of a court of record on such claim. The Contractor shall afford the Subcontractor reasonable opportunity to either present such claim himself or to assist the Contractor in the presentation of such claim to the Owner, an arbitration tribunal or a court of record. Subcontractor shall bear his proportionate share of Contractor's cost in pursuing such claim. Nothing herein, however, shall obligate the Contractor to initiate an arbitration proceeding or intitiate a claim in any court if the Contractor reasonably determines that the cost of pursuing the claim further is not justified or that the merits of the claim do not justify its further pursuit.

8.6.2 No action or failure to act by the Contractor, Architect/Engineer or Subcontractor shall constitute a waiver of any right or duty afforded any of them under the Subcontract, nor shall any such action or failure to act constitute an approval of or acquiescence in any breach thereunder, except as may be specifically agreed in writing.

8.7 TESTS

8.7.1 If the Subcontract, laws, ordinances, rules, regulations or orders of any public authority having jurisdiction require any portion of the Work to be inspected, tested or approved, the Subcontractor shall give the Architect/Engineer timely notice of its readiness so the Architect/Engineer and Contractor may observe such inspection, testing, or approval. The Subcontractor shall bear all costs of such inspections, tests or approvals unless otherwise provided.

8.7.2 If the Architect/Engineer or Contractor determines that any Work requires special inspection, testing or approval which Subparagraph 8.7.1 does not include, he will, through the Contractor, instruct the Subcontrator to order such special inspection, testing or approval and the Subcontractor shall give notice as in Subparagraph 8.7.1. If such special inspection or testing reveals a failure of the Work to comply with the requirements of the Subcontract, the Subcontractor shall bear all costs thereof, including compensation for the Architect/Engineer's and Contractor's additional services made necessary by such failure. If the work complies, the Contractor shall bear such costs and an appropriate Change Order shall be issued.

8.7.3 Required certificates of inspection, testing or approval shall be secured by the Subcontractor and promptly delivered by him through the Contractor to the Architect/Engineer.

8.7.4 If the Architect/Engineer or Contractor is to observe the inspections, tests or approvals required by the Subcontract, he will do so promptly and, where practicable, at the source of supply.

8.8 ARBITRATION

8.8.1 All claims, disputes and other matters in question arising out of, or relating to this Subcontract or the breach thereof, except as set forth in Subparagraph 3.2.4 with respect to the Architect/Engineer's decisions on matters relating to artistic effect, and except for claims which have been waived by the making or acceptance of final payment provided by Subparagraphs 10.8.4 and 10.8.5, shall be decided by arbitration in accordance with the Construction Industry Arbitration Rules of the American Arbitration Association then obtaining unless the parties mutually agree otherwise. This agreement to arbitrate shall be specifically enforceable under the prevailing arbitration law. The award rendered by the arbitrators shall be final, and judgment may be entered upon it in accordance with applicable law in any court having jurisdiction thereof.

8.8.2 Notice of the demand for arbitration shall be filed in writing with the other party to the Subcontract and with the American Arbitration Association. The demand for arbitration shall be made within a reasonable time after the claim, dispute or other matter in question has arisen, and in no event shall it be made after the date when institution of legal or equitable proceedings based on such claim, dispute or other matter in question would be barred by the applicable statute of limitations.

8.8.3 The Subcontractor shall carry on the Work and maintain the progress schedule during any arbitration proceedings, unless otherwise agreed by him and the Contractor in writing.

8.8.4 All claims which are related to or dependent upon each other shall be heard by the same arbitrator or arbitrators even though the parties are not the same unless a specific contract prohibits such consolidation.

8.8.5 These provisions relating to mandatory arbitration shall not be applicable to a claim asserted in an action in a state or federal court by a person who is under no obligation to arbitrate such claim with either of the parties to this Agreement insofar as the parties to this Agreement may desire to assert any rights of indemnity or contribution with respect to the subject matter of such action. These provisions shall also not be applicable to any claim the Subcontractor may wish to assert against the Contractor if the Contractor desires to assert that claim, either in whole or part, over against the Owner and the Agreement between the Owner and Contractor does not provide for binding arbitration or does so provide but the two arbitration proceedings cannot be consolidated. In such a case, the Contractor shall notify the Subcontractor either before or after demand for arbitration is made of Contractor's desire to assert the claim against the Owner. In such a case, the Subcontractor shall not proceed by arbitration but in a state or federal court which has jurisdiction over both the Contractor and the Owner. If a dispute arises over the application of these provisions, the question of arbitrability shall be decided by the appropriate court and not by an arbitrator.

ARTICLE 9

TIME

9.1 DEFINITIONS

9.1.1 The Contract Time is the period of time allotted in the Subcontract for the Substantial Completion of the Work as defined in Subparagraph 9.1.3 including authorized adjustments thereto.

9.1.2 The date of commencement of the Work is the date established in a notice to proceed. If there is no notice to proceed, it shall be the date of the Subcontract or such other date as may be established therein.

9.1.3 The Date of Substantial Completion of the Work or designated portion thereof is the Date certified by the Architect/Engineer when construction is sufficiently complete, in accordance with the Subcontract, so the Owner can occupy or utilize the Work or designated portion thereof for the use for which it is intended.

9.1.4 The term day as used in the Subcontract shall mean calendar day unless otherwise specifically designated.

9.2 PROGRESS AND COMPLETION

9.2.1 All time limits stated in the Contract Documents are of the essence of the Contract.

9.2.2 The Subcontractor shall begin the Work on the date of commencement as defined in Subparagraph 9.1.2. He shall carry the Work forward expeditiously with adequate forces and shall achieve Substantial Completion within the Contract Time.

9.3 DELAYS AND EXTENSIONS OF TIME

9.3.1 If the Subcontractor is delayed at any time in the progress of the Work by any act or neglect of the Owner, Contractor, or the Architect/Engineer, or by any employee of either, or by any separate contractor employed by the Owner, or by changes ordered in the Work, or by labor disputes, fire, unusual delay in transportation, adverse weather conditions not reasonably anticipatable, unavoidable casualties or any causes beyond the Subcontractor's control, or by delay authorized by the Owner or the Contractor pending arbitration, or by any other cause which the Contractor determines may justify the delay, then the Contract Time shall be extended by Change Order for such reasonable time as the Contractor may determine.

9.3.2 Any claim for extension of time shall be made in writing to the Contractor no more than twenty days after the commencement of the delay; otherwise it shall be waived. In the case of a continuing cause of delay only one claim is necessary. The Subcontractor shall provide an estimate of the probable effect of such delay on the progress of the Work.

9.3.3 If no agreement is made stating the dates upon which interpretations as set forth in Subparagraph 3.2.2 shall be furnished, then no claim for delay shall be allowed on account of failure to furnish such interpretations until fifteen days after written request is made for them, and not then unless such claim is reasonable.

9.3.4 It shall be recognized by the Subcontractor that he may reasonably anticipate that as the job progresses, the Contractor will be making changes in and updating Construction Schedules pursuant to the authority given him in Subparagraph 4.2.3. Therefore, no claim for an increase in the Contract Sum for either acceleration or delay will be allowed for extensions of time purusant to this paragraph 9.3 or for other changes in Construction Schedules which are of the type ordinarily experienced in projects of similar size and complexity.

9.3.5 This Paragraph 9.3 does not exclude the recovery of damages for delay by either party under other provisions of the Contract Documents.

ARTICLE 10

PAYMENTS AND COMPLETION

10.1 CONTRACT SUM

10.1.1 The Contract Sum is stated in the agreement between the Contractor and the Subcontractor including adjustments thereto and is the total amount payable to the Subcontractor for the performance of the Work under the Subcontract.

10.2 SCHEDULE OF VALUES

10.2.1 Before the first Application for Payment, the Subcontractor shall submit to the Contractor a schedule of values allocated to the various portions of the Work prepared in such form and supported by such data to substantiate its accuracy as the Contractor may require. This schedule, when accepted by the Contractor, shall be used only as a basis for the Subcontractor's Applications for Payment.

10.3 APPLICATIONS FOR PAYMENT

10.3.1 At least ten days before the date for each progress payment established in the Subcontractor's Agreement, the Subcontractor shall submit to the Contractor an itemized Application for Payment, notarized if required, supported by such data substantiating the Subcontractor's right to payment as the Owner or the Contractor may require, and reflecting such retainage as provided in the Subcontract.

10.3.2 Unless otherwise provided, payments will be made on account of materials or equipment not incorporated in the Work but delivered and suitably stored at the site and, if approved in advance by the Contractor, payments may similarly be made for materials or equipment stored at some other location agreed upon in writing. Payments made for materials or equipment stored on or off the site shall be conditioned upon submission by the Subcontractor of bills of sale or such other procedures satisfactory to the Contractor to establish the Owner's title to such materials or equipment or otherwise protect the Owner's interest, including applicable insurance and transportation to the site for those materials and equipment stored off the site.

10.3.3 The Subcontractor warrants that title to all Work, materials and equipment covered by an Application for Payment will pass to the Owner either by incorporation in the construction or upon the receipt of payment by the Subcontractor, whichever occurs first, free and clear of all liens, claims, security interests or encumbrances, hereinafter referred to in this Article 10 as "liens;" and that no Work, materials or equipment covered by an Application for Payment will have been acquired by the Subcontractor, or by any other person performing the Work at the site or furnishing materials and equipment for the Project, subject to an agreement under which an interest therein or an encumbrance thereon is retained by the seller or otherwise imposed by the Subcontractor or such other person. All Subcontractors and Sub-subcontractors agree that title will so pass upon their receipt of payment from the Subcontractor.

10.4 PROGRESS PAYMENTS

10.4.1 If the Subcontractor has made Application for Payment as above, the Contractor will, with reasonable promptness but not more than seven days after the receipt of payment from the Owner make payment in accordance with the Subcontract.

10.4.2 No approval of an application for a progress payment, nor any progress payment, nor any partial or entire use or occupancy of the Project by the Owner, shall constitute an acceptance of any Work not in accordance with the Subcontract.

10.4.3 The Subcontractor shall promptly pay each Sub-subcontractor upon receipt of payment out of the amount paid to the Subcontractor on account of such Sub-subcontractor's Work, the amount to which said Sub-subcontractor is entitled, reflecting the percentage actually retained, if any, from payments to the Subcontractor on account of such Sub-subcontractor's Work. The Subcontractor shall, by an appropriate agreement with each Sub-subcontractor, also require each Sub-subcontractor to make payments to his subcontractors in a similar manner.

10.5 PAYMENTS WITHHELD

10.5.1 The Contractor may decline to approve an Application for Payment if in his opinion the Application is not adequately supported. If the Subcontractor and Contractor cannot agree on a revised amount, the Contractor shall process the Application for the amount he deems appropriate. The Contractor may also decline to approve any Applications for Payment or, because of subsequently discovered evidence or subsequent inspections, he may nullify in whole or in part any approval previously made to such extent as may be necessary in his opinion because of:

.1 defective work not remedied;

.2 third party claims filed or reasonable evidence indicating probable filing of such claims;

.3 failure of the Subcontractor to make payments properly to Sub-subcontractors or for labor, materials or equipment;

.4 reasonable evidence that the Work cannot be completed for the unpaid balance of the Contract Sum;

.5 damage to the Contractor, the Owner or another contractor working at the Project;

.6 reasonable evidence that the Work will not be completed within the Contract time; or

.7 persistent failure to carry out the Work in accordance with the Subcontract.

10.5.2 When the above grounds in Subparagraph 10.5.1 are removed, payment shall be made for amounts withheld because of them.

10.6 FAILURE OF PAYMENT

10.6.1 If the Subcontractor is not paid within seven days after payment to the Contractor by the Owner, then the Subcontractor may, upon seven days additional written notice to the Contractor, stop the work until payment of the amount owing has been received. The Contract Sum shall be increased by the amount of the Subcontractor's reasonable costs of shutdown, delay and start-up, which shall be effected by appropriate Change Order in accordance with Paragraph 13.3.

10.7 FINAL COMPLETION AND FINAL PAYMENT

10.7.1 Upon receipt of written notice that the Work is ready for final inspection and acceptance and upon receipt of a final Application for Payment, the Architect/Engineer and Contractor will promptly make such inspection and, when they find the Work acceptable under the Subcontract and the Contract fully performed, the Contractor will promptly approve final payment.

10.7.2 Neither the final payment nor the remaining retainage percentage shall become due until the Subcontractor submits to the Contractor (1) an affidavit that all payrolls, bills for materials and equipment, and other indebtedness connected with the Work for which the Owner or his property might in anywaybe responsible, have been paid or otherwise satisfied, (2) consent of surety, if any, to final payment and (3), if required by the Owner, other data establishing payment or satisfaction of all such obligations, such as receipts, releases and waivers of liens arising out of the Subcontract, to the extent and in such form as may be designated by the Owner. If any Sub-subcontractor refuses to furnish a release or waiver required by the Owner or Contractor, the Subcontractor may furnish a bond satisfactory to the Owner and Contractor to indemnify them against any such lien. If any such lien remains unsatisfied after all payments are made, the Subcontractor shall refund to the Owner or Contractor all moneys that the latter may be compelled to pay in discharging such lien, including all costs and reasonable attorneys' fees.

10.7.3 If, after Substantial Completion of the Work, final completion thereof is materially delayed through no fault of the Subcontractor or by the issuance of Change Orders affecting final completion, and the Contractor so confirms, the Owner or Contractor shall, upon certification by the Contractor, and without terminating the Contract, make payment of the balance due for that portion of the Work fully completed and accepted. If the remaining balance for Work not fully completed or corrected is less than the retainage stipulated in the Subcontract, and if bonds have been furnished as provided in Paragraph 8.5, the written consent of the surety to the payment of the balance due for that portion of the Work fully completed and accepted shall be submitted by the Subcontractor to the Contractor prior to certification of such payment. Such payment shall be made under the terms and conditions governing final payment, except that it shall not constitute a waiver of claims.

10.7.4 The making of final payment shall constitute a waiver of all claims by the Contractor except those arising from:

.1 unsettled liens;

.2 faulty or defective Work appearing after Substantial Completion;

.3 failure of the Work to comply with the requirements of the Subcontract; or

.4 terms of any special warranties required by the Subcontract.

10.7.5 The acceptance of final payment shall constitute a waiver of all claims by the Subcontractor except those previously made in writing and identified by the Subcontractor as unsettled at the time of the Final Application for Payment.

ARTICLE 11

PROTECTION OF PERSONS AND PROPERTY

11.1 SAFETY PRECAUTIONS AND PROGRAMS

11.1.1 The Subcontractor shall be responsible for initiating, maintaining and supervising all safety precautions and programs in connection with the Work.

11.1.2 If the Subcontractor fails to maintain the safety precautions required by law or directed by the Contractor, the Contractor may take such steps as necessary and charge the Subcontractor therefor.

11.1.3 The failure of the Contractor to take any such action shall not relieve the Subcontractor of his obligations in Subparagraph 11.1.1.

11.2 SAFETY OF PERSONS AND PROPERTY

11.2.1 The Subcontractor shall take all reasonable precautions for the safety of, and shall provide all reasonable protection to prevent damage, injury or loss to:

.1 all employees on the Work and all other persons who may be affected thereby;

.2 all the Work and all materials and equipment to be incorporated therein, whether in storage on or off the site, under the care, custody or control of the Subcontractor or any of his Sub-subcontractors or Sub-subsubcontractors; and

.3 other property at the site or adjacent thereto, including trees, shrubs, lawns, walks, pavements, roadways, structures and utilities not designated for removal, relocation or replacement in the course of construction.

11.2.2 The Subcontractor shall give all notices and comply with all applicable laws, ordinances, rules, regulations and lawful orders of any public authority bearing on the safety of persons or property or their protection from damage, injury or loss.

11.2.3 The Subcontractor shall erect and maintain, as required by existing conditions and progress of the Work, all reasonable safeguards for safety and protection, including posting danger signs and other warnings against hazards, promulgating safety regulations and notifying owners and users of adjacent utilities. If the Subcontrator fails to so comply he shall, at the direction of the Contractor, remove all forces from the Project without cost or loss to the Owner or Contractor, until he is in compliance.

11.2.4 When the use or storage of explosives or other hazardous materials or equipment is necessary for the execution of the Work the Subcontractor shall exercise the utmost care and shall carry on such activities under the supervision of properly qualified personnel.

11.2.5 The Subcontractor shall promptly remedy all damage or loss (other than damage or loss insured under Paragraphs 12.2 and 12.3) to any property referred to in Clauses 11.2.1.2 and 11.2.1.3 caused in whole or in part by the Subcontractor, his Sub-contractors; his Sub-subcontractors, or anyone directly or indirectly employed by any of them or by anyone for whose acts any of them may be liable and for which the Subcontractor is responsible under Clauses 11.2.1.2 and 11.2.1.3, except damage or loss attributable to the acts or omissions of the Owner or Architect/Engineer or anyone directly or indirectly employed by either of them or by anyone for whose acts either of them may be liable, and not attributable to the fault or negligence of the Subcontractor. The foregoing obligations of the Subcontractor are in addition to his obligation under Paragraph 7.1.5.

11.2.6 The Subcontractor shall designate a responsible member of his organization at the site whose duty shall be the prevention of accidents. This person shall be the Subcontractor's superintendent unless otherwise designated by the Subcontractor in writing to the Contractor.

11.2.7 The Subcontractor shall not load or permit any part of the Work to be loaded so as to endanger its safety.

11.3 EMERGENCIES

11.3.1 In any emergency affecting the safety of persons or property, the Subcontractor shall act, at his discretion, to prevent threatened damage, injury or loss. Any additional compensation or extension of time claimed by the Subcontractor on account of emergency work shall be determined as provided in Article 13 for Changes in the Work.

ARTICLE 12

INSURANCE

12.1 SUBCONTRACTOR'S LIABILITY INSURANCE

12.1.1 The Subcontractor shall purchase and maintain such insurance as will protect him from claims set forth below which may arise out of or result from the Subcontractor's operations under the Subcontract, whether such operations be by himself or by any of his Sub-subcontractors or by anyone directly or indirectly employed by any of them, or by anyone for whose acts any of them may be liable:

.1 claims under workers' compensation, disability benefit and other similar employee benefit acts which are applicable to the work to be performed;

.2 claims for damages because of bodily injury, occupational sickness or disease, or death of his employees under any employer's liability law including, if applicable, those required under maritime or admiralty law for wages, maintenance, and cure;

.3 claims for damages because of bodily injury, sickness or disease, or death of any person other than his employees;

.4 claims for damages insured by usual personal injury liability coverage which are sustained (1) by any person as a result of an offense directly or indirectly related to the employment of such person by the Subcontractor, or (2) by any other person;

.5 claims for damages other than to the work itself because of injury to or destruction of tangible property, including loss of use resulting therefrom; and

.6 claims for damages because of bodily injury or death of any person or property damage arising out of the ownership, maintenance or use of any motor vehicle including those not owned by the Subcontractor.

12.1.2 The insurance required by Subparagraph 12.1.1 shall be written for not less than any limits of liability specified in the Contract Documents, or required by law, whichever is greater.

12.1.3 The insurance required by Subparagraph 12.1.1 shall include premises-operations (including explosion, collapse and underground coverage), elevators, independent contractors, products and completed operations, and contractual liability insurance (on a "blanket basis" designating all written contracts), all including broad form property damage coverage. Liability insurance may be arranged under Comprehensive General Liability policies for the full limits required or by a combination of underlying policies for lesser limits with the remaining limits provided by an Excess or Umbrella Liability Policy. The insurance required by Paragraph 12.1.1 shall include contractual liability insurance applicable to the Subcontractor's liability under Paragraph 5.18

12.1.4 The foregoing policies shall contain a provision that coverages afforded under the policies will not be cancelled or not renewed until at least sixty days' prior written notice has been given to the Contractor. Certificates of Insurance acceptable to the Contractor shall be filed with the Contractor prior to commencement of the Work. Upon request, the Subcontractor shall allow the Contractor to examine the actual policies.

12.2 PROPERTY INSURANCE

12.2.1 Unless otherwise provided, the Owner will purchase and maintain property insurance upon the entire Work at the site to the full insurable value thereof. This insurance shall include the interests of the Owners, the Contractor, the Subcontractors, and Sub-subcontractors in the Work and shall insure against the perils of fire and extended coverage, and shall include "all risk" insurance for physical loss or damage.

12.2.2 The Owner will effect and maintain such boiler and machinery insurance as may be necessary and/or required by law. This insurance shall include the interest of the Owner, the Contractor, the Subcontractors, and Sub-subcontractors in the Work.

12.2.3 Any loss insured under Paragraph 12.2 is to be adjusted with the Owner and Contractor and made payable to the Owner and Contractor as trustees for the insureds, as their interests may appear, subject to the requirements of any applicable mortgagee clause.

12.2.4 The Owner, the Contractor, the Architect/Engineer, the Subcontractor, and his Sub-subcontractors waive all rights against each other and any other contractor or subcontractor engaged in the project for damages caused by fire or other perils to the extent covered by insurance provided under Paragraph 12.2, or any other property or consequential loss insurance applicable to the Project, equipment used in the Project, or adjacent structures, except such rights as they may have to the proceeds of such insurance. If any policy of insurance requires an endorsement to maintain coverage with such waivers, the owner of such policy will cause the policy to be so endorsed. The Owner and contractor will require, by appropriate agreement, written where legally required for validity, similar waivers in favor of the Subcontractor and Sub-subcontractors by any separate contractor and his subcontractors. The policies shall be endorsed to provide waivers of subrogation.

12.2.5 The Owner and Contractor shall deposit in a separate account any money received as trustees, and shall distribute it in accordance with such agreement as the parties in interest may reach, or in accordance with an award by arbitration in which case the procedure shall be as provided in Paragraph 8.8. If after such loss no special agreement is made, replacement of damaged work shall be covered by an appropriate Change Order.

12.2.6 The Owner and Contractor as trustees shall have power to adjust and settle any loss with the insurers unless one of the parties in interest shall object in writing within five days after the occurrence of loss to the Owner's and Contractor's exercise of this power, and if such objection be made, arbitrators shall be chosen as provided in Paragraph 8.8. The Owner and Contractor as trustees shall, in that case, make settlement with the insurers in accordance with the directions of such arbitrators. If distribution of the insurance proceeds by arbitration is required, the arbitrators will direct such distribution.

12.2.7 If the Owner finds it necessary to occupy or use a portion or portions of the Work prior to Substantial Completion thereof, such occupancy shall not commence prior to a time mutually agreed to by the Owner and Contractor and to which the insurance company or companies providing the property insurance have consented by endorsement to the policy or policies. This insurance shall not be cancelled or lapsed on account of such partial occupancy. Consent of the Contractor and of the insurance company or companies to such occupancy or use shall not be unreasonably withheld.

ARTICLE 13

CHANGES IN THE WORK

13.1 CHANGE ORDERS

13.1.1 A Change Order is a written order to the Subcontractor signed by the Contractor, issued after the execution of the Subcontract, authorizing a Change in the Work or an adjustment in the Contract Sum or the Contract Time. The Contract Sum and the Contract Time may be changed only by Change Order. A Change Order signed by the Subcontractor indicates his agreement therewith, including the adjustment in the Contract Sum or the Contract Time.

13.1.2 The Contractor, without invalidating the Contract, may order Changes in the Work within the general scope of the Subcontract consisting of additions, deletions or other revisions, the Contract Sum and the Contract Time being adjusted accordingly. All such changes in the Work shall be authorized by Change Order, and shall be performed under the applicable conditions of the Subcontracts.

13.1.3 The cost or credit to the Contractor resulting from a Change in the Work shall be determined in one or more of the following ways:

.1 by mutual acceptance of a lump sum properly itemized and supported by sufficient substantiating data to permit evaluation; or

.2 by unit prices stated in the Subcontract or subsequently agreed upon; or

.3 by cost to be determined in a manner agreed upon by the parties and a mutually acceptable fixed or percentage fee; or

.4 by the method provided in Subparagraph 13.1.4.

13.1.4 If none of the methods set forth in Clauses 13.1.3.1, 13.1.3.2 or 13.1.3.3 is agreed upon, the Subcontractor, provided he receives a written order signed by the Contractor, shall promptly proceed with the Work involved. The cost of such Work shall be determined by the Contractor on the basis of the reasonable expenditures and savings of those performing the Work attributable to the change, including, in the case of an increase in the Contract Sum, a reasonable allowance for overhead and profit. In such case, and also under Clauses 13.1.3.3 and 13.1.3.4 above, the Subcontractor shall keep and present, in such form as the Contractor may prescribe, an itemized accounting together with appropriate supporting data for inclusion in a Change Order. Unless otherwise provided in the Subcontract, cost shall be limited to the following: cost of materials, including sales tax and cost of delivery; cost of labor, including social security, old age and unemployment insurance, and fringe benefits required by agreement or custom; workers' or workmen's compensation insurance; bond premiums; rental value of equipment and machinery; and the additional costs of supervision and field office personnel directly attributable to the change. Pending final determination of cost, payments on account shall be made as determined by the Contractor. The amount of credit to be allowed by the Subcontractor for any deletion or change which results in a net decrease in the Contract Sum will be the amount of the actual net cost as confirmed by the Contractor. When both additions and credits covering related Work or substitutions are involved in any one change, the allowance for overhead and profit shall be figured on the basis of the net increase, if any, with respect to that change.

13.1.5 If unit prices are stated in the Subcontract or subsequently agreed upon, and if the quantities originally contemplated are so changed in a proposed Change Order that application of the agreed unit prices to the quantities of Work proposed will cause substantial inequity to the Owner, the Contractor, or the Subcontractor, the applicable unit prices shall be equitably adjusted.

13.2 CONCEALED CONDITIONS

13.2.1 Should concealed conditions encountered in the performance of the Work below the surface of the ground or should concealed or unknown conditions in an existing structure be at variance with the conditions indicated by the Subcontract or should unknown physical conditions below the surface of the ground or should concealed or unknown conditions in an existing structure of an unusual nature, differing materially from those ordinarily encountered and generally recognized as inherent in work of the character provided for in this Subcontract, be encountered, the Contract Sum shall be equitably adjusted by Change Order upon claim by either party made within twenty days after the first observance of the conditions.

13.3 CLAIMS FOR ADDITIONAL COST

13.3.1 If the Subcontractor wishes to make a claim for an increase in the Contract Sum, he shall given the Contractor written notice thereof within twenty days after the occurrence of the event giving rise to such claim. This notice shall be given by the Subcontractor before proceeding to execute the Work, except in an emergency endangering life or property in which case the Subcontractor shall proceed in accordance with Paragraph 11.3. No such claim shall be valid unless so made. Any change in the Contract Sum resulting from such claim shall be authorized by Change Order.

13.3.2 If the Subcontractor claims that additional cost is involved because of, but not limited to, (1) any written interpretation issued pursuant to Subparagraph 3.2.2, (2) any order by the Contractor to stop the Work pursuant to Paragraph 4.3 where the Subcontrator was not at fault, or (3) any written order for a minor change in the Work issued pursuant to Paragraph 13.4, the Subcontractor shall make such claim as provided in Subparagraph 13.3.1.

13.4 MINOR CHANGES IN THE WORK

13.4.1 The Owner will have authority to order through the Contractor minor changes in the Work not involving an adjustment in the Contract Sum or an extension of the Contract Time and not inconsistent with the intent of the Subcontract. Such changes shall be effected by written order and such changes shall be binding on the Owner, the Contractor and the Subcontractor. The Subcontractor shall carry out such written orders promptly.

ARTICLE 14

UNCOVERING AND CORRECTION OF WORK

14.1 UNCOVERING OF WORK

14.1.1 If any portion of the Work should be covered contrary to the request of the Contractor or Architect/Engineer, or to requirements specifically expressed in the Subcontract, it must, if required in writing by the Contractor, be uncovered for their observation and replaced, at the Subcontractor's expense.

14.1.2 If any other portion of the Work has been covered which the Contractor or the Architect/Engineer has not specifically requested to observe prior to being covered, the Architect/Engineer or Contractor may request to see such Work and it shall be uncovered by the Subcontractor. If such Work be found in accordance with the Subcontract, the cost of uncovering and replacement shall, by appropriate Change Order, be charged to the Contractor. If such Work be found not in accordance with the Subcontract, the Subcontractor shall pay such costs unless it be found that this condition was caused by a separate subcontractor employed as provided in Article 7, and in that event the separate subcontractor shall be responsible for the payment of such costs.

14.2 CORRECTION OF WORK

14.2.1 The Subcontractor shall promptly correct all Work rejected by the Architect/Engineer or the Contractor as defective or as failing to conform to the Subcontract whether observed before or after Substantial Completion and whether or not fabricated, installed or completed. The Subcontractor shall bear all costs of correcting such rejected Work, including compensation for the Architect/Engineer's and/or Contractor's additional services made necessary thereby.

14.2.2 If, within one year after the Date of Substantial Completion of Work or designated portion thereof, or within one year after acceptance by the Owner of designated equipment or within such longer period of time as may be prescribed by law or by the terms of any applicable special warranty required by the Subcontract, any of the Work is found to be defective or not in accordance with the Subcontract, the Subcontractor shall correct it promptly after receipt of a written notice from the Owner or Contractor to do so unless the Owner or Contractor has previously given the Subcontractor a written acceptance of such condition. This obligation shall survive the termination of the Subcontract. The Owner or Contractor shall give such notice promptly after discovery of the condition.

14.2.3 The Subcontractor shall remove from the site all portions of the Work which are defective or non-conforming and which have not been corrected under Subparagraphs 14.2.1, 5.5.1 and 14.2.2 unless removal has been waived by the Owner.

14.2.4 If the Subcontractor fails to correct defective or non-conforming Work as provided in Subparagraphs 5.5.1, 14.2.1 and 14.2.2, the Owner or Contractor may correct it in accordance with Subparagraph 4.3.2.

14.2.5 If the Subcontractor does not proceed with the correction of such defective or non-conforming Work within a reasonable time fixed by written notice from the Contractor, the Owner or Contractor may remove it and may store the materials or equipment at the expense of the Subcontractor. If the Subcontractor does not pay the cost of such removal and storage within ten days thereafter, the Owner or Contractor may upon ten additional days' written notice sell such Work at auction or at private sale and shall account for the net proceeds thereof, after deducting all the costs that should have been borne by the Subcontractor, including compensation for the Contractor's additional services made necessary thereby. If such proceeds of sale do not cover all costs which the Subcontractor should have borne, the difference shall be charged to the Subcontractor, and an appropriate Change Order shall be issued. If the payments then or thereafter due the Subcontractor are not sufficient to cover such amount, the Subcontractor shall pay the difference to the Owner or Contractor.

14.2.6 The Subcontractor shall bear the cost of making good all work of the Contractor, other Subcontractors and other contractors destroyed or damaged by such removal or correction.

14.3 ACCEPTANCE OF DEFECTIVE OR NONCONFORMING WORK

14.3.1 If the Owner or Contractor prefers to accept defective or non-conforming Work, he may do so instead of requiring its removal and correction, in which case a Change Order will be issued to reflect reduction in the Contract Sum where appropriate and equitable. Such adjustment shall be effected whether or not final payment has been made.

ARTICLE 15

TERMINATION OF THE CONTRACT

15.1 TERMINATION BY THE SUBCONTRACTOR

15.1.1 If the Work should be stopped for a period of thirty days by the Subcontractor because of failure to receive payment in accordance with the Subcontract, then the Subcontractor may, upon seven additional days' written notice to the Contractor, terminate the Subcontract and recover from the Contractor payment for all Work executed and for any proven loss sustained upon any materials, equipment, tools, construction equipment and machinery, including reasonable profit and damages.

15.2 TERMINATION BY THE CONTRACTOR

15.2.1 If, after being notified of any of the following failures to perform, the Subcontractor continues to fail to commence his Work; continues to fail, except in cases for which extension of time is provided, to supply enough properly skilled workmen or proper materials; continues to fail to make prompt payment to Sub-subcontractors or for materials or labor; continues to fail to perform his Work in accordance with the Drawings and Specifications; continues to disregard laws, ordinances, rules, regulations or orders of any public authority having jurisdiction; or continues to be otherwise guilty of a substantial violation of a provision of the Subcontract; then the Contractor shall, without prejudice to any other right or remedy and after giving the Subcontractor and his Surety, if any, three day's written notice, have the right to any one or any combination of the following remedies: (1) supply such number of workers and quantity of material, equipment and other facilities as the Contractor deems advisable for the completion of the Work, or any part thereof which Subcontractor has failed to complete or perform after the aforesaid notice, and charge the cost thereof to the Subcontractor, who shall be liable for the payment of same; (2) contract with one or more additional contractors to perform such part of the completion of the Work as Contractor shall determine will provide the most expeditious completion of the total Work and charge the cost thereof to the Subcontractor, who shall be liable for the payment of same; or (3) terminate the Subcontract and use any materials, implements, equipment, appliances or tools furnished by or belonging to Subcontractor in completing the Work, or, at its option, itself or through a subcontractor or subcontractors furnish any such labor, material, implements, equipment, appliances or tools, in whole or in part, necessary for the completion of the Work, and charge the cost thereof to the Subcontractor, who shall be liable for the payment of same. The Subcontract shall be terminated, unless the Contractor subsequently otherwise agrees, upon the appointment of a receiver of the Subcontractor by reason of his insolvency or upon the Subcontractor making an assignment for the benefit of creditors. If Subcontractor files a petition under the Bankuptcy Code, the Subcontract shall terminate under (3) above if the Subcontractor or his trustee rejects the contract or, when not performing in accordance with the Project Schedule, is unable to give adequate assurance that he will complete the Subcontract in accordance with the Project Schedule. If Subcontractor is not performing in accordance with the Project Schedule at the time of filing such petition or at any subsequent time, the Contractor may, while awaiting the Subcontractor or his trustee to reject the Subcontract or to accept and provide adequate assurance of his ability to perform, avail himself of such remedies under (1) and (2) above as are reasonably necessary to maintain the Project Schedule. Contractor may offset all costs incurred by it in the pursuance of any of the remedies provided in the preceeding sentences, together with Contractor's reasonable overhead and direct job expenses incurred in pursuing such remedy or remedies, including without limitation, its attorneys' fees, and, at Contractor's discretion, a reasonable profit not to exceed six percent (6%), against any sums due or to become due hereunder. Subcontractor shall be liable for the payment of any amount by which such costs may exceed the unpaid balance of the Contract Sum.

15.2.2 If the unpaid balance of the Contract Sum exceeds the cost of finishing the Work, including compensation for the Contractor's additional services made necessary thereby, such excess shall be paid to the Subcontractor. If such costs exceed the unpaid balance, the Subcontractor shall pay the difference to the Contractor.

15.2.3 The Contractor has the option to terminate his Agreement with the Owner if the Work is stopped for a period of thirty days under an order of any court or other public authority having jurisdiction, or as a result of an act of government, such as a declaration of a national emergency making materials unavailable, or from the failure of the Owner to make payment. If the Contractor exercises such option he may then terminate the subcontracts with the Subcontractors and the Subcontractors shall be entitled to recover such amounts for his proven losses as the Contractor may be able to recover from the Owner.

THE ASSOCIATED GENERAL CONTRACTORS

STANDARD DESIGN-BUILD SUBCONTRACT AGREEMENT WITH SUBCONTRACTOR NOT PROVIDING DESIGN

This Document shall be used in conjunction with AGC Document 430 – Conditions Between Contractor and Subcontractor for Design-Build.

This Agreement made at ______________________________

this __________ day of ______________, 19_____, by and between ______________________________, hereinafter referred to as the Contractor, and ______________________________, hereinafter referred to as the Subcontractor, to perform part of the Work on the following Project:

PROJECT:

OWNER:

ARTICLE 1

SCOPE OF WORK

1.1 The Contractor employs the Subcontractor as an independent contractor to construct a part of the Project for which the Contractor has contracted with the Owner. The Subcontractor's portion of the Project, hereinafter referred to as the "Work," is set out in Exhibit A attached hereto. The Subcontractor agrees to perform such Work under the general direction of the Contractor and subject to the final approval of the Owner, in accordance with the Subcontract Documents. This Agreement and the Subcontract Documents incorporated herein represent the entire agreement between the parties and supercede all prior negotiations, representations, or agreements.

1.2 The Subcontract Documents, hereinafter referred to as the "Subcontract," include this Agreement, the Conditions Between Contractor and Subcontractor for Design Build [AGC Document 430], and documents set forth therein, all of which are more specifically identified in Exhibit B attached hereto. If any provisions of such documents conflict with the terms of this Agreement, the terms of this Agreement shall control. The Subcontractor binds himself to the Contractor for the performance of Subcontractor's Work in the same manner as the Contractor is bound to the Owner for such performance under Contractor's contract with the Owner.

1.3 In the performance of his Work, Subcontractor will:

.1 Furnish all labor and materials, along with competent supervision, shop drawings and samples, tools, equipment, scaffolding, permits and fees necessary for the construction of the Work; and,

.2 Give all notices and comply with all applicable laws, building codes, ordinances, regulations and orders of any public authority bearing on the design and construction of the Work under this Agreement.

ARTICLE 2

PROJECT SCHEDULE

2.1 Subcontractor will commence, and thereafter prosecute his Work in accordance with the Project Schedule so as not to cause any delays or interference with the completion of the Project or in the obtaining of payments by the Contractor from the Owner or the final acceptance of the Project by the Owner. If the Subcontractor does not commence the Work in accordance with the Project Schedule, or if at any time the Work is not performed in accordance with such schedule, the Subcontractor agrees, upon three (3) days' written notice from the Contractor, to provide the necessary personnel and supply such equipment, materials, overtime work, workers and other devices and facilities as necessary so as to expedite the Work. Such notice, once given, shall continue in effect until the Work specified therein has been fully completed, even though the Subcontractor has initially acted under the notice but has failed to continue to do so until complete performance thereof. Subcontractor shall work overtime, at the direction of Contractor without additional cost to Contractor if such overtime work is necessary to cure delinquency in maintaining the Project Schedule and such delinquency is due to delays by Subcontractor.

ARTICLE 3

CHANGES IN THE WORK

3.1 The Contractor may order changes in the Work consistent with the provisions of the Conditions Between Contractor and Subcontractor for Design-Build and within the general scope of this Agreement, consisting of additions, deletions or other revisions.

3.2 No claims for extra work or changes will be recognized or paid unless prior approval has been obtained in writing from the Contractor.

ARTICLE 4

GENERAL PROVISIONS

4.1 The Work performed under this Agreement is subject to the approval of the Contractor and Owner.

4.2 If the Work, or any portion thereof is not acceptable, the Subcontractor shall be responsible for the cost of remedying unaccepted Work, whether such remedial Work is performed by the Subcontractor or by any other entity at the request of the Contractor or Owner.

ARTICLE 5

CONTRACT SUM AND PAYMENTS

5.1 The Contractor agrees to pay to the Subcontractor for the satisfactory completion of Subcontractor's Work the Contract Sum of ______________________ ($____________) in monthly payments of ________ percent of the work performed in any preceding month, in accordance with estimates prepared by the Subcontractor and approved by the Contractor. Payment of the approved portion of the Subcontractor's monthly estimate and final payment shall be conditioned upon receipt by the Contractor of his payment from the Owner.

5.2 Subcontractor shall provide with his monthly applications for payment completed lien waivers and affadavits from his subcontractors and suppliers in a form satisfactory to the Owner and Contractor. Approval and payment of Subcontractor's monthly estimate is specifically agreed not to constitute or imply acceptance by the Contractor or Owner of any portion of the Subcontractor's Work. Final payment shall not constitute acceptance of defective work.

5.3 The Subcontractor agrees and covenants that money received for the performance of this Agreement shall be used solely for the benefit of persons and firms supplying labor, materials, supplies, tools machines, equipment, plant or services exclusively for this Project in connection with this Agreement and having the right to assert liens or other claims against the land improvements, or funds involved in this Project or against any bond or other security posted by Contractor or Owner; that any money paid to the Subcontractor pursuant to this Agreement shall immediately become and constitute a trust fund for the benefit of said persons and firms, and shall not in any instance be diverted by the Subcontractor to any other purpose until all obligations and claims arising hereunder have been fully discharged.

5.4 The Contractor may deduct from any amounts due or to become due to the Subcontractor any sum or sums owing by the Subcontractor to the Contractor; and in the event of any breach by the Subcontractor of any provision or obligation of this Subcontract, or in the event of the assertion by other parties of any claim or lien against the Owner, the Contractor, Contractor's Surety, or the premises upon which the Work was performed, which claim or lien arises out of the Subcontractor's performance of this Agreement, the Contractor shall have the right, but is not required, to retain out of any payments due or to become due to the Subcontractor an amount sufficient to completely protect the Contractor from any and all loss, damage, or expense therefrom, until the claim or lien has been adjusted by the Subcontractor to the satisfaction of the Contractor. This paragraph shall be applicable even though the Subcontractor has posted a 100% labor and material payment bond and a performance bond.

5.5 Final payment will be made when the completed project is accepted by the Owner; the Subcontractor has submitted completed lien waivers and affidavits from his subcontractors and suppliers in a form and to the extent required by the Owner and Contractor; and the Contractor has received final payment from the Owner.

ARTICLE 6

INSURANCE

6.1 The Subcontractor shall, within ________ days of signing this Agreement, but before performing any Work, provide the Contractor with certificates of insurance indicating coverage for Comprehensive General Liability, Comprehensive Auto Liability, claims under workers compensation, disability benefit, and other similar employee benefit acts which are applicable to the work to be performed in accordance with the Conditions Between Contractor and Subcontractor for Design-Build [AGC Document 430] for the following limits:

Comprehensive General Liability		Comprehensive Auto	
Bodily Injury	$____________	Bodily Injury	$____________
Property Damage	$____________	Property Damage	$____________

Workers' Compensation $ Legal Limit

6.2 The Builders Risk Insurance contains a deductible of $____________. Each insured shall bear his loss within the deductible unless the Contractor's Agreement with the Owner provides that the Owner shall bear any such loss.

ARTICLE 7

MISCELLANEOUS PROVISIONS

7.1 Governing Law: This Agreement shall be governed by the law in effect at the location of the Project.

IN WITNESS WHEREOF the parties hereto have executed this Agreement under seal, the day and year first above written.

____
SUBCONTRACTOR

By____________________

ATTEST:

____

____
CONTRACTOR

By____________________
(Title)

ATTEST:

____

EXHIBIT A

The Subcontractor's Work on this Project shall consist of the following portions of the Project:

EXHIBIT B

The Contract Documents include:

1. The Agreement Between the Owner and Contractor dated ________________.

2. The General, Special and Supplementary Conditions identified as:

3. The Project Schedule dated ________________

4. The following drawings, specifications, and criteria:

5. The Contract Sum includes the following allowances:

THE ASSOCIATED GENERAL CONTRACTORS

STANDARD DESIGN-BUILD SUBCONTRACT AGREEMENT WITH SUBCONTRACTOR PROVIDING DESIGN

This Document shall be used in conjunction with AGC Document 430 – Conditions Between Contractor and Subcontractor for Design Build.

THIS AGREEMENT made at ______________________________ this _________ day of _________, 19___ by and between _____________________, hereinafter referred to as the Contractor, and _____________________, hereinafter referred to as the Subcontractor, to perform part of the Work on the following Project:

PROJECT:

OWNER:

ARTICLE 1

SCOPE OF WORK

1.1 The Contractor employs the Subcontractor as an independent contractor, to design and construct a part of the Project for which the Contractor has contracted with the Owner. The Subcontractor's portion of the Project, hereinafter referred to as the "Work," is set out in Exhibit A attached hereto. The Subcontractor agrees to perform such Work under the general direction of the Contractor and subject to the final approval of the Owner, in accordance with the Subcontract Documents. This Agreement and the Subcontract Documents incorporated herein represent the entire agreement between the parties and supercede all prior negotiations, representations, or agreements.

1.2 The Subcontract Documents, hereinafter referred to as the "Subcontract," include this Agreement, the Conditions Between Contractor and Subcontractor for Design-Build [AGC Document 430], and documents set forth therein, all of which are more specifically indentified in Exhibit B attached hereto. If any provisions of such documents conflict with the terms of this Agreement, the terms of this agreement shall control. The Subcontractor binds himself to the Contractor for the performance of Subcontractor's Work in the same manner as the Contractor is bound to the Owner for such performance under Contractor's contract with the Owner.

1.3 In the performance of his Work, Subcontractor will:

.1 Furnish by properly licensed and qualified architects or engineers all necessary professional architectural and engineering design services for the design of the Work;

.2 Furnish all labor and materials, along with competent supervision, shop drawings and samples, tools, equipment, scaffolding permits and fees necessary for the construction of the Work;

.3 Give all notices and comply with all applicable laws, building codes, ordinances, regulations and orders of any public authority bearing on the design and construction of the Work under this Agreement; and,

.4 The Subcontractor shall submit for the Contractor's approval in accordance with the Project Schedule, design development documents, working drawings, specified shop drawings and samples, and data and specifications of materials proposed to be incorporated in the Work. The Subcontractor shall provide copies of approved drawings in the form and quantity specified by the Contractor. Subcontractor shall advise Contractor and other affected trades of all design development changes in a timely manner so as to preclude additional costs and conflicts with work of others on the Project. Subcontractor shall be liable for the extra costs incurred for failure to provide such timely notice.

ARTICLE 2

PROJECT SCHEDULE

2.1 Subcontractor will commence, and thereafter prosecute his Work in accordance with the Project Schedule so as not to cause any delays or interference with the completion of the Project or in the obtaining of payments by the Contractor from the Owner or the final acceptance of the Project by the Owner. If the Subcontractor does not commence the Work in accordance with the Project Schedule, or if at any time the Work is not performed in accordance with such schedule, the Subcontractor agrees, upon three (3) days' written notice from the Contractor, to provide the necessary personnel to complete the design and supply such equipment, materials, overtime work, workers and other devices and facilities as necessary so as to expedite the Work. Such notice, once given, shall continue in effect until the Work specified therein has been fully completed, even though the Subcontractor has initially acted under the notice but has failed to continue to do so until complete performance thereof. Subcontractor shall work overtime, at the direction of Contractor without additional cost to Contractor if such overtime work is necessary to cure delinquency in maintaining the Project Schedule and such delinquency is due to delays by Subcontractor.

ARTICLE 3

CHANGES IN THE WORK

3.1 The Contractor may order changes in the Work consistent with the provisions of the Conditions Between Contractor and Subcontractor for Design-Build and within the general scope of this Agreement, consisting of additions, deletions or other revisions.

3.2 No claims for extra work or changes will be recognized or paid unless prior approval has been obtained in writing from the Contractor.

ARTICLE 4

GENERAL PROVISIONS

4.1 The Work performed under this Agreement is subject to the approval of the Contractor and Owner.

4.2 If the Work, or any portion thereof is not acceptable, the Subcontractor shall be responsible for the cost of remedying unaccepted Work, whether such remedial Work is performed by the Subcontractor or by any other entity at the request of the Contractor or Owner.

ARTICLE 5

CONTRACT SUM AND PAYMENTS

5.1 The Contractor agrees to pay to the Subcontractor for the satisfactory completion of Subcontractor's Work the Contract Sum of ______________________ ($_____________) in monthly payments of _________ percent of the work performed in any preceding month, in accordance with estimates prepared by the Subcontractor and approved by the Contractor. Payment of the approved portion of the Subcontractor's monthly estimate and final payment shall be conditioned upon receipt by the Contractor of his payment from the Owner.

5.2 Subcontractor shall provide with his monthly applications for payment completed lien waivers and affidavits from his subcontractors and suppliers in a form satisfactory to the Owner and Contractor. Approval and payment of Subcontractor's monthly estimate is specifically agreed not to consititute or imply acceptance by the Contractor or Owner of any portion of the Subcontractor's Work. Final payment shall not constitute acceptance of defective work.

5.3 The Subcontractor agrees and covenants that money received for the performance of this Agreement shall be used solely for the benefit of persons and firms supplying labor, materials, supplies, tools machines, equipment, plant or services exclusively for this Project in connection with this Agreement and having the right to assert liens or other claims against the land improvements, or funds involved in this Project or against any bond or other security posted by Contractor or Owner; that any money paid to the Subcontractor pursuant to this Agreement shall immediately become and constitute a trust fund for the benefit of said persons and firms, and shall not in any instance be diverted by the Subcontractor to any other purpose until all obligations and claims arising hereunder have been fully discharged.

5.4 The Contractor may deduct from any amounts due or to become due to the Subcontractor any sum or sums owing by the Subcontractor to the Contractor; and in the event of any breach by the Subcontractor of any provision or obligation of this Subcontract, or in the event of the assertion by other parties of any claim or lien against the Owner, the Contractor, Contractor's Surety, or the premises upon which the Work was performed, which claim or lien arises out of the Subcontractor's performance of this Agreement, the Contractor shall have the right, but is not required, to retain out of any payments due or to become due to the Subcontractor an amount sufficient to completely protect the Contractor from any and all loss, damage, or expense therefrom, until the claim or lien has been adjusted by the Subcontractor to the satisfaction of the Contractor. This paragraph shall be applicable even though the Subcontractor has posted a 100% labor and material payment bond and a performance bond.

5.5 Final payment will be made when the completed project is accepted by the Owner; the Subcontractor has submitted completed lien waivers and affidavits from his subcontractors and suppliers in a form and to the extent required by the Owner and Contractor; and the Contractor has received final payment from the Owner.

ARTICLE 6

INSURANCE

6.1 The Subcontractor shall, within _________ days of signing this Agreement, but before performing any Work, provide the Contractor with certificates of insurance indicating coverage for Comprehensive General Liability, Comprehensive Auto Liability, claims under Workers compensation, disability benefit, and other similar employee benefit acts which are applicable to the work to be performed in accordance with the Conditions Between Contractor and Subcontractor for Design-Build [AGC Document 430] for the following limits:

Comprehensive General Liability		Comprehensive Auto	
Bodily Injury	$______________	Bodily Injury	$______________
Property Damage	$______________	Property Damage	$______________

Workers' Compensation $ Legal Limit

6.2 The Builders Risk Insurance contains a deductible of $___________. Each insured shall bear his loss within the deductible unless the Contractor's Agreement with the Owner provides that the Owner shall bear any such loss.

6.3 The Subcontractor shall, within _____________ days of the same time period, furnish a certificate of insurance in the amount of $_____________ to protect himself and the Contractor from claims arising out of the performance of professional services caused by any errors, omissions, or negligent acts for which he is legally liable.

ARTICLE 7

MISCELLANEOUS PROVISIONS

7.1 Governing Law: This Agreement shall be governed by the law in effect at the location of the Project.

IN WITNESS WHEREOF the parties hereto have executed this Agreement under seal, the day and year first above written.

____
SUBCONTRACTOR

By_________________________
(Title)

ATTEST:

____

____
CONTRACTOR

By_________________________
(Title)

ATTEST:

____

EXHIBIT A

The Subcontractor's Work on this Project shall consist of the following portions of the Project:

EXHIBIT B

The Contract Documents include:

1. The Agreement Between the Owner and Contractor dated _______________.
2. The General, Special and Supplementary Conditions identified as:

3. The Project Schedule dated _______________.
4. The following drawings, specifications, and criteria:

5. The Contract Sum includes the following allowances:

Glossary

Absence of Privity

Introduced into law during the Roman Empire to limit claims against an individual by unrelated or remote parties. In effect, the law stated that a contractual relationship (called privity) must exist between two parties in order to impose liability on one of the parties. In the absence of privity, liability cannot be imposed. See **Privity**.

Advertisement for Bid

The official notice of a government agency's search for qualified bidders on a government or public-sector construction project. The notice usually includes information about the project and provides the public with a contact name for details about the solicitation, rules for submission of bids, and awarding of the contract.

Agent

Under agency law, an agent is authorized by the principal to act on the principal's behalf. Generally, an agent's acts bind the principal as though the principal had acted directly. See **Principal**.

American Institute of Architects (AIA)

A national society of registered architects founded in 1857. It is the single largest representative body of architects in the United States.

Arbitration

The process by which parties agree to submit their disputes to the determination of a third, impartial party (referred to as the arbitrator), rather than pursuing their claims before a judge and jury in a court of law.

Architect

An individual who is educated, trained, and experienced in the art and technology of building planning and design, construction administration, and coordination of the specialized skills of structural, mechanical, and electrical design engineers. Use of the term is usually limited by law to those who have been licensed to practice architecture.

Assignment Clause
A clause in a contract that restricts either party from assigning or transferring all or a portion of its contractual obligations to a third party.

Associated General Contractors of America (AGC)
The largest national representative organization of contractors in the United States.

Benefit of the Bargain
An approach to determining the amount of damages a defendant must pay the plaintiff in breach of contract or warranty actions. This approach attempts to place the plaintiff in the same position as though the defendant had fulfilled his or her contractual obligations.

Betterment Rule
Often used as a defense against the imposition of liability, this rule states that if the first party fails to perform some duty that results in extra expense incurred by the second party, the first party is not liable for that extra expense if the second party would have incurred the expense regardless of whether or not the first party failed in the performance of his or her duty.

Bid Bond
A form of security offered by a bidder to the party soliciting the bid which guarantees that the bidder will enter into a contract within a specified period of time and will furnish any required performance and labor and material bonds.

Bidding
The practice of soliciting competitive cost proposals from more than one party for the design and/or construction of the project described in the solicitor's documents.

Binding Arbitration
Dispute resolution proceedings in which the nature of the agreement between the parties obligates them to the arbitrator's decision.

Bond
A form of security guaranteeing fulfillment of some obligation. In the construction industry, bonds are typically provided by surety companies to project owners. If the contractor does not perform according to the terms of the bond, the surety company will pay the project owner the amount specified by the bond.

Bonding Capacity
The amount that a bonding or surety company is prepared to put at risk in the bonds that it writes for the construction professional. Bonding capacity is based on the amount of cash, liquid or readily liquidated assets, experience, and track record of the construction professional.

Breach of Contract
The failure to perform some contractually described obligation in accordance with the terms of the contract.

Breach of Warranty
The failure of some fact, or statement about some matter, to be as promised.

Broad Form Policy

A term used to describe a Comprehensive General Liability Insurance policy which, through the policy language or through one or more endorsements to the policy, provides a wide range of coverage that can be tailored to suit the specific needs of the insured. See **Comprehensive General Liability Insurance**.

Builders' Risk Insurance

A type of Property Insurance that protects against loss from fire and other named perils during construction.

Case Law

Those laws established or interpreted by the courts. See **Common Law**.

Change Order

The client's written order to the contractor, issued after execution of the construction contract, which authorizes a change in the construction work and contract time and/or amount. Typically, the design professional also signs the change order and then issues it to the contractor.

Claim

An assertion by one party that he or she has been damaged or otherwise wronged by some act or failure to act on the part of another, and for which the party making the assertion seeks money or other recompense to make it whole for the damages suffered.

Claims Made-based Policy

A Professional Liability Insurance policy providing coverage to the design professional, named as the insured on the policy, against loss arising out of the insured's negligent acts, errors, or omissions, provided that the claim is brought against the design professional within the period of time in which the policy is in effect. It is not sufficient that the policy be in effect at the time the design professional's services were rendered, or at the time that a negligent act, error, or omissions occurs.

Client

The party who retains the design professional and/or contractor to provide design and/or construction services in connection with a given project. The client is sometimes referred to as the owner.

Code of Ethics

A set of canons, rules of conduct, or ethical prescriptions to which a body of individuals, such as the American Institute of Architects and the National Society of Professional Engineers, obligate their members to comply.

Code of Hammurabi

A set of rules in ancient Babylonia that governed the design and construction of buildings. The code provided remedies to those injured by the failure of the structure to conform to the requirements of the code, and imposed penalties on the party responsible for such failure.

Common Law

Principles of conduct based on usage, custom, or commonly held beliefs as interpreted by the courts on a case-by-case basis. Common law is not founded on the will of legislative or rule-making bodies, but on accepted standards of conduct. See **Case Law**.

Common Law Indemnification

A form of indemnification not found in or based on a contract, but implied by the courts as existing between the parties and arising out of the nature of the relationship between the parties. See **Indemnification**, and **Quasi-contractual Indemnification**.

Comparative Selection

A method of procurement in which the client selects the top three to five prequalified design/build teams, each of whom is invited to submit design concept proposals for the client's evaluation and review, along with information about the separate qualifications of each of the various design/build teams.

Compensatory Damages

Damages intended to compensate the plaintiff by granting a monetary amount equal to the loss or injury suffered.

Competitive Bidding

A method of procurement by which two or more parties are given the opportunity to submit separate bids to the client in connection with the design and construction of a project.

Comprehensive General Liability Insurance

A broad form insurance policy providing protection to the policy holder against all liability exposure except that which is specifically excluded from coverage under the policy.

Consequential Damages

Compensation for loss or injury that is not directly attributable to some wrongful act on the part of another, but is the result of one or more of the consequences of such act.

Construction Management

A project delivery method whereby the client retains a construction manager to provide certain preconstruction expertise including cost estimating, value engineering, and scheduling and, during the construction phase of the project, coordination of all construction activities.

Construction Professionals

A term used to describe the principal players retained by the client in a construction project (typically the design professional and the contractor).

Contract

A written or oral agreement between two or more parties consisting of one or more legally enforceable promises that the law recognizes as a duty to be performed by one of the parties.

Contractor

The party who is hired to perform the required construction on a project.

Contractual Joint Venture

An agreement, possessing the legal characteristics of a partnership, between two or more parties who join forces to achieve some specific, short-term goal, such as the design and construction of a project.

Cookie Cutter Projects

A term applied to a series of projects, such as standard speculative office buildings, in which the programmatic layout, the principal design features, and the methods of construction, are similar or identical.

Corporate Seal

The official mark or signature of a corporation, typically consisting of an embossed impression on paper, evidencing the formality of the corporation's execution of the document and its intention to be bound thereby. In some jurisdictions a corporate seal may carry more serious consequences than if the document were executed without inclusion of the corporate seal but with the signature of an authorized representative of the corporation instead.

Cost Plus

One of several methods of compensating a contractor for work performed in connection with a project. Using this method, the contractor is paid for actual direct and indirect costs incurred in constructing the project, plus a separately stated fee for his or her services.

Cost Proposal

The pricing information submitted by a design/build entity to a prospective client in response to the client's request for such information. Normally, a cost proposal is part of a more comprehensive proposal which may include the conceptual or schematic design of the project, and information concerning project scheduling, project organizational structure, and key project personnel.

Damages

A measure of monetary compensation that a court or arbitrator awards to a plaintiff for loss or injury suffered by the plaintiff's person, property, or other legally recognizable rights.

Defendant

An individual against whom a claim or action is brought. See **Plaintiff**.

Design/Build Method of Project Delivery

A method of construction in which a single entity provides to the client all of the services necessary to both design and construct all or a portion of the project. This single point of responsibility fundamentally distinguishes design/build from other forms of project delivery.

Design Competition

A method of procuring design/build services in which design/build teams submit detailed design proposals to the client, who then selects a team based on the ability of their proposal to meet the requirements of the project. The "winner" of the competition is awarded the contract to complete the design and construct the project.

Design Professional

A term used generally to refer to architects; civil, structural, mechanical, electrical, plumbing, and heating, ventilating, and air conditioning engineers; interior designers; landscape architects; and others whose services have either traditionally been considered "professional" activities, require licensing or registration by the state, or otherwise require the knowledge and application of design principles appropriate to the problem at hand.

Destruction of Property (damages awarded for)
Those damages that a court or arbitrator awards to a plaintiff for physical injury to, or destruction of, the plaintiff's property by the defendant.

Developer
A party who procures the right to develop real estate through purchase, lease, or other means, and who improves the real estate for later sale or lease to others. Developers engage the services of design professionals and contractors, either separately or as members of design/build teams, to provide required design and construction services for those projects.

Direct Damages
Those damages recognized by the law as the natural and usual result of wrongful conduct by the defendant. See **General Damages** and **Special Damages**.

Direct Selection
A method of procurement in which the client selects the highest ranking design/build team from those who have previously been prequalified by the client based not on price but on qualifications.

Disclaimer
The denial or rejection of any obligation or duty.

Duty
An obligation or standard of conduct established by statute, contract, or common law.

Employer's Liability Insurance
A form of insurance available to employers that provides protection against claims by the employer's employees or their dependents for damages resulting from personal injuries or illness sustained by employees during the course of their employment activities. Claims filed under Employer's Liability Insurance are not covered under Workers' Compensation statutes.

Endorsement
An amendment to an insurance policy which expands, restricts, or otherwise modifies the extent or applicability of coverage afforded by the policy.

Engineer
One who by education, training, and experience is skilled in the art and technology of site or building engineering and design. Use of the term is usually limited by law to those who have been duly licensed to practice engineering.

Equity Interest
Partial ownership interest in a project for which the design professional, contractor, or design/build entity has provided design and/or construction services.

Exemplary Damages
See **Punitive Damages**.

Express Warranty
A promise or a guarantee that a statement about some fact is true and will continue to be true, and is made by one party to another in a manner that is clearly stated, either orally or in writing.

Fast Track Construction
A method of project delivery in which the sequencing of construction activities enables some portions of the project to begin before the design is completed on other portions of the project.

Fiduciary
One in whom the confidence and trust of another has been placed and who, as a result, owes a special duty to act in scrupulous good faith for the benefit and in the best interests of the other. See **Agent**.

Fit-out
The design and completion of shell space (i.e. raw floor space bounded by walls but not specifically adapted to the requirements of its occupants) with the specific interior partitioning, floor, ceiling, mechanical, electrical, and environmental requirements of its occupants included.

Foreclosure
A legal proceeding in which a mortgage is terminated, usually by sale of the mortgagor's interest in the property secured by the mortgage.

General Conditions
A set of guidelines that define many of the rights, responsibilities, and limitations of authority of the owner and contractor, and include the general procedures governing the performance of the work.

General Damages
Those damages that the law considers to result from the defendant's wrongful conduct. They are the natural or usual result of such conduct without reference to any special circumstances concerning the plaintiff. See **Special Damages**.

Governing Law
The body of law of a particular jurisdiction which governs the rights and responsibilities of parties in a given situation. Within limits parties may, by contract, choose which jurisdiction's law will govern matters related to contract formation, interpretation, and enforceability.

Guaranteed Maximum Price
A method of limiting the design and construction costs of a project whereby the design/build team is compensated for its actual costs incurred in connection with the design and construction of the project, plus a fee—all subject, however, to a ceiling above which the client is not obligated to pay.

Honorarium
The amount paid to the design/build teams who are not chosen by a client in a design/build competition, to help defray their costs of participation.

Implied Warranty
A guarantee created not by the explicit oral or written statements of one party to another, but through a promise that is inferred under the law to exist by virtue of the nature of the transaction or the circumstances between the parties, or by the relative position one party holds with respect to another.

Impliedly Warranted
A product or service that is covered under an implied warranty.

In-the-aggregate
The total amount of proceeds available under the terms of an insurance policy, regardless of how many separate claims for damages may be made against the policy holder of the type for which the policy affords protection.

Indemnification
An obligation contractually assumed by or legally imposed on one party to protect another against loss or damage from specific liabilities.

Indemnitee
A party who is indemnified by another against loss or damage from specific liabilities.

Indemnitor
The party who is obligated to indemnify another against loss or damage from specific liabilities.

Insurance
A contract, typically referred to as an insurance policy, in which the insurer, in return for the premium stated in the policy, agrees to pay the insured up to the limits specified in the policy for losses or damages incurred by the insured.

Insured (the)
The party who receives payments under the terms of an insurance policy in the event of loss or damage of the type for which the policy affords protection.

Integration Clause
Establishes that only those provisions contained in the written agreement between the parties of which the integration clause is a part shall have any force or effect on the parties, and excludes all other provisions not contained within the written agreement.

Intentional Tort
Those acts performed by a party which both intend to cause, and result in, harm to another.

Joinder of Third Parties
The process whereby parties to separate but related disputes are voluntarily or legally compelled to join together in a single dispute resolution proceeding.

Joint and Several Liability
Where one party, typically a partner in a partnership or a member of a joint venture, is equally responsible to a third party for the acts and omissions of the other partner or member.

Joint Venture
Sometimes referred to as a contractual joint venture, whereby two or more parties join forces to form an entity with the legal characteristics of a partnership to achieve a specific objective.

Jurisdiction
The power and authority that a court, legislature, or other rule-making, interpreting, or enforcing body has to act or decide with respect to a given matter. Jurisdiction may also include a political body, such as a state, with recognized geographical boundaries which establishes and enforces its own laws.

Jurisprudence
A system of laws.

Labor and Material Payment Bond
A contract between a contractor and a surety company in which the surety, in return for a premium paid by the contractor, agrees to pay subcontractors, laborers, and material suppliers amounts due to them for their materials and services under the terms of their contractual arrangements with the contractor, should the contractor default in his or her payment obligations to them.

Liability
A situation in which one party is legally obligated to assume responsibility for another party's loss or burden. Liability is created when the law recognizes two elements: the existence of an enforceable legal duty to be performed by one party for the benefit of another; and the failure to perform the duty in accordance with applicable legal standards.

License
Permission granted by authority of the state to engage in an occupation or to practice a profession, the engagement or practice of which is unlawful without a license.

Litigation
The process by which parties submit their disputes to the jurisdiction and procedures of federal or state courts for resolution.

Lump Sum Bidding
A design/build procurement method in which the client requires the design/build teams to propose their compensation (place their bid) in the amount of a total payment for all services, costs, and expenses incurred in the design and construction of the project.

Master Builder
A term historically applied to the individual who was responsible for both the design and the construction of a project. During the Renaissance, a divergence appeared between the individual who prepared the project's design, and the individual who was responsible for its construction. With the rise of design professionals in the late 19th century, the term fell out of favor and is used infrequently today in reference to design/build firms.

Mechanic's Lien
A legislative attempt to provide a measure of financial leverage to help secure payments owed to parties whose work results in an improvement to real property. Generally, a mechanic's lien entitles the party who provides goods or services to the project to place a lien on the property which, like a mortgage, is a recognition of a debt owed by the property holder to the person who placed the lien, and which must be paid by the property owner within a statutorily prescribed period of time. If this is not done, the lien holder can sell the property and use the proceeds of the sale to pay the amount of the lien.

Modus Operandi
A method or procedure; a way of doing things.

National Society of Professional Engineers (NSPE)
A national organization of engineers founded in 1935 which, like the American Institute of Architects, publishes an extensive set of standard form construction documents that are used throughout the construction industry.

Negligence
The failure of a party to conform its conduct to the standard of care required by law. The law requires a person to exercise that degree of care that a reasonable person would exercise under the same or similar circumstances. As applied to design professionals, it is the failure to exercise that degree of skill, care, and diligence that other design professionals would exercise under the same or similar circumstances.

Negligence Per Se
Violation of a statute or regulation which may be deemed negligent without any investigation into the reasonableness of the conduct or the facts or circumstances surrounding the violation.

Negotiation Method
A method of procuring design/build services in which the client evaluates the qualifications of various design/build teams and makes a selection based on interviews or negotiations with representatives of the teams.

Occurrence-based Policy
Affords protection to the insured against any event described in the policy that occurred during the policy period, regardless of how long after expiration of the policy period the claim may arise. See **Project Policy**.

On-call Arbitrator (or Mediator)
An individual selected by the parties to a contract who agrees to be available within a prescribed time period to hear and decide the parties' disputes.

Out-of-pocket Approach
A method of measuring damages, typically in actions of negligence, in which the court attempts to place the plaintiff in the same position he or she was in immediately prior to the negligent conduct of the defendant.

Partnership
An agreement between two or more individuals or entities to pool all or a portion of their resources in a common enterprise for profit, and to share in the profits and losses of the enterprise in proportion to their contribution of resources.

Pass-through Joint Venture
A form of joint venture in which the joint venture itself is nothing more than the formal documents used to create it. A pass-through joint venture owns no assets other than its interest in those contracts it may have with its clients, nor does it perform any services. Instead, the joint venture subcontracts to each of its members or to third parties all services that it is required to provide to the client. The joint venture retains no profits. The profits, together with any losses, are passed on to the joint venture members through their respective subcontracts with the joint venture.

Penal Sum
Sometimes referred to as a bond's penalty, is the stated limit of the bond which, in turn, is the limit of the insurer's liability under the bond.

Perfecting a Lien
The statutorily prescribed steps a lienholder must take in order to establish a legally enforceable lien on the property of another.

Performance Bond
A bond issued by a surety company which guarantees the client that if the contractor fails to complete the project in accordance with the terms of the construction agreement, the surety company will either complete the contract itself, or arrange for a client-approved contractor to complete the contract. The surety company will pay the new contractor the amount required to finish the work, minus the unpaid amount under the original contract. However, the surety company is not obligated to pay more than the penal sum or limit of liability stated in the bond.

Personal Injury (damages awarded for)
Those damages that a court or arbitrator awards a plaintiff for physical injury to the plaintiff's person or for invasion of various personal rights.

Plaintiff
The party that initiates a claim or action against another party. See **Defendant**.

Practice Statute
A licensing statute that regulates what services a person may perform for others or the activities in which a person may be engaged.

Prequalification Process
The sequence of activities in which prospective design/build teams submit their credentials for the client's evaluation. If accepted, the design/build team is then qualified to participate in the selection or competition process.

Primary Contractor
An individual or entity that has a direct contractual relationship with the client or owner of the project. In design/build, the primary contractor is responsible for providing, either by itself or through subcontract arrangements with other individuals or entities, all of the design and construction services required for the project.

Principal
Under agency law, a principal is one who empowers another to act on his or her behalf and to legally bind the principal as though the principal had acted directly. See **Agent**.

Private Sector
That which is neither owned nor controlled by federal, state, or local government.

Privity
The relationship that exists between two or more contracting parties. Privity does not exist between parties who do not share a contractual relationship. See **Absence of Privity**.

Privity of Contract

See **Privity**.

Procurement Method

The procedures employed by a client to retain the services of a design/build team.

Professional Liability Insurance

Protection afforded the design professional, in the amount stated in the policy, from damages and expenses (such as attorneys' fees and court costs) arising out of the negligent acts, errors, or omissions of the design professional, the design professional's employees, or others for whom the design professional is responsible.

Professional Standard of Care

That degree of learning and skill that the law requires all professionals to exhibit and which is ordinarily possessed by professionals in good standing in that profession in the same locality and under similar circumstances.

Project Policy

An occurrance-based insurance policy that affords protection to design professionals engaged on a single project from claims that may arise during the course of the project and for a stated period of time following substantial completion of the project.

Property Insurance

Often referred to as Builder's Risk Insurance, and is typically purchased by the client to protect the client, contractor, and subcontractors from fire and other named losses that may occur during construction. See **Builder's Risk Insurance**.

Proposal Bond

Typically referred to as a bid bond, is a form of security offered by a bidder to the party soliciting the bid, guaranteeing that the bidder will enter into a contract within a specified period of time and will furnish any required performance and labor and material bonds. See **Bid Bond**.

Provide vs. Perform

The distinction some courts have made in determining whether a state's professional registration or licensing statutes, which prohibit parties from engaging in certain defined activities in the absence of a valid registration or license, have been violated by the conduct of a given individual. These courts interpret "perform" to mean "to do oneself," and "provide" to mean "to arrange for the performance by others who are properly qualified." Courts in these jurisdictions determine that it is not a violation of the state's licensing or registration statutes for an unlicensed party to "provide" required design services for a project as long as services will be "performed" by properly licensed or registered persons.

Proximate Cause

A legally sufficient causal connection between the breach of duty owed by the applicable standard of care and the injury suffered by the party to whom the duty was owed.

Public Sector

That which is owned or controlled by federal, state, or local government.

Punitive Damages
Also referred to as exemplary damages, are awarded by a judge to a plaintiff not merely to compensate the plaintiff for losses incurred, but when the defendant's conduct is aggravated by violence, malice, fraud, or wanton or wicked conduct. Punitive damages are intended to punish the defendant for wrongful conduct and to use the plight of the defendant as an example to potential wrongdoers.

Quasi-contractual Indemnification
A legal assumption invented by common law to permit recovery by one party from another in the absence of a contract, but where the nature of the relationship between the parties is such that justice warrants a recovery as though a contract exists.

Qualifications-based
The method of selecting a design/build firm by a client based on a comparative analysis of each design/build team's experience, qualifications, and credentials, and not on their fee proposal.

Registration
Formal recognition of an individual's demonstration to the state that he or she possesses the skill, knowledge, training, and other factors required by the state as preconditions to practicing a regulated activity. See **Licensing**.

Request for Proposal
A client's invitation for proposals to provide required design and/or construction services for the client's project. Requests for proposals contain information about the size, scope, and complexity of the project, the client's requirements and budgetary considerations, selection criteria, and the desired form and content of the proposals.

Risk Retention Groups
A result of recent federal legislation which permits groups of design professionals to pool their resources to cover potential losses by members of the group.

Self Insurance
That portion of a risk assumed by a party which is not insured or insurable, for which another party is not legally obligated to assume, and for which the self-insured party must bear the full impact of the cost should the risk materialize.

Single Point (Source) of Responsibility
The principal feature of the design/build method of project delivery in which a single entity provides to the client all of the services necessary to both design and construct all or a portion of the project.

Sole Proprietor
The single owner of an unincorporated business.

Sole-source Supplier
Those sources who provide highly specialized services and from which all required design and construction services must be procured. Nuclear power plants are an example of projects whose complexity requires that the client seek design and construction services from a single source that specializes in constructing facilities to house nuclear technology.

Solicitation of Interest
A request from a prospective client for the expression of interest by construction professionals in participation in the client's project.

Spec
A commonly used abbreviation of the term "speculative," referring to those projects (often office, retail, and condominium) constructed by clients not for their own use, but to market for sale or lease to others.

Special Damages
Those damages that are the natural or usual result of the defendant's conduct with respect to the special circumstances of a plaintiff. See **General Damages**.

Statement of Qualification
A statement, often provided on industry standard forms such as SF 254 and 255 published by the Government Services Administration, identifying a prospective bidder's experience, financial capacity, key personnel, a current profile of the firm's activity, and other information pertinent to a particular project.

Statutes and Regulations
Enactments of the various federal, state, and local rule-making bodies such as Congress, state legislatures, local planning and zoning boards, as well as an infinite array of administrative and regulatory bodies.

Statute of Limitations
A legislative enactment that bars a claim against a party unless the claim is brought within a specified period of time after the event giving rise to the claim has occurred, or the party bringing the claim knew or should have known of the event.

Statute of Repose
A legislative enactment that bars a claim against a party unless the claim is brought within a specified period of time following some event described in the statute, regardless of whether or not the statute of limitations period for that claim has expired.

Statutory Law
Those laws established by legislatures. See **Statutes and Regulations**.

Statutory Violation
Violation of the requirements of a statute which, in and of itself, may constitute negligence on the part of the party committing the violation.

Strict Liability
The imposition of liability on a party regardless of the existence of fault or negligence and regardless of the existence of a contractual relationship between the offending party and the injured party.

Subconsultant
An individual contracted by a consultant to provide services related to or part of those which the consultant owes to the client under his or her primary contract with the client.

Subcontractor
An individual hired by the contractor to provide a portion of the work that the contractor owes to the client under the contractor's primary contract with the client.

Surety
A person or entity who promises in writing to make good the debt or default of another. See **Bond**.

Survivorship Provision
A stipulation in a legal contract stating that the provisions of one or more clauses will remain in effect after completion or termination of all of the contract's other provisions.

Tenant Package
The set of drawings and specifications establishing standard quality, quantity, and configuration information of landlord-provided rental or lease space.

Tenant Standard Specification
See **Tenant Package**.

Title Statute
A licensing statute that regulates how someone describes themselves to the public.

Tort
A private or civil wrong or injury, other than a breach of contract, for which the court will provide a remedy in the form of an action for damages. A tort is not a criminal offense. It is a civil offense that arises not merely by the agreement of the parties, but by operation of law.

Tort of Negligence
A breach of a duty or a failure of one party to exercise the standard of care required by law, resulting in damage to the party to whom the duty was owed.

Traditional Method of Project Delivery
The most common method of construction whereby a client retains a design professional to provide all required design services required for the project, and retains separately the services of a contractor to provide all construction services required for the project.

Turnkey Projects
A method of project delivery in which a single source provides not only all design and construction services for the project, but a comprehensive set of project-related services as well, such as project financing, site procurement, securing permits, and operation and maintenance of the facility during the initial period following project completion.

Type A Design/Build
A design/build arrangement in which the client contracts directly with the design professional for all design and construction services required to complete the project. The design professional then contracts directly with the contractor to provide all required construction services.

Type B Design/Build
A design/build arrangement in which the client contracts directly with the contractor for all design and construction services required to complete the project. The contractor then contracts directly with the design professional to provide all required design services.

Type C Design/Build
A design/build arrangement in which the design professional and the contractor join forces to form a joint venture. The client contracts directly with the joint venture for all design and construction services required for the project.

Type D Design/Build
A design/build arrangement in which the client contracts with an independent legal entity for all design and construction services required for the project. Neither the design professional nor the contractor are recognized as individuals within this organization.

Uniform Commercial Code (UCC)
A body of uniform laws governing consumer and commercial transactions.

Unintentional Tort
An act that results not from an intention to cause harm or to perform some harmful act, but because the defendant did not conform his or her conduct to the standard of care required by common law. See **Negligence**.

Warranty
A promise that a statement about some fact is true and will continue to be true. See **Express Warranty** and **Implied Warranty**.

Workers' Compensation Insurance
Insurance that is statutorily required to be carried by employers with a requisite number of employees. Workers' Compensation protects employees by providing payments to an employee who is injured while performing his or her job. Payments are made independent of any fault or neglect on the part of the employer.

Wrap-up Insurance
A Comprehensive General Insurance policy that combines many types of coverage normally provided separately by different parties. In a design/build project, wrap-up insurance is usually provided by the client.

Wrongful Death (damages awarded for)
Those damages that a court or arbitrator awards to the plaintiff for the death of an individual due to the negligent or otherwise wrongful conduct of the defendant.

Index

D

T

U

V

W